DEATH
AND THE
DOLCE
VITA

Stephen Gundle is a historian with specialist interest in modern Italy. His books include *Bellissima: Feminine Beauty* and *the Idea of Italy and Glamour: A History*. Professor of Film and Television Studies at the University of Warwick, he has also lived for many years in Italy, and is a contributor to *History Today*, Radio 4's *Night Waves* and the Italian press.

'A brilliant, methodical investigation of a murder scandal that convulsed the Roman political and social establishment in the 1950s' *Financial Times*

'What Gundle captures so magnificently is how the case shed light on the intersection between the stars of public life and the dark underbelly of post-war Rome' Ben Felsenburg, *Metro*

'Gundle's intellectual energy and his capacity for research has produced a book that vibrates with the peculiarities of post-war Italy, particularly those of Rome. It is a powerful, convincing recreation of a time and a place' *Sunday Herald*

'Inspired . . . the whole gloriously unimproving narrative provides the essential backstory for the Berlusconian bunga-bunga of Italy in our own day' *Literary Review*

'There is unlikely to be a more thorough and diligently researched account of the scandal than this one' *Spectator*

Also by Stephen Gundle

Between Hollywood and Moscow: The Italian Communists and the Challenge of Mass Culture

The Glamour System (with Clino Castelli)

Bellissima: Feminine Beauty and the Idea of Italy

Mass Culture and Italian Society from Fascism to the Cold War (with David Forgacs)

Glamour: A History

DEATH
AND THE
DOLCE
VITA

THE DARK SIDE OF ROME IN THE 1950s

STEPHEN GUNDLE

CANONGATE
Edinburgh · London

This paperback edition published by Canongate Books Ltd in 2012

First published in Great Britain in 2011 by Canongate Books Ltd, 14 High Street,
Edinburgh EH1 1TE

1

British Library Cataloguing-in-Publication Data
A catalogue record for this book is available on
request from the British Library

ISBN 978 1 84767 655 9

Typeset in Bembo by Palimpsest Book Production Ltd,
Falkirk, Stirlingshire

Printed and bound in Great Britain by Clays Ltd, St Ives plc

www.canongate.tv

To the memory of my father
Arthur Gundle (1925–1971)

and for my son Alessandro

Contents

Dramatis Personae

The Montesi Family Circle

Rodolfo, Wilma's father, a carpenter and family man
Maria (née Petti), Rodolfo's wife and Wilma's mother
Wanda, first child of Rodolfo and Maria
Wilma, second child of Rodolfo and Maria
Sergio, third child of Rodolfo and Maria
Giuseppe (also known as Peppe or Peppino), Rodolfo's
  brother and Wilma's uncle
Angelo Giuliani, a policeman from Foggia and Wilma's fiancé
Mariella Spissu, Giuseppe's fiancée
Rossana Spissu, sister of Mariella and Giuseppe's lover

Personalities of the Case

Adriana Bisaccia, artists' model and Bohemian dropout
Anna Maria Moneta Caglio, socialite, aspiring actress and
  Ugo Montagna's lover
Ugo Montagna, Marchese di San Bartolomeo, a Sicilian with
  extensive business contacts in Rome and a lessee of the
  Capacotta hunting estate
Rosa Passarelli, Ministry of Defence employee who claimed
  to see Wilma on the train to Ostia
Piero Piccioni, jazz musician and son of government
  minister Attilio

Legal Officials, Police and Lawyers

Tommaso Pavone, national chief of police

Saverio Polito, police commissioner for Rome

Umberto Pompei, commandant of the Rome division of the Carabinieri, the national gendarmerie

Raffaele Sepe, head of the investigative division of the Court of Appeal

Giuseppe Sotgiu, Communist president of the Province of Rome; defence attorney of Silvano Muto

Cosimo Zinza, Carabinieri lieutenant and assistant to Raffaele Sepe

The Political World

Giulio Andreotti, Rome-born associate of De Gasperi; minister for the interior, January–March 1954

Alcide De Gasperi, founder and leader of the Christian Democrats; prime minister, December 1945–August 1953

Amintore Fanfani, Christian Democrat, leader of the party's left wing; minister for the interior, July 1953–January 1954

Attilio Piccioni, deputy leader of the Christian Democrats; foreign minister, December 1953–August 1954, and father of Piero

Mario Scelba, Sicilian Christian Democrat; minister for the interior, May 1947–July 1953; prime minister, January 1954–July 1955

Giuseppe Spataro, Christian Democrat; minister of posts, January 1950–July 1953

The Press

Luciano Doddoli, reporter, *Il Giorno*; correspondent, *Epoca*
Fabrizio Menghini, chief crime reporter, *Il Messaggero*
Silvano Muto, journalist and founder of *Attualità*
Tazio Secchiaroli, press photographer, the first paparazzo

The Arts and Entertainment

Linda Christian, actress and socialite, married actor Tyrone
  Power in Rome in 1949
Anita Ekberg, Swedish film star and queen of the Roman
  night scene in 1958.
Federico Fellini, director of the Rome-set films *Nights of
  Calabria, Il bidone* and *La dolce vita*
Novella Parigini, artist from Via Margutta and socialite
Giò Stajano, artist and provocateur, friend of Novella Parigini
Alida Valli, star of Italian Fascist cinema, who went to
  Hollywood in 1947 and returned to Italy in 1952. Lover
  of Piero Piccioni

Prologue

Rome
9 April 1953

It's a blustery spring afternoon on the Via Tagliamento, a busy residential road to the east of the city. Bicycles trundle by, while Vespas and Lambrettas occasionally zip up and down the street, manoeuvring around the slower cars and trucks. It's cold, and a light drizzle has left the pavement wet. People are wearing their winter coats to visit the local shops, which have just opened for the afternoon trade. Pedestrians hurry along, eager to get out of the wind. Halfway along the road, opposite no. 76, an imposing apartment building with a decorative façade, a group of workmen lean on their shovels, smoking and eyeing up the passing talent. It's an ordinary day in a romantic, slightly shabby city, where church bells still drown the loudspeakers of the advertising vans, and the glitz and the gutter are never too far apart.

At around five fifteen p.m., a young woman leaves her family's modest apartment upstairs in no. 76. She's twenty-one, dark-haired and pretty, with a full face and dimpled cheeks. She's wearing a distinctive yellow and green checked coat, with one button at the collar, a yellow skirt with green spots, and a pair of black antelope shoes with large buckles. On her arm she carries a bucket handbag. She makes her way down the stairwell, walks across the block's courtyard and passes through the entrance arch. The concierge sees the young woman pass her window, but after she goes out onto the street, the only people who notice her are the idle workmen, who whistle appreciatively.

When she fails to return for dinner that evening, her family panic. After making some urgent phone calls to relatives, and searching the immediate neighbourhood, they report her disappearance to the police.

Thirty-six hours later, a body is found on a beach some twenty kilometres south of Ostia at Torvaianica. Discovered early in the morning by a young man named Francesco Bettini, the woman is lying face down, head towards the sea. She is dressed in a yellow coat, still fastened at the neck, but turned inside out over her head. The body is fully clothed, apart from shoes, skirt, stockings and suspender belt. Shocked, Bettini hurries off to inform the police, telling everyone he meets along the way about his discovery. Villagers come to stare and are pushed away by local officials belonging to one of Italy's six national police forces, the Financial Police, who arrive to inspect the body. No one can give her a name.

Two officers from the nearby Carabinieri station come to take charge of the scene. At eleven a.m. a doctor arrives from nearby Pratica di Mare to certify the death. He pushes through the crowd, and notes the well-preserved condition of the corpse. Following a brief examination he concludes that death had occurred approximately eighteen hours previously – that is, some time on 10 April. Drowning is the probable cause.

The body lies on the beach for the rest of the day. Covered with a simple sheet it forms a grim focal point on that drab, windswept stretch of coastline. Finally, at eight thirty p.m. the procurator's office announces that no magistrate will visit the site, and authorises removal of the body to the Institute of Forensic Medicine in Rome.

Wilma Montesi is identified at the mortuary on the morning of 12 April by her father and her fiancé. Seeing what look like bruises on the body, the younger man cries out in anguish, 'They have killed her, my poor Wilma.'

For the following five years, the mystery of Wilma Montesi's death will preoccupy the people of Rome, and the affair will blow up into a scandal that touches almost every corner of public life. For now, her distraught family must try to work out why she came to lie dead on that lonely beach, miles from Rome.

The idea that Wilma had committed suicide was quickly dismissed as improbable – by her family at least. She had had her keys with her, and no reason to take her own life. With their honour at stake, and fearful perhaps that tongues might begin to wag, the girl's parents and sister seized on an alternative scenario: Wilma had drowned accidentally while bathing her feet at Ostia, a nearby seaside resort. Shortly before her disappearance, she had complained to her sister of irritation caused by the rubbing of a new pair of shoes and had heard that sea water might ease it. Instead of seeking the advice of the local pharmacist, whose shop was just a few yards from the entrance to the apartment block, she had resolved to go to the coast. However, Ostia was a good half-hour by train from Rome, and to reach the station Wilma would have had to cross the city by tram. Would she really have left home after five o'clock on a blowy spring afternoon to undertake such a journey alone? Wilma's fiancé, Angelo Giuliani, voiced some reservations, but he was the only one.

Regardless of its implausibility, the family decided that this was what must have happened and they would not be dissuaded. The local police, having learned that the girl had left behind her identity card and valuables, were inclined towards suicide. But when the investigation was taken over by Rome's mobile police squad, the officers went along with the family's hypothesis. They, too, found accidental death the most plausible verdict. Barely five days after the body was found – an incredibly short time in terms of police procedure – the case of the girl on the beach was closed.

In normal circumstances, the matter would have rested there. Wilma Montesi was hardly the first young woman to meet an odd death in Rome. In the years after the war, numerous stabbings, cases of strangulation and bodies dragged from lakes had hit the newspapers. Women, who had won the vote for the first time in 1946, were the usual victims. More often than not they were vulnerable servants or prostitutes, from the Lazio countryside or the south, who had moved to Rome and met the wrong man.

Wilma was different. She was neither a servant nor alone in the big city. She lived at home with her family, who claimed that she scarcely went out. She passed her time mainly in the company of her mother and older sister. She liked listening to the songs on the radio and reading magazines; she loved the movies and tried to copy the stars in the way she dressed. Neighbours and acquaintances said that her appearance was always tidy and smart.

In some respects the Montesis were typical of the old-fashioned lower middle-class. They attended church infrequently, but regularly, and the parents were highly protective of their girls, not allowing them to work outside the home, or to have boyfriends. Keen to make good marriages for her daughters, but lacking the requisite social connections, Maria Montesi decided to accompany them to a reputable dance hall. The Sala Pichetti had been a middle-class meeting ground since the 1930s, and even in the 1950s preserved its strait-laced status. It was a dance school during the day, and its director still expected girls to be chaperoned during weekend sessions. Here, Maria hoped that Wilma and Wanda might attract appropriate suitors. So it was, one Sunday in September 1952, that she escorted them, dressed in their best frocks, to the dance. And it was on this first visit that Wilma met her future fiancé.

Almost nothing was ever said of Wilma's tastes or her personality. She was, and has remained, a blank canvas, an anonymous Anygirl, whose fate almost seemed a consequence of her ingenuousness. One of the few things that is known is that she did not derive much pleasure from her relationship with her fiancé. It seemed a stilted, wooden affair, in which ritualised meetings alternated with formal declarations of affection. Although Wilma received various gifts from Angelo, including a bracelet and necklace, there seems to have been little warmth between them. They saw each two or three times a week, never alone, and if they went out they were chaperoned by Wanda or Sergio, Wilma's younger brother.

At first Wilma was taken with Giuliani and his ceremonial promises. He had proposed soon after their first meeting, after receiving assurances about her reputation. But he was a jealous man with a violent streak, and after a punch-up with a colleague who had made unseemly comments about his intended bride, he was transferred to the southern city of Potenza. After this, the couple's meetings were reduced to one a month.

In a notebook Wilma drafted the letters she wrote to Giuliani every day following his transfer. After her death, it was impounded and its contents were later revealed to journalists. Her letters were brief and simple, written in conventional style, with obvious contributions from her mother and sister. The only jarring note came in the plaintive missives she wrote after what would turn out to be their last meeting, four weeks before her death. After lunch on Sunday, 3 March 1953, Angelo and Wilma had gone – alone for the first time – to the nearby public gardens of the elegant Villa Borghese. Seizing his opportunity, Angelo had attempted to grope Wilma and to kiss her on the lips, only to be pushed away with the excuse that he would mess up her lipstick. Offended, Giuliani left in an angry mood and did not make his usual trip to Rome the following month. The next time he saw Wilma, she was laid out on a slab at the morgue.

According to her family's account, Wilma's last day had been entirely tranquil. She had had lunch at home and had done some sewing for her trousseau. Sometimes the girls and their mother went to the cinema in the afternoon. There were three picture houses within walking distance of their apartment so there was always a choice of films. On this occasion, Wilma had declined to join the other women to see *The Golden Coach*, a Jean Renoir film starring Anna Magnani, about a *commedia dell'arte* theatrical troupe performing in eighteenth-century Peru. She told the others that she would stay in and maybe later she would go for a walk on her own.

Did Wilma already have a plan for the afternoon? Did she make or receive a telephone call that led her to leave the house? By all accounts, she was as composed as usual when she passed the concierge's window and, a few minutes later, the workmen on the road outside. She did not look like a girl rushing off to an assignation.

Some of those who knew Wilma were of the opinion that something important might have happened in her life during the weeks before her disappearance. Perhaps something that affected her view of her fiancé. One of her old schoolmates observed that she had recently become more confident and sophisticated. She smoked, too, a touch of daring out of step with the naïve image her family projected of her. And there were other indicators that Wilma was not simply a quiet, obedient girl. A few days before her death, she had had an argument on the stairs with two girls who lived in the block. In the course of a loud exchange, she had used the most vulgar expressions and had received a slap in the face from her mother. What was going on in Wilma's life that had caused these changes? What was the truth behind the picture of innocence? Could Wilma have become mixed up in something sinister?

*　*　*

Rome in the 1950s is remembered for the glamour of the *dolce vita* – the high life. It was home to numerous film stars, foreign business people, playboys, artists, writers and journalists. With its vibrant night life and unique *joie de vivre*, it was an ancient city with a very modern allure. But alongside the glamour there existed a much darker side. Rome had witnessed the collapse of Mussolini's Fascist regime, endured two foreign occupations and the destruction of much of its social fabric. It had grown rapidly too. The city was a magnet, drawing people, especially the young, from all of Italy's regions. It was a place where dreams could come true, but also, inevitably, where aspirations died, young hopes were crushed, and individuals – especially young women – were exploited and discarded.

Perhaps this was why the Montesi affair, as it came to be known, resonated so deeply. It was a Roman story that offered a grand narrative of a city that was struggling to find a new sense of itself. It raised issues that affected everyone: the place of the family, the freedom enjoyed by young women, and the role of honour. Not to mention sex, drugs and corruption in high places. The press eagerly followed its twists and turns, and used the fascination the case exerted on the public to increase circulation. It also became a matter of political concern, since Italy's powerful Communist Party used it as a stick to beat the establishment and the government. It even had an international resonance, with the United States becoming increasingly afraid that it could cause a deep political crisis that might imperil Italy's fragile anchorage to the West. The lonely death of Wilma Montesi, an ordinary girl, had given rise to an extraordinary scandal.

PART ONE

I

The Body on the Beach

The Montesi family lived in a large apartment block built in the 1920s to house public employees. A handsome seven-storey building with an elegant, decorative façade, it featured eight internal stairwells and a large central courtyard embellished with palm trees and a fishpond. Wilma's maternal grandfather, a post-office clerk, had originally been allocated the three-room, third-floor apartment on Staircase 5 – no. 9. The low rent meant that Wilma's father, Rodolfo, who had moved in after his marriage, could save enough money to establish his own carpentry business.

Rodolfo was a thrifty type who liked to think of himself as a poor artisan, even though by 1953 he employed two men in his workshop. He was known for his fine furniture and cinema fittings – the Holiday cinema in Largo Benedetto Marcello, which in the 1950s was called the Astra, still boasts examples of his craftsmanship. His daughters addressed him affectionately as 'Papetto' but his parenting style was neither relaxed nor informal. He wouldn't countenance the idea of his daughters working and kept them on a short leash.

Maria, his wife, was short, rotund, and known for her showy elegance, her lively temper and her frequent emotional outbursts. She was the dominant figure in a household that, until 9 April, had included twenty-four-year-old Wanda, Wilma, their younger brother Sergio, aged seventeen, and Maria's elderly parents. Wanda wasn't as pretty as Wilma – her features were similar, but she had a large nose and a dumpy figure. She also lacked the poise that made Wilma stand out. She was closer to her mother than Wilma was, mainly because she was less argumentative and a good listener. Sergio was the cleverest of the bunch. A studious boy, he would be the first in the family to graduate from university.

The family's living conditions were cramped, but not unusually so for the time. The girls slept on narrow beds in the living room while Sergio occupied a bed in his grandparents' room. Everyone gathered at the dining table to sew, read, do homework and talk. They had a telephone, a gramophone and a radio.

Rodolfo, Maria and their offspring were accustomed to dining together at eight thirty p.m. sharp. Maria and Wanda had changed their plans at the last minute and had gone to see John Ford's *The Sun Shines Bright* at the nearby Astra cinema instead of *The Golden Coach*. When they returned to via Tagliamento they noticed that there were no lights on in the apartment – a sure sign that Wilma was still out. The two women began preparing the meal and at eight thirty, after Rodolfo and Sergio had come home, everyone sat down. By nine o'clock, when Wilma still hadn't arrived, they started to worry. What could have delayed her? Had she had an accident? Wanda stood up and walked round the apartment. She found the bracelet, necklace and photograph of Wilma's fiancé, which her sister always carried with her, on the chest of drawers in her parents' bedroom. Her identity card was there too.

In the hours that followed, they made desperate attempts to find her. Sergio went off with a neighbour on a scooter to tour the hospitals in case there had been an accident. Rodolfo, for some reason fearing suicide, rushed to Ponte Garibaldi over the River Tiber – several people had jumped off it to end their lives – and then to the district police station to report his daughter's disappearance. Finally he took the tram to the Policlinico hospital.

Meanwhile, Maria went to quiz the concierge and spread the word among the neighbours of her daughter's disappearance. At nine thirty she called her father-in-law Riccardo, the only close relative with a telephone: two of her husband's siblings lived with their father. She was told that Wilma had visited the previous day but that they hadn't seen her since. Rodolfo's sister Ida ran to the Montesis' apartment block and found Maria in the street on her knees, crying, 'Wilma, come back! I forgive you!' She wondered if a quarrel lay behind Wilma's disappearance.

Rodolfo and Sergio returned, hoping to find that Wilma had reappeared. She hadn't, and their concern continued to mount. At eleven o'clock, when Rodolfo's youngest brother Giuseppe – known in the family as Peppe or Peppino – heard the news he drove to Via Tagliamento. He owned a Fiat Topolino Belvedere and offered to take Rodolfo to search for Wilma. They patrolled nearby streets, explored a park and ended up at Rodolfo's workshop. Having found no trace of her, they phoned home, where Maria, Wanda, Sergio and Ida were waiting for news.

When Rodolfo and Giuseppe got back to the apartment, they found Wanda and Sergio trying to comfort Maria. They learned that although Wilma had left her photograph, she had taken her keys, which indicated that she had expected to return. The spectre of suicide receded.

At midday, on Friday, 10 April, Rodolfo went once more to the district police station, where the duty officer tried to reassure him. It was too early for the police to get involved, he said: lots of perfectly good girls left home for one reason or another, only to reappear after a short time. Dissatisfied, Rodolfo sent a telegram to Angelo Giuliani, Wilma's fiancé: 'Wilma missing: reasons unknown.' Perhaps he thought she might have fled to her future husband. He would soon learn that she hadn't.

Rodolfo's next move was to go to Police Headquarters. Here the police took his concern seriously but Rodolfo was horrified — and intensely angry — when the officer dealing with him checked the register of prostitutes arrested the previous night for soliciting. Wanda, meanwhile, had gone to consult a fortune-teller, who assured her that she would soon hear something.

Early on the morning of Saturday, 11 April, Giuliani phoned Rodolfo for news. On learning that there was none, he told his potential father-in-law that if he wanted him to come to Rome he had to send a more alarmist telegram. Otherwise he wouldn't be granted leave. Wilma's father obliged and in the process revived his initial fear: 'Suicide likely. Keep calm. Come immediately.' The family still had no idea what had happened to Wilma. Suicide still seemed improbable but could not be entirely discounted — Maria's mother had attempted to kill herself as a young woman and the memory of that event had entered family lore. If there had been an accident, it would surely have been reported by now.

Bereft of ideas, they searched for other explanations. Curiously, given their later insistence that Wilma had had no secrets, they even imagined an elopement. Wanda recalled that, some years earlier, during a stay at the family's holiday home at Rocca di Papa, Wilma had become infatuated with a local engineer — he had been married and probably hadn't noticed the effect he had had on the teenager. But on Sunday morning Giuseppe, with his fiancée, Mirella, and Sergio, went to Rocca di Papa. When they confronted the man, he had no recollection of Wilma, let alone information on her current whereabouts, so the trio returned to Rome.

Giuliani arrived from the southern town of Potenza early on Sunday, 12 April, having travelled through the night. He gulped some coffee, then went with Rodolfo to the local police station, where they asked if there was any news. An officer was reading a newspaper, which reported that a body had been found near the fishing village of Torvaianica: the previous morning, at seven thirty, a young building worker had come across it on his way to work. A beautiful unidentified girl had been washed up on the beach.

Fearing the worst, Rodolfo and Giuliani left the station and hastened to the mortuary. When Giuliani recognised Wilma on the slab, and noticed certain marks on her face, he cried, 'They have killed her, my poor Wilma.'

In those days Torvaianica was not the desirable resort it would one day become. It was a simple fishing village, set on a barren stretch of coastline. Early on Monday, 13 April, Giuseppe drove Giuliani, Rodolfo and Sergio there. By now the elite mobile squad of Rome's bloated police force had taken over the case. But Giuliani was not content to leave the matter to them: he and the other three men were determined to find out for themselves how Wilma had ended up in such an unlikely place.

Their minds must have been racing as they approached the coast. The so-called Zingarini area of Torvaianica where Wilma had been found was barely inhabited, apart from a few fishermen, peasants, gamekeepers and their families. They discovered, though, that it was popular with courting couples from Rome: lacking privacy at home, young people often sought out secluded spots to make love. Many used the Borghese gardens in the city, but those with their own car could venture further afield.

The four men were shown where Wilma had been found.

A makeshift cross tied with string had been stuck in the sand by a photographer keen for a picture and some flowers had been placed by it. Locals told them that the body had looked fresh, not like that of a drowned person. Two villagers had some interesting information: Jole Manzi and Anna Minniti claimed they had seen a girl wearing Wilma's distinctive coat in the area on 8 April, the day before she disappeared. Others said that a large car carrying a man and a dark-haired young woman had been spotted a few days before. They suggested that the Montesis and Giuliani make more enquiries further along the coastal road, which had not yet been formally opened to traffic, where there was a hunting estate: it was frequented by well-to-do people from the city.

The four men took this advice but struggled to find their way and had to ask for directions. Eventually, they came to a large iron gate, the estate's entrance. Convinced that there might be something to learn on the other side, they tracked the perimeter fence, calling for assistance. When a guard appeared and challenged them, they showed him a photograph of Wilma. Anastasio Lilli let them in and took them to his wife, who was in bed, unwell. She had been at the gate on 9 April and had seen a luxury saloon carrying a man and a young woman. However, when she saw the picture of Wilma, she was unable to confirm that she had been the woman on board.

Frustrated, the men made their way back to Rome. They had found nothing, but they were forced to contemplate the possibility that someone had taken Wilma to the area where her body was discovered.

This was apparently confirmed the next day when a local worker, a mechanic named Mario Piccinini, claimed that he had seen the Montesi girl in a car one night early in March. He had been approached at the nearby Castel Fusano station by a railwayman who had asked if he could help free a car that was stuck in the sand. Piccinini had helped to push it while the driver's young brown-haired female companion sat inside. Piccinini remembered the model: an Alfa Romeo 1900cc saloon, a luxury vehicle not long on the market. Thinking it might be significant, he had reported the event to the police station in Ostia soon after the body had been discovered on 11 April. When he had seen Wilma's picture in the newspaper, he had said that the girl in the car perfectly resembled her.

Had she been to that area before with a wealthy man?

In Via Tagliamento, the telephone rang constantly. One unexpected call was from a Rosa Passarelli, a clerk at the Ministry of Defence. She was sure she had seen Wilma on the five thirty p.m. train to Ostia on the Thursday afternoon. When she had read about her in the newspaper she had decided not to go to the police but to contact the family. After some hasty consultations, Rodolfo and Maria invited her to pay them a visit. Smartly dressed and articulate, the thirty-five-year-old Passarelli described to the family Wilma's unusual green and yellow coat, then commented on her neat appearance and lady-like deportment. From this portrait, the parents recognised their daughter. Aldo Morlacchi, a plainclothes officer from the police mobile squad, happened to be in the apartment when she arrived: he watched as the parents showed her some photographs, which she confirmed were of the girl she had seen on the train.

But why had Wilma taken the train to Ostia? It seemed an unlikely journey to undertake so late on a cold April afternoon, and it didn't fit the Wilma the family had known. As they pondered, Passarelli suggested it might be best for all concerned if her death were to be regarded as accidental. That way trouble would be avoided: there would be no unwanted publicity and

Wilma's reputation would not be called into question. The policeman agreed, and it was at this point that Wanda said her sister had spoken of going to the seaside to soothe her feet – Wilma had tried to persuade her to join her but Wanda hadn't wanted to go. The family quickly concluded that Wilma must have gone to the coast to bathe her feet but, perhaps due to her period, had fainted, slipped into the water and drowned.

At last the police were taking an active interest in the case. Morlacchi's superior, Alfredo Magliozzi, had heard about Angelo Giuliani's exclamation in the mortuary and wanted to find out what lay behind it – hence the policeman's presence in the apartment. He also ordered that enquiries should be made in Ostia where several people claimed to have spotted the girl. A nanny swore she had seen her on a stretch of beach immediately next to the area reserved for trainee members of the Financial Police. Two students had noticed a girl they now thought had been Wilma at the Miramare bar with two other girls and a man. The party had arrived in an Alfa Romeo 1900. A news-vendor said she had sold a postcard to a girl resembling Wilma at around seven p.m – she had lent her a pen to write a message and then had offered to post the card to the girl's fiancé, a soldier.

It was doubtful, though, that even if Wilma had been in Ostia and had somehow fallen accidentally into the water, her body could have been carried to where it was found. The harbour master's office said it was unlikely that a body could be swept, within thirty hours or so, the twenty kilometres from Ostia to Torvaianica, even on a night when the currents were flowing fast, as they had been on 9 April.

The possibility that Wilma had committed suicide still hung heavily over the family. As she had not taken her jewellery or her fiancé's photograph with her, as she usually did when she left the house, the local Salario police station in Rome initially recorded the death as suicide – and suicide meant that Wilma would be denied a religious funeral. Such a verdict would cast a cloud over the entire household, possibly even prejudicing Wanda's chances of finding a husband. Instead the Montesis embraced the theory of the accident, even though it was based on little more than conjecture. More than anything, Rodolfo and Maria wanted a plausible story that preserved Wilma's respectability.

Respectability was important to a family like the Montesis and they clung to it like limpets to a rock. The girls had been too young to be tempted by the quick cash earned by women who had consorted with American troops during the Allied occupation, or to be pimped by a desperate family. The Montesis had weathered the final stages of the war and its aftermath, facing fewer troubles than many. They had not starved or lost their home, and while work was sometimes scarce, it had never dried up completely. The relatively affluent community in the Salario area had somehow held together.

In other districts of the capital it was a different story. Prostitution had flourished as women had serviced troops with time on their hands and money to spend. In his epic film of the liberation, *Paisà*, Roberto Rossellini had chosen prostitution as the theme for the Rome episode: a middle-class girl full of hope and joy at the outset has become, by the end, a whore, unrecognisable to an American soldier to whom she had offered some welcome refreshment a few months earlier.

Respectability did not amount to morality – the Church was always prepared to forgive the penitent sinner. Once lost, respectability could not – like a young woman's virginity – be reacquired. It was a matter of social standing. In the face of the fortunes accumulated by those who had done well out of the war and the liberation, the relatively impoverished lower-middle class consoled itself with conventional markers of decorum: sexual continence went with being well dressed, attending mass at the major religious festivals, keeping the home clean, the women off the labour market, working hard and taking holidays. Although Rodolfo sometimes struggled to keep his business afloat, Maria dreamed of a splendid future for the family, and had conveyed this idea to her daughters.

So, the Montesi family were determined to defend Wilma's reputation at all costs. The case of the 'beautiful woman' whose lifeless corpse had been spewed up by the sea had been front-page news in the Roman daily *Il Messaggero* on 12 April. The following day she was named and the talk was of why she might have committed suicide. Indignant at this interpretation, the family issued a statement to the press:

> Wilma was a calm and well-adjusted girl. She was engaged to a policeman whom she was planning to marry in December. Everything was ready for the wedding, including a house in Foggia [Angelo's home town], where the couple would have moved after the wedding. Wilma was only twenty-one, life was smiling on her, and a happy event awaited her. She had no reason to give up. Besides, she had never shown signs of depression or of dejection. She did not leave a single line of explanation. We are sure Wilma did not kill herself.

Meanwhile the police continued their enquiries. They conducted searches along the coast between Ostia and Torvaianica for the missing shoes, stockings, skirt, suspender belt and handbag, on the assumption that Wilma must have removed them and left them on the beach somewhere. They found more witnesses near Ostia who claimed to have seen Wilma, although some of the testimonies were confused or referred to the wrong day. Oddly, the police did not attempt to track down the mysterious owner of the Alfa Romeo 1900cc saloon, even though there were no more than three hundred in Rome.

On 14 April, an autopsy was performed by two forensic

specialists, Dr Fracche and Dr Carelli. Those who asked why it had not been carried out sooner were told that no one had been available at the weekend. Journalists were eager to know the results – and so were the public.

It produced some new facts. Crucially, the time of death was backdated by a day and a half: Wilma had died not on 10 April, but the day before, on the Thursday on which she had disappeared. In support of the fainting hypothesis, Wilma's heart was found to be slightly smaller than normal. On the other hand, she would not have been weakened by her period since she was close to the end of her cycle. As for the foot irritation, no trace of eczema or rubbing was found. No poison, drug or alcohol was identified in the stomach, although there was evidence that ice cream had been consumed. There was no obvious sign of violence on the body, although there was some superficial bruising. Death had been caused by drowning.

This document, and the report compiled by the mobile squad that summed up their enquiries and included information about Wilma's reputation and habits, enabled the police commissioner for Rome to call a press conference. Saverio Polito was seventy-four, kept on past retirement age on account of his standing with his political bosses, and well used to handling awkward matters. A Neapolitan, with a direct manner, he informed his audience of reporters at Police Headquarters that he had delivered his opinion on the cause of Wilma Montesi's death to the national head of police, Tommaso Pavone, and was terminating the investigation. The matter was simple, he said. The girl had gone to Ostia by train. After writing a postcard to her fiancé, she had selected a quiet place on the beach and removed some items of clothing in order to paddle more easily in the sea. She had lost consciousness, was sucked into the water and drowned. Her body was carried away by a strong current and eventually washed up on the beach further down the coast.

It was a strange statement. Rather than the fruit of investigation, Saverio Polito's account mixed known facts with the version of events that the family had settled on during Rosa Passarelli's visit. But with Wilma's death now officially regarded as accidental, her funeral could take place. Satisfied that she had not killed herself, the Church agreed that there could be a religious service.

The family was keen to ensure that poor Wilma was sent to her final resting place without controversy. The press had started to comment, sometimes with a knowing air, about the Montesi girl, and there were rumours that she had been pregnant or the victim of a sex crime – the most common reasons for suicide or violent death in young women. The autopsy report offered no support to either possibility: the two experts had determined that not only was Wilma not pregnant but that she was still a virgin. While some observers scoffed at this, it strengthened the Montesi family's account of Wilma. But people's views remained divided, and the mystery surrounding the girl whose lifeless body had been found on that deserted beach deepened.

II

The Rumour Mill

Wilma's funeral took place at the Basilica of San Lorenzo fuori le Mura on 16 April. As the procession, led by a traditional horsedrawn hearse, made its way from the mortuary to the ancient church, silent but for the sobs of Maria Montesi and her remaining daughter, journalists hovered. The ordeal was too much for Maria. She had fainted when the coffin was closed in the mortuary chapel. Now, as cameras flashed, she had to be supported by her daughter and husband. Rodolfo had carefully stage-managed the funeral. He had insisted that his daughter be buried in a wedding dress that had been bought for the occasion from a department store. It symbolised her purity and the marriage she would never have. A garland of orange blossoms was placed around her head. Three wreaths lay on the coffin: one from Wilma's family, another from the tenants of Via Tagliamento 76, the third from former schoolfriends.

With press interest mounting in the beautiful girl who had died so tragically, a considerable crowd was present, mostly composed of girls like Wilma. They had never met her but they identified with her, and seemed to regard her as a sort of heroine-martyr, symbolic of the struggle for dignity and a better life. The face in the papers was a mirror for a generation.

After the funeral mass, Wilma was buried in Rome's sprawling Verano cemetery. It was the city's largest, a massive complex of gardens and alleyways punctuated with grand marble memorials. The wealthy maintained family crypts or lavish tombs, adorned with statues. For lesser folk there were simple niches where the dead lay stacked on top of each other in covered galleries. It was in one of these that poor Wilma found her final resting place.

Rodolfo Montesi ordered an inscription for the stone. Composed by a teacher friend, with some help from Giuseppe, Wilma's uncle, it had an old-fashioned, mawkish quality:

Pure creature of rare beauty, the sea at Ostia carried you away to leave you on the beach at Tor Vajanica – it seemed as though you slept the sleep of God, beautiful as an angel. Your mother, your father, your sister and your brother are near you in their great love and immense suffering.

The words, and the death date of 9 April, reflected the position the family had adopted and would never give up: Wilma had been an innocent, God-fearing girl, and she had died on the evening she had disappeared without having spent a night away from home. It was a firm response to all those who muttered that she had been led into danger, like many other young women, by her own greed and immorality.

The family had initially been willing to speak to journalists, hoping that publicity might shed some light on the precise manner of Wilma's death, but the feverish speculation had made them suspicious. The press had seized on the contradictions in the official version of the story because, as they saw it, it rested on a series of suppositions that strained credibility. If Wilma had removed her shoes and stockings before dipping her feet in the water, that was one thing, but it was hardly necessary or likely for her to have taken off her skirt or suspender belt, which were also missing. Then there was the matter of how she had drowned and why her body had been found so far down the coast. Polito's hasty conclusion of the case fuelled the first suggestions that a cover-up had occured.

After the funeral Giuseppe was the only family member to talk to the press. As they left the church, he pressed one journalist, Luciano Doddoli of Milan's *Il Giorno* newspaper and *Epoca* magazine, for his thoughts on the police investigation. Doddoli was startled. 'Why are you so concerned?' he shot back. 'Did you have something to do with it?'

Shaken, Giuseppe backed away, begging the journalist not to implicate him in any speculation about the case.

Wilma's fiancé, Angelo Giuliani, had been staying with the family since he had arrived from Potenza. Now he was brusquely shown the door. Rodolfo later said that he had been cruel to be kind. He had told Giuliani that he should look to the future and make a new life for himself. Only the family knew that there had been ill-feeling between Wilma and her fiancé in the last month of her life.

Later, when his estrangement from the family became known, it was rumoured that Giuliani had upset the Montesis by offering, on the day of the funeral, to marry Wanda. He was said to have been more interested in achieving the modest material comfort and social dignity that marriage into an artisan's family would bring than in the loss of his fiancée. He had initially impressed Maria with his claim to be a wine merchant with his own business; he had neglected to mention that the business was a small retail outlet run by his father, while he himself worked as a low-salaried policeman. Now he faced losing the house that was being prepared for him and Wilma in Foggia. Status was important to the lower-middle classes, and Giuliani knew he had been lucky to win Wilma. Now perhaps he feared he would be left empty-handed.

Also, Giuliani did not accept the theory that his fiancée had died while bathing her feet in the sea. He believed she had been murdered and wanted to continue making his own enquiries. The Montesis, however, refused him their support, and he returned, chastened, to Potenza. He would contact the family on one more occasion, purely to pay his respects, before exiting their lives for good.

If anyone had thought that the funeral would put an end to speculation about Wilma's death, they were mistaken. Rumours continued to circulate of a cover-up. Rome's leading daily newspaper, *Il Messaggero*, even suggested she had been murdered, with its headline 'Was Wilma Montesi killed before she was thrown into the sea?' *Il Tempo* dismissed the police version of events as incredible: 'Many questions still remain to be answered about the death of the Montesi girl.' Signs would keep appearing to suggest that something was being concealed. Some weeks later, journalists got hold of the notebook that police had confiscated in which Wilma had prepared drafts of her letters to her fiancé, hoping to find some clue as to her state of mind. Three pages had been ripped out. No one could say when this had occurred or who was responsible.

After the Second World War the press had boomed. In Rome alone there were twenty-five daily newspapers, plus innumerable weeklies and magazines. All of the major northern Italian papers maintained correspondents and heavily staffed offices in the capital. Initially the Allied Control Commission had carefully scrutinised all new titles and had imposed conditions on long-established papers that had become compromised during the Fascist regime. But the thirst for news and the competition for influence over public opinion were so strong that many new proprietors had rushed to found publications. The daily press followed the Montesi case closely but the story was also taken up by a new brand of illustrated magazine that flourished after 1945, along with comics and picture romances. Fame and notoriety gave rise to a new style of journalism, which was sensationalist and morbid. Features about the events and personalities of the Fascist period were popular and a striking amount of space was given to crime. Under the Fascists, gossip had spread slowly but now things were very different. The press picked up quickly on tittle-tattle: a whisper overheard in a café was the next day's headline. Reporters were sent out to check hospitals, the courts and police stations. The press room at Police Headquarters was always filled with journalists, hopeful of picking up some juicy titbit. Many were used to receiving tip-offs from their network of contacts and expected that even supposedly confidential documents would be passed to them.

Wilma Montesi's case, though, was different. The autopsy report was not released to them and only a few details found their way into the public domain. However, Fabrizio Menghini, a lawyer and a leading reporter on *Il Messaggero*, noticed something. An imposing figure who stood more than six feet tall, he had been the only journalist to view Wilma's body at the morgue. Knowing he did not fit anyone's idea of a press man, he often used his legal credentials to gain access to people and institutions that were barred to others. He saw that the body was still in its underwear, which looked new and expensive. The autopsy report described the underwear as worn and patched. His suspicions were aroused and he concluded that someone, for some reason, had effected a substitution.

Other journalists continued to ponder suicide. As one paper put it, 'Why would a girl have committed suicide when everything in her life seemed to be fine?' The family had asked the same question but the press answered it differently. On 14 April Milan's *Il Corriere della Sera* speculated: 'There is only one thing to think: that she had committed some error and that she trembled at the thought of having to confess it, or perhaps that she loved another man and rather than renounce him she preferred to kill herself.'

Cover-up stories had begun to circulate within days of the case being closed. Word was passed between journalists and their informants within the police and the Carabinieri that influential persons had been involved with the dead girl. Among high-ranking state officials and in Rome's artistic quarter, it was hinted that Wilma's death had not been the result of a simple accident. It was well known that the police force had scarcely been reformed since the Fascist period and that it was beholden to those in political power. It did not see itself as neutral; rather, its job was to serve the authorities in whatever way it could. Saverio Polito's assertion that he had handed his report to his superior indicated that there was high-level interest in the case.

Polito had held important offices under the Fascist regime, including that of police commissioner in the northern city of Bologna. After Mussolini's arrest on 25 April 1943, he had been given the task of escorting Il Duce to imprisonment on the island of La Maddalena, off the northern coast of Sardinia. He had also been responsible for the Mussolini family. During one car journey with Mussolini's wife, Rachele, he had done more than guard her: she had alleged that he had unbuttoned his flies and tried to force himself on her. Later in 1943, when Mussolini was freed to lead the puppet Italian Social Republic, Polito was arrested and sentenced to twenty-four years in gaol for this outrage. After the war, his conviction was quashed, and in 1946 he was appointed police commissioner for Rome. Perhaps grateful for this trust, he antagonised the right by enthusiastically cracking down on the efforts of Fascists to reassert their influence.

Faced with mounting rumour and speculation over Wilma Montesi, the authorities made strenuous efforts to bolster the verdict of accidental death. Unused to having their judgement questioned, the higher echelons of the justice system dismissed all talk of oddities and contradictions. But the speculation continued. Eventually, on 25 April, procurator general Angelo Sigurani reopened the investigation. In recent times it had been unknown for the procurator's office to take such a step: it signalled that the conclusion the police had reached was unsatisfactory. One newspaper commented: 'The extreme difficulty of applying a minimum of logic to the reconstruction of the tragic event presented by the police in itself offers encouragement to the formulation of many suppositions, one more uncertain than the next, also as a consequence of the scarcity of facts, each more involving than the next . . . A simple girl, as it seems Wilma Montesi was, has now become an enigma; an enigma closed in a coffin.'

Most people were convinced that someone had been with her in her final hours. Who was it? And how had they contributed to her death? Too many questions about her movements and the people she might have met on the last day of her life remained unanswered. The idea of a cover-up was nourished in a setting where suspicion about the secretiveness of authority mingled with hostility against the country's new rulers. The shift from dictatorship to democracy had taken place too quickly for old habits to die overnight. Resentment of the way some had profited from the transition mixed with the conviction that too little had changed: the authorities were not accustomed to behaving openly and it was often assumed that official 'truths' were nothing of the sort. This meant that rumours of wrongdoing immediately acquired credibility and soon it was being whispered that Wilma Montesi had led a double life. On the one hand she had been utterly respectable, a girl who had never caused her parents the slightest anxiety. On the other, her outer respectability had covered questionable activities and friendships.

The unseemly buzz infuriated the Montesis, who wished to mourn in private. Rodolfo visited several newspaper offices and pleaded for his family to be left in peace. To put off reporters, the name plaque was removed from the door of the family home and the telephone was left to ring unanswered. Friends were ignored and the press invited to communicate with an appointed lawyer. But the public refused to leave the grieving family alone. Letters poured in, containing advice, commiseration, information or insults. In one of the first to arrive, even before the funeral, its anonymous author claimed to have killed Wilma for revenge on 'the policeman', her fiancé: 'Rather than let a dog of a policeman have her I have killed her. And soon there will be another Wilma.' Not surprisingly, Wanda was terrified.

The matter of the missing suspender belt stirred the public's fantasies: despite the confirmation of Wilma's virginity, many struggled to accept that sex had not been a factor. It was odd enough that Wilma's skirt and stockings were missing but the absence of the suspender belt suggested an erotic encounter. Maria had described it as 'a belt of black satin about 20cm high at the front which gradually diminished in size as it was wrapped round the body. At the back there was a small piece of elastic that was about 6cm square.' It was fastened with five hooks on the left side. At the time, all women wore suspender belts to hold up their stockings and, as Irene Gallini wrote in *Momento-sera* newspaper the day before Wilma died, 'No elegant woman removes her stockings even if it is hot.'

In early May a rumour took hold that the man who supposedly had been with Wilma, and who had seen her die without helping her, had presented himself at Police Headquarters, and had handed the missing items in. The police strenuously denied this, but in fact on 30 April a lawyer and his eighteen-year-old son, who were walking in the area of Pratica di Mare – whence the doctor had come to pronounce Wilma dead – found a pair of women's stockings in the sand. They were not recognised as Wilma's, and neither was a badly deteriorated handkerchief bearing the embroidered initial W, which an agricultural worker found near the spot two years later.

The public also latched on to the Alfa Romeo 1900 that had been spotted near Torvaianica on 9 April, and many assumed that the owner must have taken Wilma to the coast and somehow been involved in the events that led to her death. Mario Piccinini, the local mechanic who had helped to push a car stuck in sand in early March, had said that the girl in the vehicle resembled Wilma, and that the man he had spoken to was aged around thirty and brown-haired.

The mystery was assumed to revolve around this man's identity. Basing their theory on the luxury car, journalists decided he must be someone who could count on the protection of the police and the justice system. On 4 May, *Il Corriere della Sera*, Italy's newspaper of record, reported that there was a 'widespread conviction' that the beautiful Wilma Montesi had not been alone when she went to Ostia. It advanced the suggestion of foul play and hinted that the story might be more complex than it had at first appeared. But although the article's tone was serious, its content was vague. It was left to a lesser publication to set things out in black and white.

Despite its title, *Roma* was a Neapolitan newspaper owned by the shipping magnate Achille Lauro, who was mayor of the city. Right-leaning and monarchist in sympathies, the paper was nominally supportive of the ruling Christian Democrats. Lauro gave the party his backing in Parliament in return for a free hand in his home city, where he also worked with the neo-Fascist Italian Social Movement. His business had flourished under Fascism and he had even been a member of the Chamber of Fasces and Corporations, the official Fascist business council. On 4 May, *Roma* ran the headline 'Why are the police keeping quiet about the death of Wilma Montesi?' over an article which implied that the investigation had been deliberately run into the ground. This was a shameful scandal that demanded exposure. The paper suggested that Saverio Polito had embraced the implausible foot-bathing theory in an effort to conceal the truth as a favour to a powerful government minister: 'the son of a well-known political personality' had been involved and Wilma had been drugged before being left to drown in shallow water.

Roma had a certain following in the capital and the article was immediately noticed by journalists in the press rooms at the Montecitorio Palace, home of the Italian Parliament, and in Piazza San Silvestro, from where out-of-town correspondents wired their stories. The article was a turning point: it was the first to make public what was being said in newspaper offices and in the corridors of power. It licensed everyone to talk more openly. Indeed, it obliged more cautious papers to do so since anything less would have led the public to believe that they, too, were part of the establishment cover-up.

The independent left-wing Rome evening paper *Paese Sera* made the next move. It posited that the man who had possibly handed in Wilma's missing garments, the individual who had been seen near Torvaianica around 9 April, and 'the son of a political personality' were one and the same person.

The authorities responded intemperately. Late in the evening of 5 May, the police commissioner, Polito, issued a statement attacking those newspapers that had stated the police were acting

so as not to compromise the son of a political personality – not named but clearly identifiable from clear allusions – who had been involved in the episode . . . Any news of this type is devoid of any foundation. The missing garments have not so far been found and the young man to whom allusions have been made has completely different characteristics from those indicated in the press; nor is there any evidence that he ever saw or knew La Montesi. No enquiries carried out since the body was found have had the effect of modifying the orientation of the investigations or the approach of the legal system.

This was a peculiar statement – and it did nothing to silence those who were openly speculating that Wilma had been murdered or that a high-ranking person had been involved. Who exactly was 'the young man' referred to? Some of Polito's subordinates quickly realised he had gone too far and a more neutral note was hastily composed, stating that no elements had come to light to change the conclusion that the girl's death had been the result of misadventure.

The trouble was that the official account no longer satisfied anybody. With newspapers openly airing various hypotheses, Polito received a telephone call from the interior minister, Mario Scelba, who demanded to know why he was so doggedly sticking to it. Polito's limp reply was that this was the version that had been supplied by the family.

The next day Tommaso Pavone, the chief of police, was invited by the minister to tell Polito that his force's credibility was on the line. The foot-bathing theory had become a standing joke, and the investigating authorities were beginning to look ridiculous. Procurator general Sigurani made the unusual move of summoning journalists to his office to assure them that the Montesi case was definitely not closed. The magistracy would be continuing to examine the circumstances of the girl's mysterious death.

These developments were closely followed in Via Tagliamento. A young journalist named Angelo Frignani, who lived not far away, kept tabs on the family. He knew that the Montesis had continued to wonder about Wilma's fate and that the incongruous aspects of the case had eventually undercut their desire to consign the tragic event to the past. The missing items of clothing pointed unmistakably to some sort of assault, as, possibly, did the superficial bruising on the body. Wilma's mother was firm in her belief that her daughter would never have removed her underwear or her skirt outside her home. The missing suspender belt, however, made Maria suspect 'that Wilma was approached by some brute while she was bathing her feet and that, scared, she fainted. The individual took advantage of the situation to remove the garment perhaps to abuse the girl and he went away taking it with him to avoid any fingerprint identification.' The idea that fingerprints could be obtained from clothing was nonsense, but it was clear that Maria no longer ruled out the possibility that an act, or a threat, of violence had caused her daughter's death.

In the Roman imagination, such a brute was always a man of lower-class extraction, a primitive figure of violence and instinct whom respectable girls were taught to fear. He was a criminal type, normally from the south of the Italian peninsula. It was naturally to this stereotype that Maria Montesi unwittingly made reference. But the intriguing thing about the case, and what would turn it into a drama of unprecedented proportions, was that the figures who were sketched in as the perpetrators of Wilma's death were not typical of those who made the violent attacks on women that were a feature of urban life in the post-war years. They were well-heeled and well protected. It was especially shocking that one had been identified as the scion of a government minister.

At a time when the sharp divisions of the Cold War were reverberating in the Italian political system, this cast a shadow not only over the police but also over the ruling Christian Democrats. It suggested that a party that had prospered thanks to the endorsement of the Pope, the practical support of church organisations and the United States was indirectly linked to a sleazy underworld of crime and sexual corruption.

III

Politics and Scandal

In April and May 1953, when the Montesi case was attracting an unusual level of interest from the public, an election campaign was in full swing. The first national test of opinion since 1948, it would push the ruling Christian Democrats close to breaking point.

The party had been founded in 1942, on the eve of Fascism's fall, when Italy was still a monarchy. It was conceived as a broad party of Catholic inspiration that would be firmly anchored to democratic principles. By December 1945, after a series of short-lived administrations, its leader, Alcide De Gasperi, had been well placed to take over as prime minister of a national unity government. In 1953, more than seven years later, he still held that office.

De Gasperi's deputy and foreign minister was a man called Attilio Piccioni. He was a key figure in government and one of the closest collaborators of the prime minister. Born in Rieti in 1892, he was a member of the party's old guard. With the Sicilian Mario Scelba, Giuseppe Spataro and others, he had never had any truck with Fascism, although he was conservative in many of this views and hostile to the left. A Catholic to the core, Piccioni had preferred to live quietly and practise his profession as a lawyer during the Fascist years. Scelba had adopted the same approach, while De Gasperi had toiled in the Vatican Library.

Unlike the leading figures in the left-wing parties, who had mostly spent the Fascist period abroad, these men had watched the evolution of the country closely during the years of the dictatorship. They had witnessed the enthusiasms the regime had whipped up and the disappointments it had delivered. They had seen how everyday life had changed and how the institutions of the state had developed. They had had time to reflect on the type of order they wanted to build in the post-war era and on the sort of policies that needed to be pursued. During the war and the years afterwards, Italy was a country of widespread suffering and restricted privilege. While most lived from hand to mouth, the fortunate few enjoyed great wealth and luxury. Tremendous inequalities had persisted under Fascism, despite the regime's *faux*-egalitarian nationalist rhetoric, and had worsened during the turbulent period of foreign occupations. The people who profited from the situation were not the old land- and property-owning families, but those who had taken advantage of economic links with the occupying powers or who had done well during the war from the black market.

At the other end of the spectrum, the hardships of the war years had produced an unusual sense of solidarity among some sectors of the middle and lower classes. Everyone relied on his or her neighbour for a helping hand. The salary of a teacher or a white-collar employee was no greater than that of a manual worker and, because post-war inflation had consumed the savings of the former, most categories suffered hunger and hardship. Some of the worst off were the working-class families who had been shunted out of the city centre to poorly built housing in districts like Pietralata that lacked proper services or transport connections. Even running water could not be taken for granted. Displaced families and individuals were housed in refugee camps, like the one in the Cinecittà film complex. To make matters worse, the city's population swelled as thousands flocked to it from the wider Lazio region and elsewhere in the hope of finding work.

The political parties knew they could not make headway by offering ideals to the hungry. Hardship and shortages had contributed to growing discontent with Mussolini's regime, coming to a head in July 1943 after the devastating air raids on the working-class quarter of San Lorenzo. While Il Duce had stayed in his office at the Palazzo Venezia, the Pope had taken the highly unusual step of going personally to offer comfort to those who had lost homes and loved ones. Soon after, for the first time, Mussolini had found himself in a minority in the Fascist Grand Council. King Victor Emmanuel III, who had remained head of state throughout the dictatorship, dismissed him and ordered his imprisonment. His replacement as prime minister, General Badoglio, proclaimed the end of the regime that had ruled Italy for more than twenty years and everywhere there were celebrations – which soon subsided when it was announced that the war would continue in alliance with Germany. However, on 8 September 1943, the King and Badoglio abandoned the capital and signed an armistice with the Allies. Over the following four years, Rome was occupied first by the Nazis and then, following the city's liberation in June 1944, by the Allies.

It was at this point that the first coalition government consisting of all the anti-Fascist parties had been formed. While war raged in the northern half of the country, the Christian Democrats, Socialists, Communists, Liberals, Monarchists, Republicans, the Action Party and others installed themselves in office. They were strange bedfellows but they agreed to put aside their differences over several matters, including the future of the monarchy, to achieve their shared objective of ridding the country of Fascism and the Nazi occupier. The prime minister was Ivanoe Bonomi, an old social democrat, who would later be replaced by the Resistance leader Ferruccio Parri and then, at the end of 1945, by De Gasperi.

The biggest single force in Italian politics and society during this traumatic period of transition was, without doubt, the Catholic Church. It had not so much tolerated Fascism as been its close ally, at least until the late 1930s, but for this most Italians were hardly in a position to criticise it. Wisely, it had made itself as available as it could to the people at a time of tremendous upheaval, displacement, material loss and bereavement. It showed solidarity, dispensed charity and catered to spiritual needs. Also, it was the one institution that was widely trusted and had roots in the whole national community. There was no force in the land with a more extensive organisational network and a surer place in collective life. The parish church was a reference point in all villages and towns, and it became increasingly important as other institutions dissolved.

The Pope, Pius XII, hesitated before he threw his weight behind the Christian Democrats. He had hoped that the fall of the dictator might lead to a semi-authoritarian order in which the Church's role would be central. It was only after the liberation of Rome in 1944 that he lent his support to the new party, giving it a huge advantage over its rivals. Yet the backing of the Vatican was not without its problems for the Christian Democrats: Pius had a clear agenda of his own and was not averse to invoking the duty of obedience to get his way. The Church was convinced that Italy was under mortal threat and dedicated itself to a concerted campaign to restore religious values to a society whose moral fabric was deemed to have been badly damaged during the war and foreign occupations; it saw the political transition as disorienting and insidious. Ordinary Italians were faced with choices for the first time in twenty years and, in the view of the ecclesiastical hierarchy, they needed firm guidance.

An aspect of the transition that deeply alarmed the Church,

and which justified its sense of missionary urgency, was the return of the left-wing parties. It saw the Communists, with their siren calls for equality and reform, underpinned by a lightly camouflaged ideology of atheism and revolution, as a major threat. Party leader Palmiro Togliatti, who had spent the last twenty years in France, Spain and the Soviet Union – where he had risen to become secretary of the Third International – presented himself to Italy with a surprisingly moderate face. He had opted to play a long game, and instead of preaching violent revolution, he made reassuring noises designed to calm the concerns of Catholics. With his double-breasted suits and professorial style of speaking, he seemed not so different from the grey men of the Christian Democrats, but some of his lieutenants and his party's supporters were less inclined to cultivate the virtue of patience. They openly sang Stalin's praises and believed it was just a matter of time before Togliatti would cast aside his seductive mask.

Many of those who had suffered under Fascism and the Nazi occupation flocked to the Communists as the one political force to have consistently opposed Fascism and to have maintained a skeleton presence in the country under the regime. The party was well organised and offered the promise of a genuine new start. But despite its success in building a party machine of breathtaking dimensions and efficiency, it was the Christian Democrats who gradually established their dominance in Rome and in the country. More than any other party, they understood that most people wanted a rapid return to normality and that this was more urgent than reform. In 1945, sponsored by the Vatican and the Americans, De Gasperi and the Christian Democrats took the lead in shaping government policy. In elections to the constituent assembly in 1946, the Christian Democrats mobilised the support of shopkeepers, business people, peasants, devout Catholics and many women, who were voting for the first time, and won the largest share of the vote.

The sixty-five-year-old De Gasperi and his deputy, Attilio Piccioni, were concerned to give their government as wide a support base as possible. They were convinced that their party could keep together the opposing forces of conservatism and reform in the country, so long as there was no ambiguity about the party's commitment to liberal democracy. To this end, it sought co-operation with the small centre parties, the Liberals and Republicans, which counted for little in terms of votes but which had roots in the national cultural tradition going back to the period of Italian unification in the 1860s.

Piccioni's job was to make sure the party machine was geared to achieving these objectives. As a man who had cut his political teeth in Turin and later moved to Pistoia, then Florence, he had wide experience of political organisation. Although he was a loyal Catholic, he was as concerned as others that the party should not be subordinate to the Vatican. He was known as a thinker, a man of relatively few words, and his opinion was valued. It was his idea, for example, to hold a vote of the Christian Democrat membership to decide whether to back the monarchy or the republic in the 1946 referendum — the latter won decisively. A heavy smoker until he gave up in 1948, he had something of the look of a tortoise, his bald head and weary, heavy-lidded eyes making him seem older than he was. He moved slowly and deliberately, rarely smiled and was assumed to be of a melancholic disposition.

Piccioni took a key role in the election campaign of 1948. A cautious man, he stayed in Rome for most of the campaign, directing operations. Although he was standing for election in the constituency of Perugia, Terni and Rieti, he only turned up in the area in the last few days of the contest. In a swift round of rallies, he delivered exactly the same carefully crafted speech everywhere, without changing a single sentence.

The Christian Democrats were not solely responsible for

mobilising their own electorate. The Vatican decided to turn the contest into a test of its strength and galvanised Catholics as never before in a historic battle against Communism and modernisation. In Piazza San Giovanni, the square that the left always used to gather its supporters, the normally measured Communist leader, Palmiro Togliatti, uncharacteristically invited Italians at his final rally to join him in delivering a kick in the pants to De Gasperi. The boot proved to be on the other foot. Drawing advantage from American promises of a future of prosperity if Italians voted for the Christian Democrats, and the efforts of the Church, which had thrown all its resources into rousing moderate and conservative opinion and mobilising the vote, the Christian Democrats won a historic victory. When faced with a choice between a swift restoration of order – with the threat of sanctions if the vote went the wrong way – and a future of radical change filled with uncertainty, Italians had opted for the former. In Rome the Christian Democrats scored a majority on their own, winning 51 per cent of the vote, a massive increase on the 29.5 per cent they had attracted in 1946. They had achieved it, though, not by trouncing the left, which saw its share rise from 24 per cent to 27 per cent, but by squeezing the small parties of right and centre.

For the next five years, De Gasperi headed an administration including some of those small parties. He championed adherence to the Western defence organisation, contributed to the moves that led to the founding of the European Economic Community, and renegotiated the terms of what had been a humiliating peace treaty. He also embraced measures to redistribute land and promote southern development. Other members of the government, notably the bullish Scelba, made it their business to ensure a firm state response to leftist agitation, a reactionary clampdown that was fully backed by the Church. In a remarkable declaration, Pius XII formally excommunicated anyone who belonged to or voted for the Communist Party.

The rapid turning of the Christian Democrats into the party of order caused disquiet in some quarters. Men like Giuseppe Dossetti, an influential law professor turned politician from Bologna, who was known for having joined the Resistance while refusing to bear weapons, and Giorgio La Pira, another professor who became a much-loved mayor of Florence, wanted more attention paid to social questions. They sided with the workers in industrial disputes and opposed any deals with profiteers and vested interests. Broadly in tune with them, but rather more worldly, Amintore Fanfani was an energetic Tuscan: he shared their views but was much more personally ambitious. He knew that the time would soon come when De Gasperi, who by 1953 was seventy-two and not well, would step down. The election scheduled for 7–8 June would be a big test of the party's standing after five years' domination in government. It was a test it faced with some trepidation. To minimise any risk of a weak administration, and to bolster the Christian Democrats' power, De Gasperi had forced through a law that gave 65 per cent of the seats in Parliament to any party or coalition that scored more than 50 per cent of the vote. Delighted by the excuse this gave them to accuse the ruling party of rigging elections, the Communists, who had been in the doldrums since the death of Stalin in March, went into the campaign with all guns blazing. They denounced the 'swindle law' and plastered the country's cities with posters that depicted government ministers as greedy wielders of giant spoons and forks.

It was against this background that the Montesi case first started to take shape. The sharpness of political conflict and the fear that the Christian Democrats and their allies might not do as well as hoped in the election scheduled for June 1953 undoubtedly bore on how the judicial and police authorities and the press dealt with the rumours that that had started to circulate.

There can scarcely have been a political party in the world less likely to generate a sex scandal than the ruling Christian Democrats. Its elderly leaders were upright men who were early to bed and early to rise. They were colourless, cautious individuals who were deeply religious and personally austere. Typically, they attended mass every day. Unlike Mussolini and some of his henchmen, who had made an exhibition of their virility and revelled in tales of sexual conquest, little was known about their private lives. Only De Gasperi had been drawn, somewhat against his instincts, into the magazine world, where family photographs revealed off-duty and informal moments. But the image he presented was not in the least controversial. No one imagined for one instant that the privacy of his ministers concealed anything other than routine family life.

It was a different matter with the sons of some Christian Democrat ministers. When word about the alleged involvement of a politician's offspring in Wilma Montesi's death first reached the ears of the editors of Rome's leading dailies, not all were surprised. Umberto Tupini, Giuseppe Spataro and Attilio Piccioni were known to have young adult sons, as was the mayor of Rome, Salvatore Rebecchini.

Piccioni, De Gasperi's deputy, had been a widower since 1934 and had four children. His two daughters were married, as was one son. The two young men had chosen quite different careers: Leone, the elder, was a literary critic, while the younger, Giampiero, known as Piero, was a jazz musician and composer of film scores; he mixed with actors and other musicians and was an habitué of nightclubs. At thirty, Piero still lived in his father's home, a stone's throw from the Vatican in Via della Conciliazione, one of the prestigious new highways that Fascism had imposed on Rome. The block was owned by the Vatican and the family occupied it at a concessionary rent. Relations between father and son had been strained since Piero had given up a career in the law to pursue his passion for music. Regarded as something of a black sheep by his deeply Catholic family, he performed under the pseudonym of Piero Morgan to avoid any risk of embarrassment to his father.

That was now unavoidable: Piero Piccioni was soon revealed to be the subject of rumour. But before he was named in the press, journalists and editors debated how to handle a story that could have devastating consequences for the government. The founder and editor of *Il Tempo*, Renato Angiolillo, found himself in an especially uncomfortable position. A right-winger, who was a senator for the small Liberal Party, he knew Attilio Piccioni well but was also his political rival since both men were standing for election in the same constituency of Rieti in the Lazio region. When his chief news reporter Sergio Del Bufalo came to him with the gossip he had heard from his sources in the police and the Carabinieri, he first telephoned his opposite number at *Il Messaggero*, then tried to contact Piccioni himself. When he failed to get hold of him – he was out on the campaign trail – he alerted Saverio Polito to what was being said. Meanwhile, he instructed Del Bufalo to dig out the truth. Del Bufalo spoke to a colleague on the Christian Democrats' paper, *Il Popolo*, who immediately suspected a political manoeuvre. A journalist on this paper, Clelia D'Inzillo, knew the Piccioni family well because Piero's brother, Leone, was a contributor. She rushed round to Via della Conciliazione to warn them that a potentially damaging story was about to break. The Piccionis took immediate steps to try to suppress the rumour but were too late to prevent the anti-Christian Democrat press from going public.

The first clear allusion to Piero Piccioni's potential implication in the case appeared in a right-wing satirical weekly, *Il Merlo Giallo*, published by Riccardo Giannini, the journalist who had written the piece for *Roma*. A clever but fleeting reference to carrier-pigeons in a brief article that mentioned the Montesi case was enough to put the name of Piccioni (the plural of *piccione*, the Italian word for 'pigeon') into public circulation: 'The "well-known political personalities" to whom *Roma* alludes are not numerous and, moreover, they cannot disappear without a trace like carrier-pigeons.' The article went on to suggest that the case had been hushed up for reasons to do with the election campaign.

As soon as he received a copy of the *Il Merlo Giallo*, Attilio Piccioni rushed in panic to see his long-time colleague the interior minister, Scelba, to demand its immediate seizure. Furious that his good name was tarnished, he overlooked the fact that in the democratic republic the interior minister no longer had the power to order the impoundment or censorship of newspapers. Scelba recorded in his memoirs that he advised Piccioni to instruct his son to go and see the chief of police, Tommaso Pavone, to find out what could be done. Pavone had been installed in his post by Scelba. He occupied an office at the Viminale Palace – where the prime minister and the interior ministry were housed – close to those of Piccioni and Scelba. From the start, Piccioni took a firm stance: his son was innocent. That he, a man of integrity, could take such an unambiguous position persuaded many people of the falsity of the rumour.

What is interesting, though, is that Piccioni was convinced that the story had some political source. Incensed, he was determined to get to the bottom of it. This was no easy matter since the far left and the far right were always looking to damage the Christian Democrats, and battles for influence between the parties of government sometimes took unusual forms. He had reason to be suspicious of Angiolillo, who posed as a friend but, as a political rival, could not be trusted. Within his own party, one of eclectic spirits and tendencies, internal competition was normal and low blows far from unknown. Behind the dignified senior personalities who were its public face, there were many less principled individuals who were eager to gain advantage. Some younger men thought that the old guard who ran the party should be pushed aside. And, with De Gasperi's star waning after seven years at the helm of government and his health failing, Piccioni knew he was the man to beat – indeed, as early as 1 March 1953, he had been described in *Il Corriere della Sera* as 'De Gasperi's presumptive heir'. The war of succession would begin seriously after the Christian Democrats and their allies narrowly failed to secure more than 50 per cent of the vote in the June election. The Communists were cock-a-hoop that the 'swindle law', too, had failed.

The Communists chose not to make the Montesi rumours a plank of their campaign, even though the first publication to name Piccioni's son had been the Communist weekly *Vie Nuove*, on 16 May. It was one of the soft publications of the left. It was not very ideological and it published lively stories illustrated with plenty of photographs. Actresses were more likely to feature on its covers than politicians. As such, it was the ideal place to bring the Piccioni name into the open without directly implicating the party. In a long article, which carried the sub-title 'Too many rumours about the Montesi case make us think there must be some truth in them', Mario Cesarini Sforza, one of the quite numerous sons of well-established families who had joined the Communist Party after the war, pointed the finger directly at Piero Piccioni without quoting any sources. 'Does Piero Piccioni have an alibi?' his final paragraph concluded dramatically.

IV

Via Margutta

Piero Piccioni belonged to several different worlds in Rome, but the one he found most congenial was the colourful, vivacious milieu that had as its focal point the artists and Bohemians of Via Margutta. Tucked behind the picturesque Piazza di Spagna, close to the Spanish Steps and running parallel to the busy Via del Babuino, it was a narrow street mainly populated by painters and sculptors. Today it is a peaceful pedestrian enclave, with a high wall on one side that gives it a claustrophobic air. Permanently shadowed by tall buildings and partially covered by pergolas, it seems genteel. Boutique hotels, art galleries and antiques shops have replaced most of the scruffy studios and seedy bars that made it the city's own Chelsea or Montmartre.

In the early years of the twentieth century, it was the mews for the palaces on Via del Babuino and its cobbles rang to the sound of horses' hoofs. In the inter-war years, as horses and carriages gave way to cars, the stables were taken over by artists attracted by available space and low rents. Modigliani, de Chirico and the futurists Boccioni, Marinetti and Severini all made themselves at home here. Between the 1930s and the 1970s the street enjoyed a reputation as a haven from the corrupting centres of money and power that dominated the capital.

Via Margutta was dominated by Italian artists, many of them thoroughly Roman, though there was a cosmopolitan feel to the wider Bohemian community. Foreign artists had come to

Rome since at least the seventeenth century and numerous art
students still visited the city. For northern Europeans and North
Americans, Italy was cheap and Rome offered a relaxed lifestyle
that was deeply appealing – even many quite wealthy foreigners
found themselves drawn to the alternative world of the cafés
and clubs. But it was also a refuge for many young Italians
who had fled from their families or the suffocating atmosphere
of provincial life: here people lived freely, ignoring conventions,
working as and when they chose or as need demanded. It was
one of very few places in the socially repressive Italy of the
early 1950s where anything was possible.

Unusually, a number of prominent female artists worked in,
or were associated with, the area, and they set a tone that was
more modern and emancipated than anywhere else in the capital
or, indeed, in the country. Anna Salvatore, a charismatic artist
of the realist school who started her career producing anti-war
paintings in the 1940s, was the most highly regarded. One of
her early drawings from 1946 was entitled *The Orgy*: it portrayed
a group of ugly old men and a series of flabby bodies engaged
in repellent exchanges of bodily fluids. The reference to the
final decadent phase of Fascism was transparent. Salvatore was
beautiful, with dyed-blonde hair and sultry eyes; she was just
twenty-three in 1953, and became best known for her paintings
of disaffected youth, capturing their taste for American music.
She liked to paint girls from the shanty towns on the edge of
Rome: she admired their primitive vitality and portrayed them
in vivid colours. The British *News Chronicle* dubbed her 'Anna,
the artist of the dance halls'. Her work inspired several cinematic
portrayals of lower-class young women, including Elsa
Martinelli's spiky prostitute in Mauro Bolognini's *La notte brava*
(The Big Night) and Rossana Schiaffino's gutter princess in
Francesco Rosi's *La sfida* (The Challenge). She also designed
the poster for Pier Paolo Pasolini's début film *Accattone*, which
was set partly in the shanty town of Pigneto, to the east of the

city centre. She mingled with the artists, writers and actors who counted in the city, and some of the leading lights of the period, including Anna Magnani and Alberto Moravia, sat for her. As a star of the art scene known for what fellow artist Ugo Moretti called 'her patrician eyes and revolutionary blonde hair', she would appear briefly in Fellini's *La dolce vita*, playing herself, and in his follow-up *Giulietta degli spiriti*. Salvatore was no recluse but neither was she a great fan of the cliquey atmosphere that marked the artistic community. She opened a gallery called Pincio at the end of Via del Babuino, where she hosted the work of young figurative painters as well as crafts. She was interested in art rather than influence or fame.

The role of queen bee in Via Margutta fell to another female painter, Novella Parigini. More bubbly and popular than Salvatore, but a lesser artist, Parigini was exceptionally energetic and did much to establish the public reputation of the road on which she lived and worked. Her studio at Via Margutta 53b – where her name plaque can still be seen – was a permanent open house where many talented drifters found temporary refuge. Blonde and petite, she had spent several years in Paris where she mingled with the great figures of the Left Bank – Jean Paul Sartre and Simone de Beauvoir, Jean Cocteau, Jean Genet and Juliette Greco – and visited foreigners, including Truman Capote and Ernest Hemingway. She also studied in New York. When she returned to Italy in 1949, she was taken up by no less a figure than Margherita Sarfatti, Mussolini's one-time mistress, who had played a role in launching his political career.

Parigini's paintings were not very memorable. Her greatest innovation was the invention of face and body painting. For carnival, her female models were photographed with their faces, necks and backs daubed with zigzags and animal features. Otherwise she specialised in *naïf* female portraits with cat's faces. It was more as a mover and shaker and *salonière* that she made her name. She boasted that Picasso and Dalí were acquaintances and actively cultivated the friendship of writers such as Tennessee Williams, who defined her as 'wild like the garden of the world before the creation'. Her hospitality was not ceremonious but simple and relaxed. In her seventh-floor studio, which she dubbed 'the seventh heaven', she offered local Roman produce and flasks of Frascati from the nearby hills to whoever called on her, regardless of whether they were princes or paupers. Photogenic and charming, Parigini was at the centre of an exciting and experimental set, the one-woman animator of a whole cool scene.

In later years Parigini would claim to have invented the Roman *dolce vita* single-handedly. Certainly she encouraged a type of Bohemian café society that was easy-going and joyous. Film stars, dissolute nobles, aspiring actors and writers, many of them foreign, formed part of her circle. With her impish manner and knowledge of languages, she charmed those who otherwise struggled to find a place in Roman society. She had a particular taste for Hollywood actors and enjoyed flings with George Raft, Errol Flynn and Gary Cooper among others. She delighted in provoking scandal at a time when even small transgressions caused howls of protest: *bien pensants* gasped with outrage when a photograph was published of her wearing a bikini while she was staying at the Capri villa that belonged to Prince Dado Ruspoli. To even greater astonishment, she befriended Christine Jorgensen, a former American soldier whose announcement in 1952 that she had had sex reassignment surgery in Denmark caused a media sensation. Another of her long-term guests was the young Ursula Andress – the future Honey Ryder in the first James Bond film, *Dr No*. Aged only fifteen, Andress had arrived in Rome with the French actor Daniel Gélin, a mature Don Giovanni who was contracted to film the adaptation of Moravia's novel *Woman of Rome*. Parigini fixed her up with Count Pier Ferdinando Calvi di Bergolo, and she was courted relentlessly by Marlon Brando during the months she spent in Via Margutta.

The grandson of one-time Fascist Party secretary Achille Starace, the witty and camp Giò Stajano was one of Parigini's closest friends. In his scandalous fictionalised memoirs, Stajano provided an account of homosexual life in the capital that described furtive encounters between Members of Parliament, rent-boys, artists, prostitutes and actors. Real people, he said later, were concealed behind his characters' names. Parigini and Stajano loved stunts and often staged them for the benefit of the press, which they knew loved to report on the shocking night life of Rome's alternative world. Of course, most of what went on in Bohemia did not reach the newspapers.

The veil that Stajano lifted in his memoir revealed a world that was unknown to most, and unacknowledged. Although times had changed, and the press censorship that had prevailed in the Fascist period had ended, there was a strong tendency to euphemism that concealed aspects of life that might be considered sordid or louche. Newspapers normally preferred the picturesque to the sensational, although tastes were becoming racier. Everyone in the media knew that in the small towns and villages of the peninsula, and even in the residential quarters of large cities, nocturnal entertainments of any sort existed only in naughty fantasy and sinful imaginings. RAI's radio broadcasts from Roman night spots were hugely popular precisely because the audience pictured in its mind the seductive atmospheres and sophisticated pleasures hinted at by the world-weary songs and hushed commentary.

In his portrait of the artists' Rome, Ugo Moretti described how hard-up artists, many of whom struggled to sell their works and lived in draughty attics in constant fear of the landlord's call, always kept a keen eye on the passing female talent. Whether they were runaways, students, models or aspiring artists and actors, there were always girls who found the Via Margutta alluring. Practised seducers knew that few well-to-do girls could resist the appeal of a handsome painter,

so they wooed them, thinking as much of tricking them into
paying for lunch at the Taverna degli Artisti or the Trattoria
Menghi as of getting into them into bed. Some scions of the
best Roman families and rich older men also knew that pick-
ups were easier here than elsewhere. Although many of the
regulars of the area were well-nigh penniless, they brushed up
against money and lived in constant hope that fortune would
one day smile on them and they would no longer need
humiliatingly to buy cigarettes five at a time. After dark, the
bars and clubs provided a seductive mix of sounds, smells and
bodies that frayed inhibitions.

After a period of several years in which jazz had been banned
as the incomprehensible product of a racially inferior section
of a wartime enemy, it flowered on an unprecedented scale. It
was broadcast on the radio, and played in cafés and cellar bars
where it attracted legions of fans. For Italy's existentialists, Louis
Armstrong, Duke Ellington and Benny Goodman were figures
of an alternative black America, a hidden nation they found
more congenial than the country of Truman and Eisenhower.

Among the Italian musicians who would make their mark
after the war, Piero Piccioni was one of the first to form a
band. His thirteen-piece combo, the O13, was performing a
mixture of New Orleans-style jazz and bebop soon after the
Allies liberated Rome. He played at the international jazz
festival in Paris, performed on the radio, and appeared regularly
in one of Rome's night spots, the Dancing Nilo, which he
helped set up. Piccioni was better informed than most about
American jazz and he would become one of the key conduits
between it and Italian musical culture. He was a well-known
figure in Rome's café society. Although not particularly good-
looking – he had an up-turned nose and a long face – he
was often spotted with an actress on his arm.

One of the attractions for everyone – be they the
Hollywood actors who hung around the artists' studios in

the afternoon or climbed the many stairs to Parigini's studio for a late-night *spaghettata*, or the lawyers and bankers who slipped into the milk bars of the streets around Via Margutta – was the ready availability of reefers and pills that could not easily be obtained anywhere else in Rome. Drugs were a favourite indulgence at the parties that the artists and their acolytes staged. The vogue for drug-taking among the young offspring of Rome's most famous aristocratic families influenced the young artists who hung out on the Via Margutta. Prince Dado Ruspoli became a pin-up slumming aristocrat after he was busted in 1952 and confessed to his addiction. This was the parochial news the gossipy weeklies adored: it was more colourful to feature a wayward Italian noble than the sad arrest of tormented jazz musician Chet Baker for heroin possession, or the news that arrived from across the Atlantic of actor Robert Mitchum's exposure as a devotee of marijuana.

Journalists knew that two or three bars, including the Tazza d'Oro, which also held art shows, or the tiny but more popular Il Baretto on the corner of Via del Babuino, were good sources of information. Virtually everyone who belonged to one of the Via Margutta cliques popped into Il Baretto several times a week, and some made it a permanent hangout. During the day, students and the cool existentialist crowd shared the space with workers dropping by for a coffee or a glass of red wine. After dark it became a pick-up joint, artists' bar and centre of the latest tittle-tattle about the area's personalities and the worlds of the arts and entertainment. Piero Piccioni was often seen there and so were many of the other greater or lesser figures who would take part in the unfolding of the Montesi case.

The area was also known for its several brothels and late-night clubs. These were not the polished cabarets of the wealthy Via Veneto but informal establishments of a more rough and ready nature. The most celebrated was the Piccolo Slam, a private club on two floors where members gathered to play cards, eat cold snacks and, on the lower floor, drink, throw dice and dance wildly to a jukebox. It quickly won a reputation for its collection of outcasts and misfits. It was one of the few places where black people danced, lesbians gathered, and drug-dealers were known to operate openly. Another club with a similar reputation was the Siviglia, which, like the Piccolo Slam, was closed down by the police after several raids.

A journalist, Silvano Muto, had started to sniff around the bars in pursuit of some startling stories he could use to gain the public's ear. He was a law graduate and would-be magazine editor, whose father was a senior figure in the shipping industry and also an aspiring Christian Democrat politician. Muto was no Bohemian. Although he was only twenty-four, he was tidy, conventionally dressed and formal in his manners. He had a neat moustache and, on account of his weak sight, wore tinted glasses. Despite his conservative appearance, he found a few people willing to share their tales with him. Muto's aim was to investigate the drugs traffic that everyone knew existed in Rome and, as he soon discovered, drugs and the existentialists were inseparable. It was not just that drugs could be bought in the bars and clubs where the Bohemians hung out: 'I can affirm in all calmness and certainty that in Rome there is not a single existentialist who does not use at least mefedina or who is not in some way involved in vice,' he asserted; he was referring to a synthetic narcotic used medically in pain relief, the effect of which was similar to opium.

When he learned that a stretch of coast south of Ostia was known for smuggling, he travelled there in his Fiat 1900cc car in July 1953. He struck up conversations, passing himself off as someone who was interested in buying land in the area, and soon won the confidence of some locals. He quickly found that many people knew the area was an important route for drugs and contraband cigarettes, and that Ostia was the out-of-town home to some of Rome's most decadent hedonists. Its sedate outward appearance concealed a variety of immoral pleasures, including drug consumption.

He had not begun his research with any intention of taking up the matter of Wilma Montesi's death, but he soon changed his mind. One thing he heard shook him to the core: 'The most important thing was what was being murmured in those parts, namely that the death of La Montesi was linked to these activities. Tor San Lorenzo, a place just twenty kilometres from Torvaianica, was the sorting centre. Some points of the beach between Ostia and Anzio were regularly frequented by smugglers. During the night mysterious boats left the coast and returned with boxes and cases full of contraband goods.'

As far as the locals were concerned, this was not a discovery. For some time a young priest from the parish of Ardea, Don Aldo Zamboni, had been trying to raise the alarm about the drug-trafficking in the area. There had been other strange deaths that were rumoured to be associated with it. Two years previously a petty criminal, Ettore Vari, had been found dead near Ostia as the result of a drugs overdose, which was thought to have been injected by force. A nosy photographer called Flavio Agorneri, whose body had been found near Torvaianica supposedly after a tarantula bite, was another possible victim of the traffickers.

On one of his excursions to Ostia on a sunny July afternoon, Muto was introduced by a mutual acquaintance, a champion ice-skater named Elio Pedretti, to a young woman named Adriana Bisaccia. The meeting was a set-up since Muto had been tipped off – he said later – by Franco Angioy, a clerk to the Chamber of Deputies, that she would be able to provide him with interesting information. Born in the southern town of Avellino, she seemed to have lived several lives in her twenty-three years. A typical example of the girl existentialists who populated the fringes of the artistic community, Bisaccia had arrived in Rome seven years previously after a spell in Naples, hoping for fame and success. She had worked only as a typist, and her dreams had been fuelled by her mother, a former singer. Thanks to her deep brown eyes and pretty face, she had met a film director who had been momentarily taken with her. In the course of a screen test, she had been obliged to act out a seduction, then to repeat the scene in the director's bed. A producer had subsequently tried to tempt her with the promise of a journey to Switzerland but she had turned him down. She had appeared in one comedy film in a very small role but no other offers of work had followed. Instead she was obliged to make ends meet by posing nude for artists.

Ever since Wilma Montesi's death had become the mystery that was on everyone's lips, Adriana Bisaccia had been telling anyone prepared to listen that the girl had not met her death in the manner stated by the police. As long as such opinions were expressed in the smoke-filled cafés and cellar bars, they were worth nothing. For Muto, on the other hand, they were potential gold dust.

On the day he first met her, and gave her and Pedretti a lift back to Rome in his car, he tried to get more from Bisaccia. Once they were back in the city he walked with her to the central Piazza Colonna and took her number. At eleven p.m. they met up again with Pedretti on the fashionable Via Veneto where they were joined by two of the skater's friends. After an hour or two of club-hopping, Muto proposed a trip to the coast and someone suggested a dip in the sea under the light of the moon. He drove them to Lavinio where, comforted by the warm night air, they whiled away the hours until dawn in the company of a mixed group of laughing, drunken young Americans they encountered. Later this group followed them to Tor San Lorenzo and then to Torvaianica where they all indulged themselves for a few more hours in the sea and on the empty sands. There, at around four p.m., the by now exhausted band finally called a halt to the revelry and limply made their way back to Rome. The whole sarabande had lasted some seventeen hours.

The exact nature of the relationship that formed between the journalist and this young woman is not very clear. Although Muto was married, they might have become lovers. What is clear is that Bisaccia had stories to tell and Muto was more than willing to listen. Although she knew the ways of Il Baretto, and its code of not being inquisitive about others' business and not trusting strangers, she could hardly contain herself.

Bisaccia had started to spend time in the bars after she had got a job with a building company based in Via Margutta. She stayed out late and often went to dance and drink at a painter's studio or spent the early hours chatting on the Spanish Steps. She also went to the Piccolo Slam and the Siviglia. Bisaccia's first encounter with the world of drugs had occurred, she confessed, when she met a former schoolfriend, called Claudia, who had become a pusher.

Bisaccia had tales to tell about the habits of the high rollers and money men she had known. She told Muto about the parties that took place in the Castel Porziano area and mentioned a number of people she had seen at them. Muto went back to the area and found that the modest road between Rome and Pratica di Mare saw the regular passage of luxury cars. He was told, with a wink, that at three or four in the morning high-ranking people came to 'hunt' in the vicinity. Bisaccia talked, too, of the drug parties held out of Rome on a stretch of coast to the south of Ostia. She claimed to have first experienced an orgy when she went with her friend Claudia to the house of some friends. 'There were around ten of them, divided into couples, with glassy eyes and pale faces,' Bisaccia explained. And then she told Muto that she had been invited to sex parties and that at one of them she had met a girl by the name of Wilma Montesi.

V

Hollywood on the Tiber

Young women like Adriana Bisaccia or Wilma Montesi, who were in their teens or early twenties in the 1950s, found the movies fascinating, irresistible even. The cinemas themselves, even in the major Italian cities, were not the plush palaces and exotic temples that tempted consumers in the United States and northern Europe, but the movies they screened offered alluring fantasies that fuelled the dreams and hopes of the young.

Bisaccia was not unusual in having sought to break into the industry. Thousands upon thousands of girls like her flocked to auditions or went to great lengths to make the acquaintance of a producer, director or actor, or even a director's assistant, someone who knew a director's assistant or even a porter at Cinecittà, the huge international film production centre that had been opened in 1937. Despite the stern disapproval of the Church, beauty contests were hugely popular in the post-war years because they offered a possible launch pad to a movie career. Silvana Mangano had been chosen to play the lead in the neo-realist melodrama *Bitter Rice* in 1948 after being crowned Miss Rome, and a few others had had similar good fortune. Just like in Hollywood, the fantasy of movie stardom was a powerful lure. Ambition was usually unrelated to any talent or professional training; it was an inner drive based on the assumption that youth, beauty and luck were all that were needed to swap the insufferable mediocrity of everyday life for the wonderful glare of the studio lights.

These dreams were encouraged by the first Roman girls of humble origins who were fortunate enough to make it onto the silver screen in this era of black-and-white miracles. From the way she dressed, Wilma's favourite star was probably Silvana Pampanini. Seven years older than her, the Roman actress was the immediate precursor of world-famous Italian stars such as Gina Lollobrigida and Sophia Loren. 'Nini Panpan', as the French affectionately dubbed her, never spoke with her own voice on screen, but in her physical confidence and sympathetic manner she had strong Roman traits. Usually well turned-out and buttoned to the neck, Pampanini only rarely exhibited her famously curvaceous figure. The characters she played were never negative, although they often found themselves drawn unwittingly into compromising situations. In *La tratta delle bianche* (White Slave Trade), she played the lover of a gang-master, while in *Vortice* (Vortex), she breaks with her doctor fiancé to marry a rich man who can pay off her troubled father's debts.

Elsa Martinelli was another local youngster who rose to stardom. She was a railwayman's daughter who grew up in the Salario quarter, in Piazza Vescovio, an ordinary square situated not far from Via Tagliamento. A sleek and naturally elegant young woman, she took jobs from the time she was a teenager, working at the cash desk of bars where she chatted with equal abandon to rich clients during the day and local youth in the evening. Martinelli would become an internationally famous model before making her screen début in *The Indian Fighter*, a Hollywood film starring Kirk Douglas. The magazines dubbed her Italy's answer to Audrey Hepburn. Later she would marry a count and, following their separation, become one of the uninhibited protagonists of Roman café society.

Most young people, like Wilma, did not go to any great lengths to further their ambitions. Instead they indulged their dreams in private, going regularly to the movies and devouring magazines. News kiosks in Rome were explosions of colour in an otherwise drab urban landscape. The red-and-black or black-and-white print of most of the early post-war periodicals had slowly given way to the brash hues of the illustrated magazines. Copies of these lively weeklies were hung on racks on the exterior of the kiosks by news-vendors who knew that they would draw the eye of passers-by. One of the most successful new publications was a glossy magazine called *Grand Hotel*. Filled with comic-style illustrated stories of romance and passion, movie gossip and puzzles, it was a huge hit with servant girls, hairdressers and their customers. The covers always featured a glamorous couple who resembled current American film stars, such as Rita Hayworth and Robert Taylor. Most of the weekly magazines put photographs of the stars on their covers, although politicians and the Pope sometimes got a look in. They provided a glamorous escape from the everyday, and for girls like the Montesi sisters they gave an idea of a life that was at once alluringly different yet familiar. Many young people looked to the stars as life models, collected cuttings about them and followed their every move. Some also believed that they, too, might one day join the demi-gods in the modern Olympus.

Such dreams were not as preposterous as they had been in the 1920s, when every handsome youth thought he could follow in the footsteps of Rudolph Valentino, the poor emigrant from the Puglia region who became a Hollywood star. The films of neo-realism had led people to believe that they did not need to be beautiful or even able to speak well (since voices were dubbed) to appear on screen.

In fact, subtly and slowly, the Italian film industry had been injecting some glamour into its best features. As production had started to return to normal after the disruptions of the post-war years, producers set about winning back the domestic market after the Americans had taken firm hold of it during and after the liberation. Some of the new stars were women like Pampanini, who had narrowly missed winning the first national Miss Italy pageant in 1946, or Silvana Mangano, who also caught the eye of the film world when she paraded in a swimming costume. Directors, actors and producers all sat on the juries of these competitions and picked out from them promising faces and figures. In her début role, Mangano won acclaim playing just the sort of girl who might have taken part in a beauty contest, a sexy rice-weeder in thrall to romance magazines, boogie-woogie and American movies. Gina Lollobrigida, runner-up at Miss Italia 1947, played in a lot of minor movies before her winsome smile and shapely figure were shown off to better effect in light comedies. She, Pampanini and Mangano had a little of the raw authenticity of Anna Magnani and a lot of the pin-up appeal of the Hollywood starlet. Above all, they seemed familiar, not remote demi-gods but girls next door with added charisma.

Cinema was not just a pastime in Rome. It was one of the city's most important industries and a big employer. Production had languished in the immediate post-war years, as the Americans poured hundreds of old and new movies into the market in the knowledge that after seven years of absence the thirst for Hollywood was stronger than ever. At first the Christian Democrats had ignored calls to defend the local industry. They were intent on anchoring Italy to the West under American leadership and they thought a steady diet of westerns, romances and family films would persuade the people that this was in their interests too. Grim neo-realist dramas about unemployment and homelessness were dismissed as left-wing propaganda. Angry and frustrated at being ignored, film workers staged a huge rally in Rome's

Piazza del Popolo in February 1949. Anna Magnani, Vittorio De Sica and other famous names appealed to government and people with an impassioned chant to 'Help us!' After this, it was accepted that intervention was needed – not just for the sake of the local industry but also because heavy film imports were weakening the balance of payments. A system of prizes and subsidies was introduced that was remarkably similar to the one that had operated under Mussolini. A condition of gaining support was the renunciation of politics. 'Less rags, more legs' was what Italian cinema needed, according to the otherwise pious young cinema minister Giulio Andreotti; or, to put it another way, fewer ragged-trousered anti-heroes and more cheerful eroticism.

Slowly, Italian films started to place less stress on social problems. The last neo-realist film was made in 1952 by De Sica. *Umberto D* dwells on the drama of a dignified but penniless pensioner facing eviction from his rented room. With only his dog and a servant girl as friends, he is beset by suicidal impulses that are only just tempered by the dog's affection.

The lively comedies that steadily became more popular still looked rather like the realist dramas of a few years previously. They were shot in black-and-white, they were often set in familiar lower-class environments, and they tackled everyday themes, but they were more likely to be optimistic and aspirational. For the first time since restrictions on foreign films had been lifted, Italian movies were able to compete seriously for audiences. This was just as well since the American studios, in order to comply with the ban on the export of profits reaped from the distribution of foreign films that was part of the package of support for domestic production, began making their own films in Italy. Most of the great ancient-world blockbusters were made in Rome. *Quo Vadis*, shot by MGM at great expense between 1950 and 1951, was the first, followed by *Helen of Troy* and *Ulysses*. Delightful contemporary films, such as the romantic comedy *Roman Holiday*, in which a young Audrey Hepburn plays a European princess savouring Rome incognito in the charming company of American journalist Joe Bradley, played by Gregory Peck, and the rags-to-riches Ava Gardner vehicle *The Barefoot Contessa*, also employed Italian settings and harnessed studio resources.

However, the Americans regarded the experience of filming abroad with some trepidation. In the early 1920s the filming of *Ben-Hur* in Rome had been a disaster and many scenes had had to be re-shot in California. The several hundred-strong *Quo Vadis* troupe thus arrived armed with advice about the location and quantities of items that allegedly were impossible to find in Italy, such as shoes that did not squeak and matches that ignited on being struck. The studio regarded the whole trip along the lines of a colonial expedition. It carried out its own upgrade of Cinecittà's studios, installing lighting rigs for Technicolor, and air-conditioning, and tied up the studios for a full eighteen months. Tens of thousands of extras were recruited, but very few local technical workers, and only one cast member was Italian, the half-English Marina Berti, who played the slave girl Eunice. A production on a truly grandiose scale, *Quo Vadis* was also an unacknowledged propaganda film, whose making coincided with the Holy Year of 1950. A Vatican official was present to advise on the message of Christian piety and struggle for freedom against totalitarianism, which in the film was embodied by Peter Ustinov's plump and spoilt Nero.

By 1953 Rome had become a magnet for American actors. At a time when film production was being scaled back in the United States due to shrinking post-war audiences, the production boom in Italy offered precious opportunities for work. Some, such as Robert Taylor or Gregory Peck, were at the peak of their careers. Others were just starting out and arrived hoping to land parts on the spot, perhaps even in Italian films. Among

these were the Dowling sisters, Constance and Doris. Doris was
the more fortunate as she won a leading role in *Bitter Rice*, one
of few neo-realist films that would be an international hit. Others
still were has-beens hoping for a new lease of life. Many Italians
loved Laurel and Hardy (Stanlio e Ollio, as they were known)
and even Mussolini had been a big fan, but by the time the pair
arrived in Rome their heyday was long past.

The first American star to make his mark in post-war Italy
did not come to make a film at all. Tyrone Power was a dark-
haired heartthrob in the Valentino mould, who had made the
female public swoon with his portrayal of a dashing bullfighter
opposite Rita Hayworth in *Blood and Sand*. He was so popular
that people in the suburbs who had been pushing for gas
supplies to be restored chanted 'Gas or Tyrone!' at one of their
demonstrations. Others, unable to pronounce his name well,
called him 'Tairon Povero' (literally, Tyrone Poorman). In Italy,
he met and wooed the aspiring American actress Linda
Christian, who had been educated in Florence at the exclusive
Poggio Imperiale school. The couple had met once previously
in Acapulco on a film set and perhaps even then there had
been a spark. At any rate, the Rome encounter did not occur
solely by chance. Christian later admitted that the local
representative of Metro-Goldwyn-Mayer, to whom she was
under contract, had encouraged her to put herself in the actor's
line of vision.

Although Power was already married to the French actress
Annabella, and had been conducting an affair with Lana Turner,
he began to court the flame-haired Christian within hours of
meeting her at the Excelsior Hotel. Almost immediately, the
'city of beauty and romance', as Christian described Rome,.
worked its timeless magic. He took his new conquest to *trattorie*
in the hills and in the old parts of the Trastevere district, often
riding in a traditional horse-drawn carriage. Their wedding in
January 1949 was the 'wedding of the century', a social highlight

that captured the imagination of the public and pushed politics out of the headlines for a few weeks. The magazines featured the bride's visits to the Fontana sisters' studio to inspect the making of her dress while the newsreels reported on Ty's visits to his tailor Caraceni, and his numerous stag nights. One of his Roman friends, Count Rudi Crespi, owned a newsreel company and a magazine, and he persuaded the guileless actor to pose without any payment in his pyjamas, having a shave and getting dressed.

The wedding, at the Santa Francesca Romana church, took place on 27 January, just hours after the groom's divorce had come through. It was choreographed and filmed by Metro-Goldwyn-Mayer while freelance photographers pulled out all the stops to get a good shot of the couple. Everything about it was geared to publicity. Crowds of ordinary Romans, many absenting themselves from school or work for the occasion, jostled to catch a glimpse of them. The press described them as 'gossiping girls and mop-headed adolescents', although 'elderly ladies, women of the people and old folk' were also there. There were, too, 'hundreds of youths who wear their hair like Power and who gesticulate and walk in a manner copied from his films'. With just a touch of irony, some papers commented that the American star's capacity to draw a crowd exceeded that of the Communist leader Togliatti.

Power loved Rome and often went there between films to rest and see friends. He felt at ease in the city and soon established a way of being the Hollywood star there that would be widely imitated by those who followed him. He rented a villa on the Via Appia Antica, a road that would later boast several stars' homes, and he drove a large American car of the type that Italians joked was big enough to accommodate 'three rooms and a kitchen'. In a country that had recently lost its monarchy, he was treated like royalty. Yet he also enjoyed the easy-going atmosphere of a city that welcomed him with open arms. He regularly ate in down-to-earth *trattorie*, dining on pasta washed down with white wine from the Roman castles. He also spent hours sitting at the pavement cafés of the Via Veneto soaking up the warm sun and the conversation. It never bothered him that photographers often snapped him without asking permission. He was also a regular afternoon visitor to Parigini's studio.

The Via Veneto was a realm apart for ordinary Romans, an enclave of luxury and glitter that had nothing at all to do with the workaday city or the louche vibe of the Via Margutta. Its elegant bars and hotels made it a centre of social life and a magnet for the high-born, the wealthy and the ambitious. Along the street stood a line of red-wheeled horse-drawn carriages, whose drivers waited for clients to emerge from the expensive hotels. It had something of the flavour of a foreign colony. Between the American embassy at one end and the Pincian Gate at the other, there were innumerable French cafés and American bars. Quick lunch joints and restaurants serving chicken Maryland and apple pie sprang up in the side-streets that stuck out like the legs of a spider from the main road. The travel writer H. V. Morton called it 'American Rome': 'Everything here is a little richer and more expensive than elsewhere: we are in the dollar area. Here you see the "milords" of the new age, the film stars and celluloid caesars, and those executives whose names occupy such a tedious crescendo of type before a film begins.'

The simultaneous presence in Rome of Hollywood actors and dozens of new Italian stars, who were starting to attract the loyalties of audiences, was a boon to the magazines, whose editors knew their readers were tired of the unremitting political conflict and eager for light relief. Press offices and publicity agents supplied a constant stream of pictures and stories. The lure of glamour was such that even left-wing magazines put stars on their covers. The Communist *Vie Nuove* caused some disgruntlement in the party when it featured Rita Hayworth or Marilyn Monroe on the front but sales were good.

Since Power's first marriage had not been a religious one and he had divorced in the United States, even the Catholic Church embraced the new stars. Pope Pius XII received Power and Christian after their wedding and the Church gave their marriage its blessing in the hope that it would contribute to its drive to restore moral order. Christian was also pictured on the cover of the illustrated magazine *Oggi* in the company of De Gasperi, a man not normally given to schmoozing with celebrities.

The alliance between Catholic Italy and expatriate Hollywood was always destined to be unstable, though. Despite the best efforts of the industry's own censorship system, embodied in the Production Code Administration, which had been established to reassure mainstream America of the morality of Hollywood after the scandals of the 1920s, stars always tended towards transgression.

In late March, barely two months after the Power wedding, Ingrid Bergman arrived in Italy. The Swedish star of *Joan of Arc* and *Casablanca* was one of the top female stars in America. Originally recruited to Hollywood by *Gone With the Wind* producer David O. Selznick as a replacement for Greta Garbo, she had played several different parts, including prostitutes and adulteresses. However, she had made her name as a star of radiant purity and goodness, and this image was confirmed by her role as Joan. Her family life was also held up as a model since she lived happily – it was supposed – with her Swedish husband and daughter, Pia. But all this was to change when she arrived in Italy. Bergman had seen *Rome Open City* and *Paisà* in New York and was deeply affected by the authenticity of their depiction of war and suffering. They seemed to her to offer a way out of the artificiality of the industrial set-bound films she was making in Hollywood, so she wrote an impassioned letter to Roberto Rossellini offering the services of an actress 'who only knows how to say one phrase in Italian: *ti amo*'.

Rossellini did not know who Bergman was but he was soon told. The prospect of working with her fired his Latin spirit of conquest and he immediately set about finding a suitable project and wooing her. Rossellini was married, and also entangled with Anna Magnani, but he had always maintained a variety of mistresses and was open to casual liaisons. By the time Bergman held her first press conference at the Excelsior Hotel in Rome, Rossellini had captured her professionally and was well on the way to winning her heart. The couple set off in the director's red Ferrari on a long journey down the peninsula that would conclude on the island of Stromboli, off the coast of Sicily, where filming would begin on a movie that would bear the island's name as its title.

Despite the harsh conditions on the island, the press followed the couple and photographers took shots of the location set. When a photograph was published of Bergman and Rossellini holding hands, gossip about their nascent affair began. Over the eighteen months from March 1949 an international scandal engulfed the pair. A showdown with Bergman's husband, Peter Lindstrom, in May 1949 was chronicled in detail, while Magnani's fury at being dumped for a foreign actress emerged through a rival film production directed by William Dieterle on the nearby island of Volcano.

Bergman was pilloried in the USA, where she was denounced by Senator Edwin C. Johnson on the floor of the Senate as a 'free love cultist' and a 'powerful influence for evil', and in her native Sweden. It was incomprehensible to many not only that she had abandoned her family but that she had forsaken Hollywood for Italy. The outrage was such that there were calls to ban her from re-entering the USA. Rossellini, meanwhile, was branded a 'love pirate' by Senator Johnson and depicted as a sleazy seducer of other men's wives. The scandal reached its apex in the summer when it became apparent that Bergman was pregnant (their son Robertino was born on 2 February 1950) and persisted through her divorce and subsequent marriage to the director on 24 May 1950.

Their affair was far more of a scandal abroad than it was in Italy. Italians had not had the opportunity to see *Joan of Arc*, a figure who in any case held no particular religious or political significance in the peninsula. They viewed the couple's liaison as a love match rather than an adulterous affair. The Catholic hierarchy, which was so vociferous in the USA and in Sweden, kept quiet on account of Rossellini's unique position as the one prominent film director of the post-war era who proclaimed his Catholicism. Despite his turbulent personal life, he was a useful ally the Church could ill afford to lose. For its part the press wrote up the couple's liaison in the sort of soft-focus language that appealed to readers of the picture romances.

The Power–Christian wedding and the Bergman–Rossellini scandal had drawn the attention of the American press to Italy, a country that already had a firm position in the Western imagination as the land of love and romance. Away from southern California, where the studios not only relied on a tame press but also operated in conjunction with the police and the justice system to keep potential scandals out of the public eye, the chances of any misdemeanours coming into the open were much greater. Scandal, it was discovered, sold, and with so many film stars moving to the peninsula, more stories would surely follow. Beneath the hubbub of noisy gossip, an uninhibited atmosphere became a routine aspect of the foreign film community's experience of Rome. Actors quickly succumbed to the easy charms of the Eternal City and dropped their guard. They became the prey of a certain section of the press. In his memoirs, Peter Ustinov observed that no one who spent several months in Rome, 'that glut of over-ripe peaches in a dish of hills', could ever be quite the same again. The emphasis on sin, perhaps inevitably in a place so overly dedicated to the material majesty of God, and in which the spiritual majesty took second place, increased, he thought, 'its turpitude and languor . . . The climate, the sleepy days and wide-awake nights add to this sentiment of nervous exacerbation and squalid temptation . . . One turns away from the city with a kind of weary repulsion, only to be impatient for one's return.'

In the period that followed Mussolini's fall, many filmmakers hoped they could help shape the nation's future. Idealist and left-wing, they saw cinema as a social art and neo-realism became their mission. The aspirations of many of those who tried to set themselves up as producers and directors were much more venal. Wrongly for the most part, some professionals and businessmen saw the movies as a chance to make a lot of money quickly. They also liked the thrill that involvement in the industry brought and the chance it offered to meet and seduce females. There was an entire sub-world beneath the glamorous surface of the movies that worked on the sexual exploitation of women. Adriana Bisaccia's first experience of the industry at the hands of a sleazy producer and director was typical in every respect, except that she did go on to secure one very small part.

In his diary of Rome in the mid-1950s, the journalist Carlo Laurenzi recounted the story of Maria Italia, a thirteen-year-old from the provinces who stole a sum of money from her parents and ran away to Rome, determined to get into films. Rather like Bisaccia, on arriving in the capital, she rented a room from a proprietor who evidently did not care that she was under-age. Helped by an older friend, Maria Italia started to make the acquaintance of men who might assist her. 'These "introductions" generally take place in the cafés of Via Veneto or the modest bars of the Via Tuscolana near Cinecittà,' Laurenzi noted. 'The characters you meet in these bars call themselves producers, or at least friends of producers. In any case, the aspiring actress knows that only through the benevolence of such men is there any chance of getting a screen test. They are young or youthful men, well-fed and euphoric, dressed with a fascinating and immodest elegance.'

Except for the rare occasions when a story like Maria Italia's or Bisaccia's ended up in the press, this cine sub-world was concealed from the public eye. Parents warned their daughters about cinema just as they had done in an earlier age about theatre, but they only had suspicions to go on. Italy's 'girlie' magazines were tame indeed. *Parade, Follie* and others merely provided bikini shots of smiling starlets and features on foreign burlesque artists. The articles were mostly puffery supplied by agencies or the studios. It would be *Confidential*, a US magazine that had no distribution in Italy, that would lift the veil on the darker underbelly of Rome's movie business.

It was US Senator Estes Kefauver's televised committee hearings on organised crime in 1951 that provided American publisher Robert Harrison with the inspiration for *Confidential*, a magazine that would inspire dozens of imitators and would make scandals its bread and butter. Harrison had much experience of trade and tabloid papers and had been involved in producing the girlie magazines that prospered on the back of the wartime taste for pin-ups. By the time he launched his new magazine, the public's predilection for the theme of female sexual transgression was well established. *Confidential* exploited scandalous stories about Hollywood stars, the rich and the famous, while also tackling some social issues. It profited from the unlikely conjunction of concern with morality and obscenity and thirst for plausible narratives about the stars that were spicier than those supplied by the official voices of

Hollywood. *Confidential* soon built up a vast network of spies and tipsters, many of them call-girls, while it also employed surveillance and bugging devices to secure confirmation of their stories.

Famous salacious headlines, which led to *Confidential* being charged with libel or obscenity, included 'Maureen O'Hara Cuddled in Row 35', 'Mae West's Open Door Policy' and 'Robert Mitchum – The Nude Who Came to Dinner'. Further afield, a consistent stream of reports was filed by Italian correspondents, about the misdemeanours of American stars in Rome and about the buxom home-grown actresses the peninsula had produced. The capacity of the Roman air to make the stars drop more than their guard provided a steady stream of material for more than a decade. Some stars could be guaranteed to deliver. Shelley Winters, an actress with a fiery temper who had had a string of affairs with leading men, was one. She was married to Farley Granger, but within days of setting foot in the Italian capital she had met and succumbed to the charms of a most promising young stage actor, Vittorio Gassman. The chisel-jawed thespian whisked her off on a tour of Rome by moonlight before escorting her into her room at the Excelsior. Evidently the experience was memorable. 'That night I finally understood the passionate beauty of Italy, which has lasted all through the centuries, and that, wherever you may wander, all roads lead to Rome,' she wrote later. The couple even married, although neither knew the other's language. The union lasted seven months and produced a daughter.

In typical prurient fashion, *Confidential* focused on the compromises made by rising female stars rather than the structure of exploitation that made these unavoidable. In a way, its articles on Italy harked back to wartime prostitution and exploitation. It chastised the Roman actress Silvana Pampanini for unveiling her ample charms before the cameras for shots that were cut from her films before they reached the United States ('Those Startling Nudes of Italy's Hottest Pizza – Silvana Pampanini'). It published a topless picture of a splendid Sophia Loren that was taken from the so-called French version of one of her early films ('The Nude Pic Sophia Loren Will Pay $10,000 To Get Back'). Allusions were also made to similar pictures she had allegedly posed for while still an adolescent in wartime Naples.

Confidential saw itself as blowing the whistle on the 'spoilt darlings' of the movies, telling its readers truths they would not otherwise hear. In Italy, there was not as yet much of a market for this sort of arch moralising, despite the Catholic Church's continued influence. Scandals did not emerge there automatically when some moral baseline was crossed. Rather, they exploded only if a political force or institution puffed a bellows beneath them. The Montesi case would soon reveal itself to be one of these. Its sinister complexity meant it was of limited interest to the likes of *Confidential*. But the influence of the American magazine was more than apparent in the sensational article that Silvano Muto would publish in the October 1953 edition of *Attualità*. For the first time, the lurid details of what might have happened to Wilma Montesi were revealed and printed for all to read.

VI

Girl About Town

'The Truth Behind the Death of Wilma Montesi!' The girl who 'could have been your sister, your daughter, your girlfriend'. So screamed a yellow strip on the cover of the 6 October 1953 issue of *Attualità*. Silvano Muto's magazine asserted that Wilma Montesi had not died by her own hand or by accident. Rather, she had taken drugs at a swinging party, and when she had unexpectedly lost consciousness, she had been taken to an isolated stretch of the coast and dumped in the sea.

The article named no names, but it did sketch in a striking amount of detail. It claimed that Wilma had fallen into the web of a powerful and sinister Mr X, who ran a narcotics ring and used young women to carry drugs to his customers. Also involved was a Mr Y, a man of higher social extraction. Wilma had been picked up at Ostia in a black Alfa Romeo 1900cc saloon and transported to a location where orgies regularly took place. This was the nearby Castel Porziano estate, a discreet gated villa, a place of 'delights'. The article continued:

At seven thirty on Thursday evening [9 April 1953], Mr X and Wilma are together. They are not alone: three other people are with them. Time passes and they begin to smoke drugged cigarettes of a type whose dangers the girl is unfamiliar with, only with the pleasure they bring . . . The girl smokes too much; the drug starts to take effect. Suddenly she falls senseless to the ground. Efforts to revive her are useless; she no longer gives signs of life. Suddenly the four people realise that they have a dead body on their hands, and the position in Italy of one of the four does not allow a scandal . . . The body must be got rid of: it is too embarrassing. The girl is dressed, but in the hurry her suspender belt cannot be found. The skirt is left off. Perhaps they think its absence will support the accident theory or perhaps because in the confusion of the moment no one remembers where it is. Dressed in this way, the body is bundled into the car. The sea is close and the hypothesis of an accident can seem plausible. Soon Wilma is in the sea. She will be found some time later at Torvaianica.

The article went on to suggest that Wilma had travelled in the Alfa on other occasions. There were allusions to places in Bagnoli, near Naples, and Castellammare di Stabia, where similar parties took place. Castel Porziano, it said, had become a sleazy hangout after the closure by the police of the Siviglia nightclub where morphine and cocaine were consumed openly. As for the police investigation, according to the article the cover-up had begun immediately. The girl's family was told that her death was an accident. A scandal would not benefit anyone – least of all the dead Wilma. 'Mr X knows many things and holds completely in his hand those who might talk. Influential people are set in motion so as to deal with the matter slowly in silence. In this way the Montesi case is covered in silence. A strange web of silence.'

The new, low-budget weekly that Silvano Muto had founded, and for which he wrote, revived interest in the case months after it had slipped out of the headlines, despite the investigation having been reopened in April and not yet closed. *Attualità* was not a very high-minded periodical. Like so many of the other magazines that adorned the news kiosks, it typically featured a bikini-clad starlet or a smiling actress on the cover. However, with fewer pages than major weeklies, like *Oggi* or *Epoca*, it had a cheap and flimsy feel. To compensate for the lack of resources, Muto had decided to pursue his own personal brand of investigative journalism: his article was the first to link Wilma's death to the use and traffic of narcotics. On the latter topic he had done his homework and brought into the open a clandestine and illegal trade that most people knew nothing about. But it was his description of the death of the girl that proved most sensational. It came as a bolt from the blue, not only on account of the detail it offered but because for several months – between May and September 1953 – the Montesi case had slowly disappeared from the papers. After an initial flurry of headlines and questions, things had moved on and the girl on the beach seemed to have been forgotten.

Most people probably thought that interest had declined because the case had proved to be an intractable mystery. Muto alleged that this was untrue. In a bold and direct attack on the authorities, he claimed that the whole treatment of the case, from the moment the body had been found, had been marked by suspicious delays and silences. Journalists, such as Cesarini Sforza in the Communist weekly *Vie Nuove*, who had dared timidly to advance hypotheses had been subject, according to Muto, to intimidation and threats. What was more, Muto pointed his accusing finger at the press too. If a paper like *Il Messaggero* had gone quiet, he argued, it was not because of any news-related motive. Keen to avoid causing the government embarrassment during an election campaign, it had simply eliminated the case from its pages. For Muto the delay in holding the autopsy, the failure to carry out a proper toxicological examination on the cadaver, and the subsequent press blackout, were all aspects of the same co-ordinated cover-up. In short, the treatment of the case reeked of an establishment conspiracy. Not even the victim's family was exempt from his suspicions since he had noted some strange things about the dead girl's loved ones too. Unaware of the circumstances of Angelo Giuliani's break with the Montesi family, he asked why her fiancé had suddenly disappeared. Then he pointed the finger at Wanda: there was the matter of the odd sister 'who knew and did not know'.

In the news kiosks around the Via Veneto and the Piazza di Spagna, *Attualità* sold out. The Il Baretto crowd knew about Muto's enquiries the previous summer and his friendship with Adriana Bisaccia. As a result his story was eagerly devoured.

Among those who made provocation and outrage their stock-in-trade, the magazine's bold gesture was much appreciated. Those who did not know Muto, and there were many such people in Rome since the young editor had few friends among journalists, were left wondering who had supplied him with his information. Questions were also asked about the funding of *Attualità*. To start even a modest magazine required considerable money and there was no evidence that Muto was a man of means. Was it a Trojan horse for some undeclared political operation? Few newspapers in Italy made a profit and most were bankrolled by business interests that used them as a mouthpiece or source of political influence.

Some of these insinuations were started by experienced reporters who were miffed at missing out on what seemed an astonishing scoop. They showed their resentment by pointing out that no evidence had been offered and no witness named. Others took a different tack. If previous rumours were true, then Mr Y could only be Piero Piccioni – but who was Mr X, and what about the two other people who were supposedly present at the fatal orgy?

The authorities did not sit idly by when *Attualità* hit the newsstands. Just as Cesarini Sforza had been hauled in after his article appeared in *Vie Nuove*, so Muto found himself called to account. At a meeting at the Viminale Palace on 24 October with procurator Sigurani and his deputy Leonardo Murante, whose office would take the decision about whether to prosecute anyone or not, it was spelled out to him that enquiries by busybody journalists could not be tolerated. It was the task of the legal authorities to investigate unexplained deaths and the fate of the carpenter's daughter was still an ongoing case. Withdraw your story and admit that it was based on groundless speculation, Muto was told, and you will benefit from an existing amnesty and escape prosecution.

Muto knew that he ran the risk of a heavy fine or imprisonment. Adriana Bisaccia was the only witness he could put forward and she was not likely to be a very credible or reliable one so, reassured by promises that the case had not been formally closed, Muto signed a document confessing that he had invented his story to attract attention and boost sales.

This was a major climbdown, if taken at face value. In fact, it was more akin to a tactical withdrawal, given the severe punishments that the law reserved for those who committed crimes of opinion. The use of amnesties was a long-established practice that allowed the state to threaten individuals and then, if and when it so chose, reward their compliance by showing indulgence.

But if Muto had sighed with relief as he signed his confession, that relief was short-lived. Due to a mix-up over the dates of the amnesty, only the papers that had alluded to Piccioni in the period between April and early September escaped prosecution. The *Attualità* article, with a cover date of 6 October, fell outside the amnesty and Muto would be sent for trial.

This was more than an annoyance. It meant that, in addition to having had to step back on the Montesi case, he might find himself behind bars. However, he did have a potential card up his sleeve: just two days after his meeting at the

Viminale, Muto took a phone call from breathless young woman with a Milanese accent who demanded to speak with him urgently. She had read his article about the circumstances of the Montesi girl's death and wanted to find out if he knew more than he had published. Even from their brief conversation, the woman seemed to be in a position to fill in some of the missing details.

Anna Maria Moneta Caglio was a striking, sophisticated woman of twenty-two with a sassy attitude and a confident manner. She had fire in her eyes and a head of dark-brown hair.

She had been in Rome for more than a year but she had not yet found any settled role or occupation. Like Bisaccia, she had arrived in the city in search of fame and success. She was not a hopeless wannabe, though. Since she came from a wealthy, well-connected background, she entered the social world of the capital at a higher level than most. Her family was distinguished: her great-grandfather had won a Nobel Prize in 1907, and her grandfather had been among the founders of the Popular Party, the pre-Fascist forerunner of the Christian Democrats. Her father was a prominent lawyer in Milan and a man of means who was on friendly terms with government ministers and influential people in the Church. Caglio had been given an expensive religious education and the Church was an important influence in her life. She regularly spoke with her confessor, Father Filipetto, a respected philosophy teacher at the Leo XIII high school, and exchanged ideas with him. Once she had convinced herself that she was born to grace the stage or the silver screen, she tried to persuade Father Filipetto that to realise her calling she needed to move to the capital. Neither he nor her father approved of this plan, but their opposition made her more determined. In the summer of 1952, having secured the promise of an allowance as well as a clutch of letters of introduction, she packed her bags and left.

Behind her drive for recognition lay a history of rebellion and independence. Caglio had fixed her sights on Rome, having fallen out with members of her family, including her father. She had learned to be self-reliant but she was hurt that he had never shown her the affection she craved. Her French-born mother had abandoned the family home when Caglio was a child, and she and her three brothers had been the subject of a bitter battle between their parents. Her father had secured custody of the children by virtually kidnapping them while their mother was out. His family responsibilities had not, however, prevented him from volunteering for Fascism's wars in Spain and North Africa, and finally alongside Hitler, before joining the Allies after the armistice of September 1943. But the biggest blow for his daughter came in 1946 when she was sixteen: he secretly married a much younger woman, a widow of twenty-five. She rejected her new stepmother and showed her feelings by playing truant and frequently running away from home.

Looked at from a safe distance, Rome must have seemed an easy city to conquer. Everyone knew that the film industry was in rapid expansion and that all sorts of unlikely people had been cast in screen roles. Anna Maria Caglio was as determined as anyone to live her dreams. Her background might have been elevated, but her aspirations were commonplace. What she thirsted for was acknowledgement and acclamation of her artistic talents. She wanted to be noticed. Indeed, so desperate was she that she had once submitted a photo of herself in a swimsuit to a magazine beauty contest in Milan. She had had second thoughts, though, and withdrawn from the contest, citing the stern refusal of her father to tolerate such behaviour. This brief gesture of rebellion revealed the young woman's awareness of her burgeoning sex appeal. She had a slim figure and moved well, but in truth these were not her strongest suit. She soon concluded that it was not her body that would be the key to her success but her personality. She assumed that, with her irresistible charm, it would be easy to cut a swath through the stubborn bureaucracies and webs of power that notoriously dominated the capital.

It was well known that you needed connections in the capital to get on. Merely knowing a few well-to-do individuals, however, was not enough. Caglio spent her first few months in the city living quietly in a rented room and occasionally venturing out to press her case for a film role. From time to time she met with Milanese friends who were studying art and they invited her to a few artists' parties. Bohemia was not really her thing but she enjoyed this new environment and went to some of the existentialists' bars near Via Margutta to relieve her loneliness. There, it dawned on her that she would have to beg her father to supply her with serious introductions if she was not to drift into indolence. With some reluctance, he obliged and provided her with letters to well-placed freemasons and to Giulio Andreotti, then a young but already influential associate of De Gasperi. Her father's loftiest acquaintance was an older government minister, Giuseppe Spataro, the minister of posts. On 22 August 1952, on one of the hottest days of the year, she gathered her courage and went to see Spataro at the ministry.

She was received by one of Spataro's officials, a Dr Savastano, who informed her apologetically that his superior was presently out of the capital. Caglio remonstrated that she needed to see him on an urgent personal matter. At this point, the official paused, thinking he might spare the minister a nuisance, and suggested that there was someone else who might be well placed to help her. Indicating a man who had appeared as if out of the shadows, Dr Savastano said: 'Here is a man who can do more for you than the minister himself. There is no better man, more honest and loyal, in the world.'

Somehow the hyperbole of the presentation seemed to match the man who was now facing her. His demeanour signalled that he was of a very different order from the men she had previously known. Ugo Montagna was a polished, impeccably dressed man in his mid-forties, who was introduced as 'Marchese'. Fit and athletic, he was strong-featured, with steel-grey hair and tanned skin. He spoke with a Sicilian accent and was treated with much deference by the gaggle of other men who were gathered outside Dr Savastano's office.

Towards Caglio he was at once ceremonious and attentive. His manners were perfect and his attitude correct, slightly aloof even, while his eyes surveyed her with unusual intensity. He smiled as he bent to kiss her hand and promised that he would do what he could to help. Now, though, he had to leave as he had guests coming for lunch at his castle in Fiano, some fifty kilometres from Rome. Wary of being fobbed off, she insisted on going with him. Taken aback by such bold behaviour, the marchese assented and guided her out of the building to his car, a Fiat 1900cc saloon. Over the following days, he wooed her relentlessly. She was no timid virgin, having had a number of affairs since she was seventeen, but she was not accustomed to receiving multiple bunches of flowers or being bombarded with telephone calls several times a day. The marchese's attentions were flattering and, if he was truly a man of great influence, then he might also be useful. He began to invite her out, and then to his house for intimate dinners. He gave her a diamond brooch he claimed was a family heirloom. Suitably impressed, she accepted his courtship and took the initiative in leading him to bed.

Ugo Montagna was a successful man of the world. He was always well groomed and excessively perfumed. A good conversationalist, he also knew how to listen to a woman and respond to her desires. He was a man of the south, whose way of being made him different from the closed, buttoned-up men Caglio had known in Milan. He was correct and formal but also expansive and hearty. A man of means, he lived the good life. In his company, she was escorted to the glittering establishments of the Via Veneto. The marchese seemed to know everybody. If he was not occupied in greeting acquaintances then people came over to pay their respects to him. He took her to fashionable night spots, such as Victor's, which offered its select clientele cocktails and exotic cabaret acts imported directly from Paris. He also accompanied her to the Open Gate, an exclusive club inaugurated in 1950 in Via San Nicola da Tolentino just off the Via Veneto. Founded by a consortium of lawyers, nobles and industrialists, it boasted a bar, a snack bar, a grill room, tea room, ballroom and nightclub. Novella Parigini's lawyer, Gino Sotis, organised mock trials of famous figures from history, with film stars playing the parts of the accused, while Monday evenings were reserved for private viewings of yet-to-be-released movies.

For all her apparent worldliness, Caglio was quite naïve. She was completely seduced by Montagna and she considered herself to be his fiancée, even though he was yet to be divorced from his wife. To reassure her about his intentions, which were always vague, he told her that in time he would have his marriage annulled by the Church. And Caglio – despite warnings from her landlady to be careful – went to live with him.

She did not forget her ambitions, though. Her interest in acting had not waned and she was as determined as ever to find fame. Unfortunately, although he was an enthusiastic sugar-daddy, this was the one area in which her lover was unable or, more likely, unwilling to offer much help. While he seemed to know people in government, the ministries, the police, business and the Church, Montagna's circle did not extend far into the arts or the entertainment world. But she understood from his reluctance to help that he did not really approve of her working. This was a source of considerable frustration because she knew that his friend Spataro, who was responsible for posts and communications, had direct influence over the state broadcaster RAI. Thus Caglio embarked on self-promotion. She hired the Pirandello theatre in Rome and set about putting together a production in which she would star. With a sure nose for publicity, she also paid to have her photograph appear on the front cover of Le Tout Rome, a small-circulation society magazine that was read by members of the social élite.

Despite her initial enthusiasm, within a few months Caglio had started to become disillusioned with Montagna. He was dismissive of her artistic ambitions and there were things she had begun to notice about his life and business activities that disquieted her. She guessed he was leading a double life. As well as an apartment in Via Gennargentu, another in the Flaminio district and a twenty-room villa in Via Asmara, he had a castle near Fiano, a farm, and a country house at Zagarolo. His wheeling and dealing seemed to extend into areas that were dubious, even illegitimate. On several occasions he had taken her to a hunting estate he managed on land that had once been owned by the royal family. There he entertained many male friends, with whom he would close himself off to talk business. He made frequent trips away and often talked to his contacts in a hushed voice on the telephone. He had a henchman called Luigi with whom he often conferred. At every turn, he seemed concerned to prevent his lover catching glimpses of his deals. But he was not sufficiently bothered to exclude her altogether. She sometimes went with him when he had meetings and often heard snippets of conversations. It became clear to her that Montagna relied on luck and the protection of key people. He was superstitious too and always went to give thanks at the Sanctuary of the Holy Virgin of the Rosary at Pompeii whenever a big deal had come off.

The relationship between Montagna and Caglio was tempestuous and grew more so as she became suspicious about his activities. By January 1953, she was convinced Montagna was cheating on her. On 7 January, a Wednesday, she phoned his house in the Flaminio district and was told by his butler that the marchese was out. Detecting an odd tone in the servant's voice, she surmised that he was not telling the truth. Since she was not far away, she decided to drive over in the brand new Fiat 1400 that Montagna had recently bought for her and investigate. She arrived in time to catch sight of him getting into his own car while a dark-haired woman was settling into the passenger seat. It was around five thirty p.m. She decided to follow him and embarked on what would become a high-speed chase across Rome as the marchese realised she was on his tail and accelerated. Like a scene from a film, she mounted pavements and scraped by lampposts in her determination not to lose sight of him.

Near Porta Maggiore she hit a pedestrian. Giulio Parisello, an engineer, suffered numerous minor injuries and spent two weeks in hospital. Caglio paused long enough to invite him to take note of her number-plate so he could make a claim against her later. (This he did and eventually received a payment for damages of eighty thousand lire, which he gave to charity.)

The chase at last came to an end in Via Condotti, just off the Piazza di Spagna, when Montagna, having earlier set down his passenger, stopped and got out to confront Caglio. Although she had never got a proper look at the dark-haired woman, she concluded later that the mysterious passenger had been Wilma Montesi.

Appalled by Caglio's behaviour, Montagna ended their

relationship and sent her packing to Milan. However, missing the excitement of her young body, he soon decided to summon her back.

She returned to Rome by train on the morning of 14 April. Montagna was not at the station to meet her, and when she arrived at his house by taxi, she found him in his pyjamas talking animatedly on the phone to a man he was addressing in the familiar 'tu' form. He closed the call with 'Ciao, Piero,' and apologised that urgent business had prevented him meeting her. Within minutes, their conversation turned to the case of the young beauty whose body had been found at Torvaianica. Caglio had read about it and knew that the beach was not far from the hunting club that Montagna ran. He breezily dismissed her concerns and announced that he would be taking her there that very afternoon.

While Montagna and his guests were shooting quail, Caglio chatted with the estate guards and some of their wives about the macabre discovery. Anastasio Lilli told her of the visit by the girl's fiancé and family, while one of the women talked about the body, which she had seen.

'What a shock it would have been to see it emerge from the sea,' Caglio commented.

'From the sea, my foot,' replied the woman.

When she repeated this conversation to Montagna, he went quiet and refused to comment.

Over the next two weeks she was constantly in Montagna's company. During this time, she witnessed further telephone calls between him and a man called Piero. She also overheard Montagna's comment about 'Piccioni' being in trouble but also his confident assertion that he himself was too powerful to be damaged. She recalled that he had often called round at the Piccioni apartment in Via della Conciliazione, to which he took money. On occasion she went with him, although he never invited her to come in.

Once, while she was waiting, she noticed an Alfa Romeo 1900 parked in the road, like the one that had been mentioned in the papers.

At eleven p.m. on 29 April, sitting once more in the car, she watched her lover enter the Viminale Palace. He had received a call earlier in the evening from Piccioni junior and had urged her to finish dinner quickly so he could attend to some pressing business with his friend the chief of police, Tommaso Pavone. As Caglio waited for Montagna to reappear, she saw Piero Piccioni arrive and climb the steps to the imposing entrance. An hour later Montagna emerged, expressing satisfaction that the 'trouble' would be rectified. By now, Caglio was well aware that the matter in question was the dead girl who had been found at Torvaianica but when she confronted Montagna, he sent her away for the second time. When she tried to resist, he threatened her with an internal deportation order, which would force her to return to Milan – he would ask a friend in government to issue one against her. The friend in question, she was sure, was Giulio Andreotti, then under-secretary to the prime minister.

Rome, however, had got under Caglio's skin, and before a month had passed she was back in the capital. She even took up with Montagna again, although not with the same intensity as before. She met him occasionally for sex, but she stayed in lodgings on her own account and started to try to rebuild her life. It was not a happy time for her – she seemed to have no anchor in her life and her grand plans had stalled. She found herself killing time as spring turned to summer and summer to autumn. She spent hours leafing listlessly through magazines and gazing at news kiosks in search of new stimulation. The first issue of *Attualità* immediately caught her eye. Intrigued by the yellow strip that made reference to the Montesi girl, she bought a copy. It struck her that the magazine was the first to publish full-length photographs of Wilma rather than simple face shots. She pored over Silvano Muto's article, reading it again and again. It was as though a shadowy nightmare had suddenly come sharply into focus.

As Caglio absorbed the words of the article, she came to the view that she had to meet Muto in person. She felt a compelling need to tell him all she knew. She called him at his office and arranged to see him within days.

Silvano Muto and Anna Maria Caglio met for the first time at the Mille Luci bar in Via Gentile da Fabriano off the Via Nazionale on 26 October, and for Muto, it couldn't have felt more providential. She gave him the chance to defend himself rather than rely on the mercy of the court in his forthcoming trial. Caglio told him, in a state of agitation and so hastily that she almost tripped over her words, everything about her experiences with Montagna. Not only was she convinced that the Mr X of the magazine's story was none other than her lover, but that the mysterious woman in the car with Montagna that day in January had been none other than Wilma Montesi.

VII

The Marchese of San Bartolomeo

In 1953, few Romans would have been able to point on a map to the royal estate of Castel Porziano or, indeed, the even more secluded area known as Capocotta, which was located just three kilometres north of the fishing village of Torvaianica, and one kilometre from where Wilma's body was found. There was no earthly reason why anyone should have known or cared about the existence of a stretch of wooded land that was run on concession by the St Hubert Hunting Society, formed by Marchese Ugo Montagna and five of his friends. Capocotta had been leased to them on the condition that all licensed hunters were to be admitted. But, in reality, once the agreement was settled, the society installed armed guards at the gates and banned anyone who did not have a special permit signed by Montagna. Although the Montesi men did not know it at the time, this was the estate that they had been directed to when they went searching in the Torvaianica area in the days after the discovery of Wilma's body.

Anna Maria Caglio had been there as a guest on several occasions and was familiar with the sort of people Montagna entertained. They included aristocrats, politicians, churchmen, senior state functionaries, prominent businessmen, judges, police officials and generals. These members of the Roman élite came to hunt quail, pheasant, partridge and other game,

as well as to enjoy the lavish hospitality and friendly company
of their expansive host. In the 1950s, the whole area around
Capocotta was wooded countryside. Inauguration of the coastal
road linking Ostia and Anzio in 1954 would open the way
to a major influx of people and a rash of building of dubious
legality, but before that, the roads were rough-and-ready and
boars and other wildlife roamed freely. Nevertheless, it was
not difficult to reach from Rome, and early-morning hunts
were held there regularly. Montagna often invited female
company to lighten the proceedings and to entertain his male
guests. On occasion, gambling sessions were held in the estate
buildings and some visitors stayed overnight.

For Montagna, the estate was not a source of income. Rather,
it was the core of a system of influence that was crucial to
his way of doing business. The right friends could bring
respectability, status and useful information, and Montagna
played the game brilliantly. The handsome, well-built man who
now reigned over Capocotta appeared to be a fully-fledged
blueblood. His ceremonial courtesy and substantial means
ensured that he accumulated influential friends and was
acceptable in the patrician set that still dominated Roman
society. He knew not only how to build male friendships but
also how to set hearts fluttering among the titled ladies who
hosted the capital's most glittering social events in their grand
palaces. But underneath the expensive impeccable suits the
real Montagna was very different.

The youngest of five brothers from the small town of Grotte,
near Agrigento, in Sicily, Ugo Montagna had been born in
1910 to an impoverished genteel family. Renowned for its
semi-feudal economic system, dominated by large landowners,
the island was a step or two behind the more advanced regions
of the country. As in other areas of the south, many towns
were without modern sanitation, running water, gas and
electricity. Most of the population toiled on inhospitable plots

of arid land in the same manner as their forefathers, barely scraping a living. The Montagnas had once lived off the profits generated by the sulphur mines, the area's one industry. As local gentry, they inhabited a baroque palace on the main square and maintained all the appearances of high status, but their problems began when the industry, which was run inefficiently, declined sharply in the face of American competition.

Montagna's father, Diego, decided to escape imminent poverty by moving his family to Palermo, where he traded in wood and coal to support them. His sons were put to work from an early age; only Ugo continued in education until the age of fourteen. A fine-looking boy, with a strong sense of pride and a touch of vanity, he was drawn more to the city's colourful social scene. The local aristocracy – which had been reinvigorated by wealthy industrialists, such as Ignazio Florio, whose beautiful wife Donna Franca had been hailed in the early years of the century as the queen of Palermo – lived opulently. In the 1920s, the Sicilian capital was still, just, an outpost of international high society, and it boasted elegant cafés, theatres and parks. The teenage Ugo watched the rich, learned how they dressed and walked, and did his best to emulate them. Fascinated by their talk of foreign capitals, horse racing and women, he resolved to make his own mark by building a life for himself in a place where opportunities were greater.

As the years passed, each of his brothers in turn left the island to seek employment on the mainland. Ugo Montagna, too, chose this path, as had many other Sicilians, driven from their homeland by the threat or the reality of dire poverty. In 1938, after a brief sojourn in Pistoia, he arrived in Rome. There, the ambitious young man found just the terrain he needed to reinvent himself. Mussolini was at the peak of his popularity, and the capital city was becoming home to many people from other regions. The growth of government had created jobs in the bureaucracy that educated southerners were quick to fill, and Montagna encountered many Sicilians, some of them old friends from Palermo, who were happy to help each other when needed. Whether they were clerks, administrators, police officials or churchmen, they instinctively understood that personal friendships counted more than bureaucratic hierarchies, and that favours and recommendations were a currency that could always be cashed in.

Ugo Montagna wasted no time in using his connections to start wheeling and dealing in furnishings and property. With his easy patter and personal magnetism, he quickly built up a notable business portfolio. So successful was he that he summoned one of his brothers to help him. He developed a method of operation that, while not exactly original, was so suited to his personality that he would continue to practise it after the war. He befriended those close to powerful figures and so gained access to power by the back staircase. Typically, he provided his new friends with illicit entertainments and easy sex with women he engaged for payment. Such methods rarely failed but they could be risky, as he found when he provoked Mussolini's ire by taking his sons Vittorio and Bruno to high-class brothels. But Montagna's bravado was such that not even the anathema of Il Duce deterred him. Indeed, many years later he boasted to Anna Maria Caglio that the dictator had been afraid of him.

Having been warned off by Mussolini, Montagna turned his attentions to the Petaccis. This upper-class Roman family, which was headed by one of the then pope's personal physicians, had seen a huge rise in its fortunes after the older daughter, Claretta, became Mussolini's official mistress in 1936. After securing appropriate introductions, Montagna began brazenly to woo her before he identified her mother as the most vulnerable member of the clan and changed target. He started to call on her at the family's huge modernist villa, La Camilluccia, when she was alone. Claretta's younger sister Miriam later wrote: 'I don't know how he managed to get in there but for people of his type there are no obstacles. They live among the personalities of government and sub-government never missing a chance to be photographed in their company to show their familiarity with the powerful.' He flattered Claretta's mother, who was then sixty-two, and gradually won her confidence. With his customary charm, he encouraged her to believe that he was a struggling businessman looking to earn an honest living. When he had softened her up, he proposed a deal: he would sell her twenty-nine authentic Persian carpets for a 'modest' sum – half a million lire. She laughed, saying she had no need of so many carpets and, in any case, the huge sum was way beyond their means. An agreement was eventually reached: the family would buy four rugs for twenty-nine thousand lire. When they heard about it, other family members were furious. An angry Claretta reproved her mother for gullibility while an uncle questioned the provenance of the rugs. For Miriam, from then on, Montagna was simply 'the carpet man'.

Their displeasure turned to anger when, shortly after Mussolini's fall from power in July 1943, their villa was vandalised, objects stolen, and they were arrested on charges of theft and misappropriation of public funds. They were convinced that Montagna had run into trouble for handling stolen goods and had sought to exculpate himself by giving information to the new authorities, enabling them to move against a family who had become an object of public resentment.

As the war progressed the Sicilian proved extremely adept at winning the trust of the different authorities that held power in Rome. Trade went on regardless of who was in charge, whether the Nazis, the Allies or the new democratic parties.

His greatest coup was in securing for himself the title Marchese
of San Bartolomeo. Having won the confidence of Prince
Umberto, who briefly became king on the abdication of his
father in the run-up to the referendum of 1946, Montagna
persuaded him to recognise with a royal decree his right to
use the title on account of the nobility of his mother's family.
By this means he became one of the so-called 'Ciampino
nobles', who secured their titles more or less as the plane
taking the royal family into exile was rolling down the tarmac
at Rome's airport. The title was more a matter of vanity than
legitimacy, for all titles lost legal value on the abolition of the
monarchy.

Nevertheless, it demonstrated how far the man from Grotte
had come. He was no longer another genteel but impoverished
Sicilian on the make. He moved with ease in the highest
circles and courted allies in the offices and quarters that
mattered. He knew the influential organiser of numerous
Catholic lay associations, Luigi Gedda, and kept in with bishops
and other prelates. The mere fact that he was introduced to
Anna Maria Caglio in laudatory terms by a high official at a
ministry with which he had no formal connection shows that
he was now not just accepted but sought after. He was the
dispenser of advice, the giver of gifts and the man whose
friendship was prized but never disinterested.

The post-war years were kind to men like him. On the
one hand some key institutions, first and foremost the Church
but also the banks and the professions, passed through the
national tragedy and rebirth without having to account for
their compromises with the defunct regime. Other institutions,
such as the media, government ministries and the armed forces,
were initially subject to severe control by the Allies and then
were purged. Some forty thousand people lost their jobs or
were subject to sanction due to their collaboration with
Fascism, although the vast majority returned to their original

posts in 1946. But resentment ran deep. Many people preferred to conceal what they had done in earlier years and were assisted in this by the desire of the political parties to recruit as many members as possible without asking too many questions. In society and business, people were taken at face value so long as they had means and could pass as respectable. The series of transitions – from Fascism to Badoglio's administration, to revived Fascism under Nazi occupation, to the liberation and Allied occupation, then coalition government and, finally, the rule of the Christian Democrats – was bewildering. This shifting landscape offered unprecedented opportunities to men who knew their way through the labyrinth of power, who cultivated personal contacts and who proved useful. Ugo Montagna was one of them. To put it bluntly, he was an unscrupulous businessman and deal-maker.

Montagna made much of his wealth by acquiring land and property at knock-down rates and selling them on to the state at massively increased prices. There were many opportunities for such speculative practices. As agricultural profits fell, forcing landowners to seek other income, the government was promoting large-scale building. Those who inserted themselves into this dynamic could make huge profits, especially if they had prior information about building programmes and grants. Montagna's technique was straightforward: on the surface he was the most respectable of men, courteous and ceremonial to a fault. He presented himself as a legitimate mediator and businessman, winning the confidence of aristocrats, state officials and representatives of the powerful Vatican property company, the Società Generale Immobiliare. But he also offered his contacts special incentives to deal with him that blended bribery and blackmail. Like many men of a certain standing, he was equally at home in the *beau monde* and the *demi-monde*. He attended theatres, nightclubs and brothels as well as salons, and mixed with actresses and showgirls as well as countesses.

He went to Il Baretto and the Piccolo Slam as well as the stylish Open Gate, and kept an eagle eye open for young female flesh to lend gaiety to his sinister feasts.

When Anna Maria Caglio met him, he was at the peak of his powers. This might explain his carelessness in allowing her to see more of his activities than he should have done. He came to regret this when she proved not to be the disposable plaything he had assumed. His last-minute cancellation of their dates, and his frequent journeys outside Rome, bred hostility and distrust in her. By early 1953 Montagna knew that she was becoming a problem. However, although he sent her away at the end of April – for the last time, he supposed – he was unable to get rid of her completely. He desired her and feared her, aware by now that she was watching his every move.

After her meeting with Silvano Muto, Caglio brought up the matter of the *Attualità* article with Montagna. Had he seen it? she asked him. As he drove her through the city centre, she baited him and started to read aloud passages from it. As she explained to Muto, in a subsequent meeting, it was the part of the story dealing with drugs that most enraged him. When she mentioned Piero Piccioni, he exploded: 'That's enough! I forbid you to continue!' Suddenly, his attitude towards her had changed. He was seeing her for the first time as an adversary and possible traitor, and became threatening – Caglio even suspected that he wanted to kill her. When he invited her to spend the night with him at Capocotta on 30 October, she took the precaution of leaving an envelope containing a testament with her landlady. In fact, Montagna and she did not spend the night there and instead returned to the capital. But the letter remained in the landlady's possession.

VIII

New and Old Rome

Rome was changing. The city that united the humble Montesis, the slick Sicilian Ugo Montagna, the suspicious Anna Maria Caglio, Adriana Bisaccia with her broken dreams, and young men like Piero Piccioni and Silvano Muto was not the grand Rome of ancient times; neither was it the Eternal City of the Catholic Church, nor indeed the picturesque Rome beloved of generations of tourists and recently made cinematic by Hollywood. The Rome of the Montesi case was a city of intrigue, privilege, petty ambitions and low morals; a city in which a mean-minded present had imposed itself on the achievements of history.

In 1871 when Rome became the capital of the new state of Italy, it was still a small city of 245,000 inhabitants, all of whom lived within walls that dated from the time of Marcus Aurelius. Since then, like all capital cities, it had become a city of immigrants seeking to find a niche or make a future. All the protagonists of the Montesi case had lived in Rome for no more than a generation and many of them had only arrived as adults. Theirs was a Rome of flux, not roots, of ambition, not tradition.

For nineteenth-century Italian nationalists, Rome had been not simply a place but a beacon and an inspiration. It fuelled myths of grandeur that invested the idea of Italy with a sense of purpose and aspiration. It had once dominated the world through its strength and civilisation, and might, they reasoned, do so again. Between the wars, Mussolini's Fascist regime did everything in its power to impress on the Italians the sense that a new civilisation, at least equal to that which had flowered in the past, was being created. Through urban reform, a massive building programme, the militarisation of the civilian population and a set of organised rituals without equal in modern politics, it endeavoured to change the physical face of the city and its population. However, despite the efforts of the dictatorship, Rome's image remained much as it had been before Mussolini came to power in 1922. Whatever measures were adopted to try to turn it into a modern capital to rival Paris and London, somehow Rome seemed able to absorb all changes and remain fundamentally the same.

Although the growth of industry and government refreshed the traditional social fabric, the aristocracy remained hugely influential in the city's affairs. The papal aristocracy was composed of a handful of patrician families who were tied by ancient bonds and privileges to the Vatican. They occupied the most magnificent historic palaces in a city that did not lack them and wielded a financial and patrimonial power that was trumped only by that of the Church itself.

At the other end of the social spectrum there was the lower class, composed of the workers and those not so keen on work, the people on the street and at the market, the habitués of Trastevere hostelries and the simple restaurants serving time-honoured specialities made from offal. Cheerful, indolent, lovers of life, the underclass had its own folk culture and popular music made up of ironical *stornelli* sung in Romanesque dialect. This popular Rome had been celebrated in the nineteenth century by the poet Giacomo Belli. In the middle of the twentieth, Alberto Moravia best captured it in his many Roman tales written for *Il Corriere della Sera*. Moravia's male characters are the modern heirs of the street-corner *bulli* of centuries past and of the cynical plebeians corrupted by the proximity of power. His females are beautiful and cocksure, chirpy servant girls, aspirational market traders and cheery prostitutes who know how to run rings round their men.

Moravia's romanticised Roman figures include office workers, shopkeepers and artisans, members of a middle class that, in the post-war years, was beginning to savour once again some of the leisure pursuits it had enjoyed before the war. But it is striking that most of these people are treated as part of the urban popular world, not distinguished from it by virtue of their values or moderately comfortable status. The middle class grew massively between the late nineteenth and mid-twentieth centuries, but as government expanded and took on myriad new functions, Rome's favoured image was not of clerks, shopkeepers and professionals. There seemed no reason to depict this moderately comfortable world of people who, after the end of the regime that had most represented their interests, took their cue from the Church and in politics backed the parties of the centre and right.

The 'real Rome' of the mid-twentieth century remained largely hidden from view. Lacking picturesque qualities, it was not often shown in novels or at the cinema, and escaped the attentions of the artists and songwriters. Even photographers took little interest in it. Instead it was absorbed into a picture of the city that was dominated by stock characters from the lower classes and the glittering élite. The Montesi case thrust unlikely figures into the limelight and turned nonentities into personalities. For the members of the victim's family, this was a bruising experience – but others revelled in it.

Rome had always been a city in which great opulence stood in stark contrast to the humble lives and customs of the common people. The surrounding region was not prosperous and, until the land reclamations and urban projects of the Fascist period, poverty and disease had been widespread. In the 1950s, Rome's municipal territory was one of the largest in Europe – almost as wide as Greater London. Within this area were many zones of a rural and semi-rural nature. Farms, barns, and village communities that could only be reached by rough tracks were to be found in areas that were still 'Rome'. 'The Italian capital has for a long time been a city, plus suburbs, plus a no man's land,' observed the French historian Pierre Sorlin. It had profound links with the countryside: it was not far from forests and marshland, and vineyards were visible on the famous seven hills. As late as the 1920s, sheep still grazed in the Pantheon square, barely a stone's throw from Montecitorio and the Italian Parliament. For decades afterwards, shepherds led their flocks through the city on their way to new pastures.

Yet this link to the rural world was fast changing. The writer and artist Carlo Levi commented that flocks of sheep were being replaced by flocks of motor cars. Indeed, in the mid-1950s the latter forced the former off the streets, and soon the animals were transported in trucks. By the end of the 1950s, the city had just two square metres of green space per inhabitant, compared with 7.5 square metres in Paris and 10.5 square metres in London.

The 1930s and 1940s had been boom years for house building and became crucial to Rome's transformation from an ancient town to a mass modern city. So many new housing estates sprang up that by the 1950s the majority of the population lived not in areas redolent with history but in anonymous apartment blocks. The present was erasing the past, and this change was to have far-reaching effects on the city's relationship with its own history. The process of selection was especially ruthless after 1945 since there was pressure to ignore the experience of dictatorship and foreign occupation. This meant not only that the recent past was subjected to a peculiar whitewash, with Fascist projects like the futuristic EUR quarter and the Via della Conciliazione being completed despite the fall of the regime, but also that thousands of smaller matters – membership of the Fascist Party, collaboration with the Nazis, black-market trafficking and the memories associated with them – remained wholly or partly hidden. Compromise, betrayal and cowardice were brushed over by those who profited from them and sometimes by the victims too. For this reason, Rome did not easily yield up its ghosts.

The Montesi case reflected the profound changes sweeping across the city. It seemed to have nothing to do with the war and its aftermath: it was a true-crime story that roused passions at a time when few other things united Romans. In fact, it was profoundly, and in every facet, the product of a specific moment in the city's history. It developed at a time when patterns of living and consuming were undergoing change, women were becoming emancipated and younger people were beginning to move across the city easily. It is not by chance that De Sica's film *Bicycle Thieves* shows extensive travel around the city. No jobs are available to men in the new neighbourhoods so they travel to the centre. Antonio Ricci's bicycle is stolen in Via Crispi and he chases the thief into Largo del Tritone, both central roads just a few hundred yards from the seats of power. The police station where he goes to report the theft is located at the Trevi Fountain, which does not appear in the film but which was already so famous among tourists that it was illuminated at night. He searches for his bicycle in the bustling market of Piazza Vittorio. He visits a clairvoyant across the Tiber in Trastevere, the very area where he tracks down the thief.

Mobility was a feature of the post-war years. Before the war it was unusual for a worker even to take a tram ride outside his own quarter. Indeed, it was not unknown for the poorest people to take a tram ride round the sights on their wedding day as a sort of substitute honeymoon. The rapid expansion of the area occupied by the city meant that people were obliged to travel to look for work or to go to a hospital or school. The public-transport system was good and reasonably priced but it did not extend as far as some of the newer areas. Old patterns of community solidarity – seen by Carlo Levi as typical of a certain Rome – were undermined by this sort of development and would be further eroded by the tensions of the war years and the liberation. De Sica's protagonist receives precious little help from workers' organisations, the authorities or even friends in his efforts to recover the bicycle on which his livelihood depends.

The most striking feature of Rome's new urban development was its disorderly nature. The city grew spontaneously and building was rarely directed or planned in any meaningful way. Local government was weak, so clerical power and established financial muscle dominated, which always favoured the speculator and the builder. Not that this situation went unchallenged: in 1907 a movement of opinion in support of democratisation and for greater control led to the election of the reforming mayor Ernesto Nathan. In six years, he made local government a more decisive influence in matters of economic development and construction by introducing a tax on building land. He created municipal authorities for transport and electricity. Although no administration would have more impact, the practice of interventionism continued, with a raft of policies being adopted from 1919 to promote low-cost housing, to seize unoccupied dwellings and encourage approved building. Among the vast blocks erected to house the growing numbers of state employees was the residence at Via Tagliamento 76, where Wilma Montesi's grandparents went to live in the early 1930s.

The Fascists brought democratic government in the city to an end, as they did in the rest of the country. In place of an elected council, a governorate was established that was entrusted with the task of realising Mussolini's plans to make Rome once again the centrepiece of a grand imperial power. By 1921 the population had grown to 656,000 and fifteen years later it would exceed a million. By 1941 this figure had risen to 1.4 million. Twenty years later, in 1960, the population would reach two million. Fascism knew that a grand Rome needed a large population, but it was mainly concerned to give shape to a modern city that recalled directly the civilisation of the Caesars. Mussolini personally inaugurated the extensive demolitions that were intended to free up space around the ruins of the Roman Forum and the Colosseum, allowing for the construction of a major new highway linking the ruins with Piazza Venezia, the square containing the Victor Emmanuel monument and the Altar of the Fatherland, as well as the balcony from which Il Duce was accustomed to harangue the crowds.

The Fascist plan for Rome was to make the city a beacon for all Italians. In the topographical changes the regime promoted, virtually every town and village in the country found itself with a Via Roma or a Piazza Roma. Children were taught that the city was a link between past and future greatness, and many of them still had this idea in mind when they finally visited it on organised trips. Yet, in practical terms, Rome was not an easy city in which to live. The reality, inevitably, fell short of the myth. The housing shortage meant that accommodation for incomers was often cramped and inadequate. Living costs were always higher than they were in most other cities. Given that the regime made a point of keeping wages low, the potential for mobility was limited. Its solution to this sort of problem was to provide welfare and leisure facilities at low or zero cost. They included free health care, holiday camps for children, and sports and entertainment activities. Until the later war years, which brought acute shortages, these helped absorb any latent tension.

Crime was not a serious problem under the regime but it became a huge issue in the final stages of the war and during the Allied occupation. The police force remained large, having grown under the repressive Fascist state, and expanded further as post-war ministers tried to balance Fascist appointees with new recruits, but it was not large enough to deter the various criminals who contributed to the increase in burglaries, theft, and commerce involving stolen goods, as well as the violence committed for gain or vendetta. The public latched on to gruesome stories, like the violent stabbing, in June 1945, of Maria Laffi: she was murdered by a student who wanted to get his hands on her jewellery. The perpetrator invented a tale involving the recovery of documents belonging to the King but his true motive was soon exposed. Then, four months later, Angela Barrucca and her young son Gianni were found with their throats cut in their home in the Esquilino district. Their assassins, the Cataldi sisters, aged seventeen and twenty-two, hailed from Barrucca's hometown of Colleferro outside Rome; they had been envious of Angela's success in finding a husband and achieving a good standard of living.

By the early 1950s, although there had been some improvement, there was still a real issue with criminality. Some of it was motivated by economic necessity but the role of opportunity should not be ignored. The recourse to violence had a number of causes. The cheapening of life during the war was undoubtedly one. Another was the Fascist emphasis on violence and hatred with which a generation had been inculcated. Yet another was the new link between organised crime and narcotics.

Drugs were widely seen as an affectation, an external symbol of decadence, associated in the public mind with the upper classes and Bohemians. The high stakes involved with drug-trafficking led to violence and murder. Typically, the victims had lost merchandise, appropriated profits or were suspected of betrayal. Ettore Vari, the man injected with a lethal dose of heroin near Torvaianica in 1950, and Flavio Agorneri, the photographer thought to have been bitten by a tarantula, were two. There was also Corinna Versolatto, a thirty-five-year-old former coat-check girl at the Piccolo Slam nightclub. She was found dead in Alessandria after an overdose of barbiturates. She had worked for the anti-narcotics unit of the military government of Trieste, whose chief was involved with the racket, then as secretary to a known trafficker, an Italian-Venezuelan named Mario Amelotti, who was suspected of her murder. The three cases echoed in the Montesi story.

Elsewhere, ordinary Romans, like other Italians, were beginning, in the mid-1950s, to taste some of the first fruits of economic recovery. Ten years earlier, most people had struggled to make ends meet. Food was scarce and new clothes or shoes were luxuries that one could only dream of. Cinemas and dance halls were packed since they offered an inexpensive escape from the struggles and frustrations of everyday life. Those who could not afford to pay for tickets found plenty of opportunities for free entertainment. The Communists were pragmatic enough to know that, if they wanted to draw the young people to them, they had to offer more than ideology: party sections and workers' recreational associations became known for the dances they held at weekends. The Church strongly disapproved of dancing, regarding it as an immoral pastime, and tempted people with American films. Many churches organised film shows and some even had movie theatres attached to them.

The Montesi case offered a fascinating insight into the way the social and economic relations of the city intersected with a Catholic world that, despite its centralisation under the Pope, was actually remarkably heterogeneous. In Rome, the headquarters of the Church, Catholicism was a complex reality.

Catholic politicians were men of varied sensibilities and credos, who had their own allies and friends in the Vatican. At the same time, there were twelve religious orders, each of which had its own resources and functions. The largest and most influential was the Society of Jesus, an order that had been persecuted in the past but which had always come back strongly. Founded by Ignacio de Loyola in 1534, the Jesuits regarded loyalty to the Pope as an article of faith, but that did not prevent them sometimes being seen as secretive and scheming. Intellectually inclined and rigorous, the order published the influential magazine *La Civiltà Cattolica*. Well known for its intelligent and uncompromising reflections on the problems of the world, it was one of the main instruments of Jesuit influence. The order disapproved of what it saw as the compromises the Christian Democrats had made to win and maintain power. By making friends with suspect individuals, covering up for speculators and defending privilege, they had allowed some unsavoury elements to infiltrate the party as it consolidated its position as the dominant force of government. The Church's own role as property owner, banker and political player in Rome also disquieted them.

This attitude shaped the way the order responded when it found itself faced with Anna Maria Caglio and her extraordinary stories. Father Filipetto, her confessor, was a member of the order and he advised her, when she was on the point of leaving Milan, to contact his brother Jesuits in the capital if she were to run into trouble. When she renewed contact with Father Filipetto in November 1953 to tell him of her liaison with Montagna, and her fears that he was entangled with the death of the Montesi girl, he urged her to sever all links with him and to take up his own earlier offer.

Montagna, of course, had his own network of contacts in the Church. One of his closest friends, Riccardo Galeazzo-

Lisi, was the Pope's physician, and he was on friendly terms with the lay organiser Luigi Gedda and Monsignor Fiorenzo Angelini, a Vatican official who was one of Giulio Andreotti's associates. But he had no influence among the Jesuits.

Back in Rome, Anna Maria Caglio spoke with two priests, Father Dall'Olio and then Father Rotondi, meeting the first on 17 November. Both men contributed to *La Civiltà Cattolica*, and the latter was a member of its editorial board. They were more than willing to listen to the tales she told, which lifted the veil on the very practices the Jesuits deplored. Astonished by what they had heard, they decided to bring the matter to the attention of the government and, through an intermediary in the prime minister's office, a meeting was secured with Amintore Fanfani, who had recently been appointed interior minister in place of Mario Scelba. Fanfani had softened his critique of the party leadership and forged a tactical alliance with De Gasperi. The long-serving prime minister had stepped down when he was unable, following the elections of June 1953, to form a new government. Although he was unwell, he was still leader of the party and a figure it was impossible to ignore. But few doubted Fanfani's goal. His ambition and authoritarian streak made him widely disliked within and outside his party. The Christian Democrat trade unionist Rapelli described him as 'a Fascist hierarch after his time, who grew up compromising with Fascism; he is driven by ambition and presents himself as falsely humble'. For *Don Camillo* author Giovannino Guareschi, he was 'the anti-de Gasperi: Napoleonic in terms of height but Stalinist in mental outlook'. Nevertheless, his energy and determination to build his party into a force to rival the Communists, and his willingness to look for new political allies beyond the small parties of the centre, won admirers at a time when the Christian Democrats desperately needed a new strategy.

As interior minister, Fanfani took a keen interest in the

Montesi case. Even before the Jesuits came to him he was receiving reports about developments. It frustrated him, though, that he constantly found himself dealing with Scelba's appointees. In forging a tool to help him face down political and industrial agitation, the Sicilian had stamped his mark on the ministry and especially on the police. For this reason, Fanfani did not trust some of those he was obliged to work with and decided that the conduct of the police merited verification. The action he took became public during the trial of Silvano Muto. For decades afterwards it would lead to accusations that he had unleashed a bitter conflict within the state and used the case in the most cynical way to discredit the one man who stood between him and leadership of the Christian Democrats. The Montesi case was about to explode in the most public setting imaginable.

PART TWO

IX

Muto on Trial

The first hearing of the trial of Silvano Muto on charges of 'spreading false and tendentious news to disturb public order' was held on 28 January 1954. The assumption was that Muto would recite a *mea culpa* and be dealt with swiftly. In fact, he coolly announced that he no longer stood by the withdrawal he had been forced to sign the previous October, and astonished the court by proclaiming his intention – with the help of key witnesses – to demonstrate that his story was true. Muto's surprise announcement brought Adriana Bisaccia and Anna Maria Caglio into the public eye for the first time, and public interest in the case flared anew. The trouble was that neither woman could be found. Bisaccia had been taken to hospital after swallowing fifty pills of the anti-inflammatory drug quinine on 10 January. The reason for her suicide attempt was unknown but, after discharging herself from medical care, she had disappeared into thin air. As for Caglio, she was assumed to be out of Rome but not even her father in Milan knew where she was. As a result the hearing was adjourned after just over two hours and the police were ordered to find the women without delay.

When the case resumed on 4 March everything was set for a major contest. Muto's choice of defence lawyers reflected his determination to play to the gallery. One was a leading Sardinian-born Communist, Giuseppe Sotgiu, who had alarmed the Vatican by winning election to the presidency of the Rome provincial council. The second was a younger man, Giuseppe Bucciante, a general's son from Chieti, who was associated with the political right. The prosecution and the judges were determined there would be no grandstanding and did everything to block the defence in its tracks. First, the defence lawyers were granted virtually no time to consult the case files, which amounted to some two thousand pages. The prosecutor openly scoffed at a request that numerous witnesses be called. But Sotgiu and Bucciante were not easily thrown off their stride: knowing they had public opinion behind them, they succeeded in presenting most of their witnesses to the court.

Although they were not on trial, Ugo Montagna and Piero Piccioni took a very keen interest in the proceedings and their lawyers tried to ensure that the impact of possible revelations in court or the press was minimised. On 13 February they had been summoned separately to see Procurator Sigurani, who was still conducting his inquiry into the circumstances of the Montesi woman's death, and had stated their extraneousness to events. Piccioni's lawyers issued a statement acknowledging that Piccioni and Montagna were distant acquaintances while Montagna's lawyer, Girolamo Bellavista, admitted that his client had conducted a relationship with Anna Maria Caglio. It had ended, and the woman was motivated by resentment in speaking against him now, he claimed. To prove that she had loved him, he surreptitiously passed to the press extracts from some of her letters, in which, among other things, she addressed him tenderly as *ciccio patata* (loosely: spud).

But at the same time some other awkward facts surfaced by different means. Two of the guards at the Capocotta estate, it was discovered, had been dismissed in the days immediately following the discovery of Wilma Montesi's body, while an officer of the Carabinieri at Ostia, who had conducted enquiries of his own, had been briskly transferred elsewhere. And when the spotlight fell on the whereabouts of Piccioni on the crucial dates of 9 and 10 April 1953, his lawyer said first that he had been in Milan, then changed his statement to say that he had been ill. It seemed that the early concessions made by Piccioni and Montagna would not be enough to prevent them being on the back foot when the trial reopened.

The politicians and justice officials went to work frenziedly behind the scenes. A succession of leading Christian Democrats had attempted to form a government after the June 1953 election but the reluctance of the small centre parties to join a coalition made stability impossible. Ministers changed office every time a new attempt was made. Government interest in the case was related to the fact that Attilio Piccioni had become foreign minister in the reshuffle of December 1953. The office of prime minister was now occupied by Mario Scelba. A political strongman, Scelba was expected to stamp his administration with his characteristic firmness. However, on 18 February, the newspaper *Paese Sera*, which was financed by the Communists, printed a photograph that depicted him standing near to a smiling Ugo Montagna at the wedding in Sicily of Alfonso Spataro, the son of cabinet minister Giuseppe. The positions occupied by the two men made it clear they were both official witnesses. By this time Montagna had been painted in the press as a sinister figure and no politician wanted to be exposed as knowing him.

It fell to one of the Communists' ablest propagandists and orators, Gian Carlo Pajetta, to denounce the matter in Parliament. The photograph, he said, was proof that the man who was suspected of being implicated in the Montesi girl's death was a friend of the prime minister. Incensed, Scelba shouted back at him, 'I have also been photographed with you, but I am not your friend!' Despite the unwelcome publicity, Scelba won the confidence vote that was held in Parliament that day.

Yet further bad news came when it was revealed, also on 18 February, that a Sicilian bandit, Gaspare Pisciotta, had been poisoned in the Ucciardone gaol. The man had achieved notoriety when he had betrayed his chief, Salvatore Giuliano, who had won a following on his native island by championing independence. Pisciotta had expected to be rewarded for his collaboration but instead had been sentenced to a long term with other gang members. Furiously, he had shouted in court that he would reveal the deals he had done with the authorities and the Mafia. It was widely surmised that he had been murdered to prevent this. As prime minister and a Sicilian, Scelba was held doubly responsible.

These developments only served to fuel mounting concern. On 3 March, the eve of the trial's resumption, the Procurator's Office, directed by Angelo Sigurani, closed its investigation into the death of Wilma Montesi. It had been on the case for nearly ten months and now confirmed earlier conclusions that the girl had died as the result of an accident in which no one else was involved. Whatever the intention, the timing of the announcement was not enough to take the heat out of the impending trial. Few were surprised when, on the morning of Thursday, 4 March 1954, a huge crowd gathered on the banks of the Tiber outside Rome's enormous Palace of Justice. A building of monumental ugliness, it had been inaugurated in 1911, on the fiftieth anniversary of Italian unification. It was one of many pompous declarations of grandeur in bricks and mortar on the part of a state that had failed to fulfil the romantic hopes of early nationalists. In Rome, as elsewhere, big trials always drew the curious, but this was the first time that such a vast crowd had converged on the monstrous 'Il Palazzaccio'. As it was a weekday, the crowd was not composed of workers, although some girls looked as if they had slipped out from offices or shops. Lawyers and journalists

jostled with students, chic youngsters in duffel coats from the
Parioli district, men about town, existentialists from the artists'
district, and many women. *Paese Sera* concluded: 'It is truly the
trial for beautiful women. Never before have so many stupendous
ladies been seen at a legal proceeding.'

This was just the sort of mixed crowd that had pressed for
a glimpse of Tyrone Power five years earlier when he had
married Linda Christian. And although the mousy-looking
Silvano Muto was no Tyrone Power, he had achieved notoriety
and was fast becoming something of a hero now it was known
that he would contest the charges that had been laid before
him. In truth, no one wanted the trial, least of all the authorities,
but the mix-up over the dates of the amnesty had set the
judicial wheels in motion and nothing now could stop the
young editor being hauled into the dock. When Muto stepped
out of his taxi outside the palace, he was cheered by the crowd.
A quiet, reserved young man, he wore dark glasses and a silk
scarf, and tried to disappear into his overcoat.

Inside the court, three judges sat behind a large bench,
wearing black and gold robes. All eyes fell on the members
of Wilma Montesi's family as they walked into the court and
took their places. Rodolfo, Maria and Wanda were accompanied
by Rodolfo's sister Ida. Things had been difficult for them.
Sergio had given up school as a result of hurtful taunts and
had been helping his father. Rodolfo had not been well and
his business had suffered. 'My poor daughter,' Maria sighed.
'At least no one can make you die a second time.' Journalists
drew lots for a place in court, and a handful huddled around
a small table.

The first witnesses to take the stand were the journalists
who had written about the case. Then it was Anna Maria
Caglio's turn. When the police had searched for her, they had
drawn a blank. Eventually, with the assistance of her father,
who was also keen to know where she had got to, they had

tracked her down to the Maria Santissima Assunta convent in Florence where she had spent the entire month of January in retreat. There was nothing holy about her appearance. The burning sex appeal that had caught Montagna's eye now drew the attention of the public. She wore a dark tailored suit that fitted her figure closely and, with her bright red lipstick and intriguing aura, she seemed like a *femme fatale* who had stepped off the movie screen. The journalist Camilla Cederna was quick to give her a name: the Black Swan. It referred to her dark hair and clothes, her elegant deportment and the disturbing nature of her evidence.

On this, the first of her three appearances before the court, she detailed her meetings with Muto and spoke of the beginnings of her friendship with Montagna. But it wasn't until 6 March that she got fully into her stride. On that day her testimony lasted for six hours – and the Montesi affair caught fire. Caglio talked freely about herself, seeming entirely uninhibited even when discussing her previous lovers. And when asked about Montagna, there was scarcely a vice of which she did not accuse him: nepotism, corruption, deception, gambling, bribery, sexual perversion and accessory to murder. Everything was precisely presented, complete with names, dates, places and times.

In what was intended as a deadly blow, she even accused him of trafficking in cocaine without a thought for the consequences that addiction had on people's lives. 'I heard that his money came from drugs,' she told the court. 'He was ruining people with them. I would have gone to hell for Ugo, but more than once I told him, "Over and above the love I have for you, there is justice. If it is true what they say about you, you must pay for it." I would not allow him to ruin people. Cocaine drives people crazy. I didn't care if he had other women. I knew he wasn't faithful, but he needed me too. It is true that he went out with others, but he took me to his house.'

She blurted her testimony almost without taking breath.

'He said, "I do business only with those who are up to their necks in trouble." But spreading cocaine in Italy, think of it! He even asked me if I would like to take drugs but I always refused. "Keep it for yourself," I said.'

In the course of her time on the witness stand, Caglio revealed that she had overheard telephone conversations between Montagna and Piero Piccioni: 'We are suspected in the Montesi affair,' Montagna allegedly told Piccioni. Step by step she led the court towards Montagna's connections with authority. As she did so a buzz of whispers spread over the courtroom and audible gasps of surprise greeted what she had to say about some of the country's top law-enforcement officials.

Caglio's account of events on 29 April 1953 was crucial in suggesting that a cover-up had been orchestrated. On that evening, she asserted, Montagna had driven with her to the Ministry for the Interior and left her to sit in the vehicle while he entered the building with Piero Piccioni. Some time later she saw the two men emerge and leave each other with a handshake. She knew that they had been to see her lover's friend, the chief of police, Tommaso Pavone. The two men had history. Pavone had arrived in Rome from Milan in 1952 at the behest of interior minister Scelba with an enviable record of success as the city's first post-war prefect. He had opposed Fascism, and this gave him credit with the left, but he also understood the need to restore order and to get industry back on its feet. His businesslike attitude made him acceptable to the bourgeoisie, who showed their appreciation by welcoming him and his elegant wife into their salons. Montagna addressed him familiarly as 'Masino' and behaved in a way that showed favours were expected. And Pavone owed him a great deal: Montagna had intervened to secure his release after he had been arrested by the Nazis in 1943 and therefore had probably saved his life. He was thus in a position to call in favours. According to Caglio, the favour this time was to make sure that Piero was not incriminated for his part in Wilma Montesi's death. If she was right, it showed that the state was open to corruption and that there had been a conspiracy to cover up the real circumstances of the girl's death.

Following the meeting, Pavone was supposed to have told the police commissioner for Rome, Saverio Polito, to sort things out. Polito was used to receiving oblique orders and took his superior's words to be an instruction to focus on the hypothesis of accidental death and leave Piccioni out of all enquiries. He had sought to wrap the matter up quickly, only to be forced into a reversal by growing public curiosity in the case.

Caglio had travelled to Rome from Florence on 6 February and chatted on the way to journalists. A crowd was waiting for her at Termini railway station so she was advised to alight at Tiburtina instead. According to the journalist Angelo Frignani, who witnessed the scene, she lowered the window of the car that took her away and proclaimed, 'No one will convince me to keep quiet!' The next day she went to the Procurator's Office in the Palazzaccio and spent several hours telling her story to Angelo Sigurani. She told him how Montagna often made strange visits to seaports, particularly Genoa where he claimed to have put harbour officials on his payroll. Those in the know were aware that Sigurani had once been posted to Milan and knew the Moneta Caglio family, but this did not make him well disposed to her.

'I saw Sigurani on two occasions but he refused to do anything. All he said was "You keep out of this affair,"' Caglio told the court.

'Do you realise what you're saying?' interjected the judge.

'I'm just telling the truth,' she replied.

The public prosecutor jumped up several times and dismissed Caglio's testimony as pure fantasy. He was ferocious in his attacks on her credibility. But, like everybody else, he was amazed by the woman who held the court in the palm of her hand with revelation on revelation. Meanwhile, Muto sat quietly taking notes.

She had one final bombshell. During one of her separations from Montagna, she had sought refuge in the convent in Florence where she had been discovered on 5 February. She had not spent her time there in spiritual seclusion.

'I went to see the mayor, Giorgio La Pira,' she informed the court, 'who told me to reveal everything to the prime minister, Mr De Gasperi. I sat down and wrote two letters, one to the Pope and the other to the government. Shortly afterwards, I was called to Rome by Mr Fanfani.'

'*Who* did you say?' demanded the judge, with incredulity.

'Mr Fanfani, the minister of the interior,' was the response. 'I was received by the Carabinieri officer Colonel Pompei who, under orders from Fanfani, has been investigating everything I have told you about Montagna.'

Pandemonium erupted. Could this be true? Some mused that the woman should be taken to the Bocca della Verità, a well-known monument from ancient Roman times, which, according to legend, would bite any liar who placed their hand in its open mouth.

With her sensational revelations, Anna Maria Caglio instantly became the most talked-about woman in the country. She was also the most sought-after subject of the photographers who gathered every day at the Palazzaccio. Her racy tales of sex, drugs and corruption lifted the veil on a hidden world of debauchery that threatened to tarnish a hitherto untouchable élite.

★   ★   ★

For all the in-built advantages the Italian legal system gave it, the prosecution was losing the argument. The key issue was whether Colonel Pompei's report actually existed. While enquiries were ordered, the trial proceeded. More journalists were called and some minor witnesses given the chance to say their piece. Some were out-and-out eccentrics.

The first was a certain Luigi Bruzzone from Genoa, whose letters arrived at the Palazzaccio in the opening days of the trial and were read out in court. In them he claimed to establish the guilt of Montagna in the matter of Wilma's death. Then it was discovered that he had convictions for extortion, had spent time in lunatic asylums, and had been expelled from the Communist Party.

Sensational revelations were also promised by Piero Pierotti, a thirty-one-year-old miner working in Luxembourg, who got in touch with Muto and told him a fantastic story of how he had met Wilma at Ostia station. The girl, he said, had asked him to work for some of her influential friends; the job consisted of carrying a ten-kilo bag of cocaine over the frontier on his next foreign journey. Muto took him seriously: he sent his wife to meet Pierotti and accompany him to Rome by plane. Hoping that he would prove to be a star defence witness, he kept him in hiding, away from the clutches of other journalists. But Pierotti could not contain himself and, before he was called to court, he spoke to some left-wing newspapers. He offered a detailed tale, but as soon as he went public his friends let it be known that he had made everything up.

As the trial got into its stride, it was Muto's lawyer Sotgiu who emerged as the star of the show. Backed by the left-wing press, he did his best to turn the hearing into political theatre. He claimed that the cover-up and the trial itself were a dramatic indictment of the corruption of the government, the bourgeoisie and the Church. His method was to discredit the entire establishment, which he memorably branded

'Capocottari' – accomplices of Ugo Montagna and his fellow hunters at Capocotta.

Sotgiu and Bucciante's aim was to demolish the hypothesis that Wilma had died accidentally while bathing her feet. In this, they were greatly assisted by a demolition job that had been performed on it by Rinaldo Pellegrini, professor of forensic medicine at Padua University. In an analysis he published as a book, he was scathing in his criticism of the report's inconsistencies and omissions. He pointed out that the drug test had concerned only the girl's stomach, not the blood or the spinal cord. He noted that, in discarding the possibility of a sexual motive, the hypothesis of anal penetration had not been investigated. He dwelt at length on the fact that Montesi's vagina was stuffed with sand. This could be proof, he argued, that she had been the victim of a pervert who derived pleasure from abusing dead women. This necrophiliac twist added a macabre note to his testimony.

On 10 March, Adriana Bisaccia's moment arrived and expectations were high. After leaving hospital she had gone to see Silvano Muto's secretary, who had given her two thousand lire, to tide her over, and then had met up with a painter of her acquaintance, Duilio Francimei, who had taken her in. She had stayed with him for two weeks during which time their relationship had taken an intimate turn. However, when she realised he was a morphine addict she had persuaded him to seek medical help. With him now in a psychiatric clinic, she was homeless. Adriana had been found by the police on 30 January, living in a squalid basement in Via Melozzo da Forli in the Flaminio district, just a few hundred yards from Montagna's house in Via Rabirio and Caglio's lodgings. In the weeks prior to the trial she had been courted by the press and her ghosted articles had appeared, complete with numerous photographs, in the weeklies. She had even been interviewed in *Il Messaggero* by a high-profile female journalist, Flora

Antonioni. This, then, was the girl from the existentialist set who had first-hand experience of the debauched secret life of the capital.

But as she took the stand, Bisaccia looked shabby and her once lustrous hair was dull. A small woman with a cute, almost childish face, she appeared downtrodden and insignificant. When she spoke she sounded as if she were in a trance. She was hazy about the drug parties she was supposed to have attended at Capocotta. She had previously asserted that Piccioni was with Wilma when she died, but now she would not confirm that. She offered a pathetic spectacle. Eventually she tried to extricate herself from the whole business: 'I see Wilma's mother in the court. I should like to talk to her and tell her I never met her daughter,' she cried. 'Call the others – call Piccioni, call Montagna – but I have nothing to do with it.'

Her account of events and of her own previous statements to the police was incoherent. She claimed not to remember where she had been on 9 April 1953, and she denied she had told Muto anything. 'I only expressed hypotheses to Muto, as lots of others did too,' she said. Suddenly she seemed to be afflicted by amnesia.

Bisaccia was a fragile individual who was obviously shocked by the changes to her life that notoriety had brought. In the weekly *Oggi* the one-time model lamented that she felt completely alone. Not even her own mother called her by her pet name of Titti any more. She had become 'La Bisaccia, the one linked with orgies and drugs'. Interestingly, *Oggi* introduced her story under the banner title 'Youth of Today'. Although she claimed not to have known Wilma, the article suggested there was a sort of connection between them: 'There are no links between her, me and Anna Maria Moneta,' it read. 'Or perhaps there are some. Perhaps it is that link that unites all modern girls, those who never know where to take their restlessness. La Caglio took it on to the stage, but her love affair finished badly anyway. Wilma took it on to the beach at Torvaianica; probably like me and Anna Maria she did not want to live according to tradition.' There was a suspicion that she had been got at. Her whole demeanour suggested she had been intimidated and that some form of harassment was still going on.

The presiding judge, exasperated by Bisaccia's denials, decided to bring her face to face with Silvano Muto. Once on the stand, Muto pleaded that his only interest had been in the dope-smuggling that was known to take place on the part of the coast between Ostia and Anzio, and it had been Bisaccia who had drawn his attention to the link with the Montesi girl's death.

His attempt to attribute a role to her caused Bisaccia to explode and, enraged, she used the informal 'tu' when she addressed Muto. This was tantamount to a confession of intimacy, though her rage seemed to indicate that it belonged to the past.

For several days during the trial she was put up at the smart Hotel Plaza, where she met Anna Maria Caglio. To one right-wing magazine, Caglio and Bisaccia were both 'poor girls hyponotised by the glory of the illustrated magazine who have lived in these recent weeks the great moment of their lives'. For Bisaccia this was certainly true, but for Caglio it was just the start.

Press coverage of the personalities in the case gave an incentive for more eccentrics to come forward. A radio technician from Verona, Francesco Tannoia, told police that he had been approached while in Rome on business by a young woman who had pleaded with him, 'Please help me get away. I am being followed.' He went on: 'The girl told me her name was Wilma Montesi and that I was fortunate not to live in Rome, a city where slowly she was having the life sucked from her.' Few believed this timid man's tale, but others seemed more plausible.

Maddalena Caramello, a sixty-year-old writer and prominent supporter of the political ideal of federalism, claimed to have seen Wilma in the company of Montagna on a number of occasions in the spring of 1952. She stated in interviews that, while sitting on the terrace of the Caffè Valente, she had seen the pair arrive by car in Via del Viminale and go into the Hotel Impero. Caramello was a serious woman, who had been sent to internal exile under Fascism, but her stock had fallen and she was living modestly. Some suspected that she wanted to return to the centre of things and the Muto trial offered a platform.

A more serious witness was Bisaccia's one-time lover, the painter Duilio Francimei. If anyone was in a position to comment on the truth or otherwise of her affirmations, it was him. Before he got a chance to say anything of note, however, he was suddenly seized by police and committed to an institution for the criminally insane. There, his hair was shaved off and he was put in a strait-jacket. When he was released he was issued with an internal deportation order and given just a few days to leave town. As soon as the defence team heard about this, they subpoenaed him. A manic talker with staring eyes, he stood before the court with his shaven head and told all he knew about Adriana's phone calls, nightmares and relations with unnamed high-placed persons.

The attempt to get Francimei out of the way showed the government's determination to prevent the characters of Via Margutta from throwing mud around. This tactic failed as far as the painter was concerned, but a more general clampdown was still enforced. On the evening of Francimei's testimony, the police raided the Bohemian bars in a well-planned operation and rounded up some two hundred people, most of whom were non-Roman. Il Baretto and the Tazza d'Oro found their entire clienteles arrested. As many as possible were sent back to the towns they had come from. Such action was without precedent since the war, and it seemed to have been designed to scare people into keeping their mouths shut.

Many were convinced that Bisaccia had been paid fabulous sums to keep quiet at the trial. In reality she lived from hand to mouth and had no fixed abode. But she did receive significant cash payments and benefits from the press. Even Francimei was able to cash in on his tawdry moment of glory and sold his story for a hundred thousand lire.

Bisaccia's amnesia, whether real or feigned, was a setback for the defence. It soon bounced back, though. Some rapid enquiries showed that a Colonel Pompei was commander of the Rome division of the Carabinieri and he had indeed compiled a report. While the police had been eager to close the Montesi investigation, the Carabinieri had begun to look into the case, which they suspected was one of murder. The state police, who did not enjoy wide respect and were seen as inefficient, were a civilian force. The Carabinieri were the national gendarmerie founded by King Victor Emmanuel I of Savoy. Formally a branch of the army, they had responsibilities for policing both civilian and military populations. Historic rivals of the police, they were the one law-and-order force in Italy that enjoyed universal respect. Renowned for their integrity and relative autonomy from politics, they had a strong ethos that was completely different from the flexible morality of the police.

Pompei's report had been commissioned by interior minister Fanfani after he was approached by Father Rotondi following Caglio's meetings with him and Father dall'Olio. Whether, as some suspected, the ambitious minister had chosen to act as he did to discredit his main rival for the leadership of the Christian Democrats or because he was genuinely concerned about the influence acquired by a man like Montagna, it was unprecedented for a minister of the interior to go behind the backs of the police. Far from acting officially, Fanfani had in effect commissioned a private inquiry. Caglio's Catholic connections had proved strong enough to get her a hearing at the highest levels.

As for the report itself, the defence and the prosecution crossed swords over whether it should be read to the court, but in the end the prosecutor was forced to give way when printed copies of the most salacious passages were posted up on walls around the city during the night of 8 March.

Colonel Pompei, a corpulent fifty-seven-year-old who had served for ten years in Libya and worked for the secret service under the Fascists, arrived in court in uniform on 10 March. He read line by line every word of a report that was a stark indictment of Marchese Ugo Montagna. His steady rise up the social ladder was documented carefully until he had reached his present giddy position as the intimate of cabinet ministers, friend of top policemen and generals, favoured guest of countesses and *salonières*. It also catalogued the darker side of Montagna's activities, his black-marketeering, corruption, bribery and debauchery.

The Pompei report painted a picture of Montagna's past that was deeply unsavoury. According to the colonel, Montagna had been arrested in 1937 and charged with using a false name and falsified documents. In 1939 he was reported to have run a brothel from his home, catering to the libidinous desires of leading Fascists. The police had received complaints from neighbours about rowdy behaviour at the house but failed to intervene. Later, he had entertained German officers and spied for them while also being an agent of the Fascist secret police. Following the liberation, he had ingratiated himself with the Allies and used his connections to run a black-market operation. At each juncture during the dramatic political changes of the later war years, he had managed to keep a foot in both camps and had profited from every opportunity that came his way. He always ended up on the winning side.

The report confirmed that the marchese's money had come mostly from property. Using inside information, he bought and sold land and blocks of flats, often making fantastic profits. He also ran a rental operation, leaning on his police friends to help him oust tenants and reclaim properties. He relied on tip-offs from those in the know to buy up land destined for public-works projects that had not yet been announced. And for years, it was revealed, he had scarcely paid any taxes at all.

Montagna, it was also confirmed, was very gifted at forging valuable friendships. The report listed a few of his high-placed associates in business or pleasure. They included Piero Piccioni, cabinet minister Giuseppe Spataro, the Pope's personal physician Riccardo Galeazzi-Lisi, the governor of Vatican City Prefect Mastrobuono, the head of the state sulphur corporation, chief of police Pavone, and another police official who moonlighted as manager of some of Montagna's property companies. Although the list was short, such public exposure was potentially intensely damaging to his whole mode of doing business.

Unsurprisingly, Pompei also had damning things to say about the police, and especially about Rome's police commissioner, Saverio Polito, who had since been retired. This man, who had once been well regarded, was little more than a thuggish street cop who had been promoted far beyond his competence. He had 'reached the highest levels not on account of his intellectual qualities or his moral qualities but due to a certain elasticity of conscience that permitted him to show compliance towards every personality, of whatever political colour, distorting and bending facts'. For his part Pavone was exposed as someone who had had ill-considered dealings with Montagna.

Such statements brought politics even more directly into the case. By this time, the forces of the left, which closely followed Sotgiu's politicised management of the defence, were

ecstatic. They made a connection between the handling of the
Montesi case and the highly suspicious way in which the
Sicilian bandit Gaspare Pisciotta had met his end, poisoned
while in gaol in Palermo. The Communists warned the
Christian Democrats that they could not obstruct the course
of justice a second time. The editor of the party paper *L'Unità*,
Pietro Ingrao, had fuelled the flames of class hatred in an
incendiary editorial on 7 February, in which he asserted that
the case had brought about the discovery of a hidden and
undisturbed world of drugs, black masses, orgies, buying and
selling of young bodies, and fast money. In an Italy in which
there were four million unemployed, and some regions were
marked by chronic backwardness, there was shock and disbelief,
he added, that a privileged caste lived in luxury villas, went
hunting with noblemen, took drugs, and had even destroyed
the life of a luckless young woman.

Left-wing papers published the Pompei report in full. It
was widely read too, since public interest in the Montesi case
had reached a crescendo. Never had the job of the *strilloni*,
the street paper-sellers who shouted the day's news to attract
custom, been easier. As the trial progressed, the press brought
out special editions, news kiosks demanded more copies and
even the reject copies that had been retained by the printers
were snapped up. Huge headlines, sensational revelations, daily
dramatic developments, and page after page of coverage fuelled
an appetite that was without recent precedent. In the bars and
cafés of Rome, people talked of little else.

The authorities did their best to force the genie back into
the bottle. Colonel Pompei was hauled into the Viminale Palace
and subjected to a haranguing by Tommaso Pavone and Angelo
Musco, Polito's successor as police commissioner for Rome.
They angrily accused him of including facts about Montagna
in his report that had not been brought to their attention.
And, for what it was worth, newspapers that published the

Pompei report in full were accused of threatening public order. Prime Minister Scelba sensed that the future of the government was on the line and moved quickly to show that he had no intention of tolerating Montagna. One of his problems, though, was that he had personally called Pavone to Rome to head the police, and to save his own political skin he needed to ditch him: when a further photograph appeared showing the chief of police arriving in the capital with a grinning Montagna standing just behind him, he had his weapon – and ordered Pavone to resign. Meanwhile, aware that his presence in government might become an embarrassment, Attilio Piccioni offered to resign, but Scelba refused to allow him to go.

The crowds gathering outside the Palazzaccio grew day by day. Such was the clamour that even the highly cautious *Settimana Incom* newsreel devoted time to the case. The exposure of Montagna's corrupt conduct ensured that, before the court of public opinion at least, he was seen as irredeemably guilty. Montagna grasped this, and took prompt action to limit the damage. His strategy was to do his utmost to discredit the woman who was responsible for the original assault on his reputation, and in this he was helped by his friends in the police, who passed him a copy of another confidential report that he did not hesitate to hand over to the press. This one, compiled not by the Carabinieri but by the police themselves, contained information about Caglio's sexual partners and was complete with dates and details of the hotel rooms she had stayed in. The aim was to show her up as a floozy, a woman who was 'not serious' and whose word could no more be trusted than her virtue. Unfortunately for Montagna, her star turn in court, her personal magnetism and elevated social extraction somehow protected her from attempts to depict her as a fallen woman.

In a way, Montagna was fortunate that the Pompei report

was anything but a complete account of his various activities. Interviewed outside the court, Silvano Muto pointed out that it contained no mention of his role in drug-trafficking, or – Muto went further – his arms-smuggling or deals with Eastern-bloc countries. The actions he was accused of were sleazy and indecorous but not enough to alienate many of his friends. Montagna managed to hold his head high and keep officials at his beck and call. He dined out in his customary fashion and kept up his usual social round. People talked, as they always did, in the salons and in the cafés of Via Veneto, but he was not given the cold shoulder. Nevertheless, his nerves showed.When a photographer moved to take his picture, he simply snapped his fingers and had the man arrested by a watching policeman.

Now everyone was waiting for the testimonies of Montagna, Piccioni and Polito. The three men were summoned to court on the same day, 20 March. The authorities rightly anticipated that the public would arrive in huge numbers to see those who were allegedly behind the conspiracy, but their response was overkill. Jeeps full of armed soldiers and numerous mounted police were placed strategically in front of the Palace of Justice, ready to tackle any disturbances. The special armed units had been formed by Scelba to tackle left-inspired protests but it was unusual to see them used preventively or to defend public institutions. This heavy-handed reaction showed just how dangerous the situation had become in the eyes of the government.

The three men arrived at the court by a secondary entrance. With the elderly Polito hobbling on a stick, they were ushered into a side room from where they could hear the tail end of the testimony of Anna Maria Caglio's landlady, Signora Marri. This nervy woman had trouble with dates but she remembered vividly how her tenant had gone warily to Capocotta with Montagna after she had confronted him with her suspicions.

She had even put razor blades in her bag in case she needed to defend herself. The landlady learned afterwards that Caglio had begged a taxi driver to remember her face in case she did not return. Frightened, the man had found an excuse not to continue the journey.

Signora Marri also disclosed the existence of a document that Caglio had given to her for safe-keeping the previous October. She had been instructed to reveal its contents only in the case of the girl's death.

'Where is the letter now?' asked the judge.

'I posted it this morning to Anna Maria.'

'Who told you to do it?'

'It was my own idea. I gave it to my daughter to post. I didn't want the responsibility of presenting it in court.'

The judge was incensed, and the sitting was immediately suspended while the police were sent to retrieve the letter from the post office. It was found and delivered to the court within the hour. After some exchanges about confidentiality, the envelope was opened. Inside, the judge found a single sheet of pale blue paper; Caglio had written on both sides. It was dated 30 October 1953.

The entire court strained forward as the contents were read out.

I have too many Christian principles to commit suicide, but knowing both Montagna and Piero Piccioni I do not want to disappear without leaving any trace. Ugo Montagna is the head of a dope ring responsible for the disappearance of many women. He is the brains of the ring, while Piero Piccioni is the assassin.

Caglio was summoned to confirm that she had written the document. When she confirmed that she had, the prosecutor demanded, above the turmoil, that the trial be suspended indefinitely. The judge assented and everyone jumped up, leaving Caglio still on the stand.

Thus the Muto trial abruptly ended. There was now no case to answer. The three star witnesses, Polito, Montagna and Piccione, who had been called to account, never gave evidence. Whether they were relieved at being spared or angry at not having the chance to respond under oath to the allegations that had been levelled against them was not known. They cannot have been pleased, though, to be thrust to the very centre of the stage of public opinion and to have been left there with the most serious of question marks hanging over them.

If there had been any doubt before, now there could be none. The fate of the girl from Via Tagliamento had become an affair of state. The cry for justice was on the lips of all those who felt excluded from the feast of the privileged. The onus was on the government to show that it would not now stand in the way of the most thorough investigation of the murky background to Wilma Montesi's unexplained death.

Wilma Montesi, the 21-year-old carpenter's daughter whose body was found on the beach at Torvaianica, 38 kilometres from Rome, on 11 April 1953.   © Michael Ochs/Getty Images

In the days after Wilma Montesi's body was discovered, journalists flocked to Torvaianica with the photographers whose pictures appeared in the illustrated magazines. The location later became a tourist attraction for curious Romans.

Wilma's mother points to a picture of her daughter in the family home at Via Tagliamento 76. Maria Montesi always defended Wilma's reputation against insinuations that she was a call girl or drug pusher.

Wilma's 28-year-old uncle, Giuseppe Montesi, assisted his brother with the first enquiries but later was regarded as a suspect. A government employee with a complicated love life, he was the first male in the family not to become a carpenter.

© *Keystone/ Getty Images*

Angelo Giuliani was engaged to Wilma Montesi between August 1952 and her death. A policeman originally from the South, he had tried to impress the family by claiming to be a wine merchant.

© *Author's own collection*

Silvano Muto briefly became a folk hero when he was put on trial for alleging that members of Roman high society had been involved in the death of Montesi. The sensational suspension of his trial in March 1954 opened the way to a new investigation.

© *Bettmann/CORBIS*

A crowd gathers on the steps of the Palace of Justice in Rome during the trial of Silvano Muto.

© *Bettmann/CORBIS*

Escorted by police, the Montesi family leaves the Palace of Justice after being interrogated by magistrates. Maria Montesi is at the centre of the group and Wilma's sister Wanda is to her right. Father Rodolfo is partly concealed by the policeman whose arm is raised.

© Bettmann/CORBIS

Silvano Muto's chief defence attorney, Giuseppe Sotgiu, surrounded by newsmen after it was revealed that he and his artist wife had frequented a house of ill repute in the company of a minor. Sotgiu was a prominent Communist and president of the Rome provincial council.   *© Bettmann/CORBIS*

Piero Piccioni, the jazz-musician son of the Christian Democrat foreign minister, was arrested in 1954 and tried in 1957 for his part in the death of Wilma Montesi. He always protested his innocence.

© Author's own collection

Ugo Montagna, the Marchese of San Bartolomeo, was a playboy and networker with unrivalled contacts in the Roman establishment. He was accused of helping cover up the death of Wilma Montesi after an orgy held at his hunting estate.

© Keystone/Getty Images

The photographer Tazio Secchiaroli, who would later become the model for the character Paparazzo in Fellini's *La dolce vita*, made his name with the Montesi case. Piccioni and Montagna reacted furiously when he snapped them conferring furtively in a parked car. *© Tazio Secchiaroli/Photomovie*

DETECTIVE CRIMEN

SETTIMANALE DI POLIZIA SCIENTIFICA

NAPOLI

C'ENTRA CON IL "CASO MONTESI"
LA MORTE DEL MAGLIARO POLLIO?

Le confidenze di un'amica
di **ADRIANA BISACCIA**

"LA TAZZA D'ORO era disciolta in una casa, il solo posto dove potevo scambi... raccontava Trieste Rossi, una ragazza romana di 37 anni di cui le cronache si s... Squadra del Buon Costume nel noto bar di via della Croce. Fu lì che ai primi di ... nascita e alcuni anni intimi amici divenuti poi personaggi di primo piano nel pr... aspirazione di fare del cinema. Ora la "ragazza del secolo" sta realizzando il suo s... te la lavorazione del film: I TRE LADRI, in cui essa ha interpretato la parte di u...

The illustrated press covered the Montesi case extensively. True crime magazine *Detective Crimen* features a still from the only film made by Adriana Bisaccia, a witness in Silvano Muto's trial. Family weekly *La Domenica del Corriere's* cover drawing evokes the unsolved mystery of Wilma Montesi's death following the acquittal of the accused in 1957.

© *Author's own collection*

LA DOMENICA DEL CORRIERE

Supplemento settimanale illustrato del nuovo CORRIERE DELLA SERA · Abbonamenti: Italia, anno L. 1970, semestre L. 1000 · Estero, anno L. 3000, semestre L. 1470

Anno 59 — N. 22   2 Giugno 1957   L. 40.

Chi l'ha uccisa? Alla Corte d'Assise di Venezia è terminato il processo per la morte di Wilma Montesi, il cadavere della quale fu rinvenuto l'11 aprile 1953 sulla spiaggia di Tor Vajanica. Il P.M., dottor Cesare Palminteri, a macchinine di una requisitoria in cui ha sostenuto che Wilma fu vittima di un crimine e ha tacciato la principale accusatrice, Anna Maria Moneta Caglio, di falsità, ha chiesto che Piero Piccioni, Ugo Montagna, Saverio Pollio e altri imputati fossero assolti per non aver commesso il fatto. Ma il mistero della morte di Wilma Montesi non è stato svelato. (Dis. di W. Molino)

Milanese socialite Anna Maria Caglio was mobbed by crowds in Venice during the 1957 trial. Her astonishing allegations about her former lover Ugo Montagna's numerous illicit activities and millionaire lifestyle shocked public opinion and turned her into the star of the Montesi case. © *Keystone/Getty Images*

X

A New Investigation

On 26 March, four days after the sensational Muto trial had ended, the judicial authorities acknowledged that it was impossible to keep insisting on the foot-bathing theory without making further efforts to establish exactly what had happened to Wilma Montesi. A new inquiry would begin immediately and the job was to be entrusted to Dr Raffaele Sepe, head of the investigative division of the Court of Appeal in Rome, a magistrate who had no personal axes to grind and was respected for his independence and thoroughness. During the war Sepe had been active in the field of military justice and had reached the rank of general. Then, following the liberation, he had served with distinction on the high commission that had been entrusted with purging Fascist loyalists from the state apparatus.

A fifty-six-year-old widower and father of three, he lived quietly with his daughter in the middle-class Prati quarter, a stone's throw from the Vatican. Personally wealthy, he lived comfortably, employing two domestic servants and a driver, who took him every day to his office at the Palace of Justice. He was, like a surprisingly large number of his senior colleagues in the police and the judiciary, a man of considerable bulk. It was almost as if the law required a physical manifestation of its importance to acquire respect in Italy. People seemed to find Sepe's substantial presence reassuring. Here was a man who could be relied on to gather evidence, interview witnesses and decide who, if anyone, should be sent for trial in connection with Wilma Montesi's death. And, of course, it was expected at the top levels of the state that he should do this without creating embarrassment for the powers that be.

His task would not be easy since interest in the case had reached such a level that the small village of Torvaianica was no longer the quiet place it had been when Wilma Montesi's body was found there. A year on, the landscape had completely changed. From the last Sunday in March 1954, people began making weekend pilgrimages to the coastal location, with pleasant spring weather favouring day trips. From around ten in the morning, numerous vehicles would arrive. As the journalist Renzo Trionfera wrote in *L'Europeo* magazine:

> Whole families invaded the beach and bags and packs full of food for lunch were opened under the sun. The rough and ready wooden cross that had marked the place where the body of Wilma Montesi was found was no longer there. The waves had swept it away some time before. Local people were obliged to respond dozens of times to the same questions: 'Was she found here?'; 'How was she exactly?'; 'Is it true that she did not seem dead, just sleeping?' Only those who asked: 'And the orgies? Where did they hold the orgies?' were left disappointed. Up until sunset each day the beach became the setting of the classic Roman 'country trips'. The adults ate and drank while the younger folk were in an exuberant holiday mood. Some organised beach ball games; others launched the 'footbath game'. There were races to see who could get their feet in the water up to the ankle first.

Oggi magazine wrote:

> The 'Montesi case' has become the most colossal comic book novel that has ever been written, a novel that arouses the

passions of seamstresses and university professors, typists and intellectuals. A simple tale, a banal fact of crime news, has become a thing of huge proportions and has turned the whole country upside down, giving rise to a massive wave of morbid curiosity and giving the Communists a pretext to accuse the government, the Christian Democrats, the Vatican, the whole ruling class and the whole bourgeoisie.

Wilma's mysterious death had fired the public imagination to the extent that a whole flock of madmen, liars, maniacs, dreamers, exhibitionists and publicity-seekers attempted to use it to secure a fragment of fame or make some quick cash. The case also revived the practice of anonymous denunciations, which had been common in the Fascist period. All the protagonists – Sepe, the Montesi family, Muto, Montagna and the rest – and many journalists found themselves on the receiving end of hundreds of letters promising sensational revelations or the names of people who were supposedly caught up in the case. The authors were either envious of the celebrity won by Anna Maria Caglio and Adriana Bisaccia or were pursuing personal vendettas. 'Doctor PM and Miss NR, a noted call-girl, know everything about the death of Wilma Montesi,' stated one letter, while another asserted: 'Mrs T, who has a double life and is a cocaine addict, saw La Montesi die because she was there at the orgies of Capocotta.'

Like the American detective writer Rex Stout's rotund investigator Nero Wolfe, to whom he was often compared, Sepe went about his task with energy. He had always worked long days and now he routinely put in sixteen hours. His enquiries, unlike so many Italian investigations, were not, initially at least, based on deductions and theories; rather they were thorough and empirical. Hypotheses were tested, not just weighed for plausibility, alibis were checked, journey times and distances measured and locations inspected. Sepe worked mostly in his office on the second floor of the Palace of Justice. He was assisted by a small roving team, headed by a battle-hardened lieutenant of the Carabinieri, who was soon promoted to major, Cosimo Zinza, who filled the part of the fictional Wolfe's trusty assistant Archie Goodwin. A southerner from the coastal city of Bari, Zinza had been recommended to Sepe by Colonel Pompei. Like many others, he had served the Fascist regime. Some twenty-five years earlier, he had been among those who had signed a large volume of grovelling tributes to Mussolini, promoted by local dignitaries in his home city. Zinza was not without his eccentricities: he spent his spare time cultivating a grapevine on the roof of the Palace of Justice. But he aided Sepe loyally as a servant of the state.

In line with practices that dated back to the Fascist period, Sepe was kept under close surveillance by the police. Documents held in the Central State Archives in Rome show that spies reporting to the head of the police unit based in the Palace of Justice kept a close watch on everyone who came and went from his office. Policemen even listened at his door. Their reports on what they heard were followed closely by senior legal officials and, most probably, by Giulio Andreotti, who was now the interior minister. Sepe discovered what was going on and, furious, took measures to disguise the identities of witnesses and collaborators. He showed no signs of being rattled even though he must have known that these measures dramatically underlined just how politically sensitive the case was.

Wilma's alleged movements after she left Via Tagliamento 76 at five fifteen p.m. on 9 April 1953 were checked once more. It was found that she simply could not have caught the five thirty p.m. train to Ostia on which – just after the body was discovered – Rosa Passarelli, the Ministry of Defence clerk who had visited the Montesis, claimed to have seen her. By no route and no means of transport was it possible to cross the city to reach the station at rush-hour in such a short time.

Passarelli, moreover, was found to be short-sighted. Therefore her claim to have recognised Montesi on the train was doubtful. Also, with her dark hair and round face, Wilma was quite similar to many Roman girls of her age. Either it was a case of mistaken identity or someone had sent Passarelli to see the family and offer them an explanation of Wilma's last hours that they would find acceptable. Could Ugo Montagna's network have extended into the Ministry of Defence? This suspicion was revived later when it emerged that the clerk had bought an apartment for cash not long after her visit to the family.

Sepe ordered that experiments be undertaken to see if a body entering the sea at Ostia could in fact have been carried by the currents down the coast to Torvaianica. Local coastguards had their views on this matter, but the magistrate opted to conduct tests. It was found that the container he used always travelled north not south. By the same token, when it was dropped into the sea at or near Torvaianica, it always returned to the same beach.

Wilma's clothing, which was still held by the police, was sent for analysis, but produced no insights. The question of her clothing had become problematic ever since Fabrizio Menghini had suggested that her underwear had been substituted. The coat that was now produced was of a different colour from the one found on her body on the beach, and the undergarments were the worn and plain ones referred to in the autopsy report – which Menghini had queried at the time since he had seen pretty and expensive ones on the cadaver at the mortuary. Tests showed that the items now in Sepe's possession had not been in sea water at all. There were a few possible explanations for this odd state of affairs. Perhaps the original garments, including the underwear, had been disposed of by a careless official and, to cover this, replacements provided. It is also possible that a conspiracy was indeed at work to divert the investigations; there were plenty of other signals to this effect. Certainly this instance of evidence being destroyed or tampered with seemed to offer a striking confirmation that someone was obstructing the progress of the magistrate's work.

One of Dr Sepe's most significant moves was to order a new autopsy. This was a controversial decision, which was taken without consulting the Montesi family and which gave rise to protests from them. In the dead of night on 28 April 1954, the girl's body was exhumed. To avoid press intrusion, cemetery employees were instructed to maintain complete secrecy. Three forensic experts, Professors Ascarelli, Macaggi and Canuto, subjected Wilma's remains to a five-hour examination. They then asked for a period of five months to examine the evidence in order to respond definitively to the magistrate's questions.

Sepe recalled every witness. His policy was to leave no possibility unchecked, and no offer of information was refused. Everyone who had been involved in the case to this point was interviewed, and so was everyone else who came forward. Sepe was cordial and kind as long as he felt his interlocutors were co-operating; as soon as he suspected he was being taken for a ride, he clamped down hard. The first to fall victim to this policy was poor Adriana Bisaccia, who told a neo-Fascist newspaper that she had had a relationship with Piccioni and that he had forced her to have three abortions. She also claimed to have been beaten up by a former government minister, Umberto Tupini. Sepe immediately set up an American-style identity parade at which Tupini was placed among a selection of other men. Bisaccia failed to pick him out. On 18 June, she was arrested and sent to jail, where she would remain until 8 August. She made no further contribution to the enquiries.

The magistrate personally interviewed all the inhabitants of the Torvaianica area, even gathering twenty together on one occasion to ensure that accounts were immediately subjected to the verification of collective opinion. Sepe's determination to reach the truth exposed him to fantasists and opportunists. No one came forward to confess to killing Wilma Montesi, but literally hundreds of people claimed to be in possession of relevant information. Already a variety of odd and disturbed individuals had been drawn into the case. Sepe's open-door approach, combined with a press ever eager to grant a platform and payment to potential witnesses, in effect opened the investigation to all-comers.

The cast of witnesses was as wide as that of a variety show. A wine salesman claimed to have been her lover and produced photographs of the site of their secret assignations. A circus performer said she had known the girl as a young teenager. An English teacher said he had given her lessons at the request of Interpol. A dentist and a waiter with records of dope-peddling claimed that Wilma had belonged to a large ring of traffickers. A dancer, who went under the name of Rudy Valentino, spoke of the time he had gone boating with Wilma, while a guitar player from the region of Calabria told a complicated story of his meetings with her. A French prostitute announced that she had seen her at a brothel catering to rich clients.

In the absence of concrete information about what had happened to Wilma Montesi, visions, dreams and wild suppositions all found an audience. One of the more curious aspects of the Montesi case was the variety of magicians and clairvoyants who claimed a direct connection with the protagonists. During the war and occupation years, the Church had been a rock that provided continuity and practical assistance for the needy. Through the 1950s, participation in Church activities remained high and the Catholic press, especially the illustrated weekly *Famiglia Cristiana*, enjoyed a large readership.

Yet other forms of belief also prospered. In Rome, every district had its share of mediums and mystics, which showed how Rome remained, even in the early 1950s, a city with profound links to the countryside. In a famous scene in the film *Bicycle Thieves*, Antonio Ricci, the worker who has lost his bicycle, pushes through crowds of waiting women to ask a clairvoyant if he will ever find it. Before taking his money, the woman tells him, with an off-hand air of wisdom, 'Either you will find it straight away, or not at all.'

Economic change did not lead to the disappearance of practitioners of occult arts. Instead, it produced innovations in the way they operated. Women from the south or the countryside tended to be replaced by men from the cities who saw the supply of visions as a commercial activity. They were enterprising figures who seized the opportunities that came their way – and had a field day with the Montesi case. Some claimed to have received communications from Wilma herself; others offered their services to the investigators. Mainly, they had their eyes on the press, some of whose representatives, such as Renzo Trionfera, were happy to offer not merely a platform but also a fat cheque for information, no matter how dubious.

Natalino Del Duca was a former clerk at the Hotel Plaza, where both Caglio and Bisaccia had stayed during the Muto trial. He now presented himself as a master of the occult. A handsome man with a taste for silk scarves and flat caps, he was the author of pamphlets and articles in which, among other things, he asserted that Hitler had not died in his bunker but was living at the North Pole. He claimed to have met a policeman who knew that the missing items of clothing from Wilma Montesi's body had been taken to Police Headquarters by Piccioni in person. Then they had disappeared. Because he mentioned the policeman by name and stated his contribution with great confidence, he was summoned by Sepe. The fact that the policeman, one Francesco Servello, belonged to a unit headed by a major who was a friend and hunting partner of Montagna gave his testimony a certain interest. When Del Duca and Servello were brought together by Sepe, the policeman exploded and tried to attack his accuser. The magistrate duly took note and added Del Duca's account to the evidence against Montagna and Piccioni.

Orio was altogether less convincing. A short, overweight man of middle age, he had several names, including Ezio De Sanctis and the Wizard of Milan. From the start he seemed like a fantasist whose entire story was based on titbits picked up from newspapers and his own vivid imagination. He said that four people had come to consult him in his study in Milan on 9 April 1953: Montagna, Piccioni, Anna Maria Caglio and Wilma Montesi. They had flown up to see him from Rome, then flown back to take part in pagan rites. His testimony was obviously rubbish, yet Orio did not disappear from the case. His intervention, perhaps more than any other, showed how difficult it was to distinguish fact from fiction. The very outlandishness of his ramblings ensured that he won the publicity he so desperately sought.

As summer settled in and the temperature in the city rose, Sepe's determination to get to the bottom of the case strengthened. Towards the people he encountered, he was good cop and bad cop rolled into one. Suffering in the Roman heat, he would sit back and let witnesses speak. He treated them respectfully, and was content to chat too, but he turned from dove to hawk as soon as he detected hesitation or inconsistency in someone's story. His eyes opened wide – and suddenly the quiet listener was a ruthless interrogator.

The greatest test of his abilities came when he had to deal not with loquacious exhibitionists but with those who would have preferred not to be involved in the affair. Among them were the three guards of the Capocotta estate. It was widely assumed that one or more of these men had moved Montesi's body, under orders, the one kilometre from Capocotta to Torvaianica. They were rough men who spoke a mixture of Italian and local dialect. One, Anastasio Lilli, was a state employee; the other two, Venanzio De Felice and Terzo Guerrini, were in the pay of Montagna. These men, and the wives of two, proved reticent. Two of the guards had left their jobs in the weeks following the discovery of the body and had bought new houses, which suggested they had been paid off and put out of the way. Despite what Signora Lilli had said to the Montesi men when they visited the area on 13 April 1953, and the conversation some of them had had with Anna Maria Caglio the following day, they all now strenuously denied having seen a car with a man and a woman aboard on 9 or 10 April and refused to admit to any discussion with Montagna about the dead body that had been found on the nearby beach.

Frustrated but undeterred, Sepe and his assistant pursued a different line of questioning. They were keen to find out if the estate had been the site of orgies. By now Capocotta had become synonymous in the public mind with corruption and depravity. The term 'Capocottari' had even been taken up in Parliament and in rallies by the Communists. As a result, there was considerable alarm when pictures appeared in the weeklies of the hunt meetings. They showed small numbers of middle-aged men in hunting gear surrounding their cheery host. Debauchery was notable by its absence – but to be pictured at the estate was compromising and the editorial offices of the magazines were swamped with calls from former guests pleading that their names be omitted from the captions that appeared under the photographs.

The guards were unable or unwilling to say anything about the orgies and drug use that had supposedly taken place at Capocotta, so Sepe sent Lieutenant Zinza to visit the estate and its various buildings where the marchese entertained his illustrious guests. In fact, the estate itself was not very grand. It consisted of ample woodland, some clearings, a few outbuildings and a disused watchtower. In addition, there were the dwellings of the employees. Its iron gates were closed with chains and padlocks that were only opened on Montagna's orders by one of the estate guards.

Was the suggestion of orgies merely an idea that had caught on because of their role in the ancient-world movies that were so popular? Others saw the orgy fantasy as a peculiar by-product of the atmosphere of sexual repression the Church's enormous influence fostered. It may have been prompted by the magazines' obsession with Mussolini's liaison with Claretta Petacci. Il Duce's sexual habits still filled pages and pages of the weeklies, adding considerable detail to what little had been known at the time. The memoirs of his attendant, Quinto Navarra, a bestseller of the post-war years, had already informed Italians that Il Duce had been accustomed to have his way with a different woman every day in a suite adjoining his office at Palazzo Venezia. This fuelled fantasies in the popular imagination of the sordid relationship between sex and power.

Although no witness, not even Anna Maria Caglio, ever described exactly what went on at Montagna's hunting estate, fantasies ran wild. Montagna's seductive manner and smooth appearance – close-fitting suits, Brylcreemed hair, dark glasses – added plausibility to the stories. Some witnesses said that Capocotta contained few buildings comfortable enough for any form of relaxation, let alone wild parties or group sex. In fact, Zinza found that several rooms in a separate part of a gatekeeper's lodge had been reserved by Montagna for his private use. On several occasions, he had stayed there with Caglio. The annexe was not only comfortable, it was located close to an area of the coast where local people said they had seen nude bathing and a certain frolicking of men and women.

Perhaps they had even noticed the group that had included Silvano Muto and Adriana Bisaccia on their night-time jaunt in September 1953.

Truth and lies quickly became intertwined in the Montesi case, yet sufficient stories came to light for it to be clear that there was indeed a sexual sub-world that connected influential men to vice. And that unwary girls were often lured into sexual exploitation through these illicit networks.

A lesbian twist was added to the tale when a woman named Thea Ganzaroli claimed in the pages of *Attualità* that she had been with a male companion in the bushes a few metres from the Capocotta beach on the night between 9 and 10 April 1953. She had seen a car arrive and two men drag a limp body to the water's edge, where it was unceremoniously dumped. The description she gave of the men matched exactly the by now well-known faces of Piccioni and Montagna. Ganzaroli belonged to the same sub-world as Adriana Bisaccia. Indeed, the two women were friends. She lived in a boarding house on Via delle Vite, not far from Piazza di Spagna, and was known in Il Baretto and the Tazza d'Oro. A robustly built woman in her thirties who dressed in a mannish way in tailored suits with padded shoulders, she had been one of the female auxiliaries who had served in the armed forces of the Nazi-sponsored Italian Social Republic in the final eighteen months of the war. For her crimes then, she had served two years of a sixteen-year gaol sentence. With the rest of her sentence suspended, depending on good behaviour, she claimed that she had not come forward before for fear of finding herself once more in trouble. A fellow resident in the boarding house had persuaded her to go to Silvano Muto, who had paid her for her story.

Sepe wasted no time in summoning the woman but when her companion that night, one Piero Rinaldi, refused to confirm her account – indeed, he claimed he had never been near Capocotta in his life – he marked her down as a liar and ordered her arrest. She would be released with Bisaccia on 8 August.

Ganzaroli seemed in every way another implausible and unstable witness. She had aspired to a golden future on the silver screen, despite having few if any of the requisite qualities for stardom, and had contacted the actress Lea Padovani with an innocent request for an autograph. Then, however, she had proceeded to bombard her with menacing letters, telephone calls and visits to her home. She became what would later be termed a stalker. The papers that enquired into her habits in the Bohemian world discovered that she and a group of her female friends were accustomed to meet to share what were dubbed 'refined and delicate pleasures'. A mature actress was involved, who, it was hinted, was *Rome Open City* star Anna Magnani, who furiously denied it. One right-wing publication alleged that the circle had spiced up the proceedings with teenage girls recruited from the ranks of the many who flocked to Rome in the hope of getting a chance at a film part. It was this link to the sexual sub-world around the milieu of artists and musicians that gave Ganzaroli's testimony a modicum of credibility. It also gave it a unique flavour since lesbianism had never before featured in the popular press. Despite Rinaldi's refusal to support her – she later doused him with a carafe of water in a *trattoria* by the Trevi Fountain – the woman who had urged her to go to Muto in the first place, Mercedes Borgatti, always insisted that Ganzaroli had indeed come in that night in April 1953 in a state of shock after what she had supposedly seen.

As the Roman summer reached its sweltering height, Sepe turned his attentions to the clerics in whom Anna Maria Caglio had confided. He called in Father Dall'Olio and Father Rotondi. They told him that they had made their own enquiries about Montagna. When they had contacted the then interior minister Fanfani with their discoveries, they found that he was already alert to the Sicilian's behaviour. Like the Jesuits, Sepe disapproved of the wheeling and dealing, the disregard for the law and the primacy of money that had taken hold in some sections of the state and society. As a man who had inherited his wealth and preferred understatement to ostentation, the magistrate found distasteful the way in which Montagna used money to establish his status. He always behaved in such a way as to let everyone know that he had lots of it: he tipped generously, he rewarded his friends and he lavished gifts on those he favoured. He knew that public employees were not very well paid and that some were not averse to making extra on the side by turning a blind eye or issuing some necessary documentation. The Jesuits were deeply critical of the moral drift in society and welcomed the magistrate's endeavours.

Sepe eventually worked his way round to the matter of the Alfa Romeo 1900cc saloon car. From the very first days after the discovery of Wilma's body on the beach, there had been speculation about it. The exclusive focus on this vehicle implied that it was the one and only car to have passed down that road during those days. When the mechanic Mario Piccinini, had come forward to say that sometime in March he had helped a smartly dressed man free his vehicle from the sand in the early hours of the morning, it was assumed that this was the same car that been seen near Capocotta on 9 or 10 April. On seeing Wilma Montesi's picture in the papers, Piccinini had gone to the Ostia police station to report that she was the woman he had seen in the car. Later he added that the man he had spoken to might have been Piero Piccioni. Unfortunately his conviction about the identities of the people he saw was disputed by the railway worker, Alfonso Di Francesco, who had helped him that night:'I cannot understand how Piccinini can say that the woman in the car looked like Wilma Montesi. I too saw the photograph of the girl of

Torvaianica. She had nothing in common with the wife of
the gentleman. And he did not look like Piccioni.' Leone
Piccioni made it known that his brother Piero had only ever
owned a 1400cc saloon.

There was still, however, the matter of the man and woman
who had earlier been described as being on the estate on one
of the dates in question. They were not necessarily the same
couple, and neither Piccinini nor Di Francesco had seen them.
They too had been on board a 1900cc saloon. Were they Piero
Piccini and Wilma Montesi as had been implied? Montagna's
defence lawyers, who were following Sepe's enquiries closely,
passed a name to the magistrate. Both Montagna and Piccioni
had been swift to proclaim their innocence after the sudden
end of the Muto trial. Both denied ever having known or
seen Wilma Montesi, and were keen to make the most of it
whenever a shadow of suspicion fell on anyone else.

The name they pushed forward was that of Prince Maurice
of Hesse, son of the late Mafalda Savoy and grandson of the
former Italian king, Victor Emmanuel III. Italy had lost its
royal family in 1946 and both Victor, Emmanuel and his son
Umberto had subsequently gone into exile in Portugal.
Monarchist sentiment remained strong, though, especially in
the south. The illustrated weeklies fed their readers a regular
diet of pictures of Umberto, former Queen Maria José and
their children. A certain mystique even attached to minor
royals who, unlike Umberto and his male heirs, were allowed
to remain in the country. They were treated as public figures
even though they now had the status of ordinary citizens.

At twenty-four years old, Maurice of Hesse looked every
inch the prince. Tall and blond, he had an air of arrogant
insouciance. When his name was first linked to the case, as
the driver of the Alfa Romeo 1900, he was on a long cruise.
It was only after the ship had docked in Capri in mid-
September that he was made aware of the gravity of the

situation. Prince Maurice had expected to spend several days relaxing on the island, which had long been an upper-class playground and artists' colony. Instead he found himself drawn into the maelstrom of the Montesi case.

He was less than pleased to be summoned to Rome by Sepe or by Montagna's lawyers' insistence that he was the young man who had been with Wilma. He readily admitted his visit to Capocotta: it had been straightforward and innocent. He had recently bought a new car and was taking a woman friend to the sea. During the day, he had decided to show her the estate that had once belonged to his family, and to which he still had right of access. The identity of his companion, however, remained undisclosed, leading to renewed speculation that she might have been Wilma Montesi.

Another issue for Sepe was the credibility of Anna Maria Caglio. In the 1950s Italian public opinion was articulated in terms of quite stark divisions. The main divide was between the Catholics and the Communists. The popular author Giovannino Guareschi satirised their opposed world views in his tales of the battles conducted in one village between Don Camillo, a priest, and Peppone, the village's Communist mayor. Guareschi was a right-winger but he drew Peppone as a sympathetic figure who was usually equal to the challenges posed against his authority by the priest. The division between Catholics, or traditionalists, and progressives also manifested itself in the passionate support of the two cycling aces of the day, Gino Bartali and Fausto Coppi. The former was a practising Catholic who had received the blessing of the Pope, while the latter was perceived as more left-wing on account of his less conventional views and modern approach to the sport. A little later, admirers of the film stars Gina Lollobrigida and Sophia Loren would divide on a similar basis.

In the same way, opinion about the personalities of the Montesi case was shaped by political conviction. On one side there were those who believed that Piccioni and Montagna were innocent; the campaign against them had been got up by the Communists and Montagna's spurned lover Anna Maria Caglio. On the other there were those who were convinced that the pair were players in a sinister conspiracy to conceal the perverted pastimes of the caste to which they belonged.

Left-leaning sectors of public opinion regarded the voluble and lucid Anna Maria Caglio as a heroine, a latter-day Joan of Arc. Conservative people saw her as dark and untrustworthy, a snake in the grass who deserved her reputation as a *femme fatale*. They felt that, as a woman scorned, she had reason to seek revenge. Furthermore, in accord with the sexual hypocrisy of the era, she was a young unmarried woman who had taken lovers and was therefore compromised. But so powerful and passionate was her indictment of Montagna and Piccioni's misdeeds that she persuaded many. And her personal story as a young woman whose parents had divorced and left her to find her own way in life lent credibility to her accusations. Despite her troubles, it was widely thought that her comfortable background made it unlikely that she would point an accusing finger at the powerful without good reason. Moreover, she was always extremely precise and detailed in her testimony and interviews.

The credibility that Caglio acquired derived in part from the class bias that marked the Italian justice system. A lower-class woman like Adriana Bisaccia, with all her personal problems, was swiftly reduced to an irrelevance. Her inarticulacy and instability meant that she was unable to offer serious support to Muto. By contrast, Anna Maria, with her flirtatious manner and soft, seductive voice, dazzled the mostly male journalists who were covering the case. They wrote her up in a way that made her sympathetic to their readers.

Sepe, too, was inclined to give her credence. She had a grasp of Montagna's business dealings that was impressive and had stood the test of empirical verification. She listed banks, account numbers, dates on which sums had been deposited and more. She recalled how he had given her a car bought at discount from Vatican City administration, which had owned it for just a few days. She was able to cite the licence number, and reporters found on checking that her story was true. But something more was needed. To try to cut through some of the web of assertion and counter-assertion, Sepe decided on a bold move. He availed himself of a technique that was commonly used in court as well as in investigations to establish the truth when two witnesses were saying opposite things. He decided to call in Caglio and Montagna for a face-to-face confrontation.

The magistrate knew the risk he was taking in bringing the former lovers together. There might be a slanging match, or an irate Montagna might try to throttle his former mistress, but he knew that the key to the case lay with these two individuals.

The meeting took place in Sepe's office at the Palace of Justice on 1 June 1954. Journalists pressing up to the door could hear Montagna's furious cries as Caglio again detailed some of his illicit business deals. She was fearless in her denunciations and impressive in her grasp of detail. She might have had the wrong idea about Montagna at the beginning, for he proved to be no Prince Charming, but there was nothing wrong with her grasp of his way of doing business.

As always, he tried to discredit her by painting her as a sexual predator. 'You led me to the bedroom seven days after we met,' he said.

'It was eighteen days after we met!' she replied. 'The very same day you gave me half a million lire in rolls of ten-thousand-lire notes. You told me to deposit the sum in the bank and I went to the Banco di Roma, agency number ten.'

'It's not true. You only say that to make me pay more tax. I gave you money various times but never more than a hundred thousand lire at a time. You were always short of cash, so much so that you had to pawn your gold jewellery.'

'In total you gave me seven million lire. On several occasions I pawned the diamond brooch you gave me with the symbol of the marchese title, getting fifty thousand each time,' she asserted.

'I never gave you a brooch. That was yours. Often you pawned the gold bracelet that you are wearing on your wrist today and that I gave you. Even the dress you are wearing, your shoes and bag were presents from me.'

Once more she went on the attack: 'You cannot deny that you gave me a Giardinetta, number plate Rome 170970, that I then exchanged in December for a 1400, number plate Rome 171187, giving Fiat the first vehicle plus a hundred thousand lire.'

'But you always said you bought the Giardinetta with the earnings from your work in the cinema . . . And what were you doing in the month of November with a man at the Excelsior Hotel in Naples? He was called Moneta, a detective told me . . .'

'It's not true! It's not true! At that time I was in Milan.'

Montagna tried another tack: 'You knew very well who the lady was who was with me the evening of 7 January 1953, when you tailed me in the car. Now you pretend not to know so as to force me to state her name before the judge and thereby disturb the peace of a family.'

'I may have been mistaken,' Caglio conceded. 'I admit that the woman was not Wilma Montesi, but neither was she the lady you are referring to. On the sixteenth you forced me to sell the car by way of punishment.'

'What rubbish! You sold it two months later.'

Montagna left the meeting in a foul temper, having asked

Dr Sepe, he said, to hold Caglio back for five minutes, giving him time to get away. He paused long enough to mouth some disparaging comments to eager reporters.

'You want to know what impression she made on me? Well, she has got fat, cut her hair and changed perfume.'

Montagna's hatred of his former lover was limitless. He knew he had made a mistake with her, but he had rarely troubled himself to respond to her allegations. He laughed off her claims about his income and instead he continued to drag up supposed evidence of her predatory sexuality. He also released several of her letters in which it was clear that she was infatuated with her marchese. She was a hussy and a woman scorned, who, he implied, deserved none of the attention she was receiving.

This did not, however, help his position. The renewed exposure of Montagna's misdeeds was met with indignation. Commentators expressed horror at the revelation of a secret world of power and cunning so blatantly at odds with the hopes that democracy and the proclamation of the republic had heralded. The satirical weeklies *Travaso* and *Il Merlo Giallo* had a field day and for months they published cartoons featuring eager 'Capocottari' running to and from the watchtower that was the estate's only landmark. At football matches in the north, Roman teams were greeted with chanted taunts of 'Capocotta! Capocotta!' from fans who associated the corruption of the case with the capital and its channels of power. Many people, including pensioners, workers and the unemployed, were horrified by the large sums that had been associated with Montagna and the size of the allowances he was supposed to have passed to his mistress. The sheer scale of his tax evasion fuelled anger against the rich because it was known that his behaviour was typical of the well-off. In the general post-war confusion, the non-payment of tax was routine. For anyone involved in the black market or illegal commerce it was a point of principle to cover his tracks by failing to fill in tax forms or by channelling money into foreign accounts. Many Italians were poor and such flagrant abuse of the system offended them, yet it did not stop them being fascinated by the characters in this increasingly sordid drama.

XI

Via Veneto

The Muto trial had turned Anna Maria Caglio into the most famous woman in Italy. Anna Garofalo, a broadcaster and writer who had presented a series of radio programmes after the war about Italian women, was just one who found her compelling. She noted that even the most traditional Italians looked on her 'with an astonishment bordering on admiration; half angel and half demon, assisted by the clergy and disturbed by the memory of guilty love affairs. La Caglio presents, in spite of everything, an aspect of the new woman who has the courage of her opinions, who takes responsibility for her faults, who judges with lucid foresight, who refuses to be intimidated, bought or blackmailed.'

Nevertheless, her family was less impressed by her scandalous fame. Her father intervened both to deplore what had happened to her and to attempt to bring her to heel. Writing in *Oggi* in August 1954, he rejected definitions of her as a 'girl of the century' – a term that had also been applied to Adriana Bisaccia. He was appalled that, because of his own indirect influence, she had met Ugo Montagna, whom he dubbed 'an unscrupulous old libertine who took advantage of a young girl of twenty-three who wanted to make something of herself'. He continued:

I am a believing and practising Catholic and a Christian Democrat in politics. But I will never forgive those who, knowing that my daughter had a close relationship with an old man who was even married, did not inform me. I never knew anything about it and my daughter also tricked me into believing that she was pursuing a good career as an artist, and that my friends in Rome were helping and supporting her. My fault as a father is to have had faith in my daughter and in those I thought of as friends. It was a blow for me when I learned what had happened and it was a priest who told me. Even my other children and my mother, who knew about it much earlier, did not have the courage to talk to me about it.

His aim now, he said, was to rehabilitate a girl who had gone off the rails.

As for the old libertine, Montagna did his best to brazen out the scandal. Faced with attacks on his reputation, he did his utmost to continue as before, attending theatres, restaurants and nightclubs as though nothing had happened. The stage he favoured was that of the Via Veneto. There was no road in Rome, or anywhere else for that matter, quite like this half-mile stretch of hotels, bars, coffee houses and shops. It had become an open-air salon, a gathering point of the various tribes that made up the city's vibrant café society.

Politicians were rarely seen on the Via Veneto and serious business people, senior civil servants, churchmen and upstanding professionals were not numbered among the barflies and night owls. It was the shiny crowd, the daring young aristocrats, the beautiful people, the froth and sparkle of Rome, who gave it its shape and face. Writers and journalists passed the time of day at the Rosati, where they also gathered in the early hours of the morning after their respective papers had been sent to press. Roman aristocrats generally met at the Hotel Flora, while film people preferred the bar at the Hotel Excelsior. The Caffè Strega attracted theatre and variety actors – every morning the Strega functioned as an informal casting agency.

Foreigners preferred Doney, perhaps on account of its proximity to the Excelsior. The street was always buzzing with gossip. It instinctively took the side of the famous rather than the virtuous, the rich rather than the poor, although it was quick to turn its back on the disgraced. Wheeling and dealing were endemic to the Via Veneto, and some of the money men ran networks of front men, giving work to the street's humbler denizens. Thus, unlike the Bohemian Via Margutta, the Via Veneto sided with Piccioni and Montagna, not with Silvano Muto, despite his growing popularity.

Montagna was a typical habitué of the Via Veneto who knew that his stock depended on appearances. Some who had accepted his hospitality had turned their backs on him and he found this hurtful. In a display of bravado, he walked the length of the street with his head held high just days after the Muto trial collapsed, a challenge to those who dared to turn away or who failed to return his glance. It was an act that won him some admiration.

In contrast to the inveterate name-dropper and networker Montagna, Piero Piccioni claimed that he led a solitary life and liked nothing more than listening to Bach on his gramophone. In a rare public statement, he claimed that he would be amused by the whole episode were it not for the fact that it badly affected his father. 'I have never used drugs. In the evenings just before going to bed I listen to music. That's my narcotic. I have no other statement to make to the press.' In reality, he was a playboy who was seen regularly in the bars and clubs between the Piazza di Spagna and the Via Veneto. A secret police report from 1954 stated that he had acquired 'the singular habits and attitudes' of the artistic milieu, which were 'in tune with his restless and out-going temperament'. He was accustomed, the report continued, to leave home in the afternoon, 'coming back only late at night'. His musical preferences were indicative of his after-hours socialising.

Montagna also went to some lengths to defend himself. Like Piccioni, he denied ever having known Wilma Montesi. He claimed also that he had been nowhere near Capocotta on the days around which the girl's death had occurred. The weather had been bad between 8 and 10 April, he explained, and the birds had not taken to the skies. To those who claimed that he had too many friends, Montagna threw up his hands in mock surprise that such a thing could be seen as bad. He admitted to cultivating friendships in the world of politics and the state but claimed never to have sought or performed illicit favours.

Unfortunately for him, though, he had little control over the stories that continued to appear. As if on cue, a noblewoman who had been mentioned by Anna Maria Caglio suddenly appeared on the scene. This improbable creature, the bejewelled and perfumed Giobben Giò, or Jo de Yong, brought a touch of exoticism to the affair. Caglio had reported that Giobben Giò had told her she had lost a large sum to Montagna while gambling at a villa near Capocotta owned by Count Francesco di Campello. At a press conference Giò denied ever having lost money to Montagna and announced that in fact she was the Countess Massimiliani. A few days later, she withdrew her denial and admitted that Caglio had been telling the truth. She revealed to the press details of her relations with Montagna before treading the familiar path to Raffaele Sepe's door to add her testimony to the rest. In an article for *L'Europeo*, she painted a picture of the unsettling ambiguity of Roman nocturnal society:

The Roman world that Ugo Montagna belongs to is certainly one of the best, let us say, of the capital. First of all because of the people who frequent it and then for the great possibilities that one can get from it. Nevertheless, it is not an entirely healthy environment. I allude to the orgies, if they can be called orgies, certain entertainments, parties, dances of which I have heard. It is certain furthermore that among the participants in these meetings there are people who use drugs. I exclude Montagna and Piccioni, as far as I personally know, but I do not exclude certain people in the world of cinema, and I am alluding mainly to well-known actors, women above all. I remember a house in Via del Babuino where these orgies took place many times. In that house I found myself unfortunately one evening. There were only three of us but I know that in earlier gatherings there were more people. It was a very strange apartment. The rooms were full of mirrors. In front of the mirrors were dishes of cocaine. Then, bizarrely, there was a sort of tunnel that led directly from the bathroom to the bedroom. This allowed for the most extravagant surprises. I was told that the apartment was often let to painters and to mainly foreign film actresses passing through. I should point out that the other two people with whom I found myself that evening were girlfriends of Montagna or were women belonging to his environment.

Finally, it seemed, there was proof that a system of organised debauchery existed and that women of various backgrounds willingly belonged to it. 'There are not great spirals of vice in Rome 1954,' wrote the journalist Carlo Laurenzi, 'but a familiar, petulant, orgiastic spirit oppresses us. There is a small exhibitionistic world to which some degenerates, some foreigners, the odd adventurer, many young people from good families, and many ingenuous girls belong.' The Montesi case, he argued, was a decidedly Roman narrative that sprang from precisely this milieu.

The press was intrigued by the number of young and beautiful women the case brought before the public gaze. Almost every week seemed to produce a new face whose owner claimed some connection with one or more of the circles that had been bathed in publicity. After Wilma, Bisaccia, Caglio, and Giobben Giò, a young model named Lalla Ambrazejus was pushed to the fore. She was said to have been the woman in the infamous Alfa 1900 saloon with Prince Maurice. In fact, she claimed never to have met the prince but, almost inevitably, she was acquainted with the Marchese Montagna. Although Lalla had been away from Rome in April 1953, she had been a guest on other occasions at Capocotta. She told a reporter that she and another girl had been urged by Montagna to 'be nice' to a mature Member of Parliament at a party in return for a cash payment. They had both refused point blank – Lalla was convinced that this was why the gates of showbusiness had remained firmly closed to her. Although she had taken on the modelling work that was a prelude to getting parts in films, nothing else had materialised.

With more and more testimonies of the sordid private life of Ugo Montagna becoming public, the prime minister, Scelba, who was keenly aware that his personal credibility, as well as that of his party, was on the line, decided once and for all to show that he had nothing to fear from any scandal. He invited one of his cabinet colleagues, the Liberal parliamentarian Raffaele De Caro, to conduct an inquiry into Montagna's alleged relations with the government. In July, the report was presented to Parliament. De Caro read out his findings to a packed Chamber. Deputies from all parties paid eager attention while Colonel Pompei joined those who listened from the public gallery. De Caro repeated much of the information that had first come to light in Pompei's own report. He confirmed that Montagna had switched his loyalties on several occasions during the wartime occupations of Rome and had built up a series of illicit and speculative activities. He reported that he controlled no fewer than twelve companies, most of which were concerned with property. For the years 1951, 1952 and 1953, he had filed no tax return. De Caro stated the nature of Montagna's links to Pavone, the chief of police. The two men had maintained close links since the latter's release from jail during the Nazi occupation. They had met socially on many occasions. Montagna had visited his friend at the interior ministry, and on at least two occasions in the company of Piero Piccioni. He found that Pavone had been remiss in cultivating Montagna, a person with various criminal convictions from whom a police chief should have kept his distance.

The report presented a picture of secret loyalties and favours. Despite this, it was not well received. The Communists in particular were not satisfied because it repeated facts that were already known without identifying the individuals responsible for aiding Montagna's progress. Who, people wanted to know, had opened doors to him and assisted his rise? How was it possible that, in the passage from Fascism to democracy, such a man had not only conserved but expanded his influence? As they saw it, key parts of the report were a whitewash. This especially referred to the controversial relationship between Scelba and Montagna. De Caro found that Scelba had not met the man except at Alfonso Spataro's wedding, to which Montagna had invited himself. Only the sons of ministers Spataro and Piccioni were found to be his friends. As for Montagna's contracts with the government housing project INA, these were deemed valid, and his aristocratic title was legitimate.

The Communist Gian Carlo Pajetta indignantly asked if someone could invite themselves to a wedding and find himself acting as a witness of the groom. He told the Chamber that he had received information that Montagna had offered Attilio Piccioni a lift in his car to the wedding of Dr Galeazzo-Lisi, the Pope's physician. Had de Caro enquired whether Montagna was a member of the Christian Democrats? Had he looked into allegations that Montagna had contributed financially to the election campaigns of friendly politicians, including Piccioni? Others wondered about Montagna's title. A police inquiry had shown that the royal decree had not been countersigned, as required by law, by the prime minister, and Montagna himself had contributed to doubts about its validity by seeking to have it confirmed by a court.

De Caro's response to the accusation that he had not dug deeply enough was laconic. He had fulfilled his mandate and that was enough. Someone asked him why he had not interviewed Anna Maria Caglio. He screwed up his face and remarked, 'It would be against my sense of good taste.'

Montagna, who was still trying to escape the damage to his reputation caused by the Pompei report, adopted an aloof stance. 'What the Honourable de Caro said does not concern me personally. It is of no interest,' he declared pompously, no doubt hoping that his arrogance would be sufficient to see him through the storm. What he cannot have failed to note, to his dismay, was that he had become a negative symbol of corruption and vice for some parties of government as well as the opposition. He was the embodiment of everything that was wrong with Italy's incomplete transition to a democratic system.

Reporters were dispatched to Palermo, to Genoa and wherever else he had a connection in search of more salacious details. Gradually a picture was drawn of Montagna's rise to influence that left few gaps. Once again it was revealed that he had twice been arrested in Sicily for the misuse or appropriation of public funds, he had run into trouble for trafficking in false IOUs, and in 1937 he had been found guilty of illegally using an aristocratic title. An official report from the chief of police of Agrigento had described him as a person known for trafficking activities, who lived by expedients and exploited people with whom he had business or personal relationships.

His war record was even worse than initially reported. He had done deals with Jews during the Nazi occupation and betrayed them to the occupying force. He had been a major player in the black market, using official connections to divert emergency supplies of sugar and flour away from the needy. He was on good terms with the Nazis, but was able to find people to vouch for his integrity when the Allies arrived in Rome. He had two passports, Italian and Swiss; he had claimed to be a representative of the UN aid organisation UNRRA, an agent for British Intelligence, and a member of the Afghanistan Legation, a claim that had led the Allies to issue him with a diplomatic pass and permission to use diplomatic plates on his car. Black-marketeering was his main activity and he appeared to have got away with this even though it figured in reports. There were tales that he practised blackmail and extortion towards anti-Fascists first, and then towards Nazi collaborators who had been less agile at reinventing themselves than he had.

It was during this time that he had forged some of the friendships that would prove crucial later. Galeazzo-Lisi − the Pope's physician − was an associate who, it was alleged, had even joined in a scam to blackmail former Nazi collaborators. The friendship with Tommaso Pavone dated from the time when the man was imprisoned by the Nazis. Sensing that Pavone would eventually do well, Montagna had arranged for him to be brought a meal from the outside every day, earning his eternal gratitude. He had also forged at this time a bond with Luigi Gedda, a key lay Catholic organiser and a man who had the Pope's ear.

But his greatest successes came after the war when he had got in on the building boom that began with the reconstruction and continued as public and private sectors invested in new infrastructures. He realised that connections with the Church would be crucial in the new era so he had set up a company to build churches. He secured grants and subsidies through INA to build houses but chose to concentrate on profitable luxury flats. He proved expert at securing permits and was a master at forging short-lived fronts to benefit from special subsidies for co-operatives. By the early 1950s, Montagna was acknowledged and deferred to; his nobility was not questioned and his ability to make deals, far from being condemned, made him an important man to do business with. He had come a long way from trafficking in carpets.

Sepe did not hesitate to use his power to order the arrest or confiscate the passport of anyone he felt was obstructing or might obstruct his investigation. The first to face such a sanction had been Adriana Bisaccia. Events took a dramatic turn when he started to move against those he deemed could be directly implicated in the matter of Wilma Montesi's death. On 21 August the first of the guards, Venanzio De Felice, was arrested on grounds of perjury and suspicion that he might have moved the victim's body. In the first serious move against Prince Maurice, Montagna, Piccioni and Polito, their passports were withdrawn. The most surprised by this move was the twenty-four-year-old prince, but the loss of his passport did not affect him unduly: he had embarked on his cruise with the captain's permission even though he had left his passport in Rome. 'I was practically a stowaway,' the prince joked with reporters. This was more evidence that there were different rules for ordinary folk and for those who enjoyed social prestige. A few days later warrants were issued for the arrests of Piccioni, Montagna and Polito, along with the remaining guards, Anastasio Lilli, Terzo Guerrini and his wife Palmira.

Evidently forewarned that a warrant had been issued for his son's arrest, Attilio Piccioni again tendered his resignation on 18 September as foreign minister. His position had become untenable: newspapers simultaneously ran front-page stories about his efforts to negotiate the reincorporation of Trieste into Italian territory and his son's position in relation to the Montesi case. 'Italian public opinion has been so taken up in the past months by charges of skulduggery and corruption arising from the Wilma Montesi case,' the *New York Times* had written, as early as 11 April 1954, 'that foreign policy developments have been completely neglected or have received scant attention.' Piccioni left office, denouncing a 'slanderous and evil campaign'. He expressed his wish to defend freely the position of his son, who, he added, had nothing to fear from justice.

On 21 September 1954, police in civilian clothes arrived at the Piccioni family home in Via della Conciliazione. Piero was met on the stairs as he was on his way out and was read the warrant that informed him he was to be arrested on grounds of 'being responsible for the crime of manslaughter aggravated by the use of drugs, having on 10 April 1953 caused the death of Wilma Montesi by abandoning her body, which he believed to be dead, on the seashore with the aim of suppressing it'. After he was led away, his father, who was upstairs in the family apartment, sat down crushed. 'At least Piero will now be able to defend himself,' he was reported to have said. By the end of the afternoon, the Regina Coeli prison had one more internee. If there was any truth in the old saying that no man could call himself a true Roman without having crossed its threshold, then the Turin-born Piero Piccioni was now a citizen of the capital.

Severio Polito, now aged seventy-five and retired, was accused of aiding Piccioni to 'elude investigations by the judicial authorities, turning the enquiries of the police towards the hypothesis of an accidental event'. In view of his age and health, he was placed under house arrest.

Polito took his incarceration badly, but Sepe had discovered that he had lied about his role and about his relations with

Montagna. He claimed that he had scarcely taken an interest
in such a minor matter as the discovery of a dead body by
the sea: it had been handled by others. But anyone who
remembered his announcements to the press knew this was
not true. He had actively influenced the way enquiries were
made and had determined their course, responding directly
to Tommaso Pavone. It also turned out that he had made the
acquaintance of Montagna through a mutual friend and, after
his initial resistance had been overcome, had frequently
accepted the marchese's invitations to lunch and dinner. He
had no wish to be thought a friend of Montagna but it was
clear that he knew him well enough.

Montagna faced the charge of having 'jointly with Saverio
Polito helped Piero Piccioni to escape the police investigation'.
His apprehension could scarcely have been more theatrical.
When the police arrived at his home in Via Rabirio late in
the afternoon on 21 September, they found that he had gone
out at around four o'clock and had not returned. Some thirty
officers were instructed to keep watch for him. In fact he had
been tipped off and had decided to enjoy the evening on the
Via Veneto in his customary manner. Before heading there,
however, he had decided to call in to the studio of one of his
defence team, Giuliano Vasalli. While he was deep in
consultation with him, another lawyer, Filippo Lupis, burst in
with a copy of an evening newspaper reporting the arrest
warrant. What was their client to do? For the lawyers there
was just one option: Montagna had to deliver himself to the
authorities. With this intention, the three men left the building
and climbed into Vasalli's car. Before they reached the gate of
the Regina Coeli, reporters from *Il Tempo* learned what was
about to happen and gave chase in a Fiat Topolino, among
them Angelo Frignani. As they crossed Rome, others also
caught on. Vasalli's car was followed by a convoy of journalists
in cars and photographers on Vespa and Lambretta scooters.

Horns sounded and shouts of encouragement accompanied the procession as bystanders realised what was going on.

On arrival, Montagna and Lupis stepped up to the entrance and Lupis rang the bell. While they waited the photographers immortalised the moment. A man from *Il Tempo* got the best picture and claimed the scoop. The prison seemed unprepared. Incredulous guards at first wanted to turn Montagna away. The amused gaggle outside was now shouting and laughing. He insisted that the police had surrounded his house and that he had no intention of going on the run. 'Let me in or you will disappoint these journalists!' he exclaimed. It was only when prison officials were shown the front page of one of the newspapers, which had run a special edition announcing the arrests, that Ugo Montagna, Marchese di San Bartolomeo, was finally interned.

XII

Piccioni's Alibi

As Montagna and Piccioni both languished in Regina Coeli, the buzz around them continued. Montagna's theatrical arrival at the gate and delivery of himself to the prison authorities was entirely in keeping with the attention he always paid to matters of *bella figura*. To him, appearances were everything and to enter gaol with panache entirely eclipsed the ignominy of being placed behind bars. The imprisonment of a nobleman, even one whose title was of dubious authenticity, was big news. Cinema made reference to it. In one scene in the film version of Alberto Moravia's *Roman Tales*, which was shot that year, a minor trickster exclaims to his mates on his release from prison that he shared a cell with a marchese.

Piccioni by contrast found that his new-found notoriety had no up-side. The son of the former foreign minister had previously enjoyed modest celebrity as the composer of movie scores and leader of a jazz band. He had kept as low a profile as the case permitted. It was usually his extrovert brother Leone who took the lead in responding to the press. Piero, he said, did not even read the papers and this helped him to maintain his composure despite the furore surrounding him. Unlike the fit and hearty Montagna, Piccioni was rather pathetic-looking. According to Wayland Young, who covered the case for a British newspaper and wrote a book about it in 1957, he was so anonymous in appearance as to defy description. However, low visibility did not help much since his position was now so serious. Although he had allegedly been just a guest at his friend Montagna's parties, he was the principal accused, the man who, it was said, was most directly implicated in the drowning of Wilma Montesi.

From the public's point of view, Piccioni was unsympathetic. He was the spoilt son of an influential man. After graduating, he had refused to follow his father into the law and had taken his own eccentric, not to say dissolute, course. Although this decision had caused a rift in the family, he still lived in his widowed father's enormous apartment close to the Vatican. When the case broke, Piccioni retreated into his family. Since he was a bachelor, it was not easy to counteract rumours about his private life by depicting him as a family man. Nevertheless, efforts were made by the family's legal advisers to combat his reputation as an habitué of jazz clubs by trying to construct a more family-oriented image. A photograph was released showing him with his brother Leone and his young nephew. This was intended to depict him as a relaxed, domesticated uncle at ease with children. In fact, the photograph revealed a listless and disinterested man, wholly detached from the young child who had been awkwardly posed on his knee. The uneasy image was anything but reassuring.

Piero Piccioni was given extensive support by the establishment, but the political right was unsure whether he should be defended against the attacks of the left or criticised for his irregular conduct. The film *La Spiaggia* (The Beach), directed by Alberto Lattuada, for which Piccioni had composed the soundtrack, was, according to one right-wing paper, pro-Communist. The movie was set in Liguria and it starred the rising French actress Martine Carol. Filmed in 1953 and released at the very moment the Montesi case first dominated the headlines, *La Spiaggia* reinforced a common perception that Italy was governed by a corrupt élite and that only the untainted left could change things. Right-wingers were horrified that Piccioni's son should have got involved with such an obviously left-inspired project and took it as a further sign of his waywardness. 'Every move he made, every initiative he undertook was a sort of gaffe in relation to the position of his father and a challenge to the idea the Italians have of what the behaviour should be of the children of a Christian Democrat politician,' *Il Borghese* thundered. It was wholly inappropriate that he should hang about in fashionable night spots or cultivate irregular company. Not a hint of dissipation or Bohemianism was tolerable.

In fact, the exotic jazz music Piccioni favoured was beginning to acquire a wide appeal. Xavier Cugat, the smiling moustachioed band leader, was very popular in Italy, as elsewhere, always conducting while holding a Chihuahua under his arm. His sound went over well on the radio and added variety to the entertainment repertoire of early television. The rumba, the conga and the samba were all seductive novelties whose appeal was enhanced by Cugat's young wife Abbe Lane, a cocktail chanteuse who moved her curvaceous body to the rhythm of the music. So shocking were her gyrations to the Italian television broadcasters of the time that she was first ordered to be shown on screen only from the neck up, and then was banned altogether.

At a time when Italians looked to the United States as a beacon of prosperity and model society, it was inevitable that the singers and songs that were most fashionable on the other side of the Atlantic found a following among them. Frank Sinatra, Dean Martin and Tony Bennett all had Italian roots. Rome was not Las Vegas or Miami, but the links between high and low life were present nonetheless. In the fifties one club with a shady reputation was the Brick Top, run by an African–American singer, Ada Smith, who was a friend of the celebrated cabaret artist Josephine Baker. The club's name, which was also her own nickname, derived from the colour of her hair. Smith had initially set up an establishment in Paris in 1928. She moved to Rome in the early 1950s and opened a basement club at 155 Via Veneto. It was a piano bar, which featured floor shows that often included Brick Top herself. The club's tables were mostly taken by regulars but the famous names who passed through the city could also often be seen there. The club had a reputation for criminal connections that it actively played up by fostering the thrilling idea that jazz and illegal activity were natural bedfellows.

This mix was turned into a potent musical fantasy by Fred Buscaglione, a singer and Clark Gable lookalike whose *ante litteram* gangster raps romanticised, in an Italian key, the American motifs of gun crime, bars, cigarette smoke, gangsters' molls and fast cars. Born in Turin, Buscaglione enjoyed great success on the cabaret circuit nationwide and made a number of memorable appearances in movies and on live television.

As a rising composer of soundtracks, a radio performer, and son of a leading politician, Piero Piccioni had no shortage of invitations to mix with film people or with the rich or powerful. There were few doors that were not open to him. Precisely because he was so well connected, his attitude towards his predicament was more casual than might have been expected of a man who found himself accused of a serious crime. He reacted to the first articles implicating him in the affair by issuing libel writs, but he failed to formalise them to ensure they resulted in a court hearing. There was one way, though, in which he would have been able once and for all to put an end to the speculation around his name: provide an unambiguous alibi. He signally failed to do so. Advised by

Francesco Carnelutti, one of the most experienced and respected lawyers in Rome, he first denied that he knew Montagna and said that he had never been anywhere in the vicinity of Capocotta since he did not hunt. Both statements had to be quickly revised, although he admitted to having attended the hunting club only once, in 1949. Saverio Polito had announced that Piccioni was in Milan on 9 April, but Piccioni told Sepe that in fact he had spent the days up until the afternoon of 9 April 1953 first on Capri and then in the picturesque seaside town of Amalfi. After that he had returned to Rome and was so ill that he stayed in bed for four days.

His companion on that journey was the film actress Alida Valli. Mention of her name had an electrifying effect on the public. There had been some press interest in Valli, and her name had been bracketed with Piccioni's but no one had thought much about it. Only Piccioni's, father Attilio had made clear his hostility to what he knew was an adulterous liaison. Now that the musician had admitted to being romantically linked with one of the most beautiful women in Italy, his status as nonentity changed to suave seducer.

Valli had starred in numerous comedies and costume dramas that, in the early 1940s, had established her as a national treasure. She was a free spirit who had been a screen actress since the age of fifteen. At the end of the war she was briefly smeared by a rumour that she had been the lover of Il Duce or one of his sons. Despite this, she had been personally recruited by producer David O. Selznick as a candidate for Hollywood stardom, and in 1947 she had left for the United States with her husband, the musician Oscar De Mejo. After a promising début as a European *femme fatale* in Hitchcock's dark tale of a husband's murder, *The Paradine Case*, she had been loaned out for a variety of films. One of these was Carol Reed's stunning Vienna-set drama *The Third Man*, in which she played Harry Lime's girlfriend Anna Schmidt. Valli was a striking beauty, her green eyes and slightly arched eyebrows constituting the focal points of a face that Hitchcock had found sufficiently mysterious to warrant extensive close-ups.

However, she disliked Selznick's attempts to package her as a latter-day Greta Garbo and was unhappy in California. Yearning for the familiar world of Italian cinema, she broke the terms of her contract and returned home in 1952, leaving her husband behind. By the early 1950s Valli was not quite the star she had once been but she quickly resumed her film career, working with the leading directors.

Ostensibly, Valli was the very reason for Piero's fatal failure to come clean. He explained to Sepe, when pressed, that he had been reluctant to reveal his true whereabouts on 9 and 10 April 1953 not out of chivalry towards the actress but because his devoutly Catholic family strongly disapproved of his relationship with her. He had arrogantly hoped that his word that he had been in Milan would be sufficient to remove him from enquiries.

The magazines had a field day with the exposure of his affair and its role in the case. *Epoca* used its network of contacts to secure at a price a selection of photographs of the couple in a variety of enviable locations. Their assignations had not taken place just anywhere but in Sorrento, Ravello, Ischia and San Marino, as well as Capri and Amalfi, upper-class playgrounds that were some of the most idyllic Italian resorts. Piccioni had even been a regular visitor to Valli's film sets. Shots showed them in restaurants and clubs, and lunching *al fresco* on shaded terraces. Sometimes they were alone, at other times they were pictured in company. There was, however, little sign of passion or complicity. In all the photographs Valli smiled while Piccioni wore the same absent expression.

Piccioni confided to Sepe that he and Valli had attended a party on 8 April held by film producer Carlo Ponti at his magnificent villa near Amalfi. A rambling white building several storeys high and perched on a cliff above the sea, it testified to the enormous fortunes made in post-war cinema. At this time Ponti, one of the young lions of post-war cinema, was already involved with the rising Neapolitan actress Sophia Loren, to whom he had been introduced some time earlier by the artist and social networker Novella Parigini. But he had not yet abandoned his wife. One of the most powerful men in the renaissance of Italian cinema, he entertained lavishly. The party was attended by several luminaries of the film world, including Gina Lollobrigida, Roberto Rossellini and Ingrid Bergman, and Ponti's Neapolitan business crony, Dino De Laurentiis. As chance would have it, all were engaged at the time in shooting films nearby.

Piccioni claimed that on 9 April, as he was feeling unwell, he had taken his leave of his actress lover and had driven back to Rome. According to the times he supplied, he had driven at some speed, covering nearly three hundred kilometres in five hours. In the days before the construction of the Autostrada del Sole, this was quite a feat. As he reached the city, a bout of tonsillitis that had begun to develop while he was in Amalfi grew worse and he was confined to bed for four days. He could not therefore have been involved in any way in the events surrounding Wilma's death. To support his statement, Piccioni produced a prescription and affidavits from a variety of medics and household staff stating that they had seen him confined to his bed.

Valli emerged as crucial to the establishment of Piccioni's guilt or innocence. On a sweltering day in June she arrived at the Palace of Justice for an audience with Sepe. The huge interest in Sepe's enquiries meant that the building was permanently staked out by photographers. Every person entering and leaving was snapped for potential news value. With her classic profile and intriguing green eyes, Valli was one of the most instantly recognisable women in the country.

Consequently she arrived for her first meeting with the magistrate wearing a headscarf and dark glasses, in the company of a female friend, and somehow managed to slip in while reporters and photographers were still trying to work out who the mysterious woman was. That she was listed on the register of witnesses under her true name, Maria von Altenberger, did not help them.

Sepe was more than pleased to meet a star he had admired since her heyday in the early 1940s. Thanks to the investigation, he himself had become something of a celebrity. *Epoca* published several pages of photographs from his family album that showed him on holiday with his daughter. Press photographers followed him every time he left the Palace of Justice and squeezed into his car. They even tailed him when he went to mass. He beamed at Valli and, following his customary practice of a gentle opening, engaged her in conversation about her recent films.

Once the topic changed to the matter in hand, his tone became more serious. Unlike some of the other encounters that had taken place in Sepe's office, the precise dialogue did not appear in the press or in the report based on his investigation. It was revealed, though, that the actress backed Piccioni's version of events, as far as she was personally able to. She confirmed his account of their stay in Amalfi and that he had been developing tonsillitis. She also provided him with cover for the crucial evening of 29 April, when Caglio claimed that a meeting at the interior ministry had set in motion the conspiracy to cover up the circumstances of Wilma Montesi's death. Valli swore that she and Piccioni had dined together on that evening and that he had stayed at her house until late.

Sepe asked her about a telephone call that she had allegedly received in early May 1953. While she was in a bar in the Giudecca district of Venice, where she had been filming *La mano dello straniero* (The Hand of the Foreigner), she had been overheard by a local journalist named Augusto Torresin discussing Wilma Montesi with someone who was assumed to have been Piccioni. 'Are you involved with that girl's death?' she was said to have asked, before adding, 'What kind of mess have you got yourself into with that girl?' Apparently she had then exclaimed, 'That imbecile,' after hanging up. Valli firmly denied to Sepe ever having received such a call or made such a remark.

She had done all she could for Piccioni, but as the case progressed she found out that he had concealed from her many aspects of his life. Although he lived with his father, in whose house he claimed to have spent four days after his return to Rome on 9 April, he also maintained an address in the secluded residential road of Via Acherusio. He claimed that the apartment was his workplace but, contradictorily, he also said that he did not use it regularly. Originally it had been bought by Ugo Montagna and placed at the disposal of Attilio Piccioni. Valli knew nothing of this so-called *garconnière*, which was located just a few minutes from Via Tagliamento. She discovered its existence when she read about it in the newspapers. She was also less than pleased to read that Piccioni was said to be a serial womaniser. He had once got one of his father's servants pregnant and he allegedly used his bachelor apartment to entertain women he casually picked up. Even Anna Maria Caglio had been invited there on the pretext of discussing her career prospects. Still more disturbingly, there was talk of sadistic sexual interests. Then there was the matter of drugs. Privately, journalists were convinced that he was a regular user of cocaine. It was even hinted in print that his dilated nostrils and perpetually dark eyes were giveaway signs of his addiction. All this offered Valli an unwelcome insight into her lover's moody and unpredictable behaviour. It also caused her to reflect on the reasons why he had returned in such a hurry to the capital on 9 April.

Valli defended Piccioni, but she did so more out of loyalty than love. Sepe got her to admit that she had been unhappy with him because he was given to mood swings and depressive. Although almost any heterosexual man would have been happy to exchange places with Piccioni in Valli's favours, she found him cold and unresponsive. Her desire to render their liaison more stable had been met by stonewalling. Although Valli provided Piccioni with two key elements of his alibi, her testimony proved unreliable, at least in part. In October she was called back by Sepe after checks on records of telephone conversations showed that a call had indeed been made by Piccioni to a bar in the Giudecca area of Venice. Also, various other witnesses who had been in the bar gave detailed accounts of the actress's ill-tempered conversation. She was obliged to revise her evidence and admit that the call had taken place, although she would not agree that she had decried Piccioni or implied that he was involved with the Montesi affair.

Sepe also carefully checked with those present at the Ponti party whether they recalled Piccioni's presence. Lieutenant Zinza was dispatched to Amalfi to interview witnesses. Carlo Ponti and his wife Giuliana confirmed that the couple had been there, although Roberto Rossellini and Ingrid Bergman, when they were contacted in Stockholm, could not remember exact dates. The cook at the hotel, the Santa Caterina, where Valli and Piccioni had stayed in Sorrento, told Zinza that they had not dined there on 8 April and that they had left the next day. Valli had gone first to Capri before returning to Rome on 10 April.

As Sepe continued his investigation, the press were revelling in the twists and turns of the story. When Piccioni and Montagna were locked up in Regina Coeli prison, the newspapers took full advantage of public curiosity and printed thousands of extra copies. People gathered in groups on street corners to discuss the case and voices were raised on the afternoon trams. Workers were heard singing songs that had been written about those involved. Someone even coined a tongue-twister of irritating difficulty: '*Cape molta coca a Capocotta? Si, a Capocotta molta coca cape*' (roughly translated: Does a lot of coke get into Capocotta? Yes, into Capocotta a lot of coke gets).

Reporters and photographers camped outside the prison, scrutinising who went in and out. One enterprising photographer managed to gets shots of Piccioni walking in the exercise yard. They also kept watch on the Piccioni family home in Via della Conciliazione. When Leone was seen leaving with a package under his arm, probably destined for his brother, there was a fierce scramble to find out what delights it contained. No response was forthcoming from the interested party, who lashed out at the 'jackals' who snapped him and other family members every time they left home. Finally, a prison guard revealed that it contained a supply of vests to stop the prisoner catching cold.

There was ample coverage of the conditions in which he and Montagna found themselves. The two men reacted quite differently to their circumstances. Montagna sought at every turn to distinguish himself and to secure privileges. He availed himself of the opportunity to pay for a more comfortable cell and to order his meals from restaurants. At his request, his butler brought him a full armoury of toiletries and grooming equipment. Piccioni took a more modern, democratic position. On the advice of his brother and his lawyers, he announced that he would behave like a normal prisoner and would take regular prison meals. Both men wore their own clothes, as was usual for remand prisoners, but while Piccioni dressed simply, Montagna spent his days in his silk pyjamas and dressing-gown.

But it was still not clear how or why two men of different

backgrounds, tastes and ages had become so friendly. It would prove to be one of the many issues about the case that excited the press. It seemed obvious that there was something illicit or dishonourable about their association. With the revelations about the parties at Capocotta, womanising, financial malpractice, nocturnal adventures and drugs, all the pieces of the puzzle seemed finally to be falling into place. However, the press were still pondering the definitive piece of evidence. But before they could find it, they uncovered another explosive secret that might help the establishment claw back the moral high ground.

XIII

The Establishment Fights Back

Few people are more associated with the Roman *dolce vita* of the 1950s than the photographer Tazio Secchiaroli. With his camera slung over his shoulder and habitually rumpled suit, Secchiaroli hung around wherever there was a chance of a lucrative photograph, in police stations, hospitals, newspapers offices, on the Via Veneto, or in the nightclubs. Sometimes he could be seen on a Lambretta but more frequently he was to be found loitering outside cafés. Today exhibitions and books still celebrate his work. When Federico Fellini decided to base a character on him, he became the incarnation of the photographer as modern hero. But it was the Montesi case that made his name.

In the illustrated weeklies, a new flashbulb version of reality was taking shape that was at once eclectic and selective. The magazines featured a wide variety of people and events, but pride of place always went to the famous and the beautiful. Shots of episodes from their lives were concentrated doses of glamour that enchanted readers and aroused their desires for vicarious participation. Magazines started highlighting the activities of sexual adventurers instead of drawing a veil of modesty over them. King Farouk of Egypt first ran up against the photographers in Italy in 1950 when the corpulent moustachioed monarch was snapped taking a dip in his swimming trunks. After he moved to Rome following his overthrow in 1952, he was constantly pursued. Farouk was always good copy because of his short temper, vampire-like taste for young starlets, and love of the street cafes of the Via Veneto. So, too, were notorious international playboys such as Aly Khan, Baby Pignatari and Porfirio Rubirosa, the Dominican Lothario who in succession married Danielle Darrieux, Zsa Zsa Gabor, Doris Duke and Barbara Hutton. The much-reported antics of the rich and famous reinforced the idea that money brought access to fast living and easy sex. A song by Fred Buscaglione, entitled 'Porforio Villarosa', captured the popular fascination with one hero of café society. Among several films that depicted the Riviera lifestyle, *Costa azzurra* (Côte d'Azur) featured the greatest concentration of fast cars, yachts, hotels, beaches, nightclubs, rich men, beautiful women and the sexually ambiguous.

Alongside the Via Veneto was the louche milieu of Via Margutta and Via del Babuino. It was here that the intellectual tastes and fashions of Paris found ready application and, of course, where the most colourful and off-beat people could be found. Knowing well that the picturesque and the eccentric were supremely photogenic, artists and beatniks created an environment that was more experimental than anything else in Rome. It was no more down-to-earth or real than the upscale world of Via Veneto but the scruffy bars and cheap wine made it more accessible. Novella Parigini, her friend the camp artist Giò Stajano and her models were always ready to subvert convention to draw the photographers. And the photographers duly obliged, creating a version of Roman life more rich and colourful than everyday reality.

Secchiaroli was drawn into the Montesi case when he was working for the Vedo agency, founded by one of Mussolini's favourite photographers, Adolfo Porry Pastorel, which supplied material to newspapers including the Roman evening daily *Momento-sera*. Unbeknown to him, he was to play an unlikely role in the establishment counter-attack.

Throughout the period following the suspension of the Muto trial in March 1954, various strategies were put into play to ride out the scandal and defuse the case. Montagna's fellow Sicilian and 'non-acquaintance', prime minister Mario Scelba, was instrumental in them. A close ally of the former Christian Democrat leader De Gasperi, who died aged seventy-three on 19 August 1954, he was a notorious scourge of the left and of the artists and intellectuals who had been seduced by the siren calls of the Communists. He dismissed the left-leaning films, art and literature of the post-war years as *culturame*, an untranslatable term that might be rendered as 'pseudo culture'. No post-war politician had a more intimate acquaintance with the police. He had stamped his personal mark on the massive police apparatus that the republic had inherited from Fascism and he bent it without compunction to his political agenda.

Scelba was pugnacious in his defence of the government. In impassioned addresses to the Chamber of Deputies on 25 and 30 September 1954, just days after the imprisonment of Piccioni and Montagna, he attacked the Communists for scandal-mongering. The Italian-language broadcaster Radio Prague, a Communist mouthpiece, had even announced, he yelled, that the former foreign minister had been imprisoned along with his son. 'It is superfluous to point out that only madmen would even think, never mind try, to pervert the course of justice in a climate like the present one.' To those who tried to turn Piero Piccioni's arrest against the government, he proclaimed that no government could be held responsible for the acts of private citizens, no matter who they were. If they had committed crimes, they would be punished and that was that. The black legends about Tommaso Pavone were completely unjustified, he added. The former prefect and national police chief had been held in high regard by the left and personally praised for his conduct during the Nazi occupation by Mauro Scoccimarro, the Communist chairman of the post-war purge commission.

Amintore Fanfani, who had been accused of inviting Colonel Pompei to prepare his report with the intention of discrediting Attilio Piccioni, also intervened in the parliamentary debate. 'It was certainly not my intention to bypass the magistracy,' he said. 'It just seemed opportune to me to have certain things clarified. The Carabinieri, in the person of Colonel Umberto Pompei, did a good job and their work was quite rightly used by the magistrates and by the Honourable De Caro in the course of his politico-administrative investigation.' At the end of the debate the government won a confidence vote by 294 to 254 with seven abstentions.

The authorities were given an idea about how to counter-attack when, during September, the great cycling ace Fausto Coppi was revealed to be conducting an affair with a married woman, Giulia Occhini. Just as Anna Maria Caglio had been nicknamed the Black Swan, so Occhini was turned into the White Lady on account of the pale scarf she usually wore on her head. The 'White' of the appellation was not taken to be synonymous with innocence. The exposure of the illicit liaison resulted in a scandal that led to the cyclist's passport being withdrawn and Occhini being imprisoned on charges of adultery. The case stood as an example of the hypocritical attitudes that prevailed at the time. But because Coppi was strongly identified with the left, it also had an indirect impact on the political sphere. The Communists had often in the past been accused of promoting free love and wanting to destroy the family, but this was a purely ideological criticism. The Coppi scandal seemed to give it substance.

In the event, chance played a role in what ensued. A crime reporter on the Rome evening paper *Momento-sera* discovered that a girl named Maria 'Pupa' Montorsi had been taken into hospital after being beaten up by her fiancé, who had learned that she was working at a clandestine brothel. On talking to the girl, the reporter on the paper discovered that the brothel in Via Corridoni counted a number of important figures among its clients. One in particular was a man who had recently been in the news. A journalist was dispatched to the Prati quarter, near the Vatican, to keep watch on the establishment. In fact he did more that that: he befriended the madam, a young married woman from the Veneto region named Rita Fantini, who ran her business without her husband's knowledge. On confirming the story, the paper sent Secchiaroli to the address and told him to watch out for a famous person, although he was not told who his prey was.

As Secchiaroli hung around the appointed address in Via Corridoni, in mid-November, he was surprised to catch sight of the stocky figure of Giuseppe Sotgiu leaving the building. Ever since his triumph at the Muto trial earlier in the year, the lawyer-cum-politician had been riding the crest of a wave of popularity. By reflex, Secchiaroli lifted his camera and took his shot. The startled Sotgiu asked him what he was doing. When Secchiaroli explained that it was just a matter of getting some more up-to-date pictures for the files, Sotgiu even posed for more. Satisfied that this proved the infomation to be true, the paper's editor decided that the moment was right to set up the story. He informed the police, who prepared a raid that was carried out in the afternoon of 15 November. The officers burst into the apartment and caught three men and five women engaged in sexual acts. 'Mario and Pina', the names by which the fearless moralist, Sotgiu, and his artist wife Liliana Grimaldi were known, were not present but witnesses testified that the fifty-five-year-old was accustomed to watching his wife having sex with a teenage accountancy student while in the company of other women. The news was splashed over *Momento-sera* the next day and quickly taken up by other papers.

The Communist Party sprang to Sotgiu's defence in the belief that the authorities had trumped up a scandal to discredit a dangerous opponent, divert attention from official corruption, and turn a weapon against the leading party of government into a denunciation of opposition hypocrisy. But the involvement of a teenager made the matter complicated. Like so many of those drawn into the Montesi case, Sotgiu had been leading a life that was respectable only on the exterior, and his swift resignation from his public offices showed that the accusations contained some truth.

The spotlight also fell on his alluring forty-three-year-old wife, who was mobbed by photographers when she went to give evidence on her role in the possible corruption of a minor. Normally cool and composed, Liliana Grimaldi was flustered by the unwanted attention and hurried past, covering her face. She was a prominent artist with many acquaintances in the Via Margutta area. Along with Piccioni and Montagna, Adriana Bisaccia, Anna Maria Caglio and others, she had been spotted in the artists' bar Il Baretto. This was a hangout for all manner of people. Indeed, it was here that she and her husband met the young man who would join them in their erotic games, as well as the keeper of the brothel they used. The conservative press was ecstatic. The link between the Communists and the immoral world of the Via Margutta had been established for all to see.

Sotgiu's fall from grace was dramatic. *Epoca* magazine gleefully wrote that the lawyer was 'like the class swot who is caught scrawling obscene words and pictures on the wall'. Suspension from the Communist Party quickly followed. Government spokesmen and their allies in the press made the most of the opposition's embarrassment. In the Vatican there was quiet satisfaction that the man who had daringly seized power in the Rome provincial council, thus embarrassing the Church, had been brought down. After this, the left's campaign against the moral corruption of the bourgeoisie deflated like a balloon.

And, while the clamour over Sotgiu filled the papers, Piccioni
and Montagna were granted provisional liberty and released
from gaol on 19 November. A throng of journalists and others
had gathered at the prison gate. To spare them embarrassment,
the two men were driven out in a car by a side exit and taken
to a quiet location where they were met by relatives and friends.
The journalists soon caught up, though, and were in time to
see Piccioni get into his brother Leone's car. Montagna stopped
to announce his relief at being released: 'It is not good in
prison, especially now it is getting cold,' he said.

On the other side of the city, away from the flash-bulb glare
of the media, Wilma Montesi's long-suffering family were facing
further troubles. While others had revelled in the headlines, the
notoriety that had attached to them had made life difficult in
the Salario quarter. Rodolfo had been forced to close his
workshop, his two apprentices had lost their jobs, and some of
the household furniture had been taken away by bailiffs. Rodolfo
had developed an ulcer from the stress and had had to spend
time in hospital. Although the press had taken a mostly
sympathetic view of the family, some reporters felt that they
couldn't be completely blameless for Wilma's death. What ideas
did the girl have in her head and who had she been seeing?
Had she got mixed up in the sleazy *demi-monde* that had come
to light, as some were claiming? Why, reporters wondered, had
the mother been so keen to tell everyone that she was her
daughter's only friend, with the result that the police had not
even bothered to question the friends who had sent a wreath
to her funeral? The key to the case was perhaps to be found
much closer to home.

XIV

A Family Under Stress

The Montesi family struggled throughout this traumatic period to give the impression that their household was normal and upright. During the months – and years – in which they were drawn into the spotlight, they stubbornly defended this wholesome image, always denying or seeking to minimise any discrepancy or suggestion to the contrary. Wilma was an angel. For both her parents, it was a matter of honour to safeguard her reputation. Sitting through the Muto trial, the family had grown ever more horrified as the lurid theories about Wilma's fate were put forward. The suggestion that she had been mixed up with dope fiends and sexual perverts was rejected with disdain.

The family had been wary of the press from when the first speculation mounted around the time of the funeral. But journalists were persistent: they wheedled away at family members, they befriended them and offered them money. Every facet of the life and household of the humble artisan, his wife and children was picked over and discussed. How they dressed, when they ate, where they went for entertainment, their sleeping arrangements and the interior décor of their apartment were all described. They were the subject of several photographic features and were also snapped off-guard when they were spotted on the street.

Reporters soon discovered that the family was neither refined nor particularly peaceful. The household was argumentative and riven with hostility. For instance, Maria's parents, the original tenants of the Via Tagliamento apartment, who still lived with the family, had not spoken to each other for years. They continued to live in the flat because their presence entailed a rent subsidy that would otherwise be lost. Maria Montesi's own disputatious character was confirmed by neighbours. Shouting and arguments in the apartment had often been overheard. Some of the tension probably derived from the tight control that she sought to exercise over her daughters. The girls did not always see eye to eye with their mother, who was regarded in the neighbourhood as loud and coarse. Wilma had even been heard to call her '*sozzona*' (dirty old woman), a straightforward insult suggesting that her personal hygiene was not all it might have been.

Furthermore, a nasty dispute had occurred in the autumn of 1952 with Giuseppe Montesi. Rodolfo had objected strongly when he discovered that his brother had taken Wilma's younger brother Sergio to a brothel at Ostia. After several months in which Giuseppe was not welcome in Via Tagliamento, a reconciliation was arranged by Ida Montesi, his and Rodolfo's sister. At the resulting tea-party, Giuseppe's fiancée, Mariella Spissu, allegedly made eyes at Rodolfo, provoking the ire of Maria. The two women ended up kicking and abusing each other – an ugly conflict that ended when Rodolfo and his family were asked to leave. Only Wilma's disappearance brought the various components of the family briefly back into contact.

As we know, Wilma's fiancé, Angelo Giuliani, had misled the family over his job and social status, presenting himself as a wine merchant when in fact he was a policeman and his father ran a small retail outlet, because he saw the Montesis as being of solid middle-class stock. In fact, they were no less prone to exaggeration. Wilma had been trained to describe her father not as a carpenter but as a 'wood industrialist'. The mother and her daughters aspired to wealth and success. They were vain, passionate and ambitious. Exposed to modern preoccupations, such as the cult of the film star, the belief in fashion and exterior image, they longed for upward mobility in social status. On the whole they did not present a very positive picture. And while sympathetic to their tragedy, public opinion did not find them likeable.

After Wilma's death Maria had been initially suspicious of the press, but she was drawn into selling photographs as well as access to the family home. She also allowed her name to be put to articles, especially for *Epoca* magazine, in which she gave the family viewpoint on developments. Although other immediate family members avoided this sort of activity, they posed for some photographs and did not appear to resent the attention. Although nobody ever came forward to testify that they had seen Wilma Montesi in the Via Veneto milieu, it did not take much imagination to conclude that she had been led astray, like many other girls with a smart look and keen ambition. After all, the Via Veneto was only twenty minutes on foot from the Montesi family's apartment in Via Tagliamento. Certainly the glitter there would have appealed to her more than the wayward fun and pranks of the Via Margutta community.

Writing in *Epoca* in March 1954, the journalist Roberto Cantini argued that the key to the Montesi mystery lay in the collapse of traditional lower-middle-class values. How else, he asked, could such a complex tale begin from such an apparently banal household? Wilma had somehow come into contact with a world she was ill-equipped to negotiate and this had led to her destruction.

Fabrizio Menghini, the ubiquitous chief crime reporter for *Il Messaggero*, and his fellow journalist Luciano Doddoli were convinced that Wilma's uncle Giuseppe had something to explain. Twenty-eight-year-old Giuseppe was a clerical worker with a post in the Ministry of Education and a second job doing the accounts for the Casciani printing company, whose boss was Piero Piccioni's friend Franco Biagetti. He was the only male sibling not to have followed family tradition and become a carpenter. Short and dapper, he held a cigarette like a film star and exuded the self-confidence of a minor playboy. With his thick back-combed dark hair and his double-breasted suits, he had something of the air of a street corner Porfirio Rubirosa. Sometimes he posed happily for cameras; other times he appeared moody and closed. He threw himself into the family's efforts to find out what had happened to Wilma and talked freely to the press. As Doddoli had noticed at Wilma's funeral, he seemed almost too keen to get involved. One day in May 1953 deputy procurator Leonardo Murante caught him eavesdropping at his door while an interview was being conducted. Suspicious, he requested that the Carabinieri conduct an inquiry.

When Giuseppe's room in his father's apartment in Via Alessandria was searched, officers found items of lingerie that he had collected as souvenirs from his conquests, several pornographic magazines, a membership card for a private beach, and a picture of Wilma. Giuseppe claimed scarcely to know his niece and to have seen her no more than four or five times since she was an adolescent. But this was untrue. He was known to have cast his eye over Wilma and Wanda, and had taken them out in his car on several occasions. In the small circles of the Salario quarter, he had the appearance of a man of the world. The mere fact that he owned a Topolino Belvedere, a top-of-the-range version of Fiat's economical car, marked him as unusual.

Giuseppe was a textbook example of the way the publicised hedonism of the privileged was being emulated by the lower-middle class. Everyone wanted a share of the good life and especially people who were alert to matters of status. Giuseppe had been especially contemptuous of Wilma's humble fiancé. Once, after taking the couple to Termini station, where Giuliani would catch the train for Potenza, he had turned to ask Wilma, 'So, you are really going to get married?' She had smiled strangely, without responding, as if she was not convinced about her decision.

Like everyone else in the Montesi family, he presented a clean-cut image of himself, compromised only by a few indiscretions. He painted himself as a good son, a fine fiancé, a loyal worker and a caring uncle. But his financial circumstances did not quite match this. He earned eighty thousand lire per month from two jobs, a sum that would not have gone far even for a man who lived with his father and paid a modest rent. Some people were convinced that he must have other sources of income to finance his life of restaurants, car trips, private beaches, fine clothes and women.

Giuseppe's own alibi was shaky. Despite the precise testimony to the contrary of Lia Brusin, who was employed at the Casciani works where he was engaged in the afternoons, he denied ever receiving calls from someone named Wilma. On the day of her disappearance, he had left work early, which gave rise to suspicion. His fiancée stepped forward to provide him with an alibi. Yet doubts persisted. The keen interest he took in the enquiries seemed odd, and although he claimed to have barely known Wilma, he had taken her out several times. He even stayed away from work for three weeks after her death.

Sepe did not take the family's accounts at face value. Ignoring established conventions, he did not accord greater value to the evidence of people of a higher class over those of a lower. Neither did he allow even intimate details to go unchallenged. He interviewed neighbours, servants and anyone who claimed a connection with Wilma. A woman who had worked as a servant for the Montesis during 1952, before Maria sacked her because she was pregnant, offered a striking testimony. (The discovery that a family who pleaded poverty had kept a servant caused a stir.) Annunziata Gionni was a dull, brow-

beaten woman with some resentments, and the family tried
to discredit her. Sepe, however, hoped she could provide an
insight into the dynamics of the household.

Gionni painted a very different picture of Wilma from that
offered by her parents. She said that both Montesi girls dressed
up every morning to go out and that they carefully applied their
make-up. They left together but always returned separately,
suggesting they went their separate ways as soon as they were
out on the street. In the afternoon, the pattern was sometimes
repeated. If she was at home, Wilma frequently received telephone
calls, and when this occurred, she closed the door so that the
conversation would not be overheard. The implication that Wilma
had had a secret life outside the family home was reinforced by
other details. According to Gionni, Wilma used a costly foreign
perfume and owned silk underwear. In Rome in the 1950s, such
luxury items were among the repertoire of only two categories
of unmarried women: mistresses and prostitutes.

The Montesis utterly rejected Gionni's testimony. They
claimed she only ever worked for them in the afternoon and
could not have known about the girls' movements in the
morning. Who was right? If the choice is to believe the servant
or the family, there seems no reason to choose the latter, not
least because it transpired that Gionni did work in the mornings:
she was at the house between nine and eleven, as well as
between two and four. One of her duties was to do the washing,
so she was well placed to know about the family's underwear.
Gionni might have been resentful because she had been sacked,
but she was the only outsider who ever saw the Montesi family
at close quarters. They appeared to be hiding something, and
she had no interest in defending an idealised image of Wilma.

From the moment the missing suspender belt had been
mentioned, the public imagination had gone into overdrive.
Its absence suggested that Wilma had not removed her stockings
and skirt simply to bathe her feet but rather that she or

someone else had removed them as a prelude to consensual or non-consensual sex. Also, there was the issue of the colour and type of suspender belt in question. According to Gionni, Wilma had worn a one-piece black corset that had hooks at the back – an item that could not be removed easily and certainly not without undressing. Rodolfo clarified to Sepe that Wilma had worn a simple suspender belt over her knickers, not a corset. Neither did she ever wear any foreign perfume.

The new autopsy, ordered by Sepe following exhumation of Wilma's body in March 1954, showed that Wilma had not died on 9 April and that she had not been in the sea long enough to have drowned at Ostia. The body had remained in the water between four and ten hours only, indicating that the girl had died no earlier than the afternoon of 10 April. She had been unconscious when she drowned, showing that the hypothesis of accidental death while she was bathing her feet was implausible. The experts found no signs of eczema or other irritation on the feet, or of violence on the body. Neither did they find evidence of intoxication. They confirmed that the girl had a slightly smaller heart than usual and that this might have made her prone to fainting. They also found that the body had been completely immersed in water. Nevertheless, a chemical analysis showed that the sand in Wilma's lungs and stomach matched closely that of Torvaianica and not that of Ostia.

A key issue concerned the matter of sexual activity. It was confirmed that Wilma's hymen was intact so she had never had full penetrative sex. In addition, the pathologists dismissed Pellegrini's lurid suggestion that the girl's body had been abused following her death. The sand in her vagina, they said, was not unusual. Experience showed that, when a body was immersed in the sea, sand infiltrated all orifices. Yet, crucially, they declared themselves unable to comment on whether she might have had any partial vaginal sexual contact or anal sex (whether once only or repeatedly).

At a time when virginity and honour were closely intertwined, and contraception was still illegal, sexual practices that fell short of full vaginal intercourse were common. Young women who were eager for sex yet subject to social pressures not to give up their virginity before marriage often engaged in oral or anal sex. People knew this and gossip centred around the unspoken assumption that Wilma was one of those girls, a sexually experienced virgin.

Despite innovations in the labour market and attractive new jobs for young women, there was still just one possible life choice for a respectable girl and that was marriage. In order to arrive at this much-desired goal, young women were repeatedly told that they had to reject any requests even from long-standing fiancés to give them 'proof of love'. The Montesi family's insistence on Wilma's purity was intended to parade the fact that, had she lived, she would have been a virgin bride. They also hoped to safeguard her sister from insinuations that she, too, might have been lured into immorality. The assumption here was that the girls had been carefully watched and chaperoned through their teenage years and into their early twenties. They had never worked and had never been allowed to spend time alone with a man or to develop any independent interests outside the home.

The French journalist Jean-François Revel noted that the separation of the sexes determined, and impoverished, Italian social life. 'In Italy, a female is not considered to be a free human being,' he observed. Young people, he claimed, were not usually seen out in couples. By the mid-1950s, more women were going out but the streets were still dominated by men, who often congregated in intimidating groups. For Revel, this meant that sexual life took on a 'furtive and sordid character'. Men were obsessed with sex, he argued, 'which is another way of saying that they have become brutal'.

Was Wilma, as her mother claimed, a modern-day Maria

Goretti, a saintly figure who had died rather than give in to the carnal desires of a monster? Or was she rather a *faux-*innocent who had got caught up in something very murky? These questions hinge on the girl's dreams and aspirations as well as what little is known of her life. Even at the time of the case, it was not easy to get a handle on Wilma. 'I grew up near Via Tagliamento and I knew the area well,' claimed the veteran journalist Angelo Frignani, who worked on the case for *Il Tempo.* 'But even though I was the same age as the Montesi girl, I never met her. Pity, really, because I spent so much time on the case. On my first day at the paper, the news editor told me to get a snapshot of the girl. I blagged my way somehow into the family apartment and, while the father's back was turned, I pinched a photograph and beat a rapid retreat. It was a good job I was young and fast because he chased me down the stairs and up the street.'

The Montesis were not an active part of the lively community life that bound together the lower classes in the capital. In their interactions with the people around them, there was none of the fraternity that, according to Carlo Levi, marked the life of the Roman people. It is true that many people who lived in Via Tagliamento came to Wilma's funeral and offered their condolences. But, for the most part, the family appears to have been reclusive and to have entertained few friendly contacts with outsiders.

A girl like Wilma might have been expected to have numerous friends among neighbours and old schoolmates. Yet very little ever came out about the sort of company she kept. Maria Montesi cut off any questions about friends by saying that she was the one person to whom Wilma confided everything. When asked if any men had shown interest in her daughter, she was caught between issuing a denial, with the unflattering implication that Wilma was unattractive to men, and providing examples that might have undermined the carefully constructed image of moral purity. She chose to cite the innocent example of the engineer who had allegedly taken an interest in her one summer while the family was on holiday at Rocco di Papa. Revealingly, the man cited was of a higher social status.

The one person who might have shed light on Wilma's thoughts and contacts was Wanda. The girls were often together and they slept in the same room. Yet Wanda scarcely appeared in the whole case, let alone as an independent voice. She was the living proof that the girls had little autonomy of mind or spirit. Almost the only thing she revealed to Sepe was that Wilma had received attention from kerb crawlers in Via Tagliamento. Both girls deplored this sleazy practice, but in one instance the man involved had evidently left an impression because Wilma had described him to her sister and Wanda had remembered what she had said. The man had followed Wilma down the road slowly in his car, inviting her to join him for a ride. Once she had turned to enter the main arch of Via Tagliamento 76, she spun round to look at him and saw a handsome, athletic man of middle age with grey hair.

Yet while the older Wanda was still under her mother's thumb, Wilma had asserted some independence, which had ignited rows. Recently turned twenty-one, she had realised that, having reached the age of majority, she could exercise more control over her destiny. In the weeks before her death, she had started taking on airs. When she went out, she dressed up in a way that was eye-catching and moderately expensive. She had received gifts of jewellery, some of which had not been from her fiancé. In particular, the provenance of a pair of earrings remained unidentified. She had also acquired an expensive leather handbag, whose value was almost equivalent to a month's wages for a white-collar worker. Rodolfo said he had bought the bag for his wife and that Wilma had merely used it, but, given his well-known thriftiness, this was unlikely.

As a girl who spent much time at home, Wilma was especially

susceptible to the suggestions of the illustrated magazines. As a model of decorum and elegance, the aristocracy and royalty, even if dethroned, were still unrivalled. Ex-King Umberto's daughter Princess Gabriella was a regular cover girl on the weeklies. She was endorsed by style and manners expert Donna Letizia, who warned girls in a popular manual of the time not to imitate the dress of film stars or to be tempted to mistake sex appeal for elegance. Wilma seems to have paid little heed to this advice. Silvano Muto sketched out what he thought might have been the connection between the girl's dream life and her tragic fate:

The truth began from the day that Wilma started to 'dream'. There was 'someone' perhaps who pushed her along the way of dreams, a dangerous way for a girl of twenty . . . First of all dreams, first of all illusions, and then the first contacts with the crude and grey reality of life; the first not well-defined friendships, a turbulent existence beneath the tenuous veil of modest calm. It is an old story that repeats itself for all the women who want to turn their dreams into reality.

The man she met, in Muto's view, was Mr X, the man who was unveiled at Muto's trial as Ugo Montagna.

That her father was a man out of step with the changing times didn't help Wilma. He tried to ignore the modern world around him, especially where sex and sex-roles were concerned. One theme that ran through every phase of the Montesi scandal was the public position of young women. Wilma's father might not have allowed her to work outside the home, but as new professions emerged and new possibilities of economic independence and collective recognition took shape, women had begun to grasp them eagerly. Italian girls of the time demonstrated an unprecedented desire to win attention, get ahead and fulfil their dreams. After the repression of the

Fascist period, women seemed finally to be getting their chance. Female faces were everywhere, in advertisements, at the movies, in the streets. Sex appeal of a more abstract type was becoming common currency as Italy tentatively embraced the consumer society. After the war, pin-ups, beauty contests and the movies had consolidated an idea of the ideal woman. Even the plastic nativity characters on sale at the Christmas markets in Piazza Navona had the look and manner of pin-up girls, the writer and columnist Corrado Alvaro observed.

The images of women were not always benign. The prostitute, a common feature of 1950s cinema, was a dramatic, controversial figure who embodied the temptations and delusions of the big city. For every girl who got a lucky break, there were thousands more whose dreams were dashed. Dangers and traps were numerous. For example, most beauty-contest entrants, even the winners, simply returned home to a normal life, but others ended up in the photo-romance magazines, becoming models or, in some cases, prostitutes.

A key contributor to the redefinition of sexuality was the campaign to abolish state-regulated prostitution championed by the Socialist senator Lina Merlin. Although the Church was vocal in its promotion of conventional morality, prostitution remained a significant phenomenon, made legitimate by the presence of state-licensed brothels. The system dated back to Napoleonic times and persisted into the post-war years, even though France had abolished its brothels in 1946. Shocked into action by the hundreds of letters she received about girls who had been lured into vice by promises of film parts and fame, Merlin led a campaign to abolish state-approved prostitution. It aroused intense controversy. Vigorously opposed by conservatives, nostalgic older men and a band of journalists and writers, it struck a blow against a whole system of sexual double standards. For men, a rite of initiation faced abolition. At a public meeting to discuss her proposal, Merlin was asked by a worried young man, 'What will happen to those without experience?' She replied, 'You are a good-looking boy. Learn how to court girls.'

Prostitution remained widespread in cities, although the commercialisation of sex was undergoing something of a revolution. It was no longer the social plague that it had been during the occupation. The call-girl – *ragazza squillo* in Italian – phenomenon was blurring the boundaries between respectability and illicit behaviour, because call-girls were usually young women who led normal lives but earned extra cash through part-time prostitution. Hostesses who provided men with company in the clubs, bar girls, entertainers and would-be actresses occupied a similar limbo zone. A short story by the novelist Alberto Moravia describes this world. In 'The Fortune of Irene', Irene is said to be '*di naso*' (loosely: whiffy), a term that normally described meat that had gone off; in this context it implied a girl who was prepared in certain circumstances to trade sexual favours for material reward. She is a flower-seller who works in a shop in the Parioli district on a road frequented by Americans. The narrator of the story, her boyfriend, notices that Irene claims to be a simple girl with no interest in the Americans yet somehow she always seems to have new clothes or accessories. She explains that she found them or received them as gifts from the grateful old ladies to whom she delivers her blooms. Eventually he catches her out when he sees her with a bag that an American actor had bought earlier that day in the shop where he works.

All classes were affected. Anna Maria Caglio and Adriana Bisaccia had been drawn into this sexual *demi-monde*. Both had aspirations related to showbusiness, yet the former had become a mistress and the latter had been sucked into a downward spiral of degradation. This sort of system, whereby women could climb towards success only to fall from grace, was a sign that an old heritage of sexual division still weighed on Italian society. Only a few, including the mysterious Giobben Giò, seemed to emerge triumphant. Wilma Montesi was a movie-struck girl who perhaps had been drawn into a sphere that was to lead to her fatal downfall. The *Los Angeles Times* referred to her as a 'sultry-looking party girl'. The British journalist Wayland Young speculated that she was a playgirl – a sort of escort who was happy to sit in cafés and keep men company for payment. She could be invited out but you could not sleep with her. There was a place in Rome for this sort of *faux*-respectable girl, many of whom could be seen at café tables along the Via Veneto. Such ornamental women were sometimes employed by café owners to attract custom, just as hostesses performed a similar function in nightclubs. They were a few steps up from the bottom of the national glamour hierarchy, although in their dreams the big leap to success was always just one more step away.

Had 9 April been a normal day? The possibility was mentioned that a violent family dispute had occurred. Neighbours reported that raised voices had been heard in the apartment. The fact that panic had set in so quickly after Wilma failed to appear for dinner struck some as odd, as did the initial thoughts of suicide. 'Come back, Wilma, all is forgiven! Come back, even with ten lovers!' Maria was overheard to cry later that evening; a strange exclamation indeed following a daughter's disappearance. The fruit of a police phone tap on the Montesi household, which was included in a legal document prepared in 1955 by the Procurator's Office, confirmed that the family knew something that the girl's parents could not or would not admit to. In the course of a conversation with her sister-in-law, Maria had apparently said, 'Wilma has ruined herself by her own hands.' This suggested that someone in the family was aware that the girl had contacts outside the home who were at least questionable. In some way, she had put herself at risk.

The Montesis refused steadfastly to elaborate on what Maria had said or divulge any more details. After being drawn into a pact with the devil in their relations with the media, they tried to return to some sort of normality. An opportunity was provided by the engagement of Wanda on 25 October 1954 to Silvano Pucci, a carpenter from Rocca Priora, who promised to help Rodolfo in his workshop. The happy event was scheduled to take place in the San Saturnino parish church. The family were determined that this event should escape censure even from the most critical of observers. Yet somehow it became subject to the sort of negotiation that had become the norm where the Montesi family was concerned. Luciano Doddoli feigned horror when Maria asked if his magazine could meet the bill in return for coverage ('It is not me who is marrying your daughter,' he told her). In fact, such a practice was not uncommon. Everything had a price and the family wanted to make sure they received their share of cash and publicity. So, in the manner of *Hello!* or *OK!* today, the weekly *Epoca* paid for Wanda's wedding and secured exclusive coverage.

On the eve of the wedding, the ever-solicitous journalist Menghini advised the family that they should prove Wanda's virginity, just to be sure that there would be no possibility of gossip. This required that the girl be subjected to a gynaecological examination. Wanda cried in protest but was persuaded to go through with it for the benefit of all. The examination was duly carried out by a woman doctor and Wanda's perfect integrity certified. Following this humiliating prelude, Wanda married her carpenter. Menghini acted as a witness.

XV

The Long Arm of the Mafia

During his lengthy investigations, Raffaele Sepe weighed the possible connections between Wilma's fate and the murky world of drugs. Both Anna Maria Caglio and Adriana Bisaccia had touched on drugs, and the report compiled by Colonel Pompei had also alluded to them. Several other witnesses had come forward to say that Wilma had been involved in narcotics-trafficking, one of whom was Piero Pierotti, the migrant worker who had enjoyed a brief moment of notoriety as a witness at the Muto trial. He had testified that he had met Wilma with other low-level pushers. He was later killed in a motor accident. Another was Michele Simola, a Sicilian petty criminal. Simola was so persistent in his assertions that Sepe had a *carabiniere* in civilian dress accompany him unannounced to the Montesi flat. To his surprise, when the man presented himself with a bunch of flowers, Maria Montesi appeared to recognise him and let him into the family apartment.

No intoxicating substances had been found in Wilma's body, although the first autopsy had failed to carry out exhaustive tests, and the second had occurred at such a distance of time as to make them impossible. However, the witnesses suggested that Wilma was not so much a user as an accomplice of drug-dealers. Certainly, if the girl *had* been drawn into a drugs racket in some way, that might explain some of the changes in the last period of her life: her new demeanour, her detachment from her fiancé, her costly new bag and earrings. However, her mother and sister would almost certainly have been aware of something. The closeness of their everyday lives would have made it difficult for her to keep it secret. Might the family even have been complicit? The financial gain for an activity of apparently limited risk might have appealed. At the time drugs did not carry the connotation of human devastation that they acquired in the 1970s. With the deprivations of the war years, opportunism had crept into the life of the lower-middle class and the Montesis, but the family would have been torn between fear for its general respectability and its approval of an activity whose financial rewards were great yet did not appear to compromise Wilma's reputation.

Epoca journalist Luciano Doddoli was convinced of some family connection with narcotics that came via Peppino. He found that Wilma's uncle Giuseppe maintained a flat at Ostia and an office in Via Gaeta. Held in a false name, the latter was used for a variety of business transactions. Doddoli also found that members of the Montesi family had been seen there, including Wilma, Wanda and their aunt Ida. On closer questioning Giuseppe pleaded that he made money on the side by arranging property transactions, like a small-time Montagna – but Doddoli was sure he was distributing drugs.

As for Piccioni and Montagna, there was little evidence to connect either man with narcotics-trafficking. Only Anna Maria Caglio, with her controversial testimony, had pointed her finger at them. She had said that Montagna kept cocaine in his car and that he called his dog Marijuana. But was he more deeply involved? Caglio claimed that Montagna made regular trips to Genoa, Anzio and other ports, implying that most of his illegitimate business was done there. She mentioned his friendships with port masters and coastguards.

The gossip surrounding Piccioni seemed lighter. Some colleagues at the state broadcasting company RAI told

Lieutenant Zinza, Sepe's zealous assistant, that he was known behind his back as *er puzzone* (smelly) on account of his penchant for marijuana. Dope-smoking was associated with the African-American soldiers who had served with the Allies, and Piccioni's fondness for black culture was well known.

Darker stories occasionally came to Sepe's attention. Among the many individuals who approached him was a young priest from the province of Parma, in the north. Don Onnis came forward with a letter that he said an anonymous woman had given him for safe-keeping in May 1953. Since no one had claimed it in the year that followed, he could not resist opening it. He found a detailed reconstruction of the circumstances of the death of Wilma Montesi in which Piccioni and Montagna were named as those responsible. The author had begun her letter: 'When these lines are read I shall be dead. I wish it to be known that I have not died a natural death, but have been done away with by the Marchese Ugo Montagna and Piero Piccioni.' After consulting his bishop, the priest sent the letter and his account of what had occurred to Sepe.

The priest described the mysterious woman as beautiful, red-haired and aged approximately thirty. She had called on him in his sacristy and asked to use his typewriter. After completing the letter, she had sealed it into an envelope and given it to him, with half of an entry ticket to a Florence museum. She asked him to keep the letter for her and to give it up only to a person who could produce the missing half of the ticket. As she turned to leave, the priest asked her name. 'Gianna la Rossa,' (Red Gianna) was the enigmatic reply.

Lieutenant Zinza was detailed to visit Don Onnis in his parish of Bannone di Traversetolo, where he showed him a series of pictures of women in the hope that one of them might be identified as 'Gianna la Rossa'. These included Giobben Giò, Adriana Bisaccia and Anna Maria Caglio. Don Onnis did not recognise them, and the identity of his elegant visitor remained unknown. At no point would anyone be able definitively to put a face or a name to her. For many, Onnis was yet another liar or fantasist, someone who, for reasons of his own, had decided to invent a story – perhaps even writing the letter himself – in order to have his moment of fame on the public stage of the Montesi case. Unusually for a priest, but like many of the protagonists of the case, he was photographed wearing dark glasses. Giancarlo Fusco, a seasoned journalist who specialised in low-life coverage, recognised some truth in his narrative: Parma was the northern operational centre of the drugs trade and a spate of arrests showed that people of all backgrounds had become involved in it.

Left-wing newspapers advanced the hypothesis that 'Gianna la Rossa' could have been Corinna Versolatto. Hers was a name people knew because she had once worked as a coat-check girl at the notorious Piccolo Slam nightclub before it was closed down. This downbeat club, known as a place where drugs could easily be procured, was frequented by almost everyone involved in the case, as well as such personalities as Novella Parigini and Marlon Brando. After it closed in 1952, Versolatto found work in her home city of Trieste as an employee of the military government: she had also become involved with a ring of drug-traffickers. Versolatto died age thirty-five after an overdose of barbiturates. She had a train ticket for Rome in her pocket when her body was found. Among the telephone numbers in her diary were those of Montagna and Piccioni (who was ex-directory). Versolatto was a redhead: she was described as not beautiful in the classical sense but striking and memorable.

Her precise role was unclear. Some suggested she had been a government agent who had infiltrated the drug world and then been exposed. Others thought the contrary, that she was linked to big traffickers and had been placed by them inside the agency in Trieste, a city that remained under international jurisdiction until 1954. It was widely regarded as one of the biggest centres for illegal drugs and it saw a constant struggle between the authorities and criminals. In 1950 the police compiled a list of 130 people there who were engaged in the trade.

The death of Versolatto and of the two men whose bodies had been found earlier on the beaches between Ostia and Torvaianica showed that a big change had occurred in the nature of drug-trafficking – a change that had not been registered publicly. For most Italians in the 1950s, drugs were still seen as exotic – Pittigrilli, one of the most popular writers of the inter-war years, regularly featured narcotics to spice up his novels, one of which was entitled *Cocaina*. His stories were set in Paris, a city where Italians assumed that dope fiends and cocaine addicts could commonly be found. In Italy, the use of hard drugs was still clandestine, associated with bored younger members of the social élite, artists, models and musicians.

The close link between narcotics and organised crime in post-war Italy was related to the growth of the Sicilian Mafia. Subject to repression under Fascism, the families involved skilfully manipulated the American occupation from July 1943 to their advantage. Several family heads were installed as mayors of small towns on account of their standing and lack of Fascist connections. Initially they were supportive of the bandit Salvatore Giuliano's promotion of Sicilian independence, but wiser counsel prevailed and they switched their allegiance to the Christian Democrats, contributing decisively to the massive vote the party received from the island's electorate in 1948. The United States seized the opportunity offered by its close relations with Italy's post-war governments to deport to Italy a series of Italian-born men with convictions for organised crime and drug-trafficking. The American authorities always warned the Italians about the men they were deporting. One Sam (Saverio) Valenti, sent back to Italy in 1947, was described as 'one of the most notorious and persistent drug-traffickers who has come to the attention of the Treasury Department' while Larry (Armando) Pagliaro was dubbed 'a member of the underworld and one of a ring of distributors of narcotic drugs'.

The most famous of these men was Salvatore Lucania, better known as Lucky Luciano, a gangster of the Al Capone and Legs Diamond era. He had been one of the first to abandon drink and cigarettes for drugs. Later the subject of a celebrated film biography by Francesco Rosi, Luciano had been sentenced in 1936 to fifty years in gaol. He was pardoned and released in 1946 ostensibly as a reward for the advice he had offered the US authorities prior to the Allied landing in Sicily in July 1943. In fact it was publicly alleged that he was pardoned by the man who had prosecuted him, Thomas Dewey, because he used his influence to assist the latter's election as governor of the state of New York in 1942. Luciano went first to Cuba, but was expelled after the American Treasury's Bureau of Narcotics found he had resumed his old habits. Then he was deported to Italy where, after a short time in Rome, he settled in Naples and lived a quiet life running a shop selling electrical appliances.

Those men brought with them to Italy know-how about Mafia organisation, trafficking and political influence that was far superior to that of the old fragmented territorial Mafia of Sicily. In particular they understood the lucrative nature of narcotics and the potential role of the Mafia in providing channels for international distribution. Most of the deported Mafia men arrived with considerable amounts of cash and used it to establish innocuous fronts, ostensibly legitimate businesses that could conceal activity in this sphere.

Italy provided fertile terrain for the interpenetration of crime and drugs. In the post-war years, the country was often criticised by the United Nations for its laxity in the matter of drugs. At this time international co-operation to control the illicit trade was being restored. Italy was accused of holding unnecessarily high stocks of narcotics, which were supposedly for medical purposes but sometimes found their way onto the black market.

Part of the problem was that it was one of the few countries to allow the manufacture of heroin by private firms. The government contested UN reports on the situation, but when it was demonstrated beyond all doubt that large quantities of diacetylmorphine were being diverted from factories and wholesale drug houses, it accepted that firmer action was needed.

Rome was central to European drug traffic on account of its geographical position. It was strategically placed at the crossroads of five continents. Opium arrived from North Africa and the Middle East. It was transformed in laboratories in Italy or Marseille into heroin and morphine, then sent out of the country in tennis balls, food cans, petrol tanks and double-bottomed suitcases. The usual carriers were Sicilian-Americans with one foot in both countries. Ships were the conventional means of transport but soon more arrests were being made at Rome's Ciampino airport of passengers carrying illicit substances. For example, in 1949 one Vincent Trupia, who was about to board a TWA flight to New York, was discovered carrying 7.6 kilos of an unspecified 'white powder' found to be a narcotic. In addition, a further 1.2 kilos was hidden on his person. By the early 1950s, Italy was seen as having acquired a role as an aircraft carrier for drugs.

The United States was the main market for narcotics consumption because of the growing phenomenon of heroin addiction among young people in large cities. As a result, it was at the forefront of the international battle against narcotics. The Bureau of Narcotics was sure that much of what found its way onto the market was coming directly from Italy. It never admitted that the deportation of gangsters had been a mistake but such was the scale of its concern that the US Commissioner of Narcotics was in frequent contact with the head of the Italian division of Interpol, Dr Giuseppe Dosi, about clandestine factories in the peninsula. In 1950, he dispatched an agent, Mr Pocoroba, who, he said, 'in an undercover capacity or otherwise, will be able to assist your officials in ferreting out persons in Italy who are instrumental in smuggling narcotic drugs through Italy into the United States'.

Lucky Luciano was subject to extensive surveillance by the American and Italian authorities, as well as a certain degree of media attention. It was never demonstrated that he took any part in crime after his return to Italy, despite the tenacious efforts of the Narcotics Bureau's Charles Siragusa, who played himself in Francesco Rosi's film, and Senator Estes Kefauver, chairman of the US Senate's commission into organised crime, who declared in 1951 that Luciano was the head of the international Mafia. The settled view now is that, while discreet, Luciano did not abandon his old ways. He was an influential figure in the development of narcotics-trafficking, who continued to cultivate links with the Sicilian and American Mafia.

Meanwhile, some drugs remained in Italy. According to official reports, drug use was in decline and in any case was not widespread. The reality was somewhat different, especially in Rome. Cocaine had been used in aristocratic circles since the 1920s and marijuana and synthetic substances were sold under the counter at cafés in the artistic quarter. Trafficking was not heavily punished in Italy and neither the fines nor the prison sentences were remotely intimidating to the powers behind the trade. It was almost only ever the low-level pushers who ended up in the hands of the police, and many were foreigners or petty criminals.

One of the most significant players was Frank 'Three Fingers' Coppola, who had been active in Detroit in the 1930s, later becoming known as the king of the slot machines of Kansas City. Deported from the USA in 1947, he bought a villa at Tor San Lorenzo, not far from Torvaianica, where he set himself up as a gentleman farmer. Basing himself on his experiences in the United States, he built up a social circle of some note and held banquets to which he invited prominent figures from Anzio and the surrounding area, as well as politicians and state officials. The journalist Felice Chilanti, a former Fascist who wrote for the left-wing *Paese Sera* after the war, regarded Coppola as a key figure in the transformation of the Mafia: 'The bosses of the great Mafia of contraband goods became [in the 1950s] also traders in building land and construction entrepreneurs, sometimes using false names,' he argued. Coppola was such a figure, who built up a legitimate profile while retaining control of conventional Mafia activities. According to Chilanti, 'This Mafia band of traffickers in drugs, valuables and cigarettes was really powerful, a true monstrosity in which persons beyond suspicion, in a high position, were already involved.'

Chilanti took the view that the economic activities that revolved around the smuggling and distribution of contraband goods enjoyed some degree of high-level protection, since there was no concerted state action against Mafia activities before the mid-1960s. Officially, Coppola was supposed to be kept under close police surveillance but he had sufficient influence to have transferred elsewhere any local officer who did not meet with his approval. Only once was he caught out. This was in 1952 when a large trunk he sent from Anzio to his associate Serafino Mancuso, containing twenty-five kilos of heroin and several hundred million lire in currency, was intercepted by the Carabinieri. The tip-off, Mafia historian Salvatore Lupo alleges, came from Luciano, with whom he had never enjoyed good relations. At his trial Coppola was sentenced to two years in gaol.

It was to Coppola and his associates that Silvano Muto alluded in his original *Attualità* article when he wrote that 'The beach between Anzio and Torvaianica was frequented by international dope smugglers.' In a second article in the same 8 October 1953 issue, he referred to the recent arrest of the commandant of the port of Anzio. Officially the man had been taken into custody for reasons that had nothing to do

with his work, but Muto alleged it was because of his
involvement with an illegal organisation. In a subsequent article
published in 1954, he said he had never written that Wilma
had died at Capocotta, but 'rather in the area that lies between
Castel Porziano and Torvaianica', a statement that seemed to
suggest he no longer thought the men identified as Mr X and
Mr Y were the only possible culprits. In fact, Coppola was in
gaol at the time of Wilma Montesi's death but this did not
remove suspicion from his associates.

With the entry of the Mafia into the narcotics traffic, drugs
ceased to be simply a chic pastime for the idle rich. They
became a focus of conflict and violence, and a source of
enormous wealth. The distribution of drugs in Rome was run
by a clutch of powerful individuals. For decades, the name
Max Mugnani had been a byword for narcotics in Roman
high society. A Fascist official from the central Italian town of
Cento with close connections to the aviation pioneer Italo
Balbo, he resigned from his positions in the regime in the late
1920s and set himself up at the Hotel Excelsior in the capital,
from where he supplied drugs to the social élite. Through his
relationship with the soubrette Fanny Marchiò, his network
also extended into the entertainment world. Among others,
he supplied Osvaldo Valenti, a popular screen actor widely
known to be an addict. However, Mugnani came unstuck
when he offered cocaine to Queen Wilhelmina of the
Netherlands at the 1935 Venice Film Festival. Banished in
internal exile to the southern region of Puglia, he caused
further trouble by spreading drugs among local socialites.

In 1944, Mugnani pulled off an extraordinary coup when
he was made head of the American pharmaceutical warehouses
in Italy. A more striking case of a fox being appointed to guard
the chickens would be difficult to imagine. Later he resumed
his habitual activities, supplying personalities and the wealthy
in the salons and clubs of the capital. He also operated at lower

levels of society through third parties, according to the testimony of Michele Simola, who cited a Mugnani associate, Armando Amari, in his revelations about how he had come to know Wilma Montesi through drug-dealers. Mugnani continued his activities until June 1956 when he and a group of young men who bore some of the grandest surnames in the capital were arrested in a narcotics raid on the Victor nightclub, located on the Via Emilia. In the first trial Mugnani, by now well into his sixties, was sentenced to four years and ten months in gaol. On appeal, he was acquitted for lack of proof.

At a practical level, distribution was mostly entrusted to a network of ostensibly respectable people. It was estimated that around two hundred were involved in pushing or carrying drugs in Rome. They included waiters, hotel porters, doormen and nightclub staff, as well as smart women who would arouse no suspicion and could move around the city easily without the fear of being stopped by police. It was to this milieu – or, rather, to the criminal flotsam and jetsam that hovered on its outer perimeter – that several witnesses who mentioned Wilma Montesi belonged.

Only two months after he had opened his investigation Sepe decided not to pursue the matter of the narcotics trade: the numerous testimonies offered by people with some supposed link to it took him too far from Wilma. Despite this, it remained a possible trail, a pathway into the labyrinth of Roman society. The question of Mafia influence hung over the case and was shaped by the fact that not only Montagna but several of the public officials involved were Sicilian. Montagna's rapid progress from poor upper-class boy of the Sicilian backwaters to prince of drawing rooms and ministries could not have happened, some claimed, without powerful friends. Had he been sent to Rome as an emissary of the Mafia? Indeed there was evidence that Montagna's family were mixed up in Mafia matters. His older brother Diego, according to the Pompei report, had 'previous convictions and was associated with the Sicilian underworld'.

The Turin newspaper *La Stampa* claimed that Montagna was a Mafia go-between. It pointed out that his lawyer, Girolamo Bellavista, had defended a Mafia boss, Don Calogero Vizzini, and had acted as intermediary between the police and elements of the band of Salvatore Giuliano sympathetic to the Mafia. These included Gaspare Pisciotta, the Sicilian bandit who would betray his leader and meet a mysterious death in gaol. Bellavista was a well-known figure, a Sicilian who had once been a Liberal Member of Parliament, and one of the group who rented Capocotta. Such insinuations provoked angry responses in some quarters of the southern press, which objected to what were regarded as anti-Sicilian prejudices. Bellavista himself intervened to denounce the threats and vendettas that stood behind the events of the Montesi case.

In the 1950s, the very existence of the Mafia was disputed by many Sicilians, including public figures and intellectuals, who tried to paint the entire phenomenon as a figment of the northern imagination. They acknowledged that there were 'men of honour' who played a special role in some areas of the island and that on occasion they had been drawn into illegal activity. But the idea that there was a criminal organisation with tentacles that spread though Sicilian society and onto the mainland was rejected. Prominent men, such as lawyers and parliamentarians, who found themselves accused of having criminal connections, always vociferously denied any involvement in or knowledge of 'Mafia' activities.

Montagna had arrived in Rome in 1938, at a time when the Mafia was on the defensive. His way of operating was certainly mafioso. He shared the Sicilian attitude of complete distrust in lawful government and he did business through personal relations. Like Coppola, and Michele Greco, a Mafia boss who would achieve prominence in the 1970s, he enjoyed cultivating and entertaining important people. Like them, he affected a virile swagger. Among his favourite expressions were the oft-repeated 'My fatherland is the pocket wallet' and 'Before they take me, I'll shoot down twenty of them.' He was also active in one area of business that was subject to Mafia penetration, namely construction, a notorious field for the recycling and reinvestment of criminal funds. If he was only prominent in this area by chance then his position is likely to have changed as the Christian Democrats occupied the state and the Mafia began to assert its influence at all levels. At this time, if not before, Montagna, by virtue of his background and interests, would inevitably have been drawn into relations with those who represented Mafia interests in the power élite of the capital. He might even have become a 'man of honour' himself.

If Montagna was a Mafia man, he belonged to an 'enterprise syndicate' rather than a 'power syndicate'. This distinction, first formulated by Alan Block in *East Side, West Side*, a study of organised crime in New York, is crucial to an understanding of how a bourgeois Mafia linked to economic activities and politics developed as a distinct, if not entirely separate, entity from the traditional territorial Mafia, which saw protection as its main activity. Repentant mafioso Tommaso Buscetta stated in 1986 that Mafia families sometimes gave permission to members to conduct economic activities independently, especially in new areas, such as gambling, prostitution and drugs, as well as legitimate business. Some of the deported Americans, like Coppola, who had maintained close links with Partinico, his town of origin in Sicily, straddled both forms. In other cases, however, the link to conventional Mafia families was more remote.

Montagna's colourful private life and sexually predatory nature did not fit easily with Italian Mafia practice at the time. Mafia men were generally reserved and low profile. To prevent betrayal they were expected to maintain orderly personal lives. Many had no understanding of drugs and some opposed them.

Montagna's expansiveness and opportunism were unusual traits. If he was a mafioso, he was an example of the novel phenomenon for Italy: the Mafia of enterprise. The only old-style Mafia boss who seized the limelight in a comparable way was Giuseppe Genco Russo, a family head whose taste for publicity in the era of the film star led to him being mockingly dubbed 'Gina Lollobrigida' in fake homage to the actress.

Montagna was especially vulnerable to any suggestion that he had an interest in drugs-trafficking because the Capocotta estate was strategically situated on a strip of coast known to be used for receiving and distributing such consignments. Coppola's estate was nearby. The Coast Guard stopped boats and made arrests from time to time, but these were more symbolic efforts than a systematic attempt to stamp out the trade. Anna Maria Caglio had alleged that a Mafia boss by the name of Bembo was Montagna's superior and that Montagna had spoken of this man, with an air of nostalgia, as a figure of the good Mafia of old, a man who viewed the world from a chair where he sat in the sun and enjoyed widespread respect. When *Epoca* sent two journalists to Sicily to check this story they found that Bembo existed and, furthermore, that he was implicated in drug-smuggling.

But, as ever, few of these allegations stuck to Montagna, and he continued to live confidently in the full glare of the Italian media. To general astonishment, in August 1955 the ever-resourceful marchese announced plans for a feature film based on the Montesi case. A magazine printed pictures of him swimming and horse riding in rehearsals with an unknown young woman named Gianna Alfieri, whom he had chosen to cast as Caglio. A professional actress, Pina Bottin, was to play Adriana Bisaccia. The purpose of this astonishing project, the script of which Montagna had apparently written himself, was to show that the notorious Capocotta parties, far from being scandalous orgies, were simply innocent fun. In one scene he planned to shoot, the hunt is in full cry along the beach when it happens across Wilma's body. In Montagna's version of events, the chance discovery leads to Muto's accusations, which are aimed at discrediting the entire ruling class. Montagna told journalists that the film would include a triumphant restaging of his own exit from Regina Coeli prison; in this film version, unlike shabby reality, he would be mobbed by crowds of well-wishers. In the final scene, he would climb into his car and drive to Pompeii, where he would fall on his knees in gratitude before a painting of the Madonna at the Sanctuary of the Holy Virgin of the Rosary. He proclaimed that the film would go into production as soon as the threat of incrimination had been removed. Alida Valli and Piero Piccioni, he hoped, could be persuaded to play themselves in his drama.

By mid-1954 international interest in the Montesi affair had increased. Jenny Nicholson, a *Picture Post* journalist, went to see Montagna on the proposed set of his film. He greeted her with a cheery 'Hullo, baybee!' while the German photographer who accompanied her was met with a Nazi salute and a tasteless 'Heil Hitler!' She found him a disconcerting presence: 'His body, his face and voice are as nondescript as his over-furnished apartment,' she wrote. 'But everything was concentrated in his extraordinary black-brown eyes, which were luminous even in the shadows of a shuttered room.' She confessed to the magazine's readers that he sent a shiver down her spine.

Whatever can have made him think of producing a film? The answer is that the prince of the government antechamber was at a low ebb. Announcing this outrageously bold and egotistical project was his way of standing up to his accusers, of taking control.

XVI

Dr Sepe Reports

Raffaele Sepe concluded the main part of his investigation in November 1954 and delivered the mass of evidence he had gathered to the Procurator's Office for it to be evaluated formally. By this time Angelo Sigurani had been replaced as procurator general by Leonardo Giocoli, who, with his deputies Marcello Scardia and Alfonso Colonnesi, worked through thousands of documents, recorded interviews, reports and notes until the middle of March 1955. The three men found that there was a case to answer and prepared a report that requested that Piero Piccioni, Ugo Montagna, Saverio Polito, the Capocotta guards and some of the minor characters be sent for trial. The matter was then handed back to Sepe to draft his final conclusions. This cumbersome procedure was intended to allow the investigating magistrate to have the final word within the framework established by the procurators. Sepe worked through the report and drafted his own concluding document, the *sentenza di rinvio*, or 'charge sentence', which was finally deposited on 10 July 1955.

This was the crowning moment of his long trawl through the mysteries of the Montesi case, his encounter with almost every corner of Roman society. The meticulous investigator had been at work for sixteen months and in that time he had become a popular figure. He was sometimes applauded when he was spotted in public and magazines had written him up as an honest opponent of privilege and corruption. In fact, Raffaele Sepe was nothing of the sort. Born into an established Roman family, he was not naturally inclined to set himself against vested interests. More than anything, it was his physical bulk that endowed him with a jovial, pleasing image. In photographs he appeared cordial and friendly, an approachable man who went about his business with diligence and aplomb. In the course of his enquiries he had looked into a variety of matters including Wilma Montesi's background and family, the issue of her train trip to Ostia, the question of how she had come to be found at Torvaianica, and the circumstances of her death. He had explored Montagna's affairs and activities at Capocotta, and looked into Piccioni's personal life and alibi. He had listened at length to Anna Maria Caglio and the tales she had to tell of her experiences in the capital and elsewhere. He had done his best to be thorough, even welcoming into his office an endless parade of dubious witnesses in the hope that one might hold a key to the mystery. Together, he and his faithful assistant Zinza had turned over almost every plausible stone in the case.

It was not known at the time that Sepe had faced considerable attempts to thwart his progress with the case. A few politicians made snide comments and some officials briefed against him but interior ministry documents held at the Central State Archive reveal the way he was treated. As we have seen, the police unit at the Palace of Justice kept a close watch on comings and goings to his office and his movements as he went about his investigation. With their ears pressed to the door, police agents compiled reports that were channelled back to their superiors in the ministry, where, in 1955, Giulio Andreotti was the minister. Sepe discovered what was going on and took measures to disguise the identities of witnesses and collaborators. He showed no sign of being rattled, though he must have known that the surveillance showed just how politically incendiary the case was. Ministers and senior justice officials made life difficult for him and tried to turn colleagues as well as the press against him. He was accused of deliberately prolonging the inquiry in the hope that Scelba would lose power. It is easy to imagine that this sort of behaviour was part of an establishment cover-up – but most of those engaged in these attacks were mainly concerned with discrediting the Communists.

There was particular irritation concerning the relationships Sepe enjoyed with the press. Although he always maintained that he was pursuing his enquiries with discretion, Sepe was thought to have a series of contacts in the newspapers. A police report of October 1954 noted that his cousin, Arnaldo Gelardini, happened to be the Rome correspondent of *Il Corriere della Sera* and also worked for several magazines. A journalist from the leftist paper *Il Paese* had visited him at his home for three hours, while he had received others in his office. Calls from his office had been made to newspapers and he had personally supplied *Il Messaggero* with photographs of himself. Two journalists from the Communist daily *L'Unità* were permanently stationed outside his office.

However, leaks did not only come from the magistrate himself. Antonio Ghirelli, at that time a journalist on *Paese Sera*, the evening sister paper of *Il Paese*, later revealed that, in the early days at least, 'the most succulent pieces of news on the scandal were given to us by Fanfani through the intermediary of a colonel of the Carabinieri'.

Despite the campaign of harassment and denigration, Sepe remained undeterred. The report he compiled was wide-ranging and extremely thorough, detailing every step of his investigation. The three hundred plus pages of his findings demolished earlier official verdicts on Wilma's death and, in doing so, focused on three issues: Wilma's disappearance; Piccioni's possible involvement in her death, including his alibi and associated medical evidence; and the Capocotta estate.

Sepe had called in family members on several occasions and had tried to extract more information from them, some detail, some clue that might have connected the young woman to one or more of the witnesses. In this, frustratingly, he never succeeded.

Thus he could do no more than report the well-established views of the family about Wilma's reserved character, her attachment to the home and her habit of dressing well. He did record, however, that the family had conceded she had changed her habits in the last month of her life, after the transfer of her fiancé. She had adopted 'the habit of going out more often without other family members, almost every day between around 17.30 and 19.30. This behaviour did not give rise to suspicion but was considered a necessity given the girl's temperament and love of long walks.' But enquiries into her afternoon pursuits yielded nothing. Neighbours and acquaintances were not able to shed any light on them. They only reported that there had been some heated family arguments in the household.

Wilma's trip to Ostia was treated in the report as linked to the family's concern for appearances. Sepe noted that the Montesi family did not at first mention this possibility and only latched onto it 'with extreme tenacity' after the government employee Rosa Passarelli had visited them. What appealed to them most about Passarelli's testimony was that she made clear that Wilma had travelled *alone* to Ostia – that is, not in male company. Yet Sepe found that Passarelli's description of the woman she had seen did not correspond exactly to Wilma. She was described as being aged between twenty-eight and thirty, whereas Wilma was just twenty-one. Her hairstyle was not the same and, when he spoke to her, Passarelli's recollection of the woman's clothing was vague.

The report discounted suicide: there was no motive. Wilma had gone out with her keys and, in the sole new detail he had extracted from her sister, Wanda, had left a pair of knickers to soak in soapy water. As for the fiancé, it was deemed quite possible that the girl had broken off the engagement following his transfer, even if this decision had not been expressed to Giuliani directly. However, Sepe thought that perhaps the family knew this but weren't telling, since the policeman had been treated coldly when he had come to Rome to take part in enquiries after Wilma's death.

The part of the report dealing with the new autopsy stated that the likely time of death was the evening of 10 April. It could not be established whether or not the girl had taken or been given any narcotic substances, given the amount of time that had elapsed since her death. The possibility could not be excluded. In any event the three authors of the autopsy report took the view that it was likely Wilma was unconscious when she drowned since she had drowned slowly. There were a few bruises on her body – on her left arm, her left thigh and right leg. These were deemed to have been caused before death when the body was being lifted or transported. It seemed, in brief, that her unconscious body had been abandoned in a hurry.

On the question of whether Wilma was leading a double life, Sepe was forced to admit that no hard evidence had come to light to show that she was linked to 'environments marked by secret vices and high personalities'. He therefore discounted the testimonies of Bisaccia, Simola and others. By all accounts her life had been peaceful. The only hypothesis that remained therefore was the following: 'that Wilma on the afternoon of 9 April left home to meet a person with whom she was conducting an affectionate relationship, and that her death by drowning was connected to a loss of consciousness, following which she was abandoned on the beach at Torvaianica'. The fact that she left behind the photograph of Giuliani that she usually carried in her wallet 'suggests that she was meeting a person to whom she did not intend to reveal her links with her fiancé', regardless of whether or not the engagement had been broken off. He noted that she never mentioned her afternoon outings in her letters to Giuliani, although she talked about other daily events.

Wilma's sister Wanda, the report stated, was 'always reticent', even though she probably knew something. Sepe concluded that Wilma had started seeing someone. Her happiness on 9 April, singing along to the radio, suggested that this was so. Where she went on 9 April, and where she was the following day, was unknown.

This left the matter of who the man was that Wilma had been going to meet. To Sepe, this was none other than Piero Piccioni. In reaching this crucial conclusion, he gave weight to the testimony of the Torvaianica witnesses, Jole Manzi and Anna Minniti, who claimed they had seen the couple together in the area on 10 April, and to the mechanic Mario Piccinini, who had spontaneously gone to the police station on seeing Wilma's picture in the papers to report that the woman in the car he had helped free from the sand in early March 1953 closely resembled the dead girl. Later he said the driver he had spoken to looked very like Piccioni. This was taken as evidence that Wilma had visited the location on at least one previous occasion. But Sepe found no witness who would state that the female with Prince Maurice of Hesse at Capocotta on 8 or 9 April was Wilma. Despite the ambiguity of his position, there was no basis for charging him.

Sepe deemed Piccioni's behaviour to be highly suspicious and his alibis to be of dubious credibility. Piccioni appeared not to have done anything much to combat rumours about his involvement in the girl's death, issuing writs that were then not translated into court actions. The musician claimed that his illness exonerated him because he was indisposed on the days in question. Yet it was not clear at exactly what time he had returned to his father's house in Rome or if he had stayed there without ever going out. It was only known that he had arrived back in the capital at around two thirty in the afternoon of 9 April and that he was suffering from tonsillitis. He had been in Amalfi with Alida Valli since 3 April, as a guest at Carlo Ponti's villa. The couple had left early on the morning of 9 April, when Piccioni had accompanied the actress by car to Sorrento, whence she had taken the ferry to Capri. On 10 April Valli had returned to Rome: she claimed to have telephoned her lover at around ten thirty that evening and found that he was confined to bed. Piccioni had produced a doctor's prescription to prove his illness.

But the validity of his alibi was undermined by the fact that, on 9 March 1955, long after the conclusion of his investigation, Sepe received an anonymous note informing him that the prescription the musician had produced had been falsified. The tip-off, it turned out, came from the recently abandoned wife of Piccioni's lawyer, Primo Augenti. Herself a law graduate who had followed the case in detail, she knew that the date on the prescription had been modified, a detail that her husband had covered up and that had escaped Sepe's attention. Valli's own plausibility had come into question too when she had been forced to admit that she had indeed received that telephone call in a bar in Venice, in which she had discussed the Wilma Montesi case with Piccioni, despite having initially denied it.

Sepe also detected confusion in the evidence of the doctors and nurses who attended the Piccioni residence. Some had been summoned to Attilio Piccioni, who was also unwell. It transpired that, even though he had been ordered to bed, he had attended a meeting at five thirty p.m. on 10 April and another the following day. By the same token his son, too, could have left the house.

When it came to Ugo Montagna, the report showed that Sepe had been persuaded by the testimony of Anna Maria Caglio, the marchese's jilted mistress. 'The assertions of the woman have always been firm and well supported and repeated with absolute résolution even in the face-to-face confrontation with her lover, while the justifications offered by Montagna appeared vague and unconvincing, often little more than denials of the most salient facts.' Montagna had intervened in the case to help his friend Piccioni. He had mobilised his friendships and contacts among the police to ensure that the case would be steered away from him and action taken to stop press speculation. Chief of police Pavone and police commissioner Polito were the key figures here. Montagna's friendship with Pavone had been established and had led to the man being transferred to another post. Polito, too, had been exposed as having a personal link to the monied marchese. He had taken an unusually close interest in the case and had failed to promote the pursuit of full enquiries. Indeed he had deviated them: his reconstruction of the events leading to Wilma's death was preconceived rather than the product of proper police work. Sepe discovered that there was a further connection between the two men. One of Polito's friends was a certain Vincenzo Fede, a former police officer who had been a close ally and business partner of Montagna for some twenty years. Montagna's own background was far less presentable than his brilliant present life would suggest. Sepe had received Pompei's report directly from its author and accepted his findings about Montagna's unsavoury past and family connections to organised crime.

Despite the conviction of some journalists that Wilma's uncle Giuseppe had something to answer for, Sepe determined that he had not been involved in her death. The man had few positive qualities, and had run up considerable debts, but he did not appear to be implicated.

By producing such a dramatic outcome, so markedly at variance with earlier previous official conclusions about the case – either suicide or accidental death – Sepe set his face firmly against the legal and political establishments. For months he had been regarded with suspicion and now, it seemed, he had confirmed why. Some saw him as a Communist, others as an exhibitionist who had fallen in love with his public image as a fearless investigator. For years to come Giulio Andreotti would repeatedly imply that the magistrate had been swayed by gossip, and in particular by the seductive minx Caglio. He even hinted that Sepe had asked him for a job in government in July 1955 when the magistrate came to visit him while he was on holiday in the Roman hills at Grottaferrata. But Andreotti, as a former lieutenant of De Gasperi, was closer to Piccioni senior than he was to Fanfani, the emerging strongman of the second phase of Christian Democratic rule. As a Rome-born politician who had forged a network of interlocutors and allies in the Vatican and the archipelago of Catholic institutions in Rome, he had had some dealings with Montagna. He also knew Anna Maria Caglio's father. So, for these reasons, he had every interest to play the whole case down as a political manoeuvre. It was true that Sepe was not without his flaws, but he was not the malleable careerist depicted by Andreotti, a politician so Machiavellian that, later in his long career, he would acquire the nickname 'Beelzebub'.

Despite the support they still had from their friends in politics and the state, the three men on whom the glare of the inquiry had been focused were now committed for trial. Piccioni was charged with materially abandoning Wilma Montesi to a slow death in shallow water. Montagna was accused of being an accessory to her death and of having sought to pervert the course of justice. The third accused, Saverio Polito, was also committed on the latter charge. He was said to have favoured the cover-up by embracing the discredited theory of the foot-bathing and blocking other lines of enquiry in the crucial weeks following discovery of the body.

The reactions of the men to their committal for trial reflected their different temperaments. Montagna posed for photographs with his elderly father at his Faiano Romano castle and even wrote an article in which he proclaimed that he was 'innocent like Christ'. He declared stiffly that he had complete faith in the justice system. He could hardly have said otherwise. Ideally, he would have returned to his own world. Yet, once he had been brought into the open, he turned into a showman. On the day Procurator Giocoli and his deputies announced there was a case to answer, 15 March 1955, he concocted a classic spoiler. He made sure he was photographed in a run-down street near the Vatican in the company of the Regina Coeli prison chaplain, Father Luigi Cefalone, making a gift of money to a homeless child of six who had written to him while he was in gaol. To some degree, this was a response to the harassment he had experienced from the press as he tried to resume his usual socialising on the Via Veneto. Like a petulant star, he lashed out at the photographers who followed him on his nocturnal pursuits. They even snapped him once in the proximity of curvaceous Roman film star Silvana Pampanini. On this occasion the marchese could not resist a beaming smile. Like a pantomime villain, he played on his image of 'the man you love to hate'. His plans for the feature film were part of this strategy too. Meanwhile, no one seemed to mind that the legitimacy of his title had been challenged. Everyone addressed him as 'Marchese' just the same. And with his well-known expertise in the matter of young women, he was even invited to act as a judge at beauty contests.

Within weeks, Montagna's friendly demeanour had dissolved. After previously leaning on his friends, he now resorted to blackmail to scare those acquaintances and collaborators who were keeping their distance. He penned an article, entitled *Le mie prigioni* (My Prisons), which borrowed a title from a celebrated nineteenth-century Italian patriot Silvio Pellico, in which he announced that he was going to publish his memoirs. The cover of the weekly *Settimo Giorno* carried a picture of a beaming Montagna holding a mock-up of his book, which bore the title *The Memoirs of a Forgetful Man*. It would be the story of his life, he declared, in which no detail would be hidden. The one-thousand-page volume would contain revelations about six or seven thousand people. Everyone would be named, save his lovers, he added, with mock gallantry. Its aim was simply to tell the truth, he said. Lest anyone were to suspect him of cashing in on his notoriety, he promised that a share of the profits would go to the homeless. Needless to say, the book was never published. Evidently some had paid him to keep their names out of it rather than risk ignominy by telling Montagna to 'publish and be damned'.

With or without influence, Montagna knew enough about some powerful people to be too dangerous to abandon. Yet he was not the man he once was. He had accumulated debts, and legal action had led to the confiscation of some of his property. It was not just the Montesi case that dogged him. Certainly it had made it difficult for him to conduct his business, but ways of doing business were changing fast. Montagna had forged a network that had brought him into contact with the old notables who had run the Christian Democrats in the first phase of the post-war period. His aristocratic title bought him credit with a generation still impressed by such things. Yet the notables – De Gasperi, Piccioni, Scelba and others – were rapidly being eclipsed by an aggressive new grouping of political entrepreneurs. Montagna was on the verge of being left high and dry.

The other two accused behaved rather differently. Polito sank into depression and refused to leave his home. Piccioni did his best to disappear and issued no statement at all.

Montagna and Piccioni were men from different backgrounds, of different ages and different interests. People continued to wonder what could have brought them together. Some quarters of the press murmured about nocturnal raids on bars and clubs but no further details were offered.

In reality, it was not hard to work out that Montagna and Piccioni shared a taste for illicit and dangerous pleasures. Their

Rome was not at all that of the shoeshines and bicycle thieves who dominated the post-war cinema image of the city. Neither was it the sacred city that Pius XII was determined to reconsecrate to Christ. It was on the one hand a tantalising city of ministries, palaces, fashionable restaurants and private clubs frequented by only the best people. On the other, it was a world of cellar bars, brothels and drug dens where the habitués were more likely to be addicts, pushers, criminals, existentialists, prostitutes and models than politicians, state officials and senior clerics. Rome was a city where hypocrisy was routine and arrogance taken for granted.

As the son of a government minister, Piccioni was more securely a member of the new establishment, but he lacked two things that were Montagna's speciality: ready money and an unrivalled protective web of contacts and allies. Piccioni declared blandly that he had been introduced to Montagna by the nephew of a monsignor at a large gathering some time in 1946 or 1947. The basis of their friendship – which both men initially denied on account of its compromising nature – was the ability to provide things denied to the other. When Piccioni ran into trouble he turned to Montagna for help, just as Montagna relied on Piccioni to provide access to important people and new spheres.

That there might have been something suspicious or illicit about their association was thrown sharply into relief when Tazio Secchiaroli was given the chance to score a second major scoop. By this time he was well known and had become an acquaintance of Anna Maria Caglio. A photograph taken by a fellow news photographer, Attilio Porcari, shows him dancing with her one evening. Wearing his usual creased suit, his camera still slung over his shoulder, he looks at her, smiling, and she beams back at him. The relationship of complicity the two established was a forerunner of the sort of staged conflicts and faked spontaneity that would come to characterise many paparazzi shots of the stars a little later in the decade.

There was nothing staged, however, about the image that Secchiaroli was now about to take. Following a tip from an anonymous source, the photographer sent his young assistant Velio Cioni to stake out Piccioni's pad in Via Acherusio. After two days spent lurking in the horseshoe-shaped road, Cioni saw Montagna drive up in a Fiat 1100 saloon. A few minutes later, Piccioni furtively emerged, wearing dark glasses, and invited the older man to join him in his own car. The pair drove off, tailed at a distance by Cioni on his scooter. When they reached the sports stadium, they pulled over in a deserted dead-end street and began to confer animatedly. Evidently they had something to talk about that they did not wish to entrust to the telephone. They had previously admitted knowing each other but, even after a picture appeared that showed them together on a jaunt to London, they had pretended they were mere acquaintances. Clearly there was more to it than that.

Cioni dashed to a bar and called Secchiaroli, who leaped into a car and was at the location within minutes. When he arrived, the two men were still deep in conversation. Spotting him, Piccioni started his engine and stamped his foot on the accelerator. However, the photographer knew that the road had a single exit so he positioned his own vehicle to block Piccioni's escape. As the car headed back in his direction, he advanced towards the two men, his camera at the ready. So angry was Piccioni at the unexpected trap that, without thinking, he attempted to run down the photographer. Secchiaroli, sure that he would be able to sell the pictures to a weekly, stood his ground, raised his camera and seized his chance to get five or six revealing shots of the irate and flustered pair as their car skidded to avoid him, tyres screaming, and veered away into the blazing sunshine.

XVII

The Venice Trial

When the Montesi trial was finally convened in January 1957, four years after Wilma's death, it was not in Rome. The Communists had whipped public opinion into a frenzy, and the highest Italian Court of Appeal, the Court of Cassation, had decided it would not be possible for Piccioni, Montagna and Polito to receive a fair trial in the capital. Instead, it was scheduled to take place in Venice, despite the objections of the Catholic patriarch of the city, Angelo Roncalli, the future Pope John XXIII. Roncalli was fully apprised of the sleazy underbelly of Roman life that the case had brought to light and he didn't want it contaminating his historic city.

The long-awaited Montesi trial would, it was hoped, finally determine whether or not those who had been accused of causing and covering up the death of Wilma Montesi were guilty or innocent. The trial would also establish whether post-war Italy was run by a secretive, powerful and corrupt élite or whether it was an open society capable of confronting its demons. In anticipation of revelations, or at least confirmation of some of the stories and allegations that had been in circulation for several years, the press de-camped *en masse* to the lagoon city. Many of the journalists who had been following the case since 1953 took the six-hour train journey from Rome and booked into the city's hotels. They were joined by numerous photographers. In addition, the foreign correspondents from international newspapers arrived for what was expected to be a carnival of lurid tales and bizarre characters. In the icy weather at the start of the year, the city buzzed with out-of-season excitement.

The Montesi family had been turned into public property. Some of its members, notably Rodolfo, were very uncomfortable with this. They had found some comfort in a new ritual: every Sunday, they took the tram to the Verano cemetery to pay their respects to Wilma. They arrived in Venice stony-faced in heavy overcoats but evidently united in facing what would be an ordeal. Maria was heard to comment that she had never imagined she would return to the city of her honeymoon in such circumstances.

The role of the media had been controversial. They had turned the case into a long-running scandal, fed by revelations that were often of a dubious nature. They had also done what the authorities had failed to do: they had investigated the background to the case, endeavoured to find out more about what had happened to the tragic Wilma and to identify where guilt lay. Significantly the driving force behind press attention was not the left-wing papers like *Paese Sera* or *L'Unità*, although both of these played a crucial role, or the Rome titles that covered the case as a local story, but the weekly illustrated magazines that had turned it into a visual feast and a macabre soap opera. Almost without exception they were published in Milan by large corporations. They used scandal in an industrial way, not to score political points but to increase circulation. The return they expected was economic. As business, entertainment or politics, the Montesi affair had turned into the biggest show of the decade.

As soon as the court convened, the media circus was reanimated. The fact that the outcome was so unpredictable was a major factor in their interest. Lawyers for Piccioni and

Montagna had gone on the warpath in the lead-up to the trial, preparing the ground for their courtroom strategy by attacking Anna Maria Caglio and others. Meanwhile, leading witnesses and the accused were stalked by the paparazzi. Minor figures reacted to their moment of celebrity with everything from delight to weary resignation. Those who escaped the camera's eye on the street would be snapped secretly by wily photographers as they sat in the courtroom. All eyes were on Piccioni and Montagna, who were staying at the Hotel Danieli, one of the most luxurious in the city. After appearing on the first day in a dapper Prince-of-Wales check suit, Montagna was only sporadically present in court. Piccioni, by contrast, arrived wearing a sober but fashionably cut suit, and sat quietly through every session, returning from Rome each week for the hearings, which were held between Wednesdays and Saturdays.

The Tribunal of Venice formed the imposing setting for the trial. The moderately sized courtroom was located in a large old building called Fabbriche Nuove, not far from the Rialto Bridge. The layout of the court was conventional. The presiding judge and his two colleagues sat behind a table on a raised platform; to the left there was a rostrum for the public prosecutor, and to the right, the witness's chair and seating for the accused. Tables facing the judges were occupied by the legal teams, and behind them the massed ranks of up to a hundred journalists. Finally, standing at the back, two hundred members of the public followed the proceedings. Often they rumbled noisily and shouted encouragement or corrections to witnesses.

Francesco Carnelutti, aged seventy-nine, was Piccioni's godfather and his leading counsel, while Montagna had appointed his fellow Sicilian, Girolamo Bellavista. Flanking him were the lawyers Vasalli and Augenti. For Carnelutti, perhaps the most famous, and certainly the most experienced, criminal lawyer in Italy, it would be the final case of a long and generally distinguished career. The prosecution was led by Cesare Palmintieri, a plump and voluble young man of limited experience and unlimited ambition. While respectful of the authority of the judge, Mario Tiberi, a man of tolerant disposition, with clipped moustache and military bearing, the defence teams adopted a very aggressive attitude. They were prepared to attack Sepe's investigation and the Pompei report and to question the credibility of every witness whose testimony pointed towards a guilty verdict. It did little to endear them to the locals who gathered outside.

The court would go over Sepe's reconstruction of events in detail. Every witness who had come forward since 1953, with virtually the sole exception of poor, disturbed Adriana Bisaccia, was heard at length. Gatekeepers, magicians, servants, police chiefs, civil servants, drug-dealers and journalists all took their turn on the stand, as did the accused.

The first of the three to do so was Piccioni, who was interrogated about his movements in the days from 9 April 1953. Speaking in a quiet, lisped voice, in a marked Roman accent, this pale, slightly stooped man addressed the lawyers and the presiding judge as his equals. He was neither intimidated nor deferential. His aim was to remove himself from the entire context of the accusations. His approach, however, was infused with complacency. Piccioni described his tonsillitis, his drive at speed from Sorrento to Rome, the medical visits he had received and the treatments he was prescribed. For ordinary people, a home visit by a doctor was a rarity. The minister's son, by contrast, had apparently received attention worthy of a far more serious condition. No fewer than five people, including three doctors, had attended him as he lay ill. When he was questioned about his symptoms, however, the accused himself was unable to recall the precise details. Oddly, he had not even mentioned his illness several days after his recovery when a woman journalist from *Il Popolo* had warned him about the rumours that concerned him. His memory of events seemed to fluctuate, according to convenience.

Piccioni insisted that he had never set eyes on Wilma, even though he frequently drove down Via Tagliamento to reach his apartment and had occasionally walked along it. Yet, in the course of his testimony, he admitted in the vaguest possible way that he might well have spoken to Valli about her: 'I don't deny it. It's perfectly possible, but I don't remember. Maybe I told some friends about what was happening to me at that time.' As for his friendships, he admitted to knowing Montagna well: he had spoken on various occasions to him on the phone and had been to Capocotta, although not since 1949. Meanwhile, Tommaso Pavone, the chief of police, was an old family friend, but Piccioni had never met Saverio Polito, the former police commissioner.

Suddenly the judge asked him if he had known Corinna Versolatto, the dead redhead who had been mixed up in narcotics.

'I've never heard of her,' responded the accused.

'Your telephone number, which does not appear in the Rome telephone directory, was found in this woman's notebook. Who do you think can have given it to her?'

'I don't know her. Certainly not me, because the first time I heard of her was from the Judge of Instruction.'

The musician also strenuously denied calling on Pavone on 29 April, the date Anna Maria Caglio insisted she had sat outside in Montagna's car while the two men went to see him at the Viminale Palace. Piccioni said he had seen the police chief for the first time on 5 May to complain about the allusion to 'pigeons' that had appeared in a satirical weekly. He had arrived, he said, at eleven a.m. with a copy of the paper in hand. Then he had gone a second time ten days later and had coincidentally found Montagna sitting in the antechamber to Pavone's office.

Over the course of the trial, Piccioni returned to the stand twice. Otherwise he sat silently, taking notes. He was reserved, never betraying the slightest emotion even during several heated exchanges between lawyers and witnesses. His conduct came most sharply under scrutiny when the doctors who had treated him were called to testify. Sepe had taken note of the anomalies in the prescriptions and alterations to the dates on which they were issued that had come to his attention, but the doctors had explanations for everything: one prescription for the accused's father had been mistakenly included and another had been altered due to a simple error of date. Nevertheless something still smelt fishy. It was striking that the medics were all friends of the family.

Seven other people, nurses, maids and a butler, who were all members of his father's staff, testified that Piccioni had been confined to bed. Their sheer number gave the impression that the young man had been under constant guard and had never left his bed – but no one could testify that he had not been out. Although it had not been asked of them, the doctors were eager to vouchsafe for Piccioni's good name. Only one, Professor Giuseppe Caronia, the fifth and last to visit him, casually remarked, 'As for Piero, the only thing you could hold against him is the disorder of his life, but that can be explained by the fact that he is an artist.'

Piccioni did not come over as likeable. He appeared to treat public officials as private factotums, there to take his orders. When he arrived back at Via della Conciliazione on 9 April, his first action had been to call his father's secretary and ask him to arrange medical appointments rather than make the calls himself. When the rumours started to circulate about him, he did not consult a lawyer. Rather, he claimed that he went straight to see Pavone, another family friend, to ask him to do something to counter them. This first meeting took place on 5 May, he said, and a second was held, with Montagna present, on 15 May. This high-handed behaviour gave the court an insight into the easy access to power that the son of a politician could secure.

The retired former police commissioner Saverio Polito, who had initially directed enquiries into Wilma's death, was next on the stand. Old and embittered, he had come to Venice with his wife. Struggling to negotiate the steps with his walking stick, he had neither the detached air of Piccioni nor the pride of Montagna. The heavily built old policeman had never imagined that he would finish his long career in the dock. A broken man with sagging jowls, he wore his war-invalid medal on his dark jacket and repeatedly complained, in a heavy southern accent, that Sepe had subjected him to eighteen hours of humiliating interrogation. Accused of promoting a cover-up, Polito said that he had merely been following what he had taken to be orders. He had been asked by Pavone to look into the accusations that were circulating against Piccioni and he had responded by taking steps to exclude him from all investigations.

This alone was interesting. It showed that Polito regarded it as his duty to act in the interests of authority even to the point of overlooking possible crimes. He appeared to have acted on a reflex without thinking, and that, to his mind, was a sign of his loyalty to his superiors. He regarded this as correct behaviour. But others saw it differently.

'I tell you, I never bothered myself with the Montesi affair and yet every time I saw Sepe he came out with the foot-bathing story as if I had invented it myself,' he moaned. 'He insisted on that version and treated me like a criminal and a murderer. We carried out our enquiries. We interrogated the Montesi family and it was they who brought out the foot-bathing story. My inspectors reported this to me, and that was the end of it. As for the girl having gone to Ostia to wash her feet, that was what the Montesis said, and why should we object to it? Wilma Montesi turns out to have been a good girl, honest and discreet, even if certain people in pursuit of their own ends have tried to turn her into a loose woman.'

He claimed that the case of the girl was beneath his personal interest and that not even the missing suspender belt had aroused his suspicions.

Third up was the smoothest and most skilled performer of the three accused. Tanned and self-assured, Ugo Montagna, master of Capocotta and king of networking, had presence, if little of the detached refinement of the aristocrat. Many journalists saw him in person for the first time at the trial. What struck those present about him was, first, his heavily nasal Sicilian accent. The second was the intensity of his resentment towards Anna Maria Caglio. She was mad, a fantasist and little more than a prostitute, he angrily asserted. Whenever her name was mentioned, he threw back his head and spluttered, scarcely able to contain himself.

Montagna was questioned about his relations with Polito and Pavone. He stated that he had known Tommaso Pavone since 1943 but claimed that he had met Polito for the first time in June 1953. He regarded his visits to Pavone's office and frequent lunch meetings with him as a normal consequence of their friendship. It was not at all odd, in his view, that a man with no official titles or functions should call on public officials during working hours or at their place of work. He regarded it almost as a prerogative of his wealth that he should be seen by officials whenever he wished, and especially by those with whom he had some personal link.

The marchese admitted that he knew all about Piccioni's illness and circumstances because he, too, was a friend. Naturally he was told of Piccioni's indisposition and wanted to assist when the musician's name was mentioned in connection with

that of the Montesi girl. But the impression he tried to give
of ordinary routine did not last long. When he was asked
about activities at Capocotta, he tried to wave away suggestions
of wrongdoing, but was confronted with the case of a hunt
guest, Guido Celano, an actor, who had been forcibly ejected
from Capocotta on 10 May 1953. Montagna insisted that he
had had no right to stay because the member who had invited
him had already left. The fact was, though, that Celano had
been heard asking questions about Wilma Montesi's death.
Whether or not his expulsion was in the natural course of
events, the image remained of an irate Montagna angrily
throwing out a man who had dared to mention the
unmentionable.

He readily admitted that he was often at Capocotta at night,
preparing hunts. On 11 April 1953, he had arrived at around
six a.m. and had left at eleven. Although this was the very
morning when Wilma's body had been discovered just a
kilometre away, he claimed that no one had mentioned it to
him, even though he had spoken to three estate employees.

The guards, Anastasio Lilli, Terzo Guerrino and Venanzio
De Felice, were all brought to the stand on 24 and 25 January.
From the deliberate, cautious way they responded to questions,
it was clear they were reciting from an agreed script and that
they had been primed. From the days of the Muto trial, they
had benefited from the services of Montagna's lawyers. Sepe
had found them reticent and had done his best to scare them
into revealing something by having them thrown into gaol.
This time they had been coached before they took the train
to Venice and again before their appearance in court. Rather
than crack, they fell into contradiction under questioning,
raising the spectre of perjury.

Enquiries had shown that word had spread rapidly in
Torvaianica about the sensational discovery of the corpse and
that the wives of two of the guards were aware of it. Their

husbands tripped up when recalling details, but it was clear they would not betray their benefactor. They had not discussed the dead girl with him, they asserted. They also reported that Montagna had ordered the locks to be changed on the Capocotta gates at the end of 1952 and that, from then on, he had been able to let himself in and out without troubling the guards. If true, this meant he could have spoken to them before the body had been discovered and had no further contact with them before he had left later in the morning. They had no explanation for the fact that the register of vehicles entering the estate was missing.

The Montesi parents were called to testify on 30 January. They had arrived in Venice looking humble and ordinary. Impoverished, they could only afford to stay for the first few days, although the court would pay their expenses to return to the trial on two further occasions. Their legal representation, it later transpired, was paid for by the interior ministry. Their legal representative, who had the right to intervene in cross-examinations, was a small, white-haired man named Casinelli. Piccioni never once looked directly at them. They had changed their minds several times, moving from straight denial that Wilma could have known a man such as Piccioni to a willingness to listen to the evidence that had been gathered against him.

It is difficult to imagine the anguish they felt at revisiting the torment of the days of Wilma's disappearance and the discovery of her body. They had tried to return to a semblance of normality but it had not been easy. The pressure of public opinion and the insinuations about them that had appeared in the press had made them uneasy and even more suspicious of outsiders than they had been previously. In Via Tagliamento they had been treated with sympathy and some respect, but even there poisonous gossip was not wholly absent.

As always Rodolfo stood erect and proud while his squat

wife Maria, her coarse features bearing the signs of years of pain, affected the attitude of a *mater dolorosa*. They repeated what they had said many times before and about which they had even written in the press. Wilma the angel, the dutiful daughter, was their common theme. Judge Tiberi, like investigating officials before him, suspected that the family had closed ranks because it had something to hide. He did his best to cajole and harry them in an effort to get this out into the open.

He got straight to the point with Wilma's father as he took the stand, asking him: 'Did she ever sleep away from home?'

'Never, and it angers me that it has been written that Wilma used to be out at night with men. When I went to the police station to report her disappearance . . . they began to consult the register of prostitutes. I thought I was going to die of shame. I deny that my daughter had a double life and that she wanted to be taken on as a film extra. It's not true that she dressed in a luxurious way. She was modest even to her clothes, as in everything else. She made a little go a long way and I liked that. She never went to Capocotta and she never took part in orgies or parties.'

Wilma's mother, too, defended their dead daughter. Asked if Wilma had ever gone out alone, she replied: 'Sometimes she went out in the afternoon for a couple of hours' walk, but she never came in later than half past seven. She never went out with anybody that I didn't know. Wanda and Wilma told me everything. We were more like friends than mother and daughters.'

On 31 January Wilma's one-time fiancé Angelo Giuliani was called. He had married a local girl from Potenza, a jeweller's daughter, in August 1954, and his relationship with Wilma seemed but a distant memory. He presented himself to the court with the same clipped moustache he had sported in 1953, but he no longer wore his heart on his sleeve. Prodded by the prosecutor, he remained precise and unflustered. Towards the end of the trial, he was recalled to Venice. He was asked if he had loved Wilma. 'Well, she was a girl who had respect for her family. We used to talk, that was all,' he replied, as though he were speaking of a person he barely knew.

As the trial wore on, the circle of witnesses widened. Eleven Torvaianica residents told their versions of whom they had seen on the beach on 9 and 10 April 1953, several people from Ostia added their thoughts, while the worker Mario Piccinini, who had helped dislodge the car on the morning of 10 April, and a fellow worker disagreed over whether the passengers were Wilma and Piccioni. The concierge of Via Tagliamento 76, Adalgisa Roscioni, described Wilma as she left the building on her last fateful day, minus the jewellery that she usually wore. Various journalists were called to testify how they had heard rumours of Piero Piccioni's involvement in the case, and the doctors who had conducted autopsies came to offer their contrasting ideas about how Wilma had died.

Several key witnesses had yet to be called. Particular expectation surrounded the appearance of La Caglio. But, first, another star appearance was scheduled. The prospect of sighting the dashing Prince Maurice of Hesse drew a mass of Venetian women to the courthouse. There had been great speculation about his visit to Capocotta on 9 or 10 April and about the identity of his female companion. The prince's car was certainly memorable: it was a right-hand-drive beige Aurelia saloon. But, for all the insinuations, his presence in the vicinity was more or less innocent. He testified that he had gone there on an afternoon jaunt with a casual pick-up, no doubt hoping that the combination of his royal blood, a smart new car and an isolated location would favour a speedy seduction. Asked to recall the exact date of his visit to the estate, he replied: 'I don't remember if it was the ninth or tenth of April. I think it was probably the ninth.'

'Are you sure it was the ninth and not the tenth of April?' injected a defence counsel. 'Weren't there days when it was not allowed to take guns to Capocotta?'

'Capocotta was mine. I could go there whenever I wanted,' the prince shot back, asserting the residual royal privileges that applied even though the estate had passed into the hands of the state and been leased to Montagna.

Any remaining suspicion that his companion was Wilma Montesi was crushed when the woman in question arrived to give evidence. Previously the prince had gallantly withheld her name, but the seriousness of the situation obliged him to reveal it. Elsa Ceserani was twenty-two and, according to the press, very pretty. She spoke tenderly of 'Maurizio', whom she had met on Capri in March and whom she had been pleased to meet again on 9 April. But after that outing to Capocotta, to her regret, he had not called her again.

The Venetian public echoed the sentiments of Romans a few years before: they had approved servants of the state who refused to act blindly in the state's interests. Colonel Pompei was one of the few public officials involved in the Montesi case who had always enjoyed the warm embrace of popular support. The author of the report into Montagna, commissioned by Amintore Fanfani during his brief stint as interior minister, he was a public servant of a different stamp from Polito and Pavone. The former colonel, since promoted to general, was a stout, robust man, now aged sixty. In his dress uniform, he cut an impressive figure and he underscored this with his uncompromising stance. He embodied an idea of the state that was not open to corruption by well-connected men like Montagna. He had known of the marchese because he had personally received no fewer than three invitations to join him at Capocotta. He knew that prefects, police chiefs, ministers and senior civil servants were all part of the Sicilian's network. He had declined the offers because he had strong suspicions about the nature and purposes of this web of influence. This was the same Montagna, he realised, 'who had passed through all the Allied offices, for which he had taken it upon himself to organise entertainments'. He also had links with the world of narcotics and some of his friends were known traffickers. Pompei had welcomed Fanfani's invitation to investigate officially because he had long wanted to make enquiries into this whole murky set.

Pompei explained that it had not been easy to conduct enquiries into Montagna because files held on him had been removed from Police Headquarters. Nevertheless, he had discovered several past convictions and continuing illicit activities. Montagna had bought and sold land and apartments at a high profit, using funds whose provenance was unclear. He used his means to reward friends such as Pavone, to whom he had allegedly made a gift of an apartment. Montagna's generous tipping and ostentatious charity was a matter of record but the extent of the largesse drew gasps of astonishment from the public gallery.

The general had discovered one significant fact: the flat in Via Acherusio, which Piero Piccioni used as a base, had been obtained by Montagna as part of a larger property deal and had been made available to Attilio Piccioni. The latter had granted his son permission to use it. This fact highlighted not only a connection between Montagna and Attilio Piccioni but also identified a clear reason why Piero Piccioni might be beholden to the Sicilian businessman.

It was interesting that Pompei's conclusions did not rely on Anna Maria Caglio. 'I didn't pay much attention to what Caglio said,' he stated, adding, 'even though no doubt some of it was true.' Nevertheless, defence lawyers picked over the supposed facts in his report in a determined effort to show that many of them were unchecked and unreliable.

The defence had hoped to establish swiftly that Piccioni was innocent. They had attacked the outcome of Sepe's investigation as a mass of speculation without any basis in hard evidence. But as the trial moved into its third week, the emerging picture was not the one they had hoped to build. The testimonies of state officials inadvertently suggested the existence of networks, connections and mindsets that might have favoured a cover-up. The public in Venice grasped this and the atmosphere of hostility became almost tangible. The hustle and bustle outside and inside the courtoom increased by the day. The sense of expectation mounted as the moment when Anna Maria Moneta Caglio would take the stage drew closer.

In between the testimonies of people who obviously had something to contribute there were those of lesser figures, the wild cards, publicity-seekers and fantasists who lent the trial a carnival flavour. Judge Tiberi seemed inclined to give these free rein, and the defence could see advantage in allowing the theatrical element to come to the fore. Ever ready to portray the case as an absurd and politically motivated concoction, they happily allowed the magicians, fortune-tellers and low-lifes to hog the limelight. Despite the best efforts of the judge to maintain order, and to punish witnesses who were obviously lying, the conviction that money or fame could be gained by intervening in the proceedings had a major distorting effect. Many hours were wasted on the testimonies of the magicians Del Duca and Orio, who added colour but were inveterate liars. Del Duca, the wizard of Milan, was kept on the stand for no less than eleven hours. A large part of the blame for this lay with the defence. In order to undermine the seriousness of proceedings, and perhaps also to render as uncertain as possible the facts, they dragged out the testimonies of marginal witnesses with endless questions. The real contribution of such people was almost zero. At the conclusion of their testimonies, Orio and several others found themselves transferred directly from the witness stand to the cells.

Finally, on 28 February, Anna Maria Caglio made her entrance, more than a month after the opening of the trial. She arrived like a film star, sporting a fashionably short hairstyle, with cameras flashing all around her as she pushed her way through the crowds. There was a reason for this: on 30 January, a film opened in Rome with the title *La ragazza di Via Veneto* (The Girl of the Via Veneto). Its plot was unremarkable, vaguely similar to that of *Donatella*, a film starring Elsa Martinelli as an ordinary girl with ideas above her station. This time the protagonist is a laundress from the popular Trastevere district, who wants to become, first, a fashion model, and then a film star. Her boyfriend, a butcher and part-time boxer, is not keen. After being courted by a rich producer and presented with the shame of the casting couch, she gives up her dreams and returns to her simple life. The part of the laundress was played by none other than Anna Maria Moneta Caglio. She had been well paid for her performance and she hoped that it would launch her artistic career. Alas, not even her notoriety was sufficient to save this piece of tosh from flopping at the box office. Although the production featured a largely professional cast and was properly produced and directed, it was not favourably received either by critics or film-goers. Unfortunately, it is now lost. Caglio also wrote a book, which she published herself, *Una figlia del secolo* (Daughter of the Century), which was mainly about her unhappy childhood.

Now she knew she was entering a lion's den, where the defence teams would seek to savage and discredit her. She held her head high and once more impressed everyone with her memory, lucidity, sincerity and mastery of detail. She was questioned vigorously and verbally mauled by Piccioni and Montagna's experienced lawyers. After five hours, she had preserved her calm bearing and had retained the sympathy of the public. But it was clear that she had nothing new to add to what she had said at the Muto trial four years before. She offered suppositions and deductions, fragments of evidence rather than corroborated facts and circumstances. Repeatedly the judge reminded her that she was under oath, especially when she offered piquant insights into Montagna's domestic ways.

'Mina, his father's maid, gave notice because they did such disgusting things in that house,' she claimed. 'She told me they used to sit down to table totally naked.'

Having been on the receiving end of sexual slurs, she paid them back in kind. 'Ugo always told me that Piccioni was a decadent and that he procured women. One day I told Piccioni what Montagna had told me about him and Piccioni answered, "On the contrary, Ugo is the leader of the gang."'

Once more she repeated her allegations about narcotics-trafficking.

Journalists no longer referred to her as the Black Swan, even though her performance in Venice would truly be her swansong. With her polished appearance and noble bearing, she seemed more of a greyhound or a panther. Thinner and more elegant than before, she was attired in a tailored suit and her hair was softly curled. Wayland Young, who covered the case for the *Manchester Guardian*, noticed that the bold young woman of 1954 was now more mature and composed. Over the course of a week, she made several court appearances and responded to questions on every one of the episodes that she had at various stages brought to the attention of the authorities. She offered her special insights into Montagna's activities, his telephone calls, his comments on Piccioni, his lunches and dinners with influential people, and his efforts to shroud aspects of his life in secrecy.

Piccioni and Montagna went to some lengths to quibble with minor aspects of their accuser's evidence. In so doing, they inadvertently drew attention to their earlier lies and to their desperate desire to deflect suspicion from themselves.

Piccioni was obliged to admit that he had met Caglio at the broadcasting station RAI. Although this meeting had occurred at Montagna's request, it being the one and only introduction he secured for her, he denied that they had discussed his friend. Caglio had said Piccioni complained that Montagna always stole his women (while Montagna had told her the opposite). A matter of pride might have been involved here, but the notion that they had not discussed the one man who was the link between them was wholly implausible. Montagna foolishly asserted that a lunch at which he had supposedly received the gift of a crucifix from Luigi Gedda, the influential Catholic organiser, had never taken place. In fact, the lunch had been confirmed when Father Dall'Olio called one of the other guests to question him about it.

The two men left it to their counsel to expose Anna Maria's contradictions and exaggerations on larger matters. Carnelutti and Vasalli pressed her on every detail, seeking finally to separate rumour from fact. At the end of her testimony, they drew up a list of twelve lies she had allegedly told. They went directly for the jugular and demanded that she be immediately incriminated for bearing continuous false witness. This request was rejected twice by the court. Had the judge acceded, he would have admitted that the trial itself was invalid. By refusing, he showed that he believed in its legitimacy. Nevertheless, her credibility had been seriously undermined. So powerful and impressive a figure in 1954–5, she ultimately failed to persuade when she took the stand in Venice. Her supporters were left feeling like guests at a Guy Fawkes party where the fireworks had failed to go off.

Although she stated her views with no less vigour, it was clear that she had fallen in love with her own public persona. She delighted in causing sensation and was tempted to make revelations about people and refer to events that had not occurred. Whereas before her word had stood alone, now she was measured against the wealth of detail Sepe had gathered and the testimony of other witnesses. When she was caught out on some points of fact, her credibility on everything else collapsed. In one such example, she spoke of visiting Switzerland with Montagna but her passport contained no entry stamp for that country.

Undeterred, and in a move that seemed calculated to win back some credibility, she claimed that, while the trial was going on, the accused had attempted, through intermediaries, to buy her silence. She revealed that a flamboyant hairdresser named Bruno Pescatori, whose services she had recently used, had offered her money to withdraw her evidence. Pescatori was indeed a link between several protagonists in that he was Alida Valli's coiffeur and had met Piccioni (although, as usual, the latter at first denied this). Had Caglio been willing to accept a pay-off, the hairdresser could have acted as a go-between. When he was hauled into the courtroom, he exclaimed that, far from offering Anna Maria Caglio money, he had been asked to forward a request for it to Piccioni. In short, she had offered to be bought off. Who was telling the truth? As was so often the case with the volatile Caglio, her tale could not be supported and it was left to contextual factors to lend it plausibility. Only this time they were absent. Gradually, some newspapers that had taken for granted a guilty verdict started to align themselves with the other side.

Alida Valli arrived in Venice on 8 March amid photographers' flashes and the curious stares of the public. The actress was the key witness for Piccioni, the one person who could vouch for his illness in Amalfi, his whereabouts between 9 and 11 April, and also provide him with an alibi for 29 April, the evening he was alleged to have attended a meeting with Montagna at the interior ministry. Valli was no longer in a relationship with Piccioni and, over the previous year or so, she had isolated herself from friends. Her image had been damaged by the squalid details of the case into which she had involuntarily been drawn and her health had suffered. But her film-star sense of publicity had not deserted her. At the same time as she was giving evidence, *Epoca* published her diary of the events that had unfolded in Amalfi before she and Piccioni had returned to Rome.

Through these diaries and cross-examinations a crucial element of doubt emerged about the events of 9 April. Asked why Piccioni had returned separately to Rome that day, after they had spent several days together, she replied, 'I really don't know. You can see that it is what was decided.' Although he had been suffering from tonsillitis, her lover had evidently been well enough to drive alone at high speed to Rome. Had he had been at his father's house for the entire evening of 9 April? Piccioni had stated that she had called him that evening and found him at home. But on this point, too, the actress provided less than solid support: 'I don't rule it out, but I don't remember,' she said.

This important point was not followed up, although there must have been doubt as to whether the call was made. Piccioni might have invented it to consolidate his alibi, although it is unlikely that Valli would ever have personally called the house of Attilio Piccioni, a man who strongly disapproved of his son's relationship with her. The minister had insisted Piero leave the actress and, in 1953, the relationship was continuing without his knowledge.

Piccioni's brother Leone was his staunchest public defender in the family, the only relative to back him up under oath. No other sibling testified, and, curiously, neither did his father, even though he had supposedly been ill in bed too. Leone informed the court that his brother had arrived home at approximately two thirty p.m. on 9 April. He was clearly not well and neither, at that time, was their father, hence the comings and goings of doctors to the house. Leone could not, and did not, state that his brother had never left the house because he had not been there continuously himself. Instead, he mentioned the irrelevant fact that his father had, despite his influenza, attended a meeting on 10 April at which Christian Democrat election candidates were to be chosen. Leone might have mentioned this to give the impression that he knew exactly who had stayed in and who had gone out in those days. Or he might simply have been supplying irrelevant but true information to divert attention from the fact that he could not directly confirm his brother's presence. It is also possible that this was a Freudian lapse. By saying that his father had gone out, he inadvertently revealed that his brother had in fact left the house.

Valli was questioned about her telephone call from Venice on 7 May, which she had initially denied making. Allegedly, she had complained at the end of the call that Piero was an 'imbecile' who had got himself into 'a mess'. She denied this: 'Talk out loud to myself? I rule it out totally.' Five eyewitnesses, including a Socialist Member of Parliament who had been in the bar at the time, were summoned. Valli's personal assistant, who was there with her, could not remember the call. Others affirmed that she did say the key words, while one suggested she had merely asked about the stories mentioning Piccioni. Only Guido Celano, who would later find himself ejected from Capocotta by Montagna, reported that he had heard, but not with his own ears, that Valli had said during her heated conversation, 'So what will you do now, you pig?'

The actress had also provided Piccioni with an alibi for the evening of 29 April, when he was alleged to have met with Montagna at the interior ministry. She stated that Piccioni remained at her house that evening until after midnight. Normally, they took dinner together at nine thirty. On that day, she said – her memory acquiring a new precision – they had dined later. For his part, Pavone had denied that the supposed meeting at the interior ministry ever took place, although he acknowledged often receiving young Piccioni in the morning and Montagna in the evening. Anna Maria Caglio was thus left alone in sustaining that the fateful meeting had taken place, and since her credibility had been undermined this marked a major blow to the case against Piccioni.

The spotlight now swung back to the Montesi household as the former servant Annunziata Gionni took the stand on 9 March and confirmed her account of the sisters' lives. The family were not present to hear her. Small and humble, she gave her evidence in a calm, firm voice. The girls went out every morning and returned at lunchtime, she said. They changed their outfits frequently and Wilma used a foreign fragrance and face powder. 'She always went out heavily perfumed,' she confirmed. Wilma also received phone calls. One caller, 'a man with a deep voice, polite', phoned several times, but Wilma always closed the door to avoid being overheard. Her relations with her fiancé were not good, Gionni asserted: 'She didn't like him. She used to say it especially to her mother.'

On 12 March, Polito's former superior, ex-chief of police Tommaso Pavone, who had been dismissed from his post when his relationship with Montagna had been caught on camera, faced the court to defend his reputation. It was one thing to be acquainted with a rich businessman and quite another to be shown up as a friend when the same man was revealed to have a criminal history and a dubious present. Pavone was a capable man, trusted by Italy's new political rulers. He had served the state well, especially in Milan where his Sicilian origins might have been resented. He deplored the damage that had been done to his hard-won reputation and tried to minimise his role in the case. He presented himself as neutrally as possible, even toning down his accent, which was markedly less strong than that of the accused Sicilian. He stated that his only role had been to order an inquiry into the origins of the rumours about

Piero Piccioni. This action he had undertaken, he specified, not because Montagna had asked him to do it but because the request had come directly from Attilio Piccioni, foreign minister and deputy prime minister.

What had been his relations with Montagna? On this sensitive topic, Pavone revealed his snobbery and self-regard. 'With me, Montagna has always been deferential, very correct. He never introduced me to Caglio. I don't think he ever introduced her to people of a certain standing.' Although their links went back to 1943, Pavone said that he had not met the Sicilian again until 1952, when he found him in Rome 'very well inserted'. He asserted that Montagna was accustomed to mixing in 'the best milieux, *only* the best milieux'. In this way, Pavone sought to isolate his friend from the sort of criminal company in which other witnesses situated him. By so doing, he hoped also to legitimise his own connections with him. There was a cost to this, however. From his testimony, there emerged a portrait of a man quite capable of bending himself to the requirements of his political superiors.

Pavone offered an insight into the way the police conceived of their role. In obeying Piccioni senior, he had merely done his duty, he said, because 'one of the tasks of the public security police is in fact to act as an investigative service in the interests of the government'. This came as a surprise to those who assumed that, in a democracy, the job of the police was to seek the truth and apply the law. But, as had always been the case in Italy, the real priority for public officials was to defend the government. When the existence of the Pompei report became known, Pavone had been instrumental in calling the meeting at the Viminale Palace at which Pompei had been bluntly reproved for meddling in matters that were the concern of the state police. This he had done, even though he had no formal authority over the national gendarmerie, and overlaps between the police and the Carabinieri were common.

Pavone's testimony gave a glimpse of the battle that the Montesi case had unleashed in the corridors of state. These were fragmented impressions but, for those who wanted to read between the lines, it was clear that the matter had been amply discussed in the seats of power. This frenetic backstage activity was a reflection of the fear of Communism, which governed the behaviour of so many in the late 1940s and early 1950s, and the battle for influence that was taking shape within the governing party.

By 1957 the political context had changed. Within the Christian Democrats, accounts had been settled and Fanfani had taken steps to establish an organisational structure that made the party less dependent on the Church and private business for support. A new political class was taking shape that would extend its influence across the entire state sector and beyond. Fanfani had established his authority in the party while men like Piccioni, Scelba and Spataro had lost influence. The energetic Tuscan had seized his chance and taken action that undermined a man to whom he bore no personal hostility but who stood in the way of his desire to seize power and modernise his party.

The Communists' general position had been affected by developments within Eastern Europe. In February 1956, Khrushchev's secret letter to the 20th Soviet Communist Party Congress, in which he sensationally criticised Stalin's leadership, had been published. Then, in October 1956, the Soviet Union had invaded Hungary and deposed the country's independent-minded Communist government, headed by Imre Nagy. These events, and the ensuing riots in Budapest, caused consternation among Communist activists and intellectuals in Italy, as elsewhere. In Rome and other cities, party meetings filled up with angry men and women wanting to know how the great liberator could occupy a sister country. When the party leadership demanded support for the USSR, 101 mainly

Roman intellectuals signed a petition of protest that was published in a mainstream newspaper. This was a bold act, provoking widespread debate within the party. In all, about 250,000 out of a membership of two million, including nearly all of the 101 petitioners, left the party in the wake of the events of 1956.

More significantly, the enthusiasm and commitment of those who remained began to wane markedly. The level of activism diminished sharply in the late 1950s, as people migrated from the countryside, sought prosperity for their families and were able to pay for commercial leisure instead of making use of party-sponsored alternatives. Left-wing recreational facilities in Rome's working-class quarters that, just a few years before, had been filled every evening were now more sparsely attended. All this meant that Italian political parties were no longer on a war footing. The trial was thus less dramatically politicised than it would have been four or even two years earlier.

By early March, more than a hundred witnesses had been heard but almost no pertinent facts had been unequivocally established. Rarely did two witnesses agree over dates, places or the identities of people sighted. What should have been a final reckoning degenerated into confused uncertainty. Nevertheless the case struggled on.

Piccioni's faithful brother Leone, who had robustly defended his sibling, often appearing before the press while Piero shied away, was asked why so little legal action had been taken when rumours had circulated about his brother and the Montesi girl. He responded that no one in the family had realised how serious the matter was until the day Piero was arrested in September 1954. They had seen the use of his name as a political tactic to discredit Attilio. The second statement might have been true but the first was odd, given the huge publicity the Muto trial had received and the profile of Sepe's investigation. It can only be assumed that they took it for granted that the judicial authorities would confirm their initial conclusion and close the case. Anyway, Attilio Piccioni was keen to avoid the issuing of writs, fearing that they would rebound on him if it was found that the rumours had begun in the Christian Democrat party. They assumed everything would be sorted out, though it was not clear if this was because they were convinced of Piero's innocence or because they knew that mechanisms had been set in motion and people mobilised to save him.

However, although the trial seemed to be failing to pin down beyond doubt evidence linking the accused to Wilma Montesi's death, neither did it establish their absolute innocence.

The defence teams adopted diversionary tactics, much as they had during Sepe's hearings. Wherever the opportunity presented itself, the potential guilt of other parties was crudely highlighted to take the heat off Piccioni and Montagna. Prince Maurice and Giuseppe Montesi were both, at different times, made use of in this manner. This tactic did not endear the defence team to the public but, in the latter case especially, it was effective.

Under pressure from the defence, the court began to focus once more on the Montesi family. What became known as 'Operation Giuseppe' was finally put systematically into action. This involved the defence lawyers raising doubts and questions about the role of Rodolfo Montesi's brother to divert attention from the principal accused. Attention focused on him also because the brief testimony of Wilma's former fiancé Angelo Giuliani revealed a formal, rather distant relationship. Giuseppe, who was only six years older than Wilma, knew as much, if not more, about her life than the rest of her family. Moreover, it was alleged that he had received calls at work, including one on 9 April, from a woman named Wilma. Thus he was set up as the fall-guy – but no one could have expected the astonishing revelations his testimony would bring. It is no exaggeration to say that it was a sensational climax in a trial rich with dramatic moments.

Giuseppe Montesi struck observers in Venice as a short, well-dressed man with the cocksure air of a spiv. He was described by the journalist Oriana Fallaci – who would later make her name through her revealing interviews with Henry Kissinger and Colonel Gaddafi – as 'a young man with cunning eyes and a bull-like neck who lives and dresses with an elegance similar to the Sunday splendour of some Trastevere corner boy'. In court, he was coy rather than candid. He decided 'with diabolical astuteness', Fallaci said, whether to talk or keep quiet.

The Montesi parents did not like or trust Giuseppe, but they did not suspect him of harming Wilma, even if his behaviour was in some respects peculiar. He had, for example, disposed of his car a month after Wilma's death. When Maria Montesi was asked about the family's relations with him now, she replied, 'Complete breach. He is a bachelor and he amuses himself with women and girls even though he is engaged to be married.' When she was summoned back on 31 March and asked if she had ever tried to find out where he had been on 9 April, she answered, 'Never. Even if he is a libertine, he would never have done anything like that to his niece.' She denied that he had ever taken Wilma out for a car ride, although she acknowledged that he had invited her. After the prosecutor turned the screws on her, sharply telling her to stop playing the tragedienne and telling lies, she finally admitted that her daughter had been taken out for rides regularly by her uncle – the 'thirty-two-year-old government functionary who fancies himself a Don Juan', as *Time* described him. This was something that the whole Montesi clan had been trying to conceal. And when Maria cracked, Giuseppe, who had stubbornly stuck to his original alibi, changed his story.

Suspicions concerning him had been raised from early on in the enquiries but they had never found much support within the family. Rather, it was his fellow employees at the

Casciani works, and a handful of journalists, who insisted that he should be treated as a suspect. Polito's replacement as police commissioner, Arturo Musco, had looked into him and found that he had 'a morbid interest' in Wilma. Lila Brusin, a worker at the Casciani plant, testified that Giuseppe often made calls from work to girls, one of whom was called Wilma, using the telephone on her desk. Sometimes he would arrive at work dressed for an occasion and try to get off early to go to Ostia.

Giuseppe had insisted that he had spent the evening of 9 April in the company of his fiancée and the family members he lived with. When his afternoon colleagues at the print works testified that he had left early and gone to meet a woman, he had tried to sue them for slander. Events soon forced him to withdraw his suit. There were gaps in this account that did not completely satisfy the defence. Pressed hard, he was obliged to reveal that in fact he had spent part of the evening with another woman. This, he pleaded, was not his niece Wilma but someone else.

Only when he was subjected to the most unrelenting pressure did he reveal the identity of the other woman. It would scarcely have been more sensational if he had confessed that it was his own dead mother. He had been secretly seeing Rossana Spissu, the sister of his fiancée Mariella. Indeed, unbeknown to Mariella, Rossana was expecting his child. As Giuseppe's position became critical, Rossana came forward to confirm their secret liaison. She confessed that they had spent time together on 9 April in a room they rented by the hour on the Via Appia.

The press made the most of the revelations about Giuseppe's complex private life. When his domestic double-dealing was exposed, an already sceptical public opinion turned sharply against him. He quickly became a substitute hate-figure for Piccioni, while the plain Spissu sisters – well-built Mariella and thin Rossana – were merely objects of pity, women who had fallen under the spell of a man who could not even be bothered to distinguish between them. Moreover, no matter how clamorous the revelation was that Giuseppe had been having sex with his future sister-in-law, he was not yet off the hook regarding Wilma's death.

The Giuseppe trail would lead further but, first, in an effort to bring the proceedings firmly back to reality, in the early days of April the entire court made highly publicised visits to Torvaianica and to Capocotta. Accompanied by hordes of policemen, journalists and photographers, the judge and the lawyers inspected the beach, the surrounding roads and all the various buildings that were to be found on the hunting estate. Needless to say, at such a distance of time, nothing additional was added to what Sepe had garnered.

While the court was in transfer, the journalist Fabrizio Menghini published a headline-grabbing article in the weekly *L'Espresso*. He had played an ambiguous role throughout the entire case. He had managed to insinuate himself into the Montesi household early on and, after the family had been deserted by their original legal advisers, he had even become their spokesman and counsellor. This was a role he performed in a less than disinterested fashion. Now Menghini's ambiguous behaviour reached a climax. Abandoning caution, he publicly invited Giuseppe to confess his guilt. Over the four years that he had covered the case, Menghini wrote, he had formed the conviction that Giuseppe Montesi was guilty. He had surely been with Wilma in Ostia on 9 April and, indeed, he had taken her there by car.

This was a startling development. Menghini was the doyen of Montesi-case journalists, a man who had secured unrivalled access to the family. He claimed that family members now entertained terrible doubts about their relative. In a letter to the judge, the *Epoca* correspondent Doddoli backed him. Menghini's gesture showed again how the press were setting the agenda in the Montesi case and were important players in it. Menghini had not acted in accord with the family and, indeed, his intervention led to a breach in relations. Through Wanda, the Montesis made a statement in which they firmly denied harbouring any suspicions about Giuseppe.

What motivated Menghini and why did he intervene at that precise moment? He had been convinced of Piccioni's innocence from the start, a view embraced by his newspaper. His convictions about Giuseppe appeared to follow from this and, for that reason, he became a key actor in the so-called 'Operation Giuseppe'. He bolstered the strategy of the defence teams by intervening at a critical moment.

The fact that Menghini's contribution was part of a strategy was confirmed when the journalist was brought to the witness stand to explain himself. He had no new facts to present, merely his personal convictions. What had at first seemed like a bombshell was soon revealed as a damp squib.

Nevertheless, the renewed focus on Giuseppe motivated public prosecutor Palmintieri to launch an onslaught against him. He drew heavily for this on the detailed work of the journalists who had been closely concerned with the case from the beginning. He was able to count on two new witnesses located by Doddoli, Signor and Signora Piastra, friends of Rossana Spissu. They said that she had been at Termini station with them, seeing off Signora Piastra's mother at around six or seven p.m. on 9 April. If this was so, she could not have been tucked away in a hotel with Giuseppe on the Via Appia. The counterfoil of a concessionary ticket was produced to show that there had been no confusion with any other trip. The second alibi that Giuseppe had established at such a high personal cost was suddenly shaken.

By this time the courtroom was filled to capacity. A crucial point had been reached and everyone present knew it. Even the cool Piccioni strained forward with anticipation. Goaded by the public prosecutor, who had brought her face to face with Signora Piastra, Rossana stood firm. She refused to admit that she had been at the station and implored the Piastra woman to say she was mistaken. Her histrionics aroused no sympathy in the prosecutor, who dismissed her cries of desperation as mere theatre.

Rossana's emotion clearly derived not from any commitment to the truth but rather from self-interest. In Italy an illegitimate child risked passing through life with a permanent mark of shame unless it was recognised by the father. Giuseppe had evidently told Rossana that he would give their unborn child his name only if she provided him with a sure alibi. And when Palmintieri put this to her, she pathetically admitted as much.

With his alibi in tatters, the defence demanded that Giuseppe be arrested without further delay. The request was declined but everyone, from Judge Tiberi to the defence counsel, was convinced that he was harbouring a secret. After all, the only things that were certain about his movements on 9 April were his departure from work at around five p.m. and his arrival at home between eight thirty and ten past nine that evening. Although it had been determined that Wilma had died on 10 April, it was the whereabouts of witnesses and the accused at the time of her disappearance that most concerned the court.

Giuseppe's moments in the spotlight were the most tension-filled of the whole trial. Attention had fundamentally shifted away from an establishment plot and towards the Montesi family. This was enhanced when Rossana Spissu declared to the press, as Giuseppe was giving evidence, that a family secret was being concealed. Clearly, she wanted to take the heat off her fiancé. The effect, though, was different. When Rodolfo Montesi learned of it, he fired off a telegram to his brother demanding that he reveal it immediately and completely. Nothing came of this gesture. It was clear, though, that it concerned Wilma. Perhaps she had broken off her engagement and had met someone else, whose name was being concealed. This hypothesis was sustained by the established fact that Wilma had owned a pair of earrings that neither her fiancé nor her parents had given her. Or perhaps it was a reference to the rumour, restated by the family's legal representative Cassinelli, that Giuliani had offered to marry Wanda on the day of Wilma's funeral. Whatever it was, Rodolfo's challenge had the effect of keeping mouths shut.

What had seemed to be a major scandal suddenly started to look more like a squalid domestic affair. Responsibility for Wilma's death did not appear to lie with Piccioni and his friends at all. The Montesis' lawyer, however, was not convinced. 'In my opinion the campaign against Giuseppe is a distraction launched by Biagetti [his employer at the Casciani works] who is a friend of Piccioni,' he lamented. Nonetheless the proceedings were drawn unexpectedly to a close on the grounds, simply, that 'it could have gone on for ever'.

In four months little had been established beyond doubt, although a range of facts had emerged that aided one reconstruction or another. Attempts to prove that Piccioni had known the dead girl had failed. He was able to bring witnesses to show his whereabouts on 9 and 10 April and 29 April. It had not been proven that he was at Torvaianica on the earlier dates. At most, the shadow of suspicion remained over the politician's son. He had been lucky in one key respect. One of the most striking aspects of the trial was the way class had shaped the interrogations, the behaviour of the court, and the attitudes of the witnesses. The educated and articulate were challenged, harried and scrutinised far less than those whose social origins were inferior. Piccioni's life was not picked over in detail. The trajectory of his relationship with Alida Valli, for example, was not examined and neither was the substance of his peculiar friendship with Montagna. There was no journey into the mores of the Bohemian milieu of

Photographer Tazio Secchiaroli, obviously enjoying a dance with Anna Maria Moneta Caglio, one of his quarries. The pattern of complicity and conflict that marked the turbulent relationship between Paparazzi and the famous in Rome was established with the Montesi case.

Christian Democrat politician Mario Scelba, shown stepping out of the new Fiat 600, the baby car that would relaunch the Italian economy.

© Bettmann/CORBIS

Ambitious politician Amintore Fanfani manoeuvred to seize control of the governing Christian Democrats after the party suffered a setback in the 1953 election. *© Bettmann/CORBIS*

Foreign minister Attilio Piccioni (right), seen with Anthony Eden, was regarded as the man most likely to lead the Christian Democrats, until his son Piero was accused of causing the death of Wilma Montesi.

© Bettmann/CORBIS

Rome's Montmartre, Via Margutta was home to the city's artists and the focus of the Bohemian community. Painter Novella Parigini inaugurated the road's annual open-air exhibitions and pioneered face and body painting. *© Bettmann/CORBIS*

Silvana Pampanini, who was runner-up in the first Miss Italy pageant in 1946, was the precursor of stars like Gina Lollobrigida and Sophia Loren. Beautiful and feisty, she was idolised by the many Roman girls who dreamed of getting into the movies. *© Studio Patellani/CORBIS*

Elsa Martinelli preparing to pose for a sexy pin-up photo. A fashion model and film star who grew up not far from the Montesi family home, she would later be a protagonist of the city's racy café society. *© Studio Patellani/CORBIS*

The Via Veneto was the focus of Rome's high life in the 1950s. With its luxury hotels, pavement cafes and fashionable clubs, it drew foreign stars, including Ava Gardner (left), and Italian actresses such as Alida Valli (right), who provided Piero Piccioni with an alibi.

Swedish actress Anita Ekberg dances with Gerard Herter at a party at the Rugantino club in November 1958. The party later span out of control when Turkish dancer Aiche Nana performed an impromptu striptease, causing police to raid the club. Tazio Secchiaroli was on hand to record events.

Anita Ekberg was the queen of the Roman night and a magnet for photographers. Pierluigi Praturlon captured her one evening as she bathed a scratched foot in the Trevi fountain. He took the still photograph of her when she repeated the nocturnal dip in the glamorous setting of Fellini's *La dolce vita*.

© *Pierluigi Paturlon*

© *Keystone/Getty Images*

Film director Federico Fellini standing before a poster of his 1960 film *La dolce vita*. A devastating portrait of contemporary Rome, the film sharply divided opinion in Italy and was the subject of demands for censorship It won the Palme d'or at the Cannes film festival and frequently features on best-ever-movie lists.   © *David Lees/CORBIS*

Via Margutta. In these issues lay possible clues to the riddles of the case.

The final witnesses were called at the end of April. Wilma's ex-fiancé Giuliani was recalled but added nothing to what he had said before, save the curious fact that Wilma could not dance and had not wanted to be seen dancing with him. 'She could hardly move her feet at all and she said that she would certainly look terrible dancing with me,' he admitted dolefully.

Then came a handful of skirmishes with minor witnesses before the court adjourned for a month. In that time, the last cold winds of the winter were blown away and the warm spring opened the lagoon city's tourist season.

The closing speeches of the prosecutor and the defence counsel were awaited with less than bated breath. In the final stage of the trial, the prosecutor, who had played an unusually passive role until the penultimate phase, had intervened more and more assertively. He had begun timidly, perhaps over-awed by the prestige of the defence teams, but he had acquired confidence and even belligerence towards some witnesses. And now, in late May, here was his grandstand moment, his opportunity to pull the threads together and propose a conclusion.

When Palmintieri finally rose to speak, his conclusion was highly unusual. He failed to convey the grey areas and uncertainty of the lengthy Venice trial. Instead he offered a black-and-white summary. He affirmed that there was no evidence Wilma Montesi and Piero Piccioni had ever met, or that Piccioni had been near Torvaianica on 9 April 1953. He attacked the contributions of many witnesses, labelling them liars. He reserved his most ferocious comments for Anna Maria Caglio, whom he dubbed 'a perfidious woman intent on vengeance and dedicated to mud-slinging'. She had repeatedly lied over numerous issues, including the 29 April meeting. He even advanced the suspicion that, far from confirming the contents of Silvano Muto's article in *Attualità*, she had been the inspiration for it. He demanded that Piccioni should be acquitted of the crime of which he was accused and the other two should be acquitted not for 'insufficient proof' but for the 'absolute absence' of proof of their involvement in the girl's death or in any subsequent cover-up.

While he engaged in a highly irregular dismantling of the case against Piccioni, Montagna and Polito, Palmintieri glossed over the lies of the accused, the holes in their evidence and the strangeness in their behaviour. Also, he seemed to overlook the numerous interventions and meetings that, if they did not amount to aiding and abetting a crime, would have had little or no purpose. He made no mention of the corrupt practices and illicit activities that the case had brought to light involving well-placed individuals. He made it clear that he entertained strong suspicions about Giuseppe Montesi's role but in reality there was a symmetry between his situation and that of Piccioni. Both men were able to present five people who provided them with elements of an alibi for 9 April. The difference between them was that the five Piccioni presented were all respected professionals, albeit with links to his family. Therefore, it was implied, they should be believed, despite the coincidence that he had returned to Rome in curious circumstances on the very day the victim had disappeared.

On 28 May, Judge Tiberi and his two supporting colleagues withdrew to consider their verdict. After seven and a half hours of deliberation, Tiberi emerged to announce the acquittal of Piccioni, Montagna and Polito. Piccioni's alibi, regarded as unconvincing by Sepe, was found by the court to be credible. In their written justification, the judges highlighted the weakness of Anna Maria Caglio. Her testimony at the outset had seemed to provide the bridge between the inconsistencies in the accounts of Piccioni and Montagna and the specific charges that had been laid against them. But while some of her statements were undoubtedly true, her reliability had been compromised by her personality and ulterior motives. Under the cold scrutiny of the male-dominated court, she seemed emotional and vindictive. In the final analysis, her femininity, which had charmed so many in the past, made her an unreliable witness. Caglio could not demonstrate that her allegations were true and therefore all her evidence was ignored.

Also acquitted were the guards, Anastasio Lilli, Terzo Guerrino and Venanzio De Felice. Those deemed to be false witnesses were also absolved after they had retracted – Michele Simola and Francesco Tannoja included. Pierotti and Maddalena Caramello had died in the meantime. In the end, the only person found guilty was Adriana Bisaccia, who received a suspended sentence for lying under oath.

The defence team greeted Tiberi's reading of the verdict with shouts and cheers, while hordes of eager photographers were finally allowed into the courtroom. The trial was over. All that remained was for the judges to provide their extended written justification of the verdict and set out what had been established at the trial.

As *Il Messaggero* commented, 'Of all the terrible suspicions which tormented public opinion nothing is left: no orgies, no white slavery, no boatloads of prostitutes, nothing.'

PART THREE

XVIII

The Rise of the Paparazzi

As they left the court after their acquittal, Piero Piccioni and Ugo Montagna were immediately mobbed by well-wishers. Piccioni responded calmly to the verdict. He told journalists, 'Of course I am happy. What else can I say?' before announcing that he would stay in Venice to see the opening night of Shakespeare's *Titus Andronicus*, featuring Laurence Olivier and Vivien Leigh.

'Are you going on a journey to Haiti?' he was asked, following publication of a rumour to this effect.

'I would go,' he replied, smiling, 'if I won *Lascia o raddoppia?*'

His reference to Italy's first popular television quiz show, an adaptation of the American *The $64,000 Dollar Question*, which became a national craze, was the first concession he had made to popular opinion. He was angry that drugs and music had become conflated in press coverage of his life. 'I read in a weekly that because I had played in Harlem in the black jazz orchestras, it was the case that I had assumed the habit of drug-taking that many blacks have.' Such assertions were false, he claimed, but why, he wanted to know, had they been written in the first place? To his mind, questions inevitably needed to be asked about a system of justice that had allowed him to suffer three years of humiliation and judicial jeopardy on the basis of gossip.

Wilma's parents, back in Rome, issued no statements. With

Rodolfo's business to run, they had been unable to absent themselves from Rome for several weeks so had taken little part in the proceedings. Before the verdict was announced, Rodolfo had put his name to a magazine article in which he stated his faith in the theory that Wilma had gone to Ostia to bathe her feet. He demanded respect for his family and, as if to bolster this request, declared that he had always been poor and would remain so. When a journalist asked him for his opinion of the outcome, he replied, 'I have nothing to say.'

Maria was also reserved: 'What can I say? I cannot do anything except trust in the law.'

As for Raffaele Sepe, the day after the verdict he was at his desk as usual at the Palazzaccio. He took coffee in the morning and at eleven o'clock returned to matters in hand. He issued no comment. Silvano Muto, too, who had not been at the trial, was faithful to his surname and declined to say anything.

Montagna was the first of the three accused to leave Venice. Wearing the same dapper Prince-of-Wales checked suit he had worn on day one, he waved to the crowd as he made his way to the station to take the sleeping car back to Rome. He then went to his castle retreat at Fiano. A few days later, it was reported that he was travelling to Rome almost every day. He expressed the hope that he could re-establish his networks and begin to rebuild his business interests. For all his bravado, he had been badly affected by his involvement in the case.

The verdict brought sighs of relief from nearly all sections of the establishment. There had been anxiety within the state, the Church, the political and economic élites, and sectors of the press, that the outcome of the trial might tarnish the whole social order and breed resentment. Instead, for a while at least, the boot was on the other foot. Editors and journalists were denounced for being interested only in scandals and for having whipped up a campaign that had turned innocent people into monsters. Those who were now acquitted would never have been accused without press interest. Several newspapers, including *Paese Sera*, acknowledged that they had been too partisan and recited a *mea culpa* through clenched teeth.

Yet the outcome of the marathon trial did not entirely silence the critics of power. The written *sentenza* prepared by Judge Tiberi presented a picture that dismissed the construction placed on events by Sepe. But at the same time it gave no place to the foot-bathing theory that had been so eagerly adopted by earlier investigations. Piccioni and company were acquitted, but the court concluded that Wilma had died where she was found, that she had never been to Ostia, and that her death had indeed been the result of a criminal act. In brief, she had been murdered. This was a significant advance on the seemingly impenetrable mystery of the spring of 1953. Despite the extraordinary length of the trial, many questions remained unanswered and others were not even asked. Wilma's life was still a closed book. No one familiar with the family was brought to give evidence, save the former maid Annunziata Gionni and the concierge of the block in Via Tagliamento 76. No neighbours were called to resolve the dispute between Gionni and the family about Wilma's movements. In the absence of any testimonies from friends and acquaintances, the gulf remained between those who saw her as a good, home-loving girl and the various witnesses who claimed that she was caught up in a much more sinister drugs racket.

There were still unanswered questions concerning Piccioni. Despite his unprepossessing appearance and unconvincing homebody pose, he was very far from being an unworldly innocent. Yet his life and habits were not examined in any thorough way. How did he and Montagna become close friends? Why exactly did he go to visit Pavone on several occasions if the rumours about him were entirely baseless? Was he a drug addict or a sexual pervert? Despite the holes in their testimonies, the accused, in the time-honoured manner of socially well-placed defendants, were able to parade a series of declarations as to their good character. They benefited from the respect of the public prosecutor and the presiding judge. Although an inquiry into the activities and milieux of Piccioni and Montagna might have shed light on how the startling accusations against them were accorded such immediate credibility, this did not take place.

The fact that the two men had repeatedly lied about a series of details was forgotten. Also, the drugs issue was not followed up. What connections, if any, did the protagonists of the case have with a traffic whose significance remained in the background? Strong suspicions remained that there had been a cover-up. The outcome showed that old networks of power, which could not afford any association with impropriety, could close ranks and protect their own even when faced with a scandal of unprecedented proportions.

Wayland Young suggested that the Montesi affair provided a necessary outlet for the tensions of the Cold War period. It allowed, he wrote, 'the greatest possible amount of public outcry, of blowing off of steam, without positively toppling the country over into disorder ... Every true affair is the ghost of a revolution, the lightning rod of violence, a miniature, bloodless convulsion.' A year after the end of the trial, the novel *The Leopard* was posthumously published, the work of an unknown Sicilian author named Giuseppe Tomasi di Lampedusa. At the heart of this drama – set in Sicily at the time of the struggle to unify Italy, a process that culminated in 1861 – lay an interpretation of Italian history that instantly became famous. 'Everything must change,' comments the novel's aristocratic protagonist – referring to the bourgeois order that was taking shape in tandem with national unification – 'so that everything can remain the same.' Was the Montesi scandal an example of the appearance of change taking the place of substance, as Young implied?

In fact, the case was a Pandora's box that unleashed changes that could no longer be contained. The basic political and economic order remained solid but seismic shifts were occurring in social and sexual mores, the role of the press, the culture of celebrity, leisure, attitudes towards authority, and the value of money. While the case was unfolding, Italy underwent a significant period of economic growth that would accelerate in the years that followed.

The Montesi trial was part of a watershed in Italy in the late 1950s. In 1958 Pius XII died. His passing marked the end of an era. He was an austere and remote man, who was respected rather than loved. An authoritative, not to say authoritarian, figure who had been pontiff since 1938, he had tried to impose the imprint of the Church on post-war Italian government and society. An immensely powerful figure, who exercised a wide measure of political and diplomatic influence, he had disapproved of the direction taken by society after the historic Christian Democrat election victory in 1948.

By the mid-1950s, the influence of the Church was still far-reaching, but instead of offering examples and models, it was obliged to respond repressively to incidents it viewed as negative. Conservative forces increasingly found themselves fighting rearguard battles. The last few months of the Pope's life were marked by a stern campaign against film distribution companies, which had pasted up over Rome garish painted posters advertising the films *En Effeuillant la marguerite* (a Brigitte Bardot vehicle whose title became in Italy *Miss Striptease*), *Zarak Khan* and *Poveri ma belli* (Poor but Beautiful), each of which featured a daring, partially unclad female figure. At the Vatican's behest, the posters were banned and those responsible for putting them up were sent for trial.

By the tail end of the 1950s, the Pope's vision for the country was falling visibly apart. His final weeks witnessed the exposure of a catalogue of excesses and transgressions involving members of Roman society, some of whom were closely connected to the Vatican itself. The culture of concealment, which the Montesi case had done so much to break, gave way to a thirst for exposure and scandal. Even Pius himself would be a victim. The pontiff's last days were closely followed by the press and stolen pictures were published of him on his death bed. The party guilty of this outrage turned out to be none other than his personal physician, Riccardo Galeazzo-Lisi, a close friend of Montagna and a partner in the Capocotta hunting society.

Much of the new fever for excess and exposure was centred on the Via Veneto. Low life might have been picturesque but money demanded a higher quotient of glamour. During the day, the road bustled with the life of its elegant shops and cafés. Journalists, writers and tourists sat conversing with their peers and watching the spectacle of cars and carriages that cruised up and down, taking people nowhere in particular. As the sun set and cocktail hour began, the Via Veneto became more exciting, a place of adventures and encounters that, thanks first to the activities of a new breed of gossip columnists, would be written up in afternoon papers like *Momento-sera* and *Corriere dell'Informazione*. It was the latter that coined the expression '*dolce vita*' to refer to the high jinks of the denizens of the Via Veneto. Journalists like Victor Ciuffa pioneered a type of reporting that was different from the staid documenting of the formal events of high society and the publicity-driven puffery of the film world. It was a sort of participant observation that turned the journalist into an anthropologist exploring the customs of a tribe that was exotic if not at all remote. The practitioners had to be tireless night owls, able to blend with their environment and select stories to write up with wit and verve.

Silently but inexorably, a shift of focus had occurred within Roman café society from the Bohemian scene of the Via

Margutta and the surrounding area to Via Veneto. Press interest had switched as the famous preferred to congregate on the exclusive boulevard that ran from the Aurelian wall to the American embassy. The rabbit warren of streets that fed into the Piazza di Spagna and the Via Margutta did not afford the comfort, space or visibility of the Via Veneto's goldfish bowl for expensive sports cars.

The world of Roman café society consisted of a series of concentric circles. The core clan of Via Veneto *viveurs* was composed of the privileged sons and daughters of aristocratic families, the children of politicians, idle playboys and ambitious women. Their nights consisted of movable feasts, usually beginning in a bar before proceeding to a private house or palace, then to a nightclub and finally to the sea or the country. Their Ferraris and Alfa Romeo Spiders zoomed up the Via Veneto and were then ostentatiously parked outside fashionable watering-holes. Like the Bright Young Things of London in the 1920s, they revelled in stunts and outrageous behaviour.

The typical heroes of café society at the height of the *dolce vita* were the super-rich playboys who had been featured repeatedly in the magazines since the middle of the decade. Like other foreigners, the Brazilian industrialist Baby Pignatari cared little that his adventures and indiscretions were publicised in *Settimo Giorno* or *Lo Specchio*. Porfirio Rubirosa, the Dominican diplomat and polo player who married a string of heiresses and actresses, was a model of the idle playboy. 'Work?' he once responded to a journalist's question. 'I have no time for work.' The ecstasy of the instant was all that mattered to people whose boredom threshold was exceptionally low. Life seemed heightened by the conquest of a famous woman or a big win – or even a big loss – at the casino. In contrast to most of the people who populated the seedy underworld of sexual intrigue and anonymous prostitution, their activities were widely publicised.

Pignatari and Rubirosa had their imitators among the rising class of Italian industrialists. Since the early 1950s, such men had often been lured by the promise of sexual opportunities into investing their profits in films. One of the cleverer ones won the affection of visiting stars by acting as host and guide in the capital. Actress Kim Novak was even rumoured to be contemplating marriage to Mario Bandini, a thirty-seven-year-old businessman of utterly mediocre appearance who regularly escorted her and other female American stars round the tourist sights when they were in town. The owner of a large apartment on Via Margutta, situated directly opposite Novella Parigini's studio, Bandini was no sophisticate but he knew Rome and its attractions like the back of his hand. Dubbed a 'charming Roman bachelor' by Linda Christian, he would appear in *Roma capovolta* (Rome Overturned), a fictionalised memoir by Novella Parigini's artist friend, the platinum-blond provocateur Giò Stajano, as Alfredo, a closet homosexual more interested in bedding the author himself than his various famous ladyfriends. 'An industrialist who spends huge sums every evening in order to be seen around with very beautiful, elegant and sophisticated women who in fact are of no interest to him', Stajano mocked him for being chubby and not very tall, 'like a little Napoleon'.

The lions of café society often kept a *pied à terre* or a suite at the Excelsior, just as those with less wealth maintained at least a room. The serious Casanova had to have somewhere to whisk a potential conquest without delay. In fact, most of the hotels on or near the Via Veneto also discreetly rented rooms by the hour, such was the demand. While the Italian press at this time still traded in euphemisms, the American gossip magazine *Confidential* made no bones about the intense sexual traffic that took place around the cafés and bars. By night, the road turned into a classy pick-up joint. Wealthy and well-known men trained their sights on the female talent, which ranged from the visiting star to the aspirant starlet who had done a few pin-up shots for a magazine. Escort girls and high-end prostitutes mingled among them, touting discreetly for business. To cater to female tourists of a certain age, there were plenty of gigolos too, the sort of polished but impoverished Roman men that Tennessee Williams portrayed in *The Roman Spring of Mrs Stone*. In such a context, class and sleaze shook hands. 'Via Veneto is the median meeting point between declining élites and rising low-life,' the writer Guido Botta noted.

Among the foreign socialites who made Rome their temporary base were a handful of displaced royal figures. When King Farouk of Egypt was deposed and exiled by a military coup in 1952, he opted to settle in Rome, where later he became a key personality of the *dolce vita*. He first came to public attention when he honeymooned on Capri in 1951. As we have already seen, the corpulent monarch was outraged to be photographed in his swimming trunks and, from that moment on, he was very wary of the press. Yet everything about him militated against discretion. He was a large man with a gargantuan appetite, who gambled fortunes and smoked giant cigars. He lived in fabulous luxury and had exercised absolute power. He was also massively promiscuous. Deprived of his habitual trappings in exile, he became a Via Veneto regular and won an unenviable reputation for his unsubtle lechery. Although his standard of living was reduced, he acted as a magnet for models and would-be actresses, with whom he danced ungainly rumbas. Eventually, he settled on a fixed mistress, a brash nineteen-year-old Neapolitan blonde named Irma Capece Minutolo.

Princess Soraya was another royal who fell to earth in Rome. Spurned by her husband, the Shah of Iran, after her failure to produce a son, she arrived in Rome to begin a golden exile. Public fascination with her was at frenzy-point when she took up residence at the Hotel Excelsior with her mother and she was immediately offered film roles. She was cast in *Tre volti*

(Three Faces), a film produced by Dino De Laurentiis that flopped. But Soraya was living an illusion. She had assumed that, once her former husband had sired a son with a new wife, she would be allowed back to Tehran. The shah was less than pleased when she was repeatedly photographed out at night. With good reason, the twenty-seven-year-old Soraya became known as the sad princess, the royal who never smiled. She finally burned her bridges when she embarked on a well-documented affair with a Roman aristocrat, Raimondo Orsini, that fizzled out in early 1959.

In addition to the playboys and princesses, there was a mixed crowd of newcomers, temporary Romans and publicity-seekers. The international set had first become a feature of the Via Veneto's Rive Gauche in the early 1950s. With their constant comings and goings, the road was a singles bar for the rich and beautiful, a shop window and launch pad for fashions and dances (the hula hoop was launched there by British TV soubrette Sabrina, while two black American dancers introduced Italy to rock and roll dance steps). Standing alongside these groups, and occasionally blending with one or other of them, were Novella Parigini, Giò Stajano and some of the beautiful models belonging to their clique. They helped fuel a festive atmosphere by bringing outlandish clothes and hairstyles, theatrical behaviour and artful eccentricity to the mix.

The *dolce vita* was never the preserve solely of the rich. One reason the antics of aristocrats and international stars were so fascinating was the presence among them of a handful of humbler people whom fame or fortune had catapulted to the fore. This was a distinct change from the early 1950s and related to an increase in social mobility and the growing effectiveness of publicity. Maurizio Arena was a stocky, working-class young man from the proletarian quarter of Garbatella. He became an actor by chance after working as a shop assistant, a boxer and a barman. He appeared as a regular Roman youth in many sunny Italian-style comedies. *Poveri ma belli*, a youth-oriented comedy that was a huge hit of 1957, turned him into a star. Arena suddenly became 'the national he-man', a muscle-bound embodiment of ordinary Italian masculinity. He bought two sports cars, a white Triumph and a black Plymouth, in which he could be spotted about town. After neighbours complained about the noisy traffic around his sumptuous apartment near Villa Pamphili, he had a house built at Castel Fusano, a relatively deserted area near the station where Mario Piccinini had aided the driver of the infamous Alpha 1900 saloon car in March 1953. The Beverly Hills-style villa even featured a swimming pool in the shape of a champagne cork.

For two years Arena could do nothing wrong. He made films, took up directing, released a record of his songs and, above all, became a staple figure of the gossip pages. He was out every night and mixed easily with people of all categories, from students in the Villa Borghese gardens to the princes and princesses of the papal aristocracy. His love life was legendary. Among the women with whom he was briefly associated were Linda Christian, his girlish *Poveri ma belli* co-star Lorella De Luca, James Dean's last love Anna Maria Pierangeli, the aristocrat Patrizia della Rovere, the singer Mina, and numerous starlets, models and tourists. He became a stereotypical playboy, a man who, according to gossip, could maintain an erection for three hours and expected to bed any woman he met within hours, if not minutes, of meeting her.

Arena's clamorous conquest of Princess Beatrice of Savoy illustrated the breakdown of class barriers more than any other single event. As a result, he became a model for all the young men from areas like Quarticciolo and Torpignattara. 'They are the barbarian invasion of Via Veneto, repeated every evening with fine regularity, but in the end innocuous except for the annoyance they cause well-dressed people,' commented Guido

Botta. Rough and muscular, they paraded up the Via Veneto convinced that they, too, could take a starlet to bed before returning home to their mothers. Such was Arena's success that even his young butler decided to imitate him. Gianfranco Piacentini often went out with his master and posed as a marchese. He enjoyed a brief flirtation with Alicia Purdom, estranged wife of English actor Edmund Purdom, that resulted in her receiving a black eye from her husband. Incidents like this revealed the sexual inequality that ran through the *dolce vita*. While married and attached men allowed themselves infidelities, they exploded with anger if they discovered that their women had been behaving in the same way.

Walter Chiari was another Italian actor who made a second career with the seduction of famous actresses. An extrovert entertainment all-rounder who performed in variety theatre and on television as well as in movies, he first featured in the gossip pages when he became engaged in 1951 to former Miss Italia Lucia Bosé. He was subsequently linked with the actresses Anna Maria Ferrero, Elsa Martinelli and even Anna Magnani, among many others. His on-off liaison with the American star Ava Gardner brought him to international attention as a leading example of a new breed of Latin lover. Chiari was not a conventionally handsome man (but then, before she met and wed the charismatic Frank Sinatra, Gardner had married the pint-sized former child actor Mickey Rooney), but he had charm in abundance. He was boyish and enthusiastic, and he wooed his women with a combination of flattery and humour.

If gossip writers narrated the *dolce vita*, it was the street photographers who lent it a dramatic visual dimension. Tazio Secchiaroli, Rino Barillari, Lino Nanni and others were mostly enterprising, working-class young men from the outskirts of Rome. They had started in many cases as *scattini*, youngsters who took snaps of Allied soldiers stationed in the city, and had neither much education nor training. For this reason the writers often looked down on them. While men like the journalist Victor Ciuffa were still to some extent in awe of those they mingled with and wrote about, the photographers were not. They regarded them with the same resentment that the public viewed the corrupt men of the Montesi affair. They had learned some of their tricks when following the personalities of the Montesi case. They had besieged the witnesses and the accused, pursued Sepe, and subsequently even taken clandestine shots in court. To shield themselves against bright flashes and unwanted exposure, almost all those implicated in the case, even the journalists and the priests, copied the stars and wore dark glasses. The photographers contributed to the way the journalists had choreographed the case, forcing individuals to act parts and perform to a script. They prospered by scandalising *bien pensants* in an era of intolerance and censoriousness. They were opportunists who went in search of their prey on Vespa and Lambretta scooters. Like the British Teddy Boys, to whom they were compared, they were cocksure and insolent. However, the frenzy of interest in the famous enabled them to emerge as a force in their own right.

While the press treated their work as legitimate exposure, almost the photographic equivalent of investigative journalism, conservative opinion viewed their activities with alarm, for they made no distinctions between politics and celebrity, crime and entertainment, public and private, the proper and the improper. After dark, the party atmosphere of the Via Veneto enclave was enlivened by their presence. Like unwelcome and uninvited guests, they waited for the right moment to gatecrash the proceedings and grew bolder as illustrated magazines developed an insatiable appetite for off-duty shots of the famous. In Los Angeles the movie stars were cosseted and protected; their public personae were carefully controlled and managed. Studio publicity departments provided skilfully constructed images of their glamorous appearances and lives. Abroad, this level of protection could not be sustained.

The paparazzi, as they would later become known, developed a style of photograph that met the needs of magazines for movement and drama. The price of a photograph increased according to the element of scandal it offered. Magazines like *Lo Specchio*, which had its offices directly on Via Veneto, thrived on a diet of photographs of illicit celebrity couples and stars drunk or behaving badly. For the photographers, these had a commercial value far superior to the smiling shots of stars arriving at Ciampino airport or enjoying the sunny Roman atmosphere. Two thousand lire was the price of a standard snap, seventy to eighty thousand for a stolen kiss or a clash.

At first Hollywood stars came to Rome mainly for work. Then more and more came to the city on holiday. Like exotic birds, Ava Gardner, Gary Cooper and the others glided down from their suites in the Hotel Excelsior to enjoy the free and easy atmosphere and the general lack of pretension that characterised Roman social life. Period photographs show the likes of Kim Novak and Gina Lollobrigida at receptions, helping themselves to plates of *salame* and *prosciutto* and filling their glasses from straw-covered flasks. Rome was still in many respects a provincial city whose customs had not been changed by the influx of money. Pictures such as these show how the taste for pleasure and rustic simplicity often won out over the grand-hotel lifestyle.

Ava Gardner and Linda Christian were the most prominent women in Roman café society throughout most of the 1950s. The former was a genuine star, one of the most beautiful women in the world, who was known for her smouldering sexuality. Born in Ohio, she was equally at home in Spain, where she developed a taste for bull-fighters, and Rome, where she shot several films, starting with *The Barefoot Contessa* in 1954. A prodigious drinker who liked to open the champagne at four in the afternoon, she introduced tequila to Rome and pioneered the mixing of vodka and tea. When she went out on the town she rarely went home before four in the morning and was said never to sleep. Her sexual appetite so astonished Italian reporters that they gave up trying to document the complexities of her love life or all of her brief liaisons. The Americans, however, were well accustomed to her ways. She was a favourite cover girl of *Confidential*, *Whisper* and *Hush Hush* magazines, which dubbed her simply 'that girl Ava'. Ravishing and wild, the dark-haired actress often went barefoot and was careless of convention. She patronised the Fontana sisters' fashion house but caused gasps of disapproval when she modelled a figure-hugging adaptation of priest's garb they designed for her.

Christian was barely an actress at all. The seductive redhead had only had a couple of small parts before she married Tyrone Power. She had been educated in Italy, and was more at home there than other foreigners. She had two children by Power, from whom she was separated when he died of heart failure, aged forty-four, in 1958. According to one of the actor's biographers, the couple had taken to attending swingers' parties, which had undermined their marriage. In her autobiography, Christian portrayed herself as the loyal and unjustly wronged wife. In fact, while she had the poise and something of the looks of Grace Kelly, she also had the mentality of a playboy. She had flings with Edmund Purdom, Walter Chiari and Maurizio Arena, as well as Aly Khan, the immensely wealthy playboy and Rita Hayworth's former husband. She would also have a passionate affair with the racing driver Alfonso De Portago that ended abruptly when he was killed on the track.

Most famously, she embarked on a tumultuous relationship with Baby Pignatari. The pair mainly met in Rome and often argued in public. Their separations and reconciliations were notorious. Although their relationship was not exclusive, since he was petrified by the idea of being tied down, the businessman responded furiously when he discovered that she had repeatedly betrayed him, even though his own conduct had been no different. Days after a bitter row, which occurred when they were in Rio de Janeiro, he paid hundreds of people to take part in a noisy car parade beneath the actress's hotel room, in which the roofs and sides of the vehicles were daubed with slogans reading 'Go Home Linda!'

The 'pocket Venus' Novella Parigini was central to the Via Veneto scene but rarely featured in the romantic soap operas narrated by the magazines. Unlike Linda Christian, she was discreet rather than flagrant about her affairs. She did not disdain publicity but she never made a show of her private life. One evening she might be out with Giò Stajano and her model friends, on another she was hosting stars in her studio, and on a third she would be dining with wealthy playboys. The photographs of this period show that she negotiated with ease the transition from the artistic sub-world of Via Margutta to the Via Veneto high life. Her impish smile and short spiky hair feature in photographs of the smartest clubs and in images of street stunts. Parigini acted as an intermediary between the various spheres of Roman and international society. Like the older animators of high society, the battleaxes Elsa Maxwell and Dorothy di Frasso, she was something of a snob who enjoyed her associations with film stars and was delighted to gain access to the palaces of the aristocracy. In the mixing of spheres, nations, classes, genders and generations that was such a novel phenomenon of the *dolce vita*, she was a key shuffler of the social pack.

It was noticeable that most of the women in the carnival were foreign. Italian females were generally too wary of domestic public opinion to risk indiscretions. The controversy around Sophia Loren stood as a warning to others. Knowing that she wanted to be married, and fearful that Cary Grant, with whom she was filming the romantic comedy *Houseboat*, might snatch her from him, Carlo Ponti arranged a quick remote divorce from his wife Giuliana and a proxy wedding to Sophia in Ciudad Juarez, Mexico, in September 1957. At a time when there was no divorce in Italy, this action led to an outraged reaction on the part of the Church. There were calls for Ponti to be arrested for bigamy while Loren was branded a home-wrecker. There were even calls for a boycott of her films. Other stars took note: after the end of his marriage to Shelley Winters, Vittorio Gassman lived for years with Anna Maria Ferrero, but the couple only ever admitted to 'a cordial, affectionate, sincere friendship'.

The former model Elsa Martinelli was the only Italian actress who was truly uncaring of convention. Despite her lowly origins, she was arrogant in manner and expected always to do her own thing. Her striking Audrey Hepburn looks and personal elegance somehow redeemed her. Alida Valli was another social animal but experience had taught her to fight shy of publicity. For the photographers, her reserved attitude was both annoying and a relief. It meant that, despite a shift in attitudes, a scandal was still a scandal – exciting and lucrative.

The high season of the *dolce vita* exploded between the summer of 1958 and the autumn of 1959. The opening in early August 1958 of the Café de Paris endowed the Via Veneto with an institution that would soon establish itself as the most fashionable on the road. Today pictures from its heyday are exhibited in glass display cases on the exterior wall. For the socialites its opening meant that it was no longer necessary to fix appointments: it was sufficient to turn up there at cocktail hour or after midnight.

Screenwriter Ennio Flaiano noted that summer how much the atmosphere had changed since 1950. The Via Veneto was no longer a road but a beach, he observed. There was a seaside atmosphere with cafés that were more colourful and visible.

Their exaggerated umbrellas seemed like alcoves, pagodas, exhibition tents or family tombs. Open-top cars slid along it like plasterboard gondolas at the theatre.

One person who instantly elected the new café as his favourite haunt was ex-King Farouk. It was with him that the extraordinary events of the torrid night of 15 August began. Short of a story and growing impatient, photographers spotted him and advanced *en masse*, cameras at the ready, towards the pavement table where he was seated with his small entourage. Fearing some sort of attack, his bodyguards leaped into action. In the brawl that ensued, punches were thrown, cameras smashed and tables overturned. Delighted with such unregal behaviour, other photographers eagerly snapped the scene.

Next it was the turn of Ava Gardner and Anthony Franciosa. Working together on the set of *The Naked Maja*, the pair had formed a friendship that had evolved into something more when Gardner took a young American supporting actor on the film as a lover. Stung that his prerogative as leading man had been usurped, Franciosa made his move, although he was now married to Shelley Winters. Franciosa and Gardner launched themselves on Rome's night life, mostly managing to dodge photographers. On 15 August they were finally cornered, entering and then leaving the Brick Top club in the early hours. Once again an unseemly punch-up was recorded for the delectation of magazine readers.

The resulting images became the trademark paparazzi photographs. Today they seem to encapsulate the very essence of the *dolce vita*. What is not evident from these dramatic nocturnal shots is the way they heralded the onset of war between the stars and the Roman photographers. By this time the photographers operated like gangs, mounted on scooters, and no longer worked mainly by day. The night offered more potential for scandal. In their silence and fixity, these images of conflict and tantrums show their victims' rage at invasions of privacy. What is not visible is the provocation that often caused the anger. When the photographers spotted prey, they shouted abuse and sexual taunts. As the victim chased or tussled with one or more of their number, others captured the scene for posterity. Stars were horrified by this development. The bandits of the stolen snap suddenly became not just parasites but the enemy. They were, as Linda Christian put it, 'camera-fiends' who made it increasingly unpleasant to go out at night. It was their exposure of the eccentricities, misdemeanours, adventures and betrayals of the rich and famous that provided grist to the mills of moralists and gossip columnists alike. Magazines around the world could not get enough snaps of the fisticuffs, drunken outbursts and scandalous liaisons of the stars and plastic heroes of contemporary Rome.

Perhaps the star who most defined the era was Anita Ekberg, the Swedish actress whose image became indelibly imprinted on the public mind. In 1958–9 the statuesque blonde was the queen of the Roman night, the perfect expression of the uninhibited manners of the era. A former Miss Sweden, who had gone to the United States on a prize-winning journey and won a Hollywood contract, she arrived in Italy to film *War and Peace* in 1955 and spent much time in Rome afterwards. Although her screen roles had been few, she had already been turned into a fully-fledged diva. In its edition of 17 December 1955, the London *Daily Mirror* reported that 'Her conversation scintillates with stories of men, mink and money. Her clothes, [which] are artfully moulded to her general outline, encourage every curve to stand out and speak for itself.'

When she arrived in the Italian capital, Ekberg was initially aloof and uninterested in anything but herself. She was nicknamed Anita Iceberg and pop singer Tony Dallara even recorded a song dedicated to her: 'Ghiaccio bollente' (Boiling Ice). The title suggests the transformation that occurred as the actress settled in. By any standard, she was a force of nature,

an unforgettable presence. Studio publicity described her as
'a woman and a half' and, in tribute to her enormous breasts,
it was announced that 'the seven hills of Rome are now nine'.
Ekberg always solicited attention but frequently lost her temper
with photographers and reporters. She invited them to her
civil wedding in Florence on 22 May 1956 to British matinée
idol Anthony Steel. On this occasion she caused a stir by
wearing a dress that left one shoulder completely exposed
(wags commented that it would have been appropriate had
she been marrying Tarzan), but then refused to answer any of
their questions about her plans. Only after a formal protest
from journalists did she and her husband relent. Four years
later, when photographers tried to break into the grounds of
her home, she met them with a bow and arrows.

The glamorous couple were not happy for long. As her
career progressed and that of her husband declined, he turned
heavily to drink. He found it impossible to cope with the
attention she received not merely from the press but from
vocal and vulgar appreciators of female beauty. Not only was
this Cambridge graduate and former Guards officer frequently
addressed as Mr Ekberg, but he had to put up with men trying
to pick up his wife under his nose. He was frequently snapped
in public in a drunken state, on occasion even on all-fours.

After their estrangement, Ekberg threw herself into the social
whirl. In Hollywood, she had already begun a sexual career of
note. She talked openly of affairs with Gary Cooper, Frank
Sinatra and Tyrone Power. There followed Walter Chiari, Steel,
photo-romance actor Franco Silva and others. By 1958, she had
become the most desirable woman in Rome, the fantasy pin-
up of every heterosexual male. As a Swede, she had a matter-
of-fact approach to sex, but she was obliged to be discreet about
her longest-running affair. For several years, she had carried on
a secret liaison with Gianni Agnelli, the playboy Fiat heir who
was married to the beautiful Princess Marella Caracciolo.

Ekberg was a one-woman event, a cavalcade in her own right. In the summer of 1958 she moved into a large apartment on Via Tagliamento. From the roof terrace, it was possible to look out in one direction over the block where the Montesi family still lived and in the other towards the Via Veneto. She drove around Rome in an open-top Mercedes and rarely missed a fashionable party. On her own, she was capable of turning a quiet social gathering into frenetic revelry. When she kicked off her shoes to dance barefoot, it signalled the start of any evening's true festivities.

The most newsworthy event of the whole season of the *dolce vita* was started by Ekberg, although, for once, she was not the protagonist. It occurred in November 1958 at the birthday party that Peter Howard, a scion of the Vanderbilt dynasty, held for aristocratic socialite and sometime journalist Olghina di Robilant. The event took place in the basement of the Rugantino restaurant in Piazza Sidney Sonnino in the Trastevere district. On this occasion, the guests were diverse, reflecting di Robilant's desire to widen her social circle beyond the mostly young aristocrats like herself. Artists and showbusiness people mingled with bearers of some of the grandest names in Rome and danced as a jazz band played. Among them were Novella Parigini, Linda Christian, Elsa Martinelli, Mussolini's daughter Edda and the other usual suspects. The evening was comparatively sedate until Anita Ekberg came to the fore and began to dance. She shook her blonde mane free and began to move her curvaceous body to the hot rhythms of the band. When she cast aside her shoes, the princes present threw their jackets to the floor to save her feet from getting cold on the terrazzo tiles.

The atmosphere suddenly got hotter when a Turkish actress by the name of Aiche Nana stepped forward and took Ekberg's place in front of the band. Nana was later dubbed an 'unknown Turkish dancer'. In fact, although she was only twenty-two,

she had already made several films in her homeland and had
been pictured with Gary Cooper and Gérard Philipe among
others. As the music got louder and faster, she gyrated wildly
and began to remove her clothes. The routine looked
professional, and instantly a semi-circle of male revellers formed
around her to offer encouragement. At that time, striptease
was a Parisian speciality. In Rome, it was regarded as obscene.
No theatre was licensed for such performances, which only
ever occurred at parties in private houses. Thus Nana's
impromptu striptease was sensational. An enthusiastic crowd
of young men, including members of the Torlonia, Ruspoli,
Pignatelli and Borghese families, crouched around their jackets,
looking on as she stripped down to her knickers, all the while
bumping and grinding and running her hands through her
long dark hair. In the background for once, Ekberg watched
with consternation while Novella Parigini and Giò Stajano
grinned with delight. As the men cheered, and the by now
topless dancer moved to the music, Parigini tried to grab her
black knickers. While some journalists, including a suspected
correspondent for *Confidential* magazine, had been barred entry,
Victor Ciuffa and a man who would write up the story for
Whisper were watching, rubbing their hands with glee.

But then their concentration suddenly snapped. Worried by
the turn events had taken, the owner had called the local
police. Secchiaroli, who had been lurking to the side, suddenly
sprang forward, raised his camera and flashed a series of snaps
before hastily beating a retreat as the police arrived to close
the restaurant. Amid the ensuing chaos, the famous guests
scuttled away to regroup later at the Café de Paris.

The photographer's appearance might have been
premeditated, but the resulting scandal was not. After Ciuffa's
notes first appeared in *Momento-sera*, the photographs were
published by the news weekly *L'Espresso* and expressions of
outrage immediately followed. The Vatican called for the

severest measures to be taken. Indeed, the offending issue of the magazine was impounded and the publishers sued for indecency. It was not so much the dancer that shocked as the presence around her of an audience. The association of well-to-do men (pictured in the press with black strips over their eyes) and a near-naked woman suggested an atmosphere of corruption and debauchery that recalled the wild tales of Capocotta. Peter Howard was bundled out of the country by the US embassy. For her part, Nana was arrested and later sentenced to two months in gaol for committing obscene acts in a public place. She had thought she was joining the 'in' crowd and was horrified to be singled out for exemplary punishment.

One of the most striking aspects of this episode was the way it brought hitherto hidden practices into public view. Debauched parties and hedonistic behaviour were routine among the smart set, and so was the consumption of drugs, as di Robilant would later admit. It was obvious that the events at the Rugantino restaurant were the result of the copious intake of drink and various types of drug. Nana herself was probably high or she would not have taken her performance so far. The whole episode revealed that the punch-up shots so eagerly sought by the freelance photographers were merely the tame tip of an iceberg of libertinism and bad behaviour.

By this point, most of the stars had become complicit with the photographers. Now they staged events and stunts, and liaised with publicity agents. The cocky snappers and the celebrities needed each other, and the press needed both to provide the taste of the high life that the public demanded.

XIX

The 'Sweet Life' On Screen

One man who often sat reading the papers and watching the parade of stars on the Via Veneto was a film director who had recently acquired an international reputation. His name was Federico Fellini. One picture story above all had caught his attention. It featured Anita Ekberg one sultry evening in August 1958 after the end of the usual round of fun and frolics. As a result of her barefoot dancing, she had badly scratched her heel and decided to find some water in which she could bathe it. The photographer Pier Luigi Praturlon was with her and he suggested that she should dip her foot in the nearby Trevi Fountain. A baroque masterpiece and a symphony in stone, it had been an icon of Rome for visitors at least since the time of American author Nathaniel Hawthorne, who featured it in his 1860 novel *The Marble Faun*. To cast a coin into its waters was a guarantee that one day one would return to the city. Praturlon was sure that a photograph of the actress dipping her feet would be saleable. After all, she had been pictured before in conjunction with Rome's monuments. As usual, Ekberg upped the odds and climbed into the fountain, where Praturlon immortalised her. The picture appeared in *L'Espresso* and was reproduced by newspapers and magazines across the world. It was to inspire Fellini's next film, and turn the *dolce vita* into a global phenomenon. After Wilma Montesi's alleged trip to Ostia, this was the most famous foot-bathing incident in 1950s Rome.

The Montesi case had provided a platform for many who hoped to launch film careers. Ugo Montagna's announcement that he would produce and star in a feature film was not out of step with the general ethos of the moment. Everyone involved in the Montesi affair made the most of the opportunities that came their way to extract cash from the press, the publishing industry or film producers. Virtually all the protagonists had some connection with the seventh art: Piccioni was a film composer; Adriana Bisaccia had a small part in *I tre ladri* (The Three Thieves), a film starring the popular comic Totò; Anna Maria Caglio succeeded finally in getting onto the screen with her film *La ragazza di Via Veneto*.

Even the Montesi family began shooting a film in their apartment, although they soon abandoned it. The bizarre scheme was set up by the family's two keenest film-goers, Maria and Wanda, who were briefly tantalised by the prospect of seeing themselves on the silver screen. Approached by a man who presented himself as a director, they were unable to say no. Rodolfo was brow-beaten into going along with it. Their then legal advisers strongly disapproved of this pathetic example of exhibitionism and stepped down in protest. In the end filming was halted following a dispute with the director over money.

The Montesi case itself seemed to possess some of the qualities of a film plot: a beautiful girl, a mysterious death, sex parties, drugs and a marchese. Enterprising producers bought up a large number of hastily composed proposals for films resembling the case. Conspiracies and murders abounded in works with titles like *La città che uccide* (The City That

Kills), *Delitto in riva al mare* (Murder by the Sea), *L'inchiesta* (The Investigation), *Delitto di Torvaianica* (Murder at Torvaianica) and *Lo strano caso di Rita Molfesi* (The Strange Case of Rita Molfesi). Men and women came forward to offer to play various characters – like the man with the bad-guy looks who is instantly signed up by a producer in Alberto Moravia's tale 'Rascal Face'. None of these films was actually made, but aspects of the case featured in a variety of real movies. Despite severe censorship, references to crime, drugs and the murder of young women permeated the melodramas of the period. The closest thing to a representation of the Montesi case was a play by Gian Paolo Callegari entitled *Le ragazze bruciate verdi* (The Girls Who Burned Out Early), which was performed in Rome and more widely in Italy from 1956. Its central theme was juvenile prostitution.

While television offered a bland, aspirational view of the opportunities afforded by economic development, filmmakers rarely, if ever, celebrated modernity. Their left-wing allegiance made them critical of changing domestic spaces, lifestyles, aspirations and attitudes. They focused instead on the contradictions of change, the people who were left behind, the growth of crime, or unease and alienation. Directors schooled in neo-realism always engaged in long months of research on the ground before they started shooting a film. The extraordinarily realistic feel of many Italian films of this period derived from a first-hand knowledge that filmmakers had of the underbelly of Rome.

Federico Fellini was not a typical provincial, since his mother had been born and raised in Rome, but his point of view on the capital was that of an outsider and adoptive Roman. His first Roman film, *La strada*, won the award for best foreign film at the 1955 Oscars. In early 1955 he started work on *Il bidone* (The Swindlers), which he intended as an exploration of the world of the tricksters, black-marketeers and cheats of every stripe who had flourished in the 1940s. Typically such men were southerners from the regions of Campania or Calabria. As life returned to normal, opportunities receded and the confidence tricksters became a dying breed. Fellini knew some of these people, whom he encountered in the Bar Canova, one of his favourites, near Piazza del Popolo. Amused by their anecdotes, he decided to tell their story through film. As was typical at the time, the lead role was handed to an American actor, Broderick Crawford, who played a con-man on the slide.

A key scene in the film featured a New Year's Eve party in the house of a successful swindler. The gathering has the air of an elegant *soirée*, as male and female guests arrive in evening dress. But soon the tone changes and an atmosphere of debauchery takes hold, as drink flows, the music becomes more frenetic and some of the women dance with abandon. Cocaine is snorted and there is the suggestion of the beginnings of an orgy. The sleazy scene was rendered credible by the casting of a whole range of real characters drawn from the world of the tricksters. The sub-world of prostitutes, *entraîneuses*, petty criminals and drug-pushers provided a series of strikingly individual faces. Although the sequence was heavily cut before the film's release, and was restored only many years later, reviewers in the left-wing press were not slow to point out that the atmosphere of louche immorality was precisely that which had been continually alluded to by numerous witnesses in the Montesi investigation. Without the endless newspaper reports of cocaine use, drug-smuggling, orgies and prostitution, it would not have been possible to depict a world in which these things were commonplace. Such depictions, in turn, reinforced the perception that the activities were widespread.

For his next film, the thirty-seven-year-old director focused once more on the seamy underbelly of Rome. With the writer Pier Paolo Pasolini, he made the acquaintance of prostitutes, rent-boys and the downbeat inhabitants of far-flung districts like Pietralata and the Idroscalo. *Le notti di Cabiria* (The Nights of Cabiria) was eventually shot between July and October 1956. In the completed movie, the contrast between the prostitutes, who spend their nights on the street, and the glittering world of the rich is underlined in a scene in which the two worlds collide. One evening a prostitute named Cabiria, played by Giulietta Masina, Fellini's petite and elf-like wife, is picked up near the Via Veneto by a passing film star who escorts her into a private club; its anglophile feel (a neon sign announces that its name is Piccadilly) evokes that of the Open Gate to which Ugo Montagna had accompanied Anna Maria Caglio. (Today a plaque commemorates the moment the road made this appearance on screen.) The actor, who is driving a splendid open-top sports car, takes her back to his magnificent residence on the Via Appia Antica. The enormous wardrobe, the attendant butler, white telephones, aquarium and crystal bird cages are all signs of a world in which money is no object. The star was played by Amedeo Nazzari, a rugged and handsome Sardinian who had been a leading Italian male actor since the 1930s – a home-grown Clark Gable – who on this occasion simply played himself. As magazine readers well knew, Nazzari was a fast-living Casanova known for his love of luxury cars and nightclubs, his turbulent love affairs and Hollywood-style home. By casting him, Fellini incorporated a new real-life element into his filmmaking style.

Because of the relative realism and lack of romanticism with which it treated the theme of prostitution, *Le notti di Cabiria* was controversial. Even before it was completed, there were protests that it would portray Rome as a centre of vice. To avoid problems with the censors, Fellini used his connections to arrange, with the assistance of a Jesuit priest of his acquaintance, for the film to be viewed by Cardinal Siri of Genoa, a powerful figure in the Church who was seen as the

Pope's deputy. There was a sharp divide in the Church between those who believed that social evils should be denounced and those who simply thought they should be covered up. Siri was thought to belong to the first camp. After a secret midnight screening, the cardinal gave his blessing and all obstacles to the film's release fell away. What the distinguished churchman did not realise was that, in approving a film that showed an immoral environment because it had a moral message, he had unwittingly opened up wider possibilities for representing the seamy side of Italian life.

Fellini planned to make his next film, provisionally entitled *Moraldo in città* (Moraldo in the City), about the adventures of a young provincial in the Rome of the mid-1950s. This was based on an idea he had nursed since shooting *I Vitelloni* in 1953. The earlier film had been set among the idle middle-class dreamers of the seaside town of Rimini. In that movie, the men talk constantly of escaping from the constrictions of their limited world but remained incapable of breaking free of it. Only one, Moraldo, finally finds the energy to go and try his fortune in Rome. Moraldo's life in the capital was to be the subject of the new film. As Fellini and his friends chatted and developed ideas, they realised that a new world of flash money and flash cameras, shallow ideals and corruption was fast eclipsing the Rome of high-brow literary and film magazines, intellectual coteries and passionate argument that they had had in mind as a setting. The *dolce vita* was just the tip of a society that was undergoing rapid change. If Moraldo had come to Rome, he would no longer have been a writer but would have been sucked into the world of gossip magazines and scandal sheets.

Rather than abandon the project, Fellini decided to shift the focus to the 'other' worlds that inhabited the salons of Via Veneto and the distorted representations of them that were to be found in magazines and newsreels. He aimed to capture the excitement and gloss of the international stars and show how the development of the mass media and publicity was changing the fabric of Rome.

Unlike the illustrated magazines, the aim of the director and his colleagues was not merely to celebrate the momentary. They also wanted to say something more general about the type of change that was occurring and what this meant for the social order, established values, the intellectuals and religion. They aimed at the same time to illustrate the type of people and events that had come to the fore in this new context. All Fellini's previous films had oscillated between nostalgia for trades or activities in decline and critique of a present seen as illusory and corrupt. *La dolce vita* would be no exception. Veteran producer Peppino Amato offered his backing and preparations began.

Fellini had moved on from neo-realism, but he still liked to begin preparation for his films in the conventional way by enquiring into a social group. He had explored variety players, photo-romance performers and readers, idle young men, confidence tricksters and prostitutes, taking the time to get to know them. He befriended the photographers at a meeting in the famous Roman restaurant Gigetto Er Pescatore. After hearing tales of their activities, he accompanied them on some expeditions. He watched them at work and they staged some shots for him. Secchiaroli became his special adviser, and the director spent hours listening to him talk about the tricks of his trade. The name 'Paparazzo' was invented for the character of a photographer based on Secchiaroli, who, in the film, was played by Walter Santesso. Afterwards, his name became a term that would be extended in common speech to the category of press photographs as a whole. It derived from a combination of ideas. Ennio Flaiano, Fellini's scriptwriter, always said he took it from the name of a Calabrian innkeeper in a George Gissing novel. Fellini liked the waspish buzz of it, which conveyed onomatopoeically the annoying and parasitical presence of the photographers.

Fellini wanted to build his film around a strong central character – a handsome aspirant writer not unlike Victor Ciuffa who earns his crust by working as a gossip columnist and press agent. Flaiano described him as 'a man who has been absorbed by the society he despises'. The director took his cue from magazines like *Lo Specchio* and *L'Europeo*, which offered a sensational picture of the glamorous lives of the stars. The anxieties of his hero, torn between the temptations of women and celebrity on the one hand, authenticity and intellectual engagement on the other, formed the core of the narrative. The film was conceived as a collage, without a real story, that centred on the inner and outer conflicts of the central figure. Flaiano, the critic Brunello Rondi and others wrote several episodes that included the arrival of a Hollywood star in Rome, the torments of an intellectual who eventually kills his children and himself in his despair at the modern world, the rituals of the upper class, a miraculous claimed appearance of the Madonna, and a party that degenerates into an orgy.

The casting of the gossip columnist led to a dispute that was merely one of a sequence of production problems that dogged the film. Amato pulled out when Fellini refused to accept as the title *Via Veneto*, a brand name that, according to the producer, was bound to bring success. After this, Dino De Laurentiis stepped in but he and Fellini split over who should play the columnist. The director was determined that it should be an Italian actor and he already had in mind a moderately well-known workaday Italian – Marcello Mastroianni. De Laurentiis wanted an international name, perhaps Paul Newman, to draw foreign audiences. The director's refusal, other disagreements and spiralling costs eventually led to the Milanese publisher Angelo Rizzoli taking over the role of producer.

Fellini wanted to capture the authentic atmosphere of the Rome of his time. To this end, the film featured an astonishing parade of characters: actors, foreign movie stars, intellectuals, aristocrats, transvestites, gossip columnists, photo-journalists, prostitutes, artists and socialites all jostled in a giddy merry-go-round. Several French actors, including Alain Cuny, Anouk Aimée and Yvonne Furneaux, provided the film with a backbone and a solid international feel. Fellini had hoped to recruit veteran Oscar-winner Luise Rainer for the role of a mad nymphomaniac living in a tower in the vicinity of Torvaianica, but she was dropped and the scene cut when she created difficulties about the character. Many of the supporting cast simply played themselves. Members of the aristocratic Odescalchi family took parts, as did other noblemen and women, British critic John Francis Lane, Iris Tree the poet, the realist artist Anna Salvatore, Giò Stajano, the critic Leonida Repaci, future Velvet Underground singer Nico, and others. Since Fellini did not like to disappoint acquaintances, he had promised roles or cameos to hundreds of people. There was much resentment on the part of those who were excluded or whose cameos failed to make the final cut. Some, including Maurizio Arena, would find a small satisfaction when Amato gave them roles in a low-budget film entitled *Via Veneto* that he finally made three years later. Giò Stajano and one or two others appeared in both films.

Unusually, *La dolce vita* was a film whose own making was a spectacle. Shooting started on 16 March 1959 and did not finish until the late summer. The press was invited to view the shooting of selected scenes, visitors continually arrived on set and crowds gathered whenever the director, his troupe and cast took over a real-life location. It was widely written about and debated as it was being made, not just for publicity reasons but because several episodes in the film were loosely or directly based on real people or events, some of which had been

conceived to win media attention in the first place. Aiche
Nana's striptease was transmuted into an orgy scene, while
the 'miracle' was taken from a similar episode reported by the
press. Taken together, the episodes of the film portrayed Rome
as an exciting, cosmopolitan city in thrall to the flash-bulb
and celebrity, a city where truth had been corrupted and
religion deprived of meaning. The tension between celebration
and condemnation that marked the film was to some extent
the result of the contrast between Flaiano's radically pessimistic
outlook on the new Rome and Fellini's less severe one.

There were several strong female parts. Anita Ekberg, as
Hollywood star Sylvia Rank, was largely called upon to play
herself. The director was fascinated by her impulsive exuberance
and physical abundance, which corresponded exactly to his
childish notion of ideal female beauty. The first time he saw
a photograph of her, he exclaimed, 'Please, don't let me meet
her!' Although he was anything but a faithful husband, Fellini
knew that he could become dangerously obsessed with a
woman of such exaggerated proportions. 'When I met her she
was even more the character than ever I could have believed.
"You are my imagination come to life," I told her,' he later
wrote. Suspicious of such expansiveness, the actress replied: 'I
do not go to bed with you.' Ekberg's famous dip in the Trevi
Fountain was elaborated by Fellini into the signature scene of
the film. At the end of a night's revelry, the Swedish actress's
character strides into the fountain. Wearing a gravity-defying
low-cut black evening gown, she is reluctantly followed by a
bewildered Marcello Mastroianni in a dark suit. Their non-
tactile embrace, as the waters suddenly dry up behind them,
was a moving and quasi-intimate moment, rendered visually
fabulous by the baroque white exuberance of the fountain
and the contrasts of black and white captured by
cinematographer Otello Martelli. The glamour was entirely an
illusion of cinema. In fact, the water was so cold when the

scene was shot, in April 1959, that Anitona, as Fellini affectionately called her, was wearing wellington boots.

Several other famous locations in Rome were employed during filming, including the Odescalchi villa and the spa at Caracalla. Fellini tried to shoot some of the Via Veneto scenes *in situ*, but the pressure of constant crowds forced him to rethink. The filming had become an event in itself and that made it impossible for the director to have proper control. He took the unusual step of ordering a section of the street (the part directly outside the Café de Paris) to be rebuilt in the studio at Cinecittà, a costly move to which the film's producer, Angelo Rizzoli, agreed only on condition that the director renounce his percentage of the profits. Many of the interiors, including the nightclub scenes and the final episode in the villa at Fregene, were also shot in the studio. This allowed the director, in association with his set designer Piero Gherardi, to reinvent familiar locations and give them a glamorous makeover. No longer sloping downwards, as in real life, but flat, the 'Via Veneto' became a concentration of excitement with all the dull moments, the waiting, and the existential boredom of the rich and the famous, filtered out.

In contrast to Mauro Bolognini's *La notte brava* (The Big Night), a film that was shot around the same time about a trio of low-lifers who live it up for one night, Fellini's film had little downbeat realism. Bolognini included scenes shot in the lower part of Via Veneto, leading to Piazza Barberini, and in a real cellar club named the Rupe Tarpea. Gherardi's nightclubs were not improvised and sleazy, as many were in reality, but were artificial and sophisticated. They were imagined places inspired by his travels in the Far East. The décor was fantastic and Oriental, and the customers all dressed in dinner jackets and elegant gowns. On screen, those scenes almost glisten. Pier Luigi Praturlon, who had immortalised Ekberg's original dip in the fountain, took hundreds of set photographs, which were released in small numbers to magazines in the publicity build-up that preceded the film's release. The stills created an image of *La dolce vita* as a daring, acerbic, beautiful attack on a corrupt upper class. The fact that in reality it was something less than a full-blown critique did not prevent some from attacking it as an outrageous insult to Italy's reputation.

La dolce vita was widely seen as an ambitious and powerful exposé of the impact on a provincial society of glamour, fame and an intrusive press. But it was not a realistic portrait of modern Rome. Fellini originally planned to move his filmmaking style more boldly than before towards documentary. In the event, he produced a selective mix of fact, semi-fact, disguised fact and fiction. While some of the real episodes and places that informed the *dolce vita* were scarcely modified, others were so transformed as to be barely recognisable. Via Margutta, for example, was eliminated save for the camp presence of Stajano and the fleeting appearance of the artist and gallery owner Anna Salvatore. Two years later veteran director Mario Camerini would shoot *Via Margutta*, based on painter Ugo Moretti's portrait of the artists' world, with Yvonne Furneaux (who played Marcello's suffocating mistress Emma in *La dolce vita*) in the role of a female artist loosely based on Novella Parigini. But the film had none of the panache of Fellini's take on modern Rome.

The movie provoked angry comment even before it was released. The director knew his film would stir up controversy and he arranged a series of previews to try to get critics and journalists on his side before the official release. But in fact its critique was muted. To purify and simplify the visual seductions of the movie, most of the key contributors to the decadence of the time simply did not feature. In the end, Fellini did not produce an investigation into a corrupt world but a visually striking celebration of a changing Rome that was mixed with a strain of moralism and nostalgia. For all his antipathy to the transformation of the capital, Ennio Flaiano had acknowledged that Rome was still a small town where everyone seemed to know everyone else. It was not a city of great vices based on alcohol, drugs, violence or passions. It had a strong familial character even in its corruption.

However, this interpretation wasn't shared by everybody. Despite Fellini's efforts to neutralise criticism, the release of *La dolce vita* gave rise to bitter controversy. The première in the capital on 4 February passed off peacefully enough. At the Milan première the following day four spectators got up and shouted, 'Enough, enough,' one hour into the film. The director was accused of having gone over to the Communists and one spectator even spat in his face. Opinion was split between those who regarded the film as a salutary comment on the moral decline that prosperity and change had brought, and those who believed that the depiction of sex, scandal and moral vacuity was undesirable. Whereas in Rome such things no longer caused much of a stir, in Milan – Italy's 'moral capital' – they were antithetical to the core values on which economic progress was founded. While right-wingers were horrified, the left barely concealed its satisfaction. Fellini had never been a darling of the Communists but now he was warmly embraced by them. In the view of some left-wing critics, the film implied that the Eternal City had dissolved into a quagmire of corruption and sensation. The country was governed by an irresponsible élite that thought only of its own pleasures. To this extent, and regardless of its outcome, the Montesi case bore directly on the film since it had cast doubt on the integrity of the national ruling class. The sense of corruption in the film was pervasive, even if no accusing finger could be pointed at anyone in particular.

Protests in the press and from the public led to questions in Parliament. By representing a sleazy and aimless world, the film was seen as slandering the Roman people, the capital of Italy and the Catholic Church. For the Vatican newspaper, the *Osservatore Romano*, it was 'indecent and sacrilegious', a travesty that allowed 'hundreds of Roman whores, faggots, screen queens, press agents, artists, aristocrats and lawyers to play themselves or revolting caricatures of themselves'. The under-secretary responsible for cinema, a Christian Democrat named Magri, responded, saying, 'There is no doubt in fact that Fellini's film presents scenes of a crude and merciless realism and overall constitutes a dark fresco of a degraded and disoriented life that offends the sensibility of normal people and gives rise to reactions of astonishment, disgust and indignation.' But he admitted, with apparent reluctance, that the censorship commission had found no complicity with the material treated and therefore the film had passed. While the left disapproved of this ambivalent stance, conservatives increased the dose. 'Sewers exist too but they are kept closed because no one benefits commercially from opening them!' shouted one parliamentarian. 'What would Cavour and Garibaldi have said if they had seen *La dolce vita*?' enquired the Honourable Augusto Greggi of the Association of Catholic Fathers, in a speech that included condemnation of the violation of the Dome of St Peter's and the abuse of the Christ the Redeemer statue, which is carried by helicopter over Rome in the opening scenes of the film. Attacked by their fellow nobles, the Odescalchi family and other bluebloods in the film rushed to denounce it, claiming they had been tricked into taking part. The script described to them, they pleaded, bore no relation to the completed film.

Despite efforts to suppress or censor it, *La dolce vita* was the hit of the season in Italy even though ticket prices were raised on account of its unusual length of more than three hours. So great was its success that it was still making money in Italy five years after its release. Fellini had won the best foreign film Oscar in 1955 for *La strada*. Now his new film was a contender for honours. It won the Palme d'Or at Cannes after the president of the jury, detective writer Georges Simenon, championed it, and it was a critical and commercial success worldwide. The film was not merely a spectacle but a phenomenon.

The tragic dimension of the 'sweet life' was underlined by real events shortly after the film's release. One night in February 1960, cabaret singer Fred Buscaglione was killed, drunk at the wheel of his red Thunderbird. One of the key figures of the Roman nights, his gangster ballads had enlivened the city's clubs and invested the criminal underworld with B-movie glamour. His death was a consequence of his trying to live up to the persona he had created for himself. Facile observers compared it to that of James Dean, who had died at the wheel of his Porsche in September 1955.

Buscaglione was not the only protagonist of the *dolce vita* to lose his life in a car crash. In 1962 Devon-born British actress Belinda Lee, who had been the protagonist of a scandalous love affair with Count Filippo Orsini, a prominent and married member of the papal aristocracy, was killed, and in 1965 Porfirio Rubirosa smashed his Ferrari into a tree early one morning in the Bois de Boulogne.

The film transformed its stars into icons. Mastroianni had previously been a workaday actor in Italian cinema. With the aid of some skilful make-up intended to give him a sinister air, he was turned into a seductive, cynical male. He became the new Latin lover, the long-awaited successor, in the eyes of foreigners, to Rudolph Valentino. Although it would serve him well, Mastroianni hated this image, and he spent the rest of his long career playing with it, subverting and contradicting it. As the blonde bombshell Sylvia Rank, Anita Ekberg became a caricature film star, who was half child and all woman. For Italians she was, as she is for Mastroianni in the Trevi Fountain scene, the dream woman, the embodiment of a primitive, untamed nature and the promise of a future of abundance and prosperity. She would never again make a film of such note, but the shot of her striding through the fountain's waters in a low-cut evening gown has become one of the iconic images of the twentieth century.

Although the Montesi scandal was one of the decisive events

of the decade, it was only incorporated obliquely into *La dolce vita*, symbolised by a dead sea monster on the beach in the final scene. In the original conception, extended scenes at Torvaianica were to have been constructed around a contrast between the decadent nymphomaniac Dolores and an innocent teenage girl named Paola who waits tables at a seaside *trattoria*. After the character of Dolores was cut, the only remaining scene at Torvaianica was a brief interaction between Mastroianni's press agent and Paola, at her *trattoria*. The earlier contrast was shifted to the final scene, where, shortly after the sighting of the monster, Paola appears on the beach at some distance from Marcello and invites him to join her friends in joyful play. Her gesture is in vain, since Marcello, who by now is beyond redemption, cannot hear her and turns away, dismissing her with a resigned wave.

The creature was designed by Gherardi on the basis of Fellini's recollection of a strange sea beast that had been discovered by fishermen in Rimini in 1934 and which, at the time, was featured in a sketch on a magazine cover. 'Almost a monster! Attracted by a great mass floating on the surface, three fishermen spotted near the beach of Rimini a huge marine monster and after a difficult struggle they managed to stun it and carry it on to the sand. Despite being three metres long and weighing a ton, the captured beast has a tiny mouth. It is a type of sunfish very rare in our parts,' read the caption. Like the body on the beach, Gherardi's flat, dead creature was an inexplicable, embarrassing presence. It stared back as if with accusing eyes at those who saw it. In its decomposing state, it represented the putrefaction of society. Ostensibly it was a modest recognition of a complex intrigue that had preceded and informed so many elements of the hedonistic explosion of 1958, but for the journalist Tullio Kezich, who published a diary of the long months of the shoot, 'the monster of Fregene perhaps embodies the meaning of the whole film'.

XX

Aftermath

The Montesi case did not end with the conclusion of the Venice trial. The legal aftermath dragged on for years. For Wilma's uncle, Giuseppe, the nightmare was far from over. It had been expected that the acquittal of the accused in Venice would lead directly to the pursuit of fresh investigations focusing on him. Even before the trial ended, on 8 April 1957, a warrant was issued for his arrest by another court that charged him with slandering his employer and colleagues at the Casciani works: he had denounced them in August 1955 for obstructing the course of justice by saying that he had left work early on the fateful day to go to Ostia after receiving a telephone call. He claimed they knew he was innocent and had accused him falsely, perhaps because his employer Franco Biagetti was a friend of Piero Piccioni.

By this time Giuseppe had returned to Rome, resuming his main employment at the Treasury. Two policemen went to his place of work to serve the warrant. They found that he was absent, having been given permission to attend to an urgent personal matter. After checking various possible locations, the officers were tipped off as to his whereabouts and finally found him having lunch at a seaside café near Ostia, in the company of a male friend and two women. He was immediately arrested and placed in custody under a regime of solitary confinement. The severity of his treatment suggested that the authorities wanted to put him under pressure and force him to reveal the truth of his whereabouts on 9 and 10 April 1953. In total, Giuseppe spent ninety-seven days in gaol, during which he received regular visits from the Spissu sisters. At that same time he became the target of variety theatre sketches. In one, actors playing Montagna and Piccioni tuck into a sumptuous meal at a restaurant. When the waiter arrives to ask who will pay the bill, they simultaneously exclaim, 'Giuseppe will pay for us!' After his solitary confinement was relaxed he shared a cell with a drug-dealer. He revealed nothing and was finally released on 13 September, as autumn was settling in.

The charge against him stood, however, and he would be tried in December 1960. The deputy procurator concluded that there were sufficient grounds to send him for trial on the charge of aggravated slander, and made it clear that the issue of Wilma's death bore directly on the matter. 'If there were proof that the death of Wilma Montesi was caused by a criminal act, then the evidence relating to her paternal uncle Giuseppe would constitute an accusatory circle around his person so tight as to indicate beyond doubt that he was the author of that hypothetical criminal act,' he stated. The judge who led the instructional inquiry also took this view. He argued that 'the serious elements counting against him demonstrate that Giuseppe Montesi, on the afternoon of 9 April 1953 was undoubtedly involved in the events which led to the death of his niece'. In other words, although there was not sufficient proof to charge him directly with causing Wilma's death, morally he was guilty. Also accused was Rossana Spissu, who was charged with bearing false witness for having conspired with Giuseppe to create an alibi that was then demonstrated to be pure invention.

In December 1960, Giuseppe and Rossana were each sentenced to two years in gaol. At their trial Giuseppe made a point of stating, 'I only want to say that I never had anything to do with my niece Wilma.' It emerged at their trial that what had saved him from more serious charges was proof that Wilma had died not on 9 April but the following day. He had no alibi for the afternoon and evening that Wilma had disappeared, but the day after he had been fully involved with the family's search for the lost girl. And, thanks to a routine amnesty, neither he nor Rossana served any time behind bars.

Despite the firmness of the statements of the legal officials reported above, no further enquiries were conducted into the circumstances of Wilma's death, and journalists who wanted to continue digging into Giuseppe's activities were instructed to desist. Just like Silvano Muto in 1953, they were told that it was the task of the investigating authorities to deal with such matters and that press interference would provoke official displeasure.

A further legal consequence of the outcome of the Venice trial was a charge of defamation solicited by Ugo Montagna against Anna Maria Caglio and Silvano Muto. In the five years following the Venice trial, their trial was postponed no fewer than four times on various technical grounds. In 1964, it at last took place. It was essentially a reprise of Muto's original trial in 1954, with the exception that Caglio now found herself in the dock rather than on the witness stand. The hearings were brief and attracted little press attention. A guilty verdict was quickly reached. Muto was sentenced to two years in gaol and Anna Maria to two years and six months. They, too, would would not serve time, although the stain on their names would make life difficult for them for years afterwards.

The verdict of the trial of Muto and Caglio for defamation explicitly rejected the conclusions about the Montesi case that had been reached in Venice, which had discounted the possibilities that Wilma had committed suicide or met an accidental death. There was insufficient evidence for this view, the Roman judges now asserted. In this way, the entire course of the investigation into Wilma's death, from Sepe's investigation to the Venice trial, was demolished in favour of the original official conclusions. Wilma's ghost was taken back to Ostia and the fable of the fatal foot-bathing restored to its place in the official account of the case. Rejecting any hypothesis about what had happened, the court concluded that, 'The case is still shrouded in mystery.' This outcome constituted the delayed revenge of the Rome judicial authorities over their northern colleagues.

Muto and Caglio both made strenuous efforts to have their sentences overturned. They went first to the Appeal Court and then to the Court of Cassation. In both instances the verdict and their sentences were confirmed. The final legal outcome of the Montesi case therefore was this: not only were Piccioni and his alleged co-conspirators innocent of all charges, but there had been no cover-up of crimes or unseemly activities because none had occurred. The final verdict on Muto and Caglio also had the effect of lifting the shadow that still loomed over Giuseppe Montesi.

In the 1960s and 1970s, Italian cities changed: they grew in size; their shanty-town populations found regular dwellings as they expanded and most people reached a reasonable standard of living. A significant shift occurred in the way Italy was ruled, reinforced by the phase of modernisation in the Catholic Church initiated by Pope John XXIII, who died in 1963, and which would be developed by the Second Vatican Council. The decline of the tensions of the Cold War period produced a political détente that eroded some of the sharp divisions of the past, although it would not be long before economic growth and rapid urban expansion gave rise to new tensions from which the Communist Party would benefit. After the industrial heartlands of Milan and Turin, Rome was the city that grew the most. By the early 1960s, its population had reached 2.3 million, an increase of 700,000 since 1950. This resulted in a suburban sprawl that fanned out from the centre in all possible directions. A construction boom without equal enveloped isolated villas and scenic vineyards in a wave of concrete and cement. At the same time, the number of private cars increased massively, leading to the hitherto non-existent phenomenon of the Roman traffic jam. Although the term 'economic miracle' was mainly used to refer to the booming northern economy, the capital experienced no less forcefully the pressure of urbanisation and the arrival of modern consumption.

One of the places to be freed of its status as a far-flung village that few had heard of was Torvaianica. The construction of the coastal road linking Ostia and Anzio, which opened in 1954, made it easily reachable by car from Rome. The building of homes, bars, restaurants and bathing establishments turned it into a tourist destination. The notoriety the village had acquired at the time of the Montesi case provided the first impulse towards weekend visits that would soon no longer need the justification of morbid curiosity. Before he was obliged to step down, Guiseppe Sotgiv used his position as president of Rome's provincial council to build a children's holiday camp there. The provocative nature of this decision was plain to everyone.

As long as their legal situation remained unresolved, the protagonists of the Montesi case continued to appear from time to time in the weeklies. Giuseppe was photographed around the time of his trial in the company of the two Spissu sisters while he played in a park with his son Riccardo. He had still not decided which of them, if either, he would make his bride. With a glint in his eye, he said that continuing uncertainty about his situation made it impossible for him to take any steps to clarify his personal circumstances.

Gradually, however, the Montesi case was largely forgotten. It belonged to an Italy that no longer existed and, like a play from a past decade whose characters no longer seem to have contemporary resonance, it came to be regarded as a period piece. It was remembered first of all as an extraordinary manifestation of press power and public opinion that went beyond the limits of reasonable behaviour. It was a travesty that occurred because Italy was new to democracy and because there was resentment against those who had done well out of a period in which many had suffered. The press acted irresponsibly, in this view, because it was keen to win a new role and acquire a mass readership. For this reason, every snippet of information was printed, creating a dubious market in revelations.

The case was remembered also because of the undue weight given to the baseless accusations of one woman. Anna Maria Caglio was given credit by figures in the Catholic Church, at a time when the latter's power was unrivalled, so her statements were taken seriously and investigated by the legal authorities, instead of being dismissed out of hand.

There was, in addition, the political aspect. For some, the whole affair was a political strategy involving below-the-belt blows to discredit Attilio Piccioni, remove him from the race for the leadership of the Christian Democrats and create a space for a new generation of ambitious politicians.

The erasure of the Montesi case can also be explained by reference to political events. Between 1957 and 1962, Italian political life moved slowly towards the establishment of a new equilibrium between the parties. Pushed by Amintore Fanfani and his friends on the left, the Christian Democrats moved at a snail's pace towards the formation of a coalition with the Socialist Party, which was no longer allied to the larger Communist Party. This was no simple matter. In a bid to avoid the need for an opening to the left, Christian Democrat Fernando Tambroni formed a government in 1960 that was supported in Parliament by the neo-Fascist Italian Social

Movement. The riots that occurred in some northern cities famous for their role in the anti-Fascist Resistance quickly put paid to this scheme and opened the way to a collaboration that had been sternly resisted by conservatives of all stripes. In this phase Attilio Piccioni returned to office as foreign minister in 1962. However, his days as a major player in his party were over. Although the centre-left was an important development, the small size of the Socialist Party meant that the competition between Christian Democrats and Communists that had marked the mid-1950s remained the basic structural divide of Italian politics. Neither force had any desire to remember the Montesi case. The Christian Democrats preferred to think of their own history in terms of the great victory won in the 1948 election, the adherence to NATO, the contribution to the EEC. Some of the protagonists of the 1950s were still on the scene decades later and the uneasy truce between them rested on an unspoken understanding that certain topics should not be mentioned. For example, Fanfani was prime minister for the last time in 1987, Giulio Andreotti in 1992. As for the left, the outcome of the Venice trial was a setback for all those, including newspapers like *Paese Sera*, who had banked on a guilty verdict.

Soon the entire social world of the case seemed to belong to another age. In popular memory, the 1950s came to be seen as the time when the ground was laid for Italy's post-war recovery and growth into a leading industrial nation. Its symbols were the Vespa and the film star, with television and the Fiat 500 representing the first conquests of familial prosperity. The yearning for fame and reward that, at certain moments, had turned the Montesi case into pure theatre became associated most commonly with the general character of the boom years and with television quiz shows such as *Lascia o raddoppia?*. Even the broader contribution that the Montesi case made to social phenomena that marked the era has been effaced in favour of more comfortable recollections. The origins of the paparazzi are never attributed to the case, but rather to the international celebrities and their antics on the Via Veneto.

One of the key events that heralded the birth of a new Italy, an Italy no longer weighed down by the divisions and rancour of the post-Fascist period or struggling with poverty, was the 1960 Olympic Games, held in Rome. The extensive construction work and preparations were marked by the usual speculation and political manipulation, in which the name of Ugo Montagna once more came up, but the end result was positive. The organisers made sure that the most was made of Rome's classical past. A large statue of the she-wolf suckling Romulus and Remus was placed in the Olympic village and an exhibition was held commemorating sport in ancient Rome. To avoid jealousy from other Italian cities, suitable nods were paid to Italy's medieval and Renaissance civilisations, while the Vatican was appeased by appropriate references to Catholic Rome. The then minister of defence, Andreotti, in his role as chairman of the organising committee, addressed the opening ceremony in Latin. The city was invaded by competitors and spectators from every corner of the world and everything took place in an atmosphere of harmony and international friendship. For Carlo Levi, the whole experience was marked by 'the physical and visible appearance of happiness'. Rome consolidated its reputation as a city that had put its Fascist past behind it.

The Olympics heralded the beginning of the age of mass tourism. Running for three weeks from 25 August to 11 September, the Games offered ample opportunity to visitors to check out the truth of what they had heard about Rome's free-wheeling mores and piquant entertainments. The Montesi-case circus had been widely reported abroad and there had been numerous reports of the antics of celebrities, as well as colourful evocations of the latter-day Roman orgies that ostensibly happened in the city. The huge success of *La dolce vita* – the film opened in France in May 1960 and in most of Western Europe in June and July, although not until the following year in Britain and the USA – ensured that many tourists made a beeline for the Via Veneto and the Trevi Fountain.

Middle-aged tourists, students and honeymoon couples were drawn by a sense of history and romance, but their image of the city was also influenced by rumours of forbidden pleasures. Many visitors came looking for louche haunts and a taste of the illicit behaviour they had heard about and seen on the screen. At every hour of the day, the Café de Paris, Doney and other famous pavement cafés and bars were invaded by large numbers of tourists wanting to share in the atmosphere of revelry. What remained of the Bohemian élite was forced to flee with little hope of reclaiming their habitat during low season. A 1963 report in *Confidential* on Rome's night life highlighted the way the Via Veneto had become a gathering point for every type of con-artist, wheeler-dealer and tart. A male hustler named Aldo recounted the intense sexual traffic that went on and stated the view, evidently still widely held, that Wilma Montesi was a party girl who had died after an orgy.

For some who remembered the Via Veneto of just a few years before, this was all too much. The film director Ugo Gregoretti once observed that he had been walking down the street when he was approached by a young Canadian man with freckles and red hair who asked him if he could point him in the direction of an orgy. Gregoretti regarded this as a watershed, a sign that the era of the *dolce vita* was truly at a close.

The world press, however, was unwilling to drop a source of remunerative titillating stories. 'The world's tabloids can always rely on Rome. Racy pictures and copy pour out of the city in a steady flow,' observed the *New York Times*. After the 'tragi-comedy of decadence' that was the Montesi case, other scandals followed. These also occurred in other capitals, observed the paper's correspondent Paul Hofmann, 'but in the incomparable setting of the Forum Romanum and the Pantheon, of the catacombs and the basilicas, moral laxity is more conspicuous than elsewhere'.

In her 1968 novella *The Public Image*, Muriel Spark portrayed a British film star, perhaps inspired by Belinda Lee, who is sucked into 'the uninhibited ways of the Italian film world' and 'magnetised by the café life of the Via Veneto'. In this work of fiction, Rome is a corrupt whirlpool of orgies and drugs. Only in 1975 would the American press start to publish obituaries of the *dolce vita*. 'That era of the scandalous '50s and '60s no longer exists here. All that remains are the memories,' wrote the *Los Angeles Times*.

In the later 1960s, the stars became a scarcer presence. For more than ten years the huge numbers of actors and movie personnel, engaged on runaway Hollywood productions, as well as the international collaborations that had helped fuel the growth of Italian cinema, had been a staple feature of Rome's café society. The decline of Hollywood on the Tiber, following the ending of government restrictions on the export of profits that had necessitated it in the first place, contributed a change of atmosphere. But the impact of this decline was not felt immediately or dramatically. Rome would remain a centre of international film production and there was, in any case, one final blockbuster that would generate a Roman scandal that was at least the equal of earlier ones. *Quo Vadis* had been the first of a long line of American-produced movies set in the ancient world that were filmed in the city in the post-war years. After that first epic, more than a hundred foreign films were made in Rome. Some were contemporary comedies but a high proportion were toga films.

A new version of *Ben-Hur* – the first was partially shot in Rome in 1925 – starring Charlton Heston, was shot in Rome in 1958–9, using original locations. Compared to *Quo Vadis*, *Helen of Troy* and all the other historical epics of the 1950s, it was a triumph of spectacle, rhythm and drama. For audiences everywhere, the final chariot race was one of the most memorable and nail-biting sequences they had witnessed in cinema. The film was a tribute to the extraordinary technical advances of Italian filmmaking. In 1950, MGM had brought its own technical and back-up staff from California to film *Quo Vadis*. For *Ben-Hur*, Italian expertise was employed in set design and construction, costumes, camera, electrical work and other areas.

The enormous worldwide success of the film fuelled interest in Rome and its history. As a country that was able to offer the appeal of the ancient, combined with a modern tourist infrastructure, Italy was especially attractive to the newly prosperous classes of Europe and America. The city's unique history acquired a new validation in Technicolor.

The success of *Ben-Hur* contributed directly to the decision to film a new version of the Cleopatra story. Produced by Twentieth Century Fox, *Cleopatra*'s making involved struggles between four big players of the American movies: Darryl Zanuck, Spyros Skouras, Walter Wanger and the director Joseph Mankiewicz. Even though Fox was in deep financial trouble, *Cleopatra* had been conceived on a grand scale and marketed from the start in terms of the sheer size of the project. With the company's entire Hollywood lot tied up with the shooting of the biblical epic *The Greatest Story Ever Told*, it was shot wholly in Rome. Observers were amazed by some trademark excesses, the most striking of which were the decision to rebuild the Roman Forum at twice its actual size, and the engagement of an entire fleet for the battle of Actium. The large cast was complemented with some four thousand extras. What would make the filming process fascinating to the public, however, was not the film's budget or the backstage machinations, but the affair between the film's star, Elizabeth Taylor, and Richard Burton, who played Mark Anthony.

From the moment she arrived in Italy, Elizabeth Taylor took over Anita Ekberg's crown as queen of Rome. A far bigger star, now at the height of her career, she had begun as a child actor and had graduated to important films, including *Giant*, *Cat on a Hot Tin Roof* and *Butterfield 8*. Most recently she had starred with Katherine Hepburn and Montgomery Clift in *Suddenly, Last Summer*, also directed by Mankiewicz. Her fiery temperament was well known and, to appease her, an entire building fitted with every possible luxury was constructed for her personal use on the set. She was wary of what awaited her in Rome. Like every star, she had heard of the antics of the paparazzi and she also knew that it was customary to over-charge the famous for everything. Her fears would not prove groundless. The trees that surrounded the villa she rented on the Via Appia Antica did not provide privacy so much as perches for the photographers who were determined to catch her off-guard. One evening a paparazzo punched her in the stomach simply in order to snap her horrified reaction. The periodic absences of her then husband Eddie Fisher did not make it any easier for her to relax and enjoy the capital's pleasures.

Burton, at the time, was by no means as well known. He was mainly a stage actor and his film career had not brought great roles. A Welshman from mining stock, who had played Shakespeare at Stratford, he had won acclaim not so much for his matinée-idol looks (his head was large and his skin scarred by adolescent acne) as for his magnetic stage presence and the resonance of his voice. He had in common with Taylor a rebellious streak and an aversion to authority. Initially, however, he did not appear interested in her. He, too, was married, although he arrived in Rome with a mistress in tow. Several months previously he had dismissed Taylor in conversation as 'Miss Tits'. When they were introduced, he greeted her ironically, as though she were an attractive member of the supporting cast. The jest did not go down well.

Things changed after they shot their first scene together on 22 January 1962. Burton arrived on set nursing a massive hangover and was hardly in a condition to play the moment of the first meeting and *coup de foudre* between Mark Anthony and the Egyptian queen. Taylor found this amusing and warmed to him.

The public flirting between them that ensued was at first a publicity stunt, a staged 'friendship' designed to attract attention to the production, but at a certain point it became real. Both actors subscribed to the view that to portray a screen romance successfully, the actors have to fall a little in love with each other. Burton later said that somehow he felt impelled to begin a relationship with Taylor. It was not only the power of the historical romance or the suggestion of playing it in the unique context of Rome that was responsible. Each was drawn by some quality in the other. Taylor's unprecedented million-dollar fee dazzled Burton, while she was impressed with his stage credentials and fascinated by his fun-loving capacity for drink and indulgence. They both enjoyed ribald humour. He threw himself with abandon into Roman night life, and made the clubs of the Via Veneto district his second home. Unlike the great diva, he had no fear of the press and in fact enjoyed the company of journalists.

With their spouses at first oblivious to what was going on, the pair drew closer. The abundant leisure that the drawn-out production afforded gave them an opportunity to take short vacations on Ischia, an idyllic island where passion took over. Far from being private, their tryst was spotted by the paparazzi and became public knowledge.

During their stay in Italy, the two actors conducted what became known as 'the most public adultery in the world'. The affair was rich with scandal, skulduggery, intrigue, melodrama and heartache. Both the Vatican and the American Congress, as well as the international media, intervened to condemn the couple. Taylor got the worst of it: she was labelled 'an avaricious vamp', an 'erotic vagrant' and a home-breaker, whose children found themselves with a new father whenever the fancy took her. The Church condemned the 'rootless life' that she and other actors led in the age of international film production.

Fox executives were unsure whether the controversy would harm or help the movie. For old-school Hollywood, scandal was to be avoided at all costs, but things were clearly changing and controversy was not necessarily bad for business. By contrast, the Italian authorities, who had tried once more to tighten the screws of censorship after *La dolce vita*, were horrified to find themselves powerless to suppress the scandal. Rome's reputation for hedonism was dramatically reinforced by a flagrant affair that, despite early denials, soon became incontrovertible. It was a sensational culmination to the *dolce vita* season. Burton and Taylor in effect became a modern-day Anthony and Cleopatra as fiction became fact and even eclipsed it. *Cleopatra* generated huge unexpected costs and the budget increased forty-fold. Only the adultery of the central couple and the extravagance of their displays of affection attracted more attention.

Even more than the Bergman–Rossellini affair, the Taylor–Burton scandal marked the beginning of an epoch. While Bergman's affair first established post-war Italy's reputation as the home of illicit relationships, the massive sex scandal that blew up during the filming of *Cleopatra* reinforced the new image of Rome as a site of corruption, sleaze, squalid betrayal and crass materialism. In 1949–50 the Vatican had turned a blind eye to what it saw as an unusual personal drama. By the early 1960s its negative view of the rich and famous was entrenched and it was determined to combat wherever possible their negative influence.

Yet Burton and Taylor were beyond condemnation. Neither

of them allowed their conduct to be determined by what others thought of them. Burton was accustomed to referring to the controversy with ironical detachment as '*le scandale*'. The provincial prurience, wherever it occurred, that had been so disturbed by the antics of the *dolce vita* was also fast giving way to a new ethos of permissiveness that would come to be the defining feature of the decade. Whatever personal anguish the break-up of his marriage cost him, Burton benefited greatly from his association with Taylor. Suddenly he, too, was a major star whose kudos rose sky high.

With the departure of most of the American film personnel, the Via Veneto changed in character. Instead of being the salon of the beautiful people, it became a more mundane focus of business and tourism. Deprived of much of their traditional eccentric, famous and cinematic clientele, the bars and cafés of Rome's most famous road began to live off their memories, and even started putting celebrated paparazzi shots in glass-covered window displays. At the Café de Paris or the Café Strega, quiet and very ordinary places most of the time, the visitor could, through the photographs, imagine he or she was drinking a Negroni or an Americano in the company of Ava Gardner or Marcello Mastroianni.

In the 1960s London would replace Rome as the most fashionable place in the world. But Swinging London bore many a resemblance to star-struck Rome, and readily absorbed Italian styles, looks and photographic innovations. Sharp suits, dark glasses worn at night, Vespa scooters, beautiful bodies and Italian songs all conveyed an idea of sophistication that would inform both commercial culture and the image of fashionable youth. It was not perhaps a coincidence that the single film that best conveyed the spirit of London in the 1960s, *Blow-Up*, was made by an Italian, Michelangelo Antonioni. At the centre of this film there was a photographer and a mysterious corpse – the key subject and object of Rome in the 1950s.

XXI

Keys to the Case

More than sixty years after the death of Wilma Montesi, the case has not been solved. In marked contrast to other celebrated murders and assassinations, where new theories and potential guilty parties are frequently proposed, every commentator on the Montesi case has without exception refrained from advancing hypotheses. Rarely do writers re-examine the evidence or question the final inconclusive outcome of the long-running investigation and trial. Perhaps because it appeared in 1957 to have been a gigantic conspiracy theory with scant basis in fact, those who have returned to it have preferred to avoid setting down new interpretive schemes. The whole affair can be read as a distinct chapter in the social history of Rome and Italy. It occurred at a very specific moment in the development of a deeply divided society, recently emerged from dictatorship, which was experiencing rapid growth in the mass media. The variety of theories that the case generated is striking, ranging from official accounts, hearsay-based accusations, political readings, class-related interpretations, to dreams, fantasies and personal elaborations.

I have sought to review the context in which the investigations and trial occurred, the social and economic relations that bore on them, the roles played by the protagonists of the affair, including the Montesi family, the possible part played by criminal organisations, and the contribution of the mass media. I have also considered the conduct and outcomes of the legal processes. In several, if not all, of these areas it is possible to say more now than it was in the late 1950s or early 1960s. Above all, it is possible to locate the case more specifically in the time and place in which it unfolded and to read it in terms of the particular social climate that marked the period after the fall of Fascism, the establishment of the republic and the onset of the Cold War.

In my view, three factors can assist in unpicking this most impenetrable of murder mysteries. The first is the recognition that in the 1950s the state machine worked in very peculiar ways. The nature of the post-war political conflict, the continuity of state personnel and procedures from the Fascist period, and the space that existed for personal relations to condition public actions all bore on the development and handling of the case. The second is the possible role that narcotics, and the criminal networks that distributed them, played in the death of Wilma Montesi and the peculiar events that followed. Third, the outcome of the Venice trial cannot be accepted at face value. Class factors bore heavily on the way in which it was conducted and contributed to the verdict that was reached.

In terms of Rome, the case offered through its numerous protagonists a picture of a city whose population saw the world, and also their own specific worlds, in very different ways. Almost everyone seemed to be an immigrant or outsider of some sort: the Piccioni family, originating from Rieti, lived on a prestigious road that had been created following Mussolini's controversial demolition of working-class housing in the central districts. The Montesis, who hailed from the Marche region, lived in a block built for state employees, many of whom came from other parts of Italy. Marchese Ugo Montagna and Anna Maria Caglio arrived from opposite corners of the country to realise in the capital their ambitions. The horde of witnesses mostly came from the margins, hailing from the provinces or the peripheral zones of the Roman hinterland.

One thing that my investigation has not produced is any new suspect, any hitherto unknown name that might be supposed to have caused the carpenter's daughter's death. Thus any reflection on the outcome of the case must inevitably return to the two lines of interpretation that emerged between the conclusion of Raffaele Sepe's investigation and the dramatic final stages of the Venice trial.

First, there is the line that Sepe embraced in the conclusions to his instructional investigation and which resulted in the incrimination of Piero Piccioni, Ugo Montagna and Saverio Polito. Due to the outcome of the trial this should, in theory, be dead. However, it needs to be explained how Piccioni managed to turn a strong presumption of his guilt into complete absolution. This was not because his alibi was solid or because he was positively able to demonstrate his innocence. The ambiguous role of Alida Valli and other witnesses who testified in his favour needs to be weighed.

The second line of inquiry concerns the members of the Montesi family, including Giuseppe. Little was ever discovered about the family's wider links to the community or the neighbourhood. The nature of the family's dynamics and of Wilma's personal life remained blank. In addition, the role of Giuseppe Montesi was never wholly resolved. Had his niece died on 9 April, Giuseppe would undoubtedly have been tried for his involvement in her death. But, as she did not, what was his role? These matters need reflection, as do possible connections or coincidence of interest between Piccioni and Montagna on the one hand and the Montesi family on the other.

Some comment is needed on the role of the state and the way in which different branches of it operated. In the light of the many subsequent scandals and cover-ups that marked contemporary Italian political history, nothing is surprising. Complicities and connivances with organised crime and illegal activity have been revealed to be routine. The Montesi case was the precursor of the numerous scandals that would rock the Italian establishment in the 1960s, 1970s and 1980s. These scandals, which included the air crash that killed Enrico Mattei, the Lockheed bribery scandal, the exposure in 1982 of the P2 – a clandestine freemasons' lodge that included senior judges, military figures, the heads of the secret services, businessmen, politicians and journalists – all suggested that behind the scenes puppeteers were manipulating events, and that larger issues and forces were involved than ever came to the public eye. They also showed the existence of networks of interest – typically linking politics and business of some sort – that bypassed democratic forums of decision-making and scrutiny. Thus the case was not a one-off episode but the first of a long line of intrigues staining Italian public life.

From this perspective, the case highlighted certain traits of political life that would become consolidated as permanent features. These include the use of state institutions and the press for political purposes, to conceal facts and events or to discover the malfeasances of adversaries; the existence of a backstage of power populated by ambiguous personalities; the unprincipled confusion of public and private life; the existence of areas of mystery created by an extreme complexity of interlocking allegiances, loyalties, favours and obligations; the interference of foreign countries, and especially the United States, in Italy's internal affairs.

Of course, Wilma Montesi was not a mediator or a controversial business figure. She was a simple girl from a residential area of Rome. So there could have been no interest on the part of any organ of the state in bringing about her death. However, the pattern needs to be mapped. The police and the judicial authorities were mobilised from the very earliest days after her death in April 1953 to direct enquiries towards a verdict of accidental death. Once an interpretation – the foot-bathing – was formulated that fitted with this, it was embraced and never dropped. Why should the authorities have adopted this course?

There are several reasons. At the top level, there were functionaries such as Tommaso Pavone and Saverio Polito, who were well aware that power worked in ways that were not always transparent. They had a sense of the structure of élite influence that passed through the state but was essentially the prerogative of people who belonged to a recognised but informal network of authority. Functionaries like Pavone and Polito were men with different personal stories but they had held posts since the Fascist period and they were both used to operating in a context in which there was always a higher purpose than the application of the law. Indeed, they saw it as their role precisely to facilitate, where necessary, shortcuts and cover-ups.

Beneath men of this type, there were loyal state officials. Procurator Sigurani and his deputy Murante were also men formed in the Fascist period but they possessed a sense of state rather than the contingent view outlined above. They did not have a notion of the need to respond to civil society and thought of the state as the embodiment of authority. This meant that what in fact was a political truth became by default a state truth that was transmitted down to all levels of the police. In such a context, it was entirely possible that a decision taken at the first level to protect a figure related to the élite would be endorsed by the second level as a political decision and applied at all other levels. In the climate of anti-Communism that was rampant in the early 1950s, such an attitude found an ideological as well as a hierarchical justification.

The return of democracy and public opinion had brought expansion of the press. Alongside established titles, political newspapers, illustrated weeklies and satirical sheets flourished. However, in the 1950s Italy was still living under a form of police regime. Jean-François Revel said that Rome pullulated with policemen; it contained more of them than any other city he knew. The strategy deployed to discredit Giuseppe Sotgiu was proof of what could be achieved with this level of control.

Revisiting the case involves exposing power's pacts and assumptions, bringing them to the surface and showing how they worked. In later decades, several men would weave webs of intrigue and influence within business, the state and the Church. These included Licio Gelli, the organiser of the subversive freemasons' lodge, the P2; Michele Sindona, a Sicilian banker and businessman who was poisoned in jail; and Roberto Calvi, the Vatican banker who was found dead under Blackfriars Bridge in London in 1982. Ugo Montagna was a precursor of these figures, a man who wove networks of power behind the scenes.

It is known that criminal activities multiplied in the 1950s in the Italian capital and that some of these were a manifestation of Mafia penetration. There was a political dimension to this, since the Christian Democrats forged alliances with the Mafia for electoral gain in Sicily and this brought a renewed Mafia influence to the capital. There was also a dimension of straightforward corruption. Through bribes of a material kind or lavish hospitality, poorly paid state officials and politicians could be induced to turn a blind eye or even to favour illegal activities.

Beneath the case there was a factor that did not receive systematic attention at the time. The power of the Christian Democrats was based on the support it received from the Church and the United States. But the role of other forces, including the Mafia, was important. The party turned itself into an institution that attracted and covered a whole series of interests that had gathered in and around the state in the period between Fascism and the declaration of the republic. These unspoken pacts required a blind eye to be turned in the cause of anti-Communism. It is striking that both the Department of State files for the period and the papers of the American embassy in Rome contain almost nothing on the Montesi case. In the Italian archives there is also very little on narcotics, though this was even then a matter of considerable concern to the Americans. In brief, the Americans chose not to interfere too much; they did not address narcotics issues through diplomatic or political channels but left the matter to dedicated specialist forums.

Ugo Montagna was a man of passion and vanity, an opportunist and a social climber who was involved in myriad illegal and illicit activities. He conquered Rome at a time of uncertainty and flux, and he maintained his influence through a mixture of blackmail, graft and friendship. This was possible because Rome had never experienced a strong and productive bourgeoisie able to impose its leadership on society. Instead it had a flaccid aristocracy and a state-related political and administrative class. Its élite was malleable and corruptible. The journalist Revel noted that there was in Rome 'a rich and cosmopolitan minority which is in contact with the outside world, through foreign languages, relations, travel, alcohol, drugs, sex', whose members 'never cease to be Roman, because they know that Roman life is easiest for them'. The younger members of this élite could be listless and idle, hedonists looking for ever newer stimuli to excite them and awaken them from their torpor. Like Piccioni, they were used to using class privilege to escape reproof or retribution.

Anna Maria Caglio referred to Montagna's taste for violence, his collection of guns and his willingness to use them if he were ever to find himself attacked. She also said that he shared 'depraved tastes' with Piccioni, although it was never specified what they were. In the sexual culture of the time, it might have been a reference to homosexuality (she claimed Montagna's true inclinations were of this nature). It might equally have meant a liking for orgies, cocaine-charged sexual activity, cynical seduction of women for amusement, or voyeurism. She asserted, probably referring principally to herself, that Montagna's mistake was to focus his attention on girls from good families and use the promise of marriage as a means to have sex with them.

The lack of a strong bourgeois morality or ethical code meant that episodes of brutality involving privileged men were not unknown. Indeed, one of Alberto Moravia's most famous short stories 'Crime at the Tennis Club', published in 1927, dealt with the theme. It tells of a group of young and not so young men who decide to invite an older, unattractive woman they term 'the princess' to a ball they are organising. When she arrives, they take her to a private room where they ply her with drink, induce her to strip and finally kill her. They then return to the festivities as though nothing has happened.

The brutal element in Italian men was not confined to one class only, even if the bandit with the knife between his teeth, an image much loved of foreign travellers in the nineteenth century, was always southern and lower class. In 1975, a nasty case came to light that involved young well-off men of neo-Fascist views from the Parioli district, who had tortured and killed a lower-class girl, leaving another for dead, at the Circeo Park not far from Rome. Moravia compared this to the events of his story. Fellow writer Pier Paolo Pasolini contradicted him, arguing that Moravia had written of an élite setting: the current crime was one that had occurred in mass society. Wilma's death contained elements of both because it was both secret and a source of spectacle. It occurred at a point of transformation.

Capocotta was a cover. The hunting estate had a central purpose in Montagna's system of influence. But it also had the advantage of running along a stretch of coast that could be closed to prying eyes. It was a well-known Mafia practice for bosses to set up as gentlemen and entertain, particularly through hunting, an activity that had the additional benefits of affirming masculinity and prowess with guns. Such estates also allowed for other activities, such as the heroin refinery that was located within Mafia boss Michele Greco's Sicilian estate. Montagna was not a boss, but the whole area, including the coastline within his estate, was used for drug-running. It is inconceivable that he did not know Frank Coppola or that he was unaware of the traffic in narcotics. If he was aware of it, he was also inevitably involved. It makes sense to see Montagna as belonging to a criminal 'enterprise syndicate', rather than to the Mafia as a territorially based 'power syndicate'. Much of what Anna Maria Caglio said about Montagna was confirmed by Pompei and by the parliamentary report prepared by De Caro. He had made a lot of money quickly through means that were not transparent, and cultivated a wide range of contacts in high and low spheres. It was shown that it was entirely possible for sexual encounters of one sort or another to take place at Capocotta, as his own overnight stays with Caglio, and Prince Maurice demonstrated.

Montagna cared nothing about legality or state authority. Indeed, it was essential to his *modus operandi* that there should be a stratum of illegality that was untouchable and that functioned with impunity. At Venice, his lawyers were highly active in piloting the trial and steering suspicion away from Piccioni and himself. The guards were clearly involved in a conspiracy to which he was party, or there would have been no need for them to be so reticent and contradictory. The information that he was present at Capocotta on the very early morning of 11 April came out almost in passing. It showed not only that he was a regular visitor in the very early hours but that the excessive emphasis on the presence of the car that was seen on 9 or 10 April was unnecessary. No one observed Montagna arrive, so any number of vehicles could have been in the area over those days. That Montagna was only accused of being party to a cover-up, not of materially being implicated in the girl's death, meant that his actions on the days in question were absolved from close scrutiny. But steps had been taken to ensure that no one was caught.

Montagna knew he could count on the silence of his collaborators. Because of the influence he had established, he was less concerned about the authorities than his associates in the dope racket. The Mafia would have known that Montagna was a sexual adventurer and it would have disapproved. It would have been furious to discover that he had compromised a multi-million-dollar traffic by his taste for illicit pleasures. But, as usual, Montagna was playing a double game. No longer was he a Nazi-partisan or an anti-Fascist Fascist as he had been in 1943–4. He pursued his own interests, using his own methods, as well as providing coverage and assistance to the Mafia.

This brings us to Piero Piccioni, the principal accused in Venice. Piccioni has widely been seen as the scapegoat of the case and he liked to portray himself in that way. In Italian reconstructions, it has always been assumed that the Venice verdict that found him extraneous to the death of Montesi was correct. He was an innocent, a simple musician, whose moderately unconventional lifestyle exposed him to suspicion and victimisation in the bigoted climate of the 1950s. Is this accurate?

Looking over the case, it is clear that Piccioni's versions of events were riddled with inconsistencies and lies. He lied about not knowing Montagna, about having been in Milan on 9 April and about the purpose of his flat in Via Acherusio. The battery of medical witnesses who appeared and testified, not without inconsistencies, that he had been under constant medical treatment between 9 and 13 April was excessive, a ridiculous parade. The need to construct an iron-clad alibi arose from the unlikely coincidence that Piccioni had returned to Rome in an unusual manner on precisely the day that Wilma Montesi had disappeared. It led to absurd exaggeration. As a consequence, the suspicion remained that he had been seeking to cover his tracks by mobilising the support of men loyal to his family. He was never able to explain why he had left Alida Valli in Amalfi and had driven almost three hundred kilometres at high speed back to Rome on 9 April.

Piccioni had seduced a servant and was the lover of a film

star. He enjoyed the high life with a dangerous edge. He and Montagna were creatures of Rome's night life and were at home in its louche, low-light atmosphere. Outwardly respectable, they were in fact deeply corrupt. A photograph appeared in the press of them together in London with Prince Pignatelli, a Roman aristocrat who would be among those surrounding Aiche Nana as she performed her impromptu striptease at the Rugantino restaurant in 1958. The three have the same bug-eyed look, as though they were on a mission to discover the sleazier pleasures of the metropolis. Several years before the full hedonism of the decade exploded, and Fellini turned the *dolce vita* into a spectacle, men like them regarded debauchery as their private prerogative.

Ultimately, Piccioni's acquittal depended on the evidence of Alida Valli, who provided him with cover for 9 and 29 April. One of the central platforms of Anna Maria Caglio's evidence concerned the alleged meeting that took place at the interior ministry on 29 April. During the trial, this issue was presented in terms of dates, for Piccioni admitted that he had been to see Pavone more than once at the ministry, on one occasion in the company of Montagna. If the meeting took place on 29 April (that is, before the rumours about Piccioni appeared in the press), then it was designed to cover up a crime. If it took place several weeks later, its purpose was to address the matter of the press campaign. Valli provided Piccioni with an alibi for the evening of 29 April. For the second time, she saved him.

By 1957, Valli was thirty-six and the best films of her career were behind her. Giving evidence under her real name of Maria von Altenberger, she still had much of the glamour that had dazzled Sepe. In fact, she had been out of work for two years and was nervous and contradictory. She was no longer with Piccioni and looked at him coldly in the courtroom. But she provided him with a lifeline that went beyond her formal testimony. The lawyer Bucciante later wrote that no one who saw Valli could ever believe that the man who was lucky enough to be her lover could possibly be interested in an ordinary girl like Wilma Montesi. Yet Piccioni, as we have seen, was anything but a devoted and appreciative companion.

Valli later made clear that she felt she had been used. She had realised in the course of the investigations that Piccioni was a sexual predator and probably also a drug-user. The moodiness and depression to which he was subject suddenly found an explanation other than his artistic temperament. If she ever asked herself what had drawn him back to Rome so urgently, she must have wondered if it was the need to score some cocaine or the desire to keep an appointment with a girl.

It would be too easy to speculate that her unease was caused by the lengths to which she was obliged to go to save her lover. But she lied at least once for him and quite possibly more than once. She did this out of loyalty and because she was convinced he could not have been caught up in a murder. Yet, due to the case, she discovered things about him that she had not known, which must have shaken her inner conviction that he was innocent.

Did the meeting of 29 April in fact take place? Looking back, the issue of dates does not seem so significant. The most striking fact is that such meetings took place at all. The fact that several did makes it by no means implausible that a meeting occurred to address the matter of Wilma's death, either on 29 April or around that time. Of course, Montagna and Piccioni would not have asked explicitly for there to be a cover-up of a woman's death. They would have spoken by allusion and referred to an incident that, if appropriate action was not taken, might cause great embarrassment to the government.

This brings us to the matter of motivation. If such a meeting – 29 April – did not take place, the question arises as to why the police so insistently pursued the conclusion of accidental death. The case was closed quickly on the basis of an implausible hypothesis that the authorities never abandoned. It is unlikely, given the highly developed police apparatus that existed in Rome, that this was simply a result of incompetence or laziness. The hypothesis of the foot-bathing took shape as a result of a conversation between the Montesi family, who wanted peace of mind, and two public employees: a clerk at the defence ministry and a policeman, Aldo Morlacchi, who kept his identity secret from the other. The clerk, Passarelli, was unlikely to have been acting on her own initiative. Italy's bureaucrats were and are notorious for never doing more than the minimum required; for never taking risks or sticking their necks out. If Passarelli visited the Montesi household, instead of going directly to the police, it was for a purpose. The policeman was not there by chance; he had been sent to check that she performed her task and also to reinforce her advice. Their interventions suggest that connections were already being mobilised at a low level to steer the inquiry towards a rapid resolution.

The reason for this concerted action was not to save Piccioni. This was always assumed to be the purpose, but in fact there was a larger one. Important though he was, due to his father's position, he was not a Mussolini (unlike Montagna's old friends Bruno and Vittorio, Il Duce's sons). For Montagna, the crucial issue was not to extricate his friend from a mess, although he was ready and able to try to perform such a favour. What worried him mainly was that the clumsy manner of Wilma Montesi's death might lead to inquiries that would put the spotlight on Capocotta and the various private and illegal activities that took place there. This occurred anyway, catapulting an unwilling Montagna into the public eye, but he was not to know that this would happen. In the end, he only just got away with it when he was acquitted in Venice.

A key factor in ensuring that the Montesi case remained a mystery was the role of the family and the notion of *omertà* (complicit silence). The family was a vital institution in Italian society, more important to many than anything else. The right-wing journalist Leo Longanesi once observed ironically that the motto 'I have got a family to support' (*Tengo famiglia*) should be emblazoned on the Italian flag. While Montagna was an example of how disruptive a role someone who had no family could play, there was a strange symmetry between the Piccioni and Montesi families. The family of the victim never once accused Piccioni of involvement in her death, even though at times they were suspicious. Both families closed like clams to preserve some respectability and survive. For the Montesis, it was less important to win justice for Wilma than it was to protect the angelic image of her that they had constructed. For the Piccioni family, the possible accidental misdemeanour of one of their members involving a lower-class woman was not worth the disgrace of the whole household. By closing ranks and keeping quiet everyone gained something.

The Montesi family could not easily be defined in terms of social position. The father was an artisan who had known good times and bad. The mother was a woman who liked the external markers of a refined lifestyle (car, servant, holidays) but who lacked the social connections to attach herself and her daughters properly to the middle class. Thus her perceptions were external and aspirational. She did not have a rounded sense of the modestly contented ways of the established lower-middle class, which had been shaken and undercut by war and foreign occupation. She sought respectability but was also loud and vulgar. She was impressed by good manners but ill-mannered herself.

Maria Montesi dreamed of making a good match for her daughters, especially for Wilma – the younger and better-looking of the two. The cinema and photo-romances showed that, for a woman, beauty could be the key to social mobility. Both bathed the higher social echelons in a golden glow and therefore played on the anxieties of the lower-middle class as well as the hopes of the working class. Maria Montesi would never have entered her daughters in beauty or photographic competitions; rather, she sought more conventional forms of social mobility. She kept control of Wilma and Wanda because she knew that virginity was a requirement of respectability and of a good match. She gave her approval to Angelo Giuliani's proposal because, although he was not well-off or well-to-do, he behaved correctly. He was not an ideal fiancé but he would do, unless a better opportunity presented itself. The acceptance of this relationship showed the tensions in Maria Montesi's outlook: forced to choose between ambition and respectable ordinariness, she chose the latter – but all the while, she yearned for more.

Wilma was naïve and malleable. She led a reasonably protected life, but her mother's attitudes did not provide her with any protection against material temptation. She might initially have been taken with Giuliani but her engagement to him was in every way almost absurdly old-fashioned. She tried to imagine him as her handsome prince, but two things broke the spell. His transfer to distant Potenza dramatically reduced their meetings to one per month: they had never been close but now they saw each other rarely; and the prospect of leaving her family and everything she knew for a life in a remote town with him alarmed her. The other problem was Giuliani himself. They shared no bond and he was formal rather than affectionate with her. What was more, he was neither romantic nor very respectful. The only time he had tried to kiss her – in a public park – he could not resist an awkward fumble. Wilma might have suspected that her mother had rushed her into an engagement to keep her out of trouble.

I believe that in her mind, if not more explicitly, Wilma had broken off her engagement. After Giuliani's transfer, she had started to think and to reassess her situation. Inside and outside the family, she was surrounded with examples of vanity, cynicism, opportunism and materialism. In the last few months of her life, she underwent a change. People who had known her earlier commented that she was better dressed, more sophisticated and more self-confident. She was spending more time out of the house and had acquired some costly accessories. The previously passive Wilma had responded aggressively to girls in the stairwell. She had argued with her mother. These changes seemed to date from around the time of her twenty-first birthday. It is quite possible they manifested themselves before that.

Wilma had found new ways to fill her time. She had come into contact with new people. This would only have occurred through someone she knew. She was emerging from the restrictions of her life but she had been taught to be diffident towards outsiders. The indications are that this person was her uncle, Giuseppe.

According to the plausible accounts of the Casciani workers, he had something of an obsession with his niece: he telephoned her and he had disapproved of her engagement. He would have been more than pleased to establish a special connection with her and detach her from her unworthy fiancé. In this way he could also have expressed the disdain he felt for his brother Rodolfo. He had introduced Wilma's brother Sergio to prostitutes, and tried to turn him into a *protégé*. This had led to a rift with the boy's father. For this reason, and because of Giuseppe's various other women, his relationship with Wilma would have been secret. His motives were complex. Giuseppe was attracted to his niece but he was not just an incorrigible ladies' man. He cultivated a wide range of activities and connections, and the presentable Wilma could serve other purposes. He introduced her to new people in the mixed society that was his world. It was through him that she started to frequent the cafés and to meet men. The secretiveness of the family, and the repeated suggestion, even from peripheral members, that there was a secret that could not be revealed alludes to this developing connection between Wilma and Giuseppe.

It was very easy, in a context such as Rome in the 1940s and 1950s, to fall into bad company, although this did not normally occur within one's own family. The smashing of conventional petty-bourgeois values saw ambition and individualism triumph over a culture of restriction and acceptance of one's lot. As the journalist Roberto Cantini put it in 1954: 'Let us be clear about it: what sort of families do the "existentialists" of the Baretto, the runaway wives, and the girls who, in one way or another, have celebrated their "anarchy" and been the subject of notoriety, come from? They are daughters of functionaries, teachers and respectable widows.' Wilma, the film fan and reader of photo-romances, believed that the higher people were on the social scale the better they were. She did not realise that the ladders on the game board of social mobility were balanced by snakes that could transport the unlucky player back to the depths. The beautiful people had vices that in 1953 had not yet been exposed or turned into entertainment.

It was assumed the case was all about sex. The journalist Indro Montanelli, writing in 1956, adopted the idea that Wilma was not quite as innocent as she was made out to be. 'Beyond Sin, in Italy, there is no Virtue,' he wrote. 'Instead there is Vice. There is Capocotta. There are girls who die on beaches who, to be sure, are virgins, but only on one side.' As he saw it, the declining value attributed to female purity heralded the end of the Italian family.

In fact, the source of Wilma's undoing in all probability was drugs. If it is assumed that narcotics were at the heart of the mystery then the fragments start to fall into place. The drugs traffic boomed in Italy as never before in the years after the war. It wormed its way into various social milieux and furnished a network of contacts between high society, the artistic community and the criminal underworld. Together, the components of this network formed a secret society or parallel world. Large sums of money were at stake; national and international interests were involved. These were fronted at every level by ostensibly respectable people: the nobleman with connections in the bureaucracy and the political world, the gentleman farmer with a hunting estate, the accountant, and the well-dressed woman who would not arouse anyone's suspicion.

In the Montesi case, several minor characters were associated with narcotics. Montagna, Piccioni and Giuseppe Montesi were also taken to be involved, in different ways, with drug consumption or diffusion. Wilma surely had little personal knowledge of narcotics, but for that very reason she had her uses. Trusting and naïve, she was attracted by the prospect of financial gain and tempted by the excitement of a secret activity. Her changing appearance, expensive bag and jewellery showed that she had a new source of money. It gave rise to rumours that she was a call-girl, but her virginity proved that this was not so. She was most likely a carrier, one of those women who moved silently across the city, taking packages from one place to another.

Ultimately, we can never know exactly what happened on 9 and 10 April 1953. All the elements are there, though, for us to imagine a scenario that cannot be too different from what really occurred.

At approximately five fifteen p.m., Wilma Montesi walked away from Via Tagliamento 76 for the last time. She left behind her fiancé's photograph, her identity card and her jewellery. This might have been seen as a sign of an intention to commit suicide, had she not taken the house keys with her. Instead of planning to quit her life, Wilma was responding to two imperatives. The first was an instruction not to bring her identity card and to wear nothing that would give away her status as being engaged to be married. The second was an inner voice that told her she was about to step outside her life as it had been and, in particular, outside the prospect of a future life with Giuliani. The row of a month earlier had been the tipping point: Giuliani was not for her.

Wilma turned left outside the block and walked up towards Piazza Buenos Aires, where she found Giuseppe waiting for her with his car. Giuseppe told Wilma that she was going to meet some people who would give her instructions on the delivery of the merchandise. The two drove to Ostia, where Giuseppe bought Wilma an ice-cream. Another car pulled up, containing at least one person known to Wilma. This might have been Simola, although his uncouthness makes it unlikely Wilma would have trusted him. It could have been 'Luigi', the name Anna Maria Caglio gave to a man Montagna frequently called as his fixer. Giuseppe might have left at this point, as Wilma stepped into the new vehicle. Or he may have continued with the group to their destination.

Wilma believed not only that she was going to meet some people responsible for the activity in which she was getting involved, but that she would meet people connected with the film world. In fact, the scenario was more complicated. There was no need for a special meeting at which Wilma would be inducted into the company of drug-dealers. The sort of task that was entrusted to a girl like her required her to know as little as possible about what she was doing, what she was carrying or who was involved. The meeting had been organised on a pretext so that Wilma could be seduced and turned into one of the women of easy virtue who added spice to the entertainment at Capocotta.

Two hypotheses may be advanced about this. It is possible that the arrival on the scene of a good girl, a virgin, one whose compliance was guaranteed by Giuseppe, was a new thrill. It stimulated the jaded appetite of the shadowy men who ran the show. In this case a sexual-induction rite also had the advantage of linking her to the band and guaranteeing her silence. Perhaps, more probably, there was a tragic misunderstanding. Wilma dressed ostentatiously and, even without her jewellery, looked like a girl of experience rather than a virgin. She visited cafés and had met men. It is possible that she was mistaken for an available girl who was quite comfortable with sexual commerce.

Two things went wrong with the plan. Wilma went to Capocotta with Giuseppe's friends but she became nervous. When a man who had been described to her as being of high status arrived, something happened. Perhaps he failed to charm her. To make matters worse, Wilma rebelled. She had learned in recent times that she was attractive to men. This gratified her and she had developed a taste for flirting. But she had no intention of compromising her precious virginity, the one thing – her mother had told her – that she must never do. As the atmosphere of business evaporated amid drinks, music and low lighting, she realised that the evening was not unfolding as she had expected. She made a fuss and demanded to be taken home. As she lunged for the door, she was seized and restrained.

The crucial moment in the story of Wilma's last hours is the evening and night of 9 April. Wilma knew that to stay out overnight was inconceivable. Her honour would be fatally compromised and her family would panic. It is clear that she was detained against her will. Worried, her captors drugged her while they considered what to do. They could have had no idea that she had an unusually small heart and that she was prone to fainting. Instead of reviving after a few hours, Wilma remained unconscious. This time, it was her hosts who were seized by panic. To facilitate her breathing, they loosened her clothes, removing her skirt, her suspender belt and her stockings.

By this time, the would-be seducer had left the scene, leaving it to Montagna's underlings, the estate guards, to get rid of her. The following day, the girl had become a problem of major dimensions. Those who had brought her to Capocotta were now guilty of kidnap and assault. It was not possible to allow her to revive and denounce her assailants because that would imperil the illegal traffic they were running. It was decided to take her to the sea and dump her in, or close to, the water. Her fate would be determined by the tides and, if she was ever found, her demise would look like an accident or suicide. Wilma's coat was hastily thrust over her shoulders and she was bundled into a car, then covered with a blanket. She was driven the kilometre or so to an abandoned stretch of beach. Montagna's henchmen organised themselves so two of them kept a lookout while two others carried the unconscious girl to the beach. Perhaps someone held her head down in the water. This amateurish strategy shows that the Mafia was probably not directly implicated in her death.

On 11 April the body of a young woman was washed up at Torvaianica. Those responsible evidently hoped that the case would be reported as a minor local news item and would be quickly forgotten. In this, they were disappointed.

It has often been wondered if Wilma's immediate family was in any way implicated in her death. Her sister and mother surely knew something of the turn her life was taking. Maria Montesi's exclamations and suggestions that Wilma had 'ruined herself with her own hands' implied some awareness that she had exposed herself to danger. She might even have encouraged her daughter to seize an opportunity that had come her way, while offering the usual warnings. After all, she had opened the door to Simola. Her insistence on Wilma's angelic qualities was heartfelt but forced. It was a Pavlovian response to the aspersions that were cast on her character rather than the affirmation of a truth.

Rodolfo Montesi was the one figure who understood nothing of what had happened. A simple man, he wandered expressionless and glassy-eyed through the maze of events that followed Wilma's death. He neither acknowledged nor comprehended the collapse of the value system on which he had tried to found his family.

The Montesis went into shock when Wilma failed to come home on 9 April and was found dead two days later. Giuseppe was appalled at what had happened. He knew he was partly responsible. His first instinct, however, was to protect himself and it was in this spirit that he took part in the family's searches and followed the investigation. If he was ever afflicted by remorse, he did not show it. He was a coward, as well as a traitor and a liar, and he lived in mortal fear of the criminal gang with which he had incautiously become involved. He had been chosen as the fall-guy, the one who would have to take the flak if a potential guilty party was needed. He appears to have been quite aware of this. He repeatedly asked journalists how the investigation was going and even, during the Venice trial, was heard saying, 'Something must be done to save Piccioni.' Giuseppe never cracked, even after three months in solitary confinement. He knew that if he ever broke down he would face a retribution more ruthless than that of the Italian state.

Epilogue

I first came across the Montesi case more than fifteen years ago when I visited the vast Porta Portese market, which takes place every Sunday in the Trastevere district of Rome. Thousands of Romans and others visit the stalls that snake along the roads leading from one of the historic gates of the ancient city to the Viale Trastevere. People come to rummage for discount clothes and shoes, kitchen equipment and pirated CDs and videos. Towards the north of the market, a more select clientele can be found surveying antique furniture and pictures. Surprisingly large pieces – bed frames, wardrobes, dining tables – sit in the road as the sellers slump in chairs disinterestedly responding to requests for prices. Beyond the antiques, further rows of stalls are weighed down with second-hand books and magazines, postcards, bric-à-brac and jumble.

It was at one of these stalls that I stopped to inspect some magazines. As I leafed through copies of the defunct weekly *Epoca*, several stories of now forgotten events jumped to my eye: the assassination attempt on Communist leader Togliatti in 1949, the launch of the Fiat 500 in 1957, the birth of Sophia Loren's son in 1968. Personalities who have since faded seemed to enjoy a surprising prominence. Who today remembers Soraya, the sad princess whose fairytale marriage to the Shah of Iran ended suddenly and tragically when she failed to produce an heir to the Peacock Throne? Yet in the

1950s everyone knew about her, and in Italy, where she arrived to spend her exile, she was one of the first stars of the illustrated weeklies. A lot of magazines featured pictures and articles about a set of people I had not heard of, and who did not appear to be forgotten stars: Anna Maria Caglio, a dark-haired young woman who smiled to camera with evident pleasure; Ugo Montagna, a silver-haired nobleman with a prominent nose and a taste for close-fitting suits; an insignificant-looking young man with odd teeth whose name was Piero Piccioni; and a lot of people claiming a connection with a remote intrigue that evidently had been a matter of great public concern – the Montesi scandal.

Amid a disorderly pile of magazines and books on one stall, I unearthed a bundle of newspapers and press cuttings bound together by string. Looking more closely at the yellowed pages, I could see they were all concerned with the Montesi case. On the top was a smudged page bearing a faded photograph of a woman with a round face and a neat appearance. This, the caption told me, was Wilma Montesi, a young woman who had died in mysterious circumstances. Her fate had sparked a scandal that had rocked the Roman establishment in the mid-1950s. After some bartering, the stall-holder sold me the pack for the equivalent of twenty pounds.

Looking through the cuttings, I felt I was entering a world that had disappeared. Place names were the same and a few personalities – such as Loren – had lasted over time. But the human Rome of the early twenty-first century bears only a passing resemblance to the bustling, class-divided city of the post-war years. Yet there are also continuities. The politicians are still there and so are the legions of state employees. It still matters to know people. To have some connection to a powerful interest or person is not just an advantage but often a necessity for those who need a home or a job. The arrogant swagger of the well-connected and the permatanned beauty of the rich still contrasts with the careworn resignation of the ordinary population. But, among Romans, there is no longer the dramatic gulf between haves and have-nots. It is the immigrants from North Africa and Eastern Europe who today form the underclass.

The Montesi affair was the subject of two books published in English in the 1950s: Wayland Young's *The Montesi Scandal* and Melton Davis's *All Rome Trembled*. In their pages there was a real-life crime story with elements of Italian melodrama, the political thriller and the courtroom drama. It was a Roman story that offered a grand narrative of the changing city, as well as a series of snapshots of the political conflict and the social and economic inequalities of the Italian capital in the post-war years. In 2003, Karen Pinkus explored the affair in *The Montesi Scandal*, a text that approaches the death of Wilma Montesi and the events that followed through the medium of notes for a film project that is destined to remain unrealised, except on the printed page.

Although largely forgotten abroad today, the Montesi case was a defining moment in the post-war period in the same way that the murder in 1924 of Giacomo Matteotti, an opposition Member of Parliament, was a watershed for Mussolini's Fascist regime. It somehow symbolised the widespread belief that, even after the end of the dictatorship, the powerful and the well-connected could get away with anything. It also showed that Italy's new democracy would not easily allow this to happen. As such it has been revisited a number of times in Italy, especially by journalists. In 2003 Angelo Frignani, who covered the case for *Il Tempo*, published *La strana morte di Wilma Montesi* (The Strange Death of Wilma Montesi), while in 2005 Vincenzo Vasile's *Wilma Montesi: la ragazza con il reggicalze* (Wilma Montesi: The Girl with the Suspender Belt) appeared. A year later Francesco Grignetti of the Rome office of the Turin newspaper *La Stampa* wrote *Il caso Montesi* (The Montesi Case), a detailed analysis of the unfolding of the legal investigations using archival documents as well as press reports. Each of these works added something to the understanding of the case without dealing with its aftermath or seeking to question its inconclusive outcome. The Montesi affair also features in books dealing with Italy's mysteries (Carlo Lucarelli, *Nuovi misteri d'Italia* – New Italian Mysteries – 2004) and its biggest crime stories (Massimo Polidoro, *Cronaca nera* – True Crime – 2005; Cesare Fiumi, *L'Italia in nera* – Italian True Crime – 2006), the country's most dramatic trials (Sabina Marchesi, *I processi del secolo* – The Trials of the Century – 2008), the entwinement of sex and politics (Filippo Ceccarelli, *Il letto e il potere* – Sex and Politics – 1994), and political corruption (Sergio Turone, *Corrotti e corruttori dall'Unità al P2* – Corruption and Corruptors from Unification to the P2 – 1984). It has appeared in some contemporary fiction, notably Wu Ming, *54*, where it is fleetingly referred to in a discussion set in a bar in Bologna, and Simone Sarasso, *Confine di Stato* (State Border). The latter is the only work of any genre in which there is an attempt to imagine what might have happened. All the protagonists of the case appear in fictional guises. The author describes the death of 'Ester Conti' as the work of a trainee secret agent who must prove he is capable of committing murder on demand. In the novel, Ester is filmed being sodomised while a character named 'The Baron' watches, masturbating and drinking champagne.

The actual fate of those who were drawn into the case varied. Anna Maria Caglio returned to Milan, where she married a man called Mario Ricci and had a daughter, Alessandra. Later they separated. In 1967 she enrolled at university and studied law. She was disqualified from practising due to her court conviction for slander, but she ran a legal studio for many years. Alessandra, too, became a lawyer. From time to time Caglio agreed to be interviewed. Her conviction, she confessed in 1987, 'left me humiliated, destroyed. I had told the truth and even today I am willing to swear to the statements I made.' In March 2010, she announced to a journalist from *Il Corriere della Sera* that she was planning to try to overturn the final confirmation by the Court of Cassation in 1966 of her conviction. She showed the reporter a book with a signed dedication: the judge who had pronounced her guilty had given it as a gift to Ugo Montagna. By condemning her, she claimed, he had done a favour for his friend. Silvano Muto, the journalist whose article first launched the scandal, struggled for years to find work. Later, in the 1980s, he was elected to Rome city council on a Socialist ticket and became a committee chairman.

Once the case was over, Ugo Montagna sank back into the shadows and was never heard from again, save for a brief brush with the law at the time of the Rome Olympics. Soon after the dust had settled he married Iolanda Petrini and, at the second attempt, embraced family life. He quietly resumed his place in the top drawer of Rome society. His death was announced in February 1990 and his funeral was attended by various elderly aristocrats. Today the plaque on the burial niche of 'Marchese Ugo Montagna di San Bartolomeo' in the Flaminio cemetery is adorned with a picture of him beaming in black-and-white, from his heyday in the 1950s. His son currently lives on Via della Camilluccia not far from where the villa constructed for the family of Mussolini's lover Clara Petacci used to stand (it was demolished in the 1970s) and where Montagna, before he became a marchese, used to come to call.

Piero Piccioni resumed his career as a musician and composed more than two hundred original scores for Italian movies. Much later he married a former musical star Gloria Paul, with whom he had two children. He commented publicly on the case just once. In 1980 RAI TV broadcast a reconstruction of the events surrounding the death of Wilma Montesi. He issued a statement in which he denounced his own implication in the affair as a political manoeuvre designed to undermine his father. He died in July 2004 and received generous obituaries. Respectful mention was made of his work on film scores but, as with his old friend Montagna, his connection with the Montesi affair was accorded most space. For all their efforts to shrug off their incrimination and trial, the two men were forever marked in the public mind by their involvement in the scandal.

The Montesi family left Via Tagliamento and went to live in a new block near Rodolfo's workshop. They put the past behind them and moved on. Wilma's sister Wanda had two children by her 1955 marriage to Silvano Pucci, the carpenter. Her brother Sergio, the youngest and cleverest of the siblings, went to university and became an army officer. Rodolfo Montesi died in October 1977 and his wife Maria in February 1995. Neither of them is buried in the Verano cemetery where Wilma was interred. The family never again spoke to the press about the tragedy that befell them in 1953. Wanda and Sergio are both still alive and are firm in their refusal to speak to anyone about it. When I located Dr Sergio Montesi, he declined to answer any of my questions. The whole matter, he said, was simply 'too painful' even today for him to revisit it. As for Giuseppe, Wilma's family had nothing further to do with him. Eventually he had married Rossana Spissu and, in addition to their first son Riccardo, they had had two more boys. Rossana's sister Mariella did not marry and remained a member of this unusually long-lasting *ménage à trois*. Today Rossana Spissu will hear no ill of her late spouse and refers to him simply as 'a good man and a fine husband'.

In the years after its release, Fellini's film established itself as the biggest movie money-spinner of the period between 1960 and 1965. The film is repeatedly revisited, and celebrated on anniversaries. As long as he lived, Fellini was called on to talk about it on these and other occasions. Tazio Secchiaroli, too, the original paparazzo, became party to the commemoration of the film that introduced a new idea of Italy. Despite this, most of the protagonists of both the *dolce vita* and of *La dolce vita* moved on and escaped imprisonment in the specific narratives of the period. Fellini made several more great movies and Secchiaroli became his friend and set photographer. The two men died in 1993 and 1998 respectively.

La dolce vita acquired an aura in the popular imagination as a film that described the sexual antics of an aristocratic and Bohemian élite. In Pietro Germi's satire *Divorce Italian Style*, the film arrives in the Sicilian town of Cefalù preceded by its legend. 'There are orgies worthy of Tiberius, wife-swapping, striptease!' exclaims one excited local man to his friends, as he voices the film's supposed attractions. In fact, the so-called 'orgy scene' depicts a louche gathering in a seaside villa. Its culmination is an impromptu horizontal striptease performed by Nadia Gray in the role of the lady of the house. The controversy this scene aroused, in the context of a film that was already itself controversial, shows how easily fantasies of sexual transgression could take hold.

As Italian customs evolved, and the sexual prudishness of the 1950s gave way to a more tolerant atmosphere, the complex intrigues and fantasies were replaced by more relaxed attitudes to sex on the one hand and its commercial exploitation on the other. Only briefly in the 1970s did orgies once more capture the public imagination, this time as a representation of the practices in alternative living associated with Italy's hippie movement. In the prosperous but conservative climate of the 1980s this fantasy declined. Instead opportunities to step beyond conventional behaviour were institutionalised. Capocotta beach, stretching from Ostia to Torvaianica, became a well-known gathering point for nudists, who in turn became a target for voyeurs and police raids. With its rich vegetation and natural beauty, it was one of the few areas of the coast not colonised by unlicensed kiosks and bathing establishments. With this pressure the naturists abandoned the area, which instead became used by those who regarded nudism as an excuse to have sex in public. It is claimed that a number of pornographic films were shot there.

In 1996 the municipality of Rome cleaned up the area and proclaimed it a nature reserve. Then in 2000 it became the first authorised nudist beach in Italy. An opinion poll conducted in 2005 revealed that 70 per cent of Italians regarded naturism as completely normal.

In 2009 orgies returned to the headlines in Italy when it was revealed that prime minister Silvio Berlusconi was in the habit of hosting parties at his Roman residence and his Sardinian villa at which dozens of young women were paid to flatter him and attend to his requirements. The story first appeared when one prostitute, who had been paid by a businessman seeking to win favours and privileges from his association with the prime minister, went public. She had taped her encounter with Berlusconi and sold it to a magazine. Further revelations exposed an entire system of hospitality based on the procurement of women for the gratification of the septuagenarian media mogul and politician. Some of the women were minors, such as Noemi Letizia, a young woman from the province of Naples whose eighteenth birthday party he attended, an act that led his wife to announce she was leaving him. While some of the women were simply party guests, others confessed to having sex with him or to participating in sex games in which the prime minister was the only male present. These were not precisely orgies, as the prostitute who went public, Patrizia D'Addario, clarified, because there was not an equal number of male and female participants and the events were geared towards the pleasure of just one person. They were, she suggested, more akin to the practices of a sultan and his harem.

These revelations unavoidably brought the Montesi case to mind. Some of Berlusconi's political allies saw in them an attempt to use scandal to bring him down, in the way that political intrigue had informed the earlier case. What was striking was the way in which those involved in this affair resembled some of the protagonists of the Montesi case. D'Addario, with her angry denunciations, took the part of Anna Maria Caglio; the businessman who supplied and paid female guests was a latter-day Ugo Montagna; and the young and ostensibly innocent Noemi Letizia, a girl whose association with the prime minister was encouraged by her parents, was in some, but fortunately not all, respects a modern Wilma Montesi.

If Berlusconi was able, astonishingly, to get away with such behaviour without being obliged to resign, at least for the time being, it was a sign of his power. But it was also an indication of the extent to which Italians were willing to close their eyes to the excesses of the powerful. This in turn has something to do with the way *La dolce vita*, the imagery and themes it presented, has become rooted in Italy's self-image. There is somehow something Italian and even worthy of celebration in the shameless fun-loving lifestyle of a prime minister who always presented himself as an anomalous figure, an anti-politician and embodiment of popular desires. Aged seventy-five in 2011, Berlusconi is a man with his roots in the 1950s. The myth of the playboy and the hedonism of that time are part of his make-up.

Most of the celebrities from that era are long forgotten or soon put the past far behind them. Only a few failed to escape and remain as permanent monuments to their past selves. One of these was the face of *La dolce vita*, Anita Ekberg, who would never equal her success in this film. She was an international star who distilled into a single moment the frenetic hedonism that the American film world brought to Rome in the 1950s. Like the forgotten diva played by Gloria Swanson in *Sunset Boulevard*, she would remain in Rome as age and neglect withered her beauty, a permanent witness to a time that would come to be remembered as heroic.

Behind her was the more disturbing image of Wilma Montesi, the phantom whose lonely death haunted the period. In the condescension of memory, she would be even further dehumanised than in the immediate aftermath of her death. A distant, accusing face in a few oft-reproduced press photographs, she would be remembered only as a pretext, a news item that gave rise to a media circus. Wilma Montesi and Anita Ekberg apparently had nothing in common. Montesi was not a film goddess from the land of dreams, but a girl like many others who fantasised about getting into the movies. In contrast to the Swede's celebrated dip in the Trevi Fountain, the night-time bathe that resulted in her untimely death was anything but glamorous.

Ekberg and the girl from Via Tagliamento represented two sides of the same coin: one the ecstasy of fame, the other the tragedy of broken dreams; one surface waywardness, the other deep scandal. They were both heroines of the press, whose respective life and death provided raw material for journalists, photographers and filmmakers. They were bound together in another way. Without Montesi's death, much of what became known as the *dolce vita* would have remained hidden and it is unlikely that a film like *La dolce vita* would ever have been made.

Today the image of Rome in the years of the *dolce vita* is one of the most powerful marketing tools of Italian products abroad. Foodstuffs, property, holidays, music, fashion, drinks, sunglasses, watches and scooters have all been advertised using images derived from the Via Veneto in the 1950s. Black-and-white evocations of cool people in glamorous locations carry a special charge that is evocative of Rome. The key scene of Anita Ekberg's dip in the Trevi Fountain has been acted out again and again by aspirant actresses seeking attention, by tourists, and by enterprises that include the Valentino fashion label, Peroni beer and Longines watches, all seeking to add period allure to their products. The sun and the outdoors have their place, but the idea of a nocturnal adventure always carries a more adult appeal.

For the city of Rome, one person only is to be thanked for fashioning this alluring image. This is because it is not real but rather is derived from a film that had already filtered out the least acceptable aspects of the corruption of the era. Fellini's name has been given to the small triangular piazza at the top of the Via Veneto just inside the Porta Pinciana and by Harry's Bar. It is called 'Largo Fellini'. At the end of the more fashionable stretch of the road a plaque was placed on the wall in 2002 on which the inscription reads as follows: 'Here on the Via Veneto in 1959 Federico Fellini invented the theatre of the "dolce vita".'

There is no plaque to the memory of Wilma Montesi in Via Tagliamento.

Bibliography

1. ARCHIVAL SOURCES

Archivio Centrale dello Stato, Rome
  Ministero dell'Interno, Direzione Generale Pubblica Sicurezza, Divisione Polizia amministrativa e sociale, 1945–75; B.454, Fascicoli personali –Montagna, Piccioni, Polito 1954; B. 455, Fascicoli vari 1954–7; Polizia criminale Interpol, B.6 La tratta delle bianche (1923–49), B.10 Interpol, affari generali (1946–61); B.14 Stupefacenti – Pubblicazioni ufficiali; Gabinetto, Archivio generale 1953–4, B. 31
Centro documentazione *Il Corriere della Sera*, Milan
  Folder: Caso Montesi
Centro documentazione *Il Messaggero*, Rome
  Folder 236: Montesi, Wilma
Centro documentazione Rizzoli SpA, Milan
  Folders: Arena, Maurizio; Christian, Linda; Ekberg, Anita; Montesi; Paparazzi; Parigini, Novella; Roma, Via Veneto
National Archives and Records Administration, College Park, Maryland
  RG 59, General Records of the Department of State, B.3860 (1954)
  RG 84, Records of the Foreign Service Posts of the Department of State; Italy, Rome Embassy. Records of Clare Booth Luce, 1953–6, B. 1
Public Record Office, Kew
  Foreign Office FO371, RTI551/2, RT1651/2, T1651/5 (1955) 'Montesi Case'

2. Unpublished Sources

Angelo Frignani, unpublished extended draft manuscript and working notes for *La strana morte di Wilma Montesi*. Cited below as: Frignani MS. Frignani was a journalist on *Il Tempo* from 1953 until his retirement.

Wayland Young (Lord Kennett), personal scrapbooks and cuttings. Young was a reporter for the *Manchester Guardian*; he covered the case and wrote *The Montesi Scandal* at the end of the Venice trial.

3. Newspapers And Magazines

Attualità (Rome, illustrated weekly)
Borghese, Il (Milan, right-wing monthly)
Confidential (American monthly)
Corriere della Sera, Il (Milan, daily newspaper)
Detective Crimen (Rome, true crime weekly)
Epoca (Milan, illustrated weekly)
Europeo, L' (Milan, illustrated weekly)
Gazzetta del Popolo, La (Milan, daily newspaper)
Lowdown (American monthly)
Merlo Giallo, Il (Rome, satirical weekly)
Messaggero, Il (Rome, daily newspaper)
Momento-sera (Rome, evening newspaper)
Novella (Milan, illustrated weekly)
Oggi (Milan, illustrated weekly)
Paese, Il (Rome, left-wing daily newspaper)
Paese Sera (Rome, evening sister paper of *Il Paese*)
Popolo, Il (Rome, Christian Democrat daily newspaper)
Roma (Naples, daily newspaper)
Settimana Incom, La (Rome, illustrated weekly)
Settimo Giorno (Milan, illustrated weekly)
Specchio, Lo (Rome, illustrated weekly)
Tempo, Il (Rome, daily newspaper)
Unità, L' (various cities, Communist daily newspaper)
Vie Nuove (Milan, Communist illustrated weekly)

Whisper (American monthly)

4. Books and Articles (by Topic)

The Montesi Case

Ceccarelli, F., *Il letto e il potere: storia sessuale della Prima Repubblica* (Milan, Longanesi, 1994).

Enzensberger, H. M., *Politica e gangsterismo* (Rome, Savelli, 1979)

Davis, M. S., *All Rome Trembled* (New York, Putnam, 1957)

De Luca, M., 'Lo scandalo Montesi' in L. Violante (ed.), *Storia d'Italia, Annali 12, La criminalità* (Turin, Einaudi, 1997)

Frignani, A., *La strana morte di Wilma Montesi* (Rome, Adnkronos, 2003)

Galli, G., *Affari di stato* (Milan, Kaos, 1991)

Grignetti, F., *Il caso Montesi: sesso, potere e morte nell'Italia degli anni '50* (Venice, Marsilio, 2006)

Lucarelli, C., *Nuovi misteri d'Italia* (Turin, Einaudi, 2004)

Pellegrini, R., *Il caso Montesi* (Parma, Guanda, 1954)

Pinkus, K., *The Montesi Scandal: The Death of Wilma Montesi and the Birth of the Paparazzi in Fellini's Rome* (Chicago, University of Chicago Press, 2003)

Vasile, V., *Wilma Montesi: la ragazza con il reggicalze* (Rome, L'Unità, c.2005)

Young, W., *The Montesi Scandal* (London, Faber & Faber, 1957)

Italian Society and Politics

Allum, P., *Politics and Society in Postwar Naples* (Cambridge, Cambridge University Press, 1973)

Baldassini, C., *L'ombra di Mussolini: L'Italia moderata e la memoria del fascismo (1945–1960)* (Soveria Mannelli, Rubbettino, 2008)

Bellassai, S., *La legge del desiderio: il progetto Merlin e l'Italia degli anni Cinquanta* (Rome, Carrocci, 2006)

Bernabei, E., with G. Dell'Arti, *L'uomo di fiducia* (Milan, Mondadori, 1999)

Boiardi, F., 'Mario Scelba', *Appunti*, 98, March–April 1992

—, 'Attilio Piccioni', *Appunti,* 99, May–June 1992

Bosworth, R., *Mussolini's Italy: Life Under the Dictatorship* (London, Allen Lane, 2005)

Capussotti, E., *Gioventù perduta: gli anni Cinquanta dei giovani e del cinema in Italia* (Florence, Giunti, 2004)

Cremoncini, R., and others, *Against Mussolini: Art and the Fall of a Dictator* (London, Estorick Collection of Modern Art, 2010)

De Felice, R., *Mussolini l'alleato 1940–1945,* I. *L'Italia in guerra, 1940–1943,* tome 2, *Crisi e agonia del regime* (Turin, Einaudi, 1990)

—, *Mussolini l'alleato* 1940–1945, II. *La guerra civile, 1943–1945* (Turin, Einaudi, 1997)

De Giorgio, M., *Le italiane dall'Unità a oggi* (Rome, Laterza, 1992)

Di Nolfo, E., *Le paure e le speranze degli italiani (1943–1953)* (Milan, Mondadori, 1986)

'Donna Letizia', *Il saper vivere* (Milan, Mondadori, 2000; first published 1960)

Forgacs, D., and S. Gundle, *Mass Culture and Italian Society from Fascism to the Cold War* (Bloomington, Indiana University Press, 2008)

Franco, M., *Andreotti* (Milan, Mondadori, 2008)

Gabrielli, P., *Il 1946, le donne, la Repubblica* (Rome, Donzelli, 2009)

Garofalo, A., *L'italiana in Italia* (Bari, Laterza, 1956)

Ghirelli, A., *Democristiani: storia di una classe politica dagli anni Trenta alla Seconda repubblica* (Milan, Mondadori, 2004)

Ginsborg, P., *A History of Contemporary Italy: Society and Politics 1943–89* (London, Penguin, 1991)

Giovagnoli, A., *Il partito italiano: la Democrazia cristiana dal 1942 al 1994* (Rome, Laterza, 1996)

Gundle, S., *Between Hollywood and Moscow: The Italian Communists and the Challenge of Mass Culture 1943–1991* (Durham, NC, Duke University Press, 2000)

—, *Bellissima: Feminine Beauty and the Idea of Italy* (London and New Haven, Yale University Press, 2007)

—, 'Anecdotes and historiography: From Traiano Boccalini's strange death to Benito Mussolini's sexual proclivities', *Incontri,* 24:1(2009)

La Rovere, L., *L'eredità del fascismo* (Turin, Bollati Boringhieri, 2008)

Liucci, R., *L'Italia borghese di Longanesi* (Venice, Marsilio, 2002)

Logan, O., 'Pius XII: romanità, prophesy and charisma', *Modern Italy*, 3:2 (1998)

Marino, G. C., *La Repubblica di forza: Mario Scelba e le passioni del suo tempo* (Milan, Franco Angeli, 1995)

Marsili, M., 'De Gasperi and Togliatti: political leadership and personality cults in post-war Italy', *Modern Italy*, 3:2 (1998)

McCarthy, P. (ed.), *Italy Since 1945* (Oxford, 2000)

Montanelli, I., *Addio Wanda! Rapporto Kinsey sulla situazione italiana* (Milan, Longanesi, 1956)

Morris, P. (ed.), *Women in Italy 1945–60: An Interdisciplinary Study* (New York, Palgrave, 2006)

Parca, G., *Le italiane si confessano* (Milan, Feltrinelli, 1959)

Parlato, G., *Fascisti senza Mussolini: le origini del neofascismo in Italia, 1943–1948* (Bologna, Il Mulino, 2006)

Pizzinelli, C., *Scelba* (Milan, Longanesi, 1982)

Preda, G. (ed.), *Il "chi è?" del "Borghese" (vecchi fusti e nuovi fusti)* (Milan, Edizioni del Borghese, 1961)

Radi, L., *La DC da De Gasperi a Fanfani* (Soveria Mannelli, Rubbettino, 2005)

Reggiani, C., *Fanfani* (Palermo, Edizioni Sud Europa, 1958)

Scarpellini, E., *L'Italia dei consumi: dalla Belle Epoque al nuovo millennio* (Rome, Laterza, 2008)

Scelba, M., *Contro lo scandalismo* (Rome, Centro documentazione della Presidenza del consiglio dei ministri, 1954)

—, *Per l'Italia e per l'Europa* (Rome, Cinque lune 1990)

Sorlin, P., *European Cinemas, European Societies 1939–1990* (London, Routledge, 1991)

Taviani, P. E., *Politica a memoria d'uomo* (Bologna, Il Mulino, 2002)

Venè, G., *Vola Colomba: vita quotidiana degli italiani negli anni del dopoguerra, 1945–1960* (Milan, Mondadori, 1990)

Rome

Augias, C., *I segreti di Roma* (Milan, Mondadori, 1995)

Bachmann, I., *Quel che ho visto e udito a Roma* (Macerata, Quodibet, 2002)

Bizzarri, E. and others, *Tempo libero e regime: storia del Dopolavoro a Roma negli anni Trenta* (Rome, Pisani, 1997)

Botta, G., *Appuntamento a Via Veneto* (Bologna, Cappelli, 1964)

Bartolini, F., *I rivali d'Italia: Roma e Milano dal settecento a oggi* (Rome, Laterza, 2006)

Brice, C., *Histoire de Rome et des Romains de Napoleon 1er à nos jours* (Paris, Perrin, 2007)

Cusani, F., *Roma: una capitale in cerca d'autore* (Venice, Marsilio, 1990)

d'Hospital, J., *Roma in confidenza* (Milan, Rizzoli, 1963)

Fagiolo dell'Arco, M., and C. Terenzi (eds), *Roma 1948–1959: arte, cronaca e cultura dal neorealismo alla dolce vita* (Milan, Skira, 2002)

Grioni, J. S., *Via Margutta: ritratto di una strada* (Rome, Palombi, 1970)

Insolera, I., *Roma moderna: un secolo di storia urbanistica, 1870– 1970* (Turin, Einaudi, 1976)

Levi, C., *Roma fuggitiva: una città e i suoi dintorni* (Rome, Donzelli, 2002)

Mafai, M. 'Roma, dal 18 aprile alla dolce vita' in Fagiolo and Terenzi, *Roma 1948–1959*

Mughini, G.., *Che belle le ragazze di Via Margutta* (Milan, Mondadori, 2004)

Morton, H.V., *A Traveller in Rome* (London, Methuen, 1957)

Padellaro, G., and A. (eds), *I non romani e Roma* (Milan, Rizzoli, 1970)

Partridge, B., *A History of Orgies* (London, Spring, 1958)

Piccioni, L., and others, *Anna Salvatore – testimonianze* (Florence, 'La Gradiva', 1974)

Patti, E., *Cronache romane* (Milan, Bompiani, 1962)

Prete, A. T., *Istantanee romane* (Rome, ERS, 1954)

Rhodes, A., *A Sabine Journey: To Rome in Holy Year* (London, Century, 1987; first published 1952)

Sette, A. M. and others, *Roma in nera: i grandi delitti tra cronaca, storia, costume* (Rome, Palombi, 2006)

Vidotto, V., *Roma contemporanea* (Rome, Laterza, 2006)

Crime and the Law

Armati, C., and Selvetella, Y., *Roma criminale* (Rome, Newton Compton, 2005)

Bertieri Bonfanti, G., *La guerra all'oppio* (Milan, Sironi, 1964)

Bucciante, G., *Il Palazzo: quarant'anni di scandali e di corruzione* (Milan, Leonardo, 1989)

Canosa, R., *La polizia in Italia dal 1945 a oggi* (Bologna, Il Mulino, 1976)

Chilanti, F., *La Mafia su Roma* (Milan, Palazzi, 1971)

Costantini, C., *Sangue sulla Dolce Vita* (Rome, L'Airone, 2006)

Dickie, J., *Cosa Nostra: A History of the Sicilian Mafia* (London, Hodder & Stoughton, 2004)

Franzinelli, M., *I tentacoli dell'Ovra: agenti, collaboratori e vittime della polizia politica fascista* (Turin, Bollati Boringhieri, 1999)

Gundle, S., and L. Rinaldi (eds), *Assassinations and Murder in Modern Italy* (New York, Palgrave, 2008)

Lupo, S., *Storia della mafia dalle origini ai nostri giorni* (Rome, Donzelli, 1996)

—, *Quando la mafia trovò l'America: storia di un intreccio intercontinentale, 1888–2008* (Turin, Einaudi, 2008)

Marchesi, S., *I processi del secolo* (Florence, Olimpia, 2008)

Musi, G. C., *Il contrabbando degli stupefacenti* (Milan, De Vecchi, 1967)

Oliva, G., *Storia dei carabinieri* (Milan, Mondadori, 2002)

Polidoro, M., *Cronaca nera: indagine sui delitti che hanno sconvolto l'Italia* (Casale Monferrato, Piemme, 2005)

Sannino, A., *Le forze di polizia nel dopoguerra* (Milan, Mursia, 2004)

Silj, A., *Malpaese: criminalità, corruzione e politica nell'Italia delle prima Repubblica* (Rome, Donzelli, 1994)

Turone, S., *Corrotti e corruttori: dall'Unità d'Italia al P2* (Rome, Laterza, 1984)

The Press and Photography

Blessing, J., 'Paparazzi on the Prowl' in G. Celant (ed.), *The Italian Metamorphosis, 1943–1968* (New York, Guggenheim, 1995)

Bonito Oliva, A., *A Flash of Art: fotografi d'azione a Roma, 1953–1973* (Milan, Photology, 2003)

Bravo, A., *Il fotoromanzo* (Bologna, Il Mulino, 2003)

Ciuffa, V., *La dolce vita minuto per minuto* (Rome, Ciuffa, 2010)

Coen, F., *Una vita, tante vite* (Soveria Mannelli, Rubbettino, 2004)

Costantini, C., *La storia del Messaggero* (Rome, Gremese, 2008)

Desjardins, M., '*Confidential* Magazine, Stardom, and the State of California', in A. L. McLean and D. A. Cook (eds), *Headline Hollywood: A Century of Film Scandal* (New Brunswick, Rutgers University Press, 2001)

Fiumi, C., *L'Italia in nera: la cronaca nera italiana nelle pagine del Corriere della Sera* (Milan, Rizzoli, 2006)

Gambetti, F., *La grande illusione, 1945–1953* (Milan, Mursia, 1976)

Magista, A., *Dolce vita gossip: star, amori, mondanità e kolossal negli anni d'oro di Cinecittà* (Milan, Bruno Mondadori, 2007)

Mormorio, D., *Tazio Secchiaroli: Greatest of the Paparazzi* (New York, Abrams, 1999)

Murialdi, P., *La stampa italiana del dopoguerra, 1943–1972* (Bari, Laterza, 1973)

Nemiz, A., *Vita, dolce vita: storia in Via Veneto e dintorni nelle foto di Marcello Geppetti, Ivan Kroscenko, Mario Pelosi e Bruno Tartaglia* (Rome, Network, 1983)

Nemiz, A., *Vita di Paparazzo: Rino Barillari il 'King'* (Rome, Nuova arnica, 1997)

Rava, E., *Roma in cronaca nera* (Rome, Manifestolibri, 2005)

Reteuna, D., *Cinema di carta: storia fotografica del cinema italiano* (Alessandria, Falsopiano, 2000)

Talamo, G., *Il Messaggero e la sua città: cent'anni di storia* (Florence, Le Monnier, 1979)

Cinema and Entertainment

Adinolfi, F., *Mondo Exotica: sounds, visions, obsessions of the cocktail generation* (Durham, NC, Duke University Press, 2008)

Bertelli, G., *Divi e paparazzi: La Dolce Vita di Fellini* (Genoa, Le Mani, 2009)

Bondi, D., *Sottobosco del cinema* (Bologna, Cappelli, 1965)

Christian, L., *Linda: My Own Story* (New York, Dell, 1962)

Chandler, C., *I, Fellini* (London, Bloomsbury, 1995)

Colasanti, A., and C. Siniscalchi, *La dolce vita: scandalo a Roma e Palma d'oro a Cannes* (Rome, Fondazione Scuola Nazionale di Cinema, 2003)

Cottrell, J., and F. Cashin, *Richard Burton* (London, Barker, 1971)

David, L., and J. Robbins, *Richard & Elizabeth* (London, Barker, 1977)

De Santi, P. M., *La Dolce Vita: scandalo a Roma e Palma d'oro a Cannes* (Pisa, ETS, 2004)

Dufreigne, J-P., *Le Style Dolce Vita* (Paris, Assouline, 2005)

Fellini, F., *Le notti di Cabiria* (Milan, Garzanti, 1977)

—, *La dolce vita* (Bologna, Cappelli, 1960)

Gordon, R.S.C., *Bicycle Thieves* (London, BFI, 2008)

Guiles, F. L., *Tyrone Power: The Last Idol* (London, Granada, 1979)

Gundle, S., 'La Dolce Vita', in D. W. Ellwood (ed.), *The Movies as History* (Stroud, Sutton, 2000)

— 'Saint Ingrid at the Stake: Stardom and Scandal in the Bergman–Rossellini Collaboration', in D. Forgacs, S. Lutton and G. Nowell-Smith (eds), *Roberto Rossellini: Magician of the Real* (London, BFI, 2000)

Gundle, S., *Glamour: A History* (Oxford, Oxford University Press, 2008)

Kashner, S., and J. McNair, *The Bad and the Beautiful: A Chronicle of Hollywood in the Fifties* (New York, Norton, 2002)

Kashner, S., and N. Schoenberger, *Furious Love: Elizabeth Taylor, Richard Burton and the Marriage of the Century* (New York, Harper, 2010)

Kaufman H., and G. Lerner, *Hollywood sul Tevere* (Milan, Sperling & Kupfer, 1980)

Kezich, T., *Il dolce cinema: Fellini & altri* (Milan, Bompiani 1978)

—, and A. Levantesi, *Dino: De Laurentis, la vita e i film* (Milan, Feltrinelli, 2001)

Kezich, T., *Federico: Fellini, la vita e i film* (Milan, Feltrinelli, 2002)

Levy, S., *The Last Playboy: The High Life of Porfirio Rubirosa* (London, HarperCollins, 2005)

Mingozzi, G. (ed.), *Dolce dolce vita: immagini da un set di Federico Fellini* (Bologna, Giorgio Menna, 1999)

Pellizzari, L., and C. M. Valentinetti, *Il romanzo di Alida Valli* (Milan, Garzanti, 1995)

Rondi, B., *Il cinema di Fellini* (Rome, Bianco e Nero, 1965)

Reich, J., *Beyond the Latin Lover: Marcello Mastroianni, Masculinity and Italian Cinema* (Bloomington, Indiana University Press, 2004)

Sanguineti, T. (ed.), *La spiaggia* (Genoa, Le Mani, 2001)

Server, L., *Ava Gardner: Love is Nothing* (London, Bloomsbury, 2006)

Ternavasio, M., *Il grande Fred: Fred Buscaglione – una vita in musica*

(Turin, Lindau, 1999)

Wagstaff, C., *Italian Neorealist Cinema* (Toronto, University of Toronto Press, 2007)

Walker, A., *Elizabeth* (London, Weidenfeld & Nicolson, 1990)

Literature and Memoirs

Alvaro, C., *Itinerario italiano: Roma vestito di nuovo* (Milan, Bompiani, 1957)

Caglio, A. M. M., *Una figlia del secolo* (Rome, private publication, 1956)

di Robilant, O., *Snob: sine nobiltate* (Milan, Mursia, 2007)

Flaiano, E., *La solitudine del satiro* (Milan, Rizzoli, 1973)

Flaiano, E., *Diario notturno* (Milan, Adelphi, 1994; first published 1956)

Fusco G., *Il gusto di vivere*, edited by N. Aspesi (Rome, Laterza, 2004)

Guareschi, G., *Don Camillo* (Milan: Rizzoli, 1948)

Laurenzi, C., *Due anni a Roma (1954–55)* (Venice, Neri Pozza, 1957)

'Lo Duca', *The Sweet Life* (London, World Distributors, 1960)

Martinelli, E., *Sono come sono: dalla dolcevita e ritorno* (Milan, Rusconi, 1995)

Modugno, B., *Roma by Night* (Rome, Vito Bianco, 1959)

Moravia, A., *Racconti romani* (Milan, Bompiani, 1985; first published 1954)

—, *Nuovi racconti romani* (Milan, Bompiani, 1982; first published 1959)

—, *La romana* (Milan, Bompiani, 1993; first published 1947)

Moretti, U., *Artists in Rome: Tales of the Babuino* (New York, Macmillan, 1958)

Napolitano, G. G., *I racconti della dolce vita* (Rome, Studio 12, 2005)

Navarra, Q., *Memorie del cameriere di Mussolini* (Milan, Longanesi, 1946)

Patti, E., *Cronache romane* (Milan, Bompiani, 1962)

Petacci, M., *Chi ama è perduto: mia sorella Claretta* (Gardolo di Trento, Reverdito, 1988)

Revel, J. F., *As for Italy* (London, Weidenfeld & Nicolson, 1958)

Russo, G., *Oh, Flaiano!* (Cava de' Terreni, Avagliano, 2001)

Russo, G., *Con Flaiano e Fellini a via Veneto* (Sovera Mannelli, Rubbettino, 2005)

Sarasso, S., *Confine di Stato* (Venice, Marsilio, 2007)

Spark, M., *The Public Image* (London, Macmillan, 1968)

Stajano, G., *Roma capovolta* (Rome, Quattrucci, 1959)

—, *Pubblici scandali e private virtù: dalla Dolce Vita al convento* (Lecce, Manni, 2007)

Ustinov, P., *Dear Me* (London, Heinemann, 1977)

Williams, T., *The Roman Spring of Mrs Stone* (London, John Lehmann, 1950)

Winters, S., *Shelley* (London, Granada, 1980)

'Wu Ming', *54* (Turin, Einaudi, 2002)

Filmography

Barefoot Contessa, The (J. Mankiewicz, 1954)
Ben-Hur (W. Wyler, 1959)
Bidone, Il (The Swindlers) (F. Fellini, 1955)
Blow-Up (M. Antonioni, 1966)
Costa azzurra (Côte d'Azur) (V. Sala, 1959)
Dolce vita, La (F. Fellini, 1960)
Donatella (M. Monicelli, 1956)
Ladri di biciclette (Bicycle Thieves) (V. De Sica, 1948)
Modelle di Via Margutta, Le (The Models of Via Margutta) (G. M.
    Scotese,1945)
Moralista, Il (The Moralist) (G. Bianchi, 1959)
Notte brava, La (The Big Night) (M. Bolognini, 1959)
Notti di Cabiria, Le (Nights of Cabiria) (F. Fellini, 1957)
Paisà (R. Rossellini, 1946)
Poveri ma belli (Poor but Beautiful) (D. Risi, 1957)
Principe fusto, Il (Prince He-Man) (M. Arena, 1960)
Quo Vadis (M. Le Roy, 1951)
Racconti romani (Roman Tales) (G. Franciolini, 1955)
Ragazza di Via Veneto, La (The Girl of the Via Veneto) (M.Girolami,
    1955)
Riso amaro (Bitter Rice) (G. De Santis, 1949)
Roma città aperta (Rome Open City) (R. Rossellini, 1945)
Roman Holiday (W. Wyler, 1953)
Sfida, La (The Challenge) (F. Rosi, 1958)
Spiaggia, La (The Beach) (A. Lattuada, 1954)
Tratta delle bianche (White Slave Trade) (L. Comencini, 1952)
Tre ladri (Three Thieves) (L. De Felice, 1954)
Via Margutta (M. Camerini, 1960)
Via Veneto (G. Lipartiti, 1964)
Vortice (Vortex) (R. Matarazzo,1953)

Notes on Sources

Each chapter is informed by extensive reading from the sources in the Bibliography. The short explanations below offer a guide to some of the materials used in the chapters, and precise references to all significant quoted items, except where these are from the press. Most of the facts and opinions cited are taken from a wide range of contemporary press reports. With just a handful of exceptions, these are not detailed individually. Archival material has been used where possible, especially the legal documents produced by the instructional inquiry of 1954-5. I have also made use of Angelo Frignani's manuscript. Published sources are indicated by the name of the author only, plus year where more than one item appears in the Bibliography.

PROLOGUE AND I: THE BODY ON THE BEACH

The basic facts of the events immediately following Wilma's disappearance are recounted in all of the books that deal with the case and press articles of the time. *Il Messaggero* provided local coverage in the initial phase, while the Milan paper *Il Corriere della Sera* offered extensive reports. On intra-family relations, the behaviour of young women and respectability, I have drawn on a number of sources, including the oral interviews conducted for Forgacs and Gundle, in addition to De Giorgio, Parca, Capussotti (especially Chapter 3 on representations of women), and Bellassai. On the living standards of the lower-middle class at this time, see

Scarpellini, Chapters 2 and 3, and Venè, who is also useful on leisure. On youth and violent crime in the post-war years, see La Rovere, pp. 149–52.

II: The Rumour Mill

On the press in the post-war years, I have mostly drawn on Murialdi. I have also used Frignani and Grignetti, two journalists with first-hand knowledge of the sector, the former also of the period. The portrayal of Wilma in the press owed much to a post-war obsession with female beauty. See Gundle, 2007, Chapters 5 and 6. Garofalo offers a contemporary denunciation of what she called 'the dictatorship of beauty', pp. 29–30. Another obsession, that with true crime, is explored in Rava. On Fascists in post-war Rome, their links to *Il Tempo*, and Saverio Polito's actions against them, see Parlato, pp. 278–95. On Polito's behaviour in relation to Mussolini and the members of his family, see De Felice, 1997 pp. 3–19, and Grignetti, p. 46. On Achille Lauro, the shipping magnate and mayor of Naples, see Allum.

III: Politics and Scandal

On the post-war political situation, including the elections of 1946, 1948 and 1953, see Ginsborg, Chapters 1–4. The reasons for the success of the Christian Democrats are further explored in Di Nolfo, Chapter 7. On the images of De Gasperi and Communist leader Togliatti, see Marsili. For Attilio Piccioni, information has been drawn from Boiardi, May–June 1992, and Radi, pp. 52, 89, 90, 102, 105–6, 113–14. On Scelba, see Pizzinelli, Boiardi, March–April 1992, Marino. On the post-war police and Scelba's role in its expansion, see Canosa, pp. 131–2. Pope Pius XII's role is considered in Logan. On the fall of Mussolini and Rome, see Mafai, and Vidotto (Chapter 7). On the Christian Democratic left, see Giovagnoli, and Radi. It is worth pointing out that every book on the Montesi case refers to a cartoon supposedly published by the satirical weekly *Il Merlo Giallo* on 5 May 1953. It is said to have featured a carrier pigeon with a suspender belt in its beak. No such cartoon has even been reproduced and the reason is that it was never published. Instead there was the textual allusion to carrier pigeons contained in the chapter. Rapelli and Guareschi's judgements on Fanfani are quoted in Reggiani, p. 80.

IV: Via Margutta

The most complete contemporary portrait of the Bohemian community, Via Margutta, and the streets surrounding the Via del Babuino in contained in Moretti. The film adaptation of this book, *Via Margutta*, conveys little of the vitality of this sub-world but, together with *Le modelle di Via Margutta*, it is the only film to feature it. Grioni, *Via Margutta*, offers some insights, as does Prete, pp. 49–52 and Ciuffa, pp. 36–7, 56–8, 70–72. On the post-war art scene and its social world, see Mughini, and Fagiolo dell'Arco and Terenzi. For a brief additional insight into the sexual mores of this milieu, see Rhodes, p. 185. Adinolfi provides a very complete account of the night scene in Rome and Italy in the post-war years and the types of music that were played in the clubs. On Anna Salvatore, see Piccioni. Material on Novella Parigini is drawn from several interviews she gave looking back on the 1950s. See *Novella*, 6, 13, June 1972; *Oggi*, 27 April 1983; and *Oggi*, 6, 13 and 20 April 1988.

V: Hollywood on the Tiber

This chapter mostly draws on memoirs (especially those of Linda Christian, Shelley Winters and Peter Ustinov), biographies and the press of the period. On the American presence in post-war Italian cinema, see Forgacs and Gundle (Chapter 5), and, for an anecdotal account, Kaufman and Lerner. Tyrone Power's wedding is covered in Guiles (pp. 247–55) and analysed by Gundle in McCarthy, pp. 190–92. The Bergman–Rossellini scandal is analysed in my article 'Saint Ingrid at the Stake'. On post-war illustrated magazines and *Grand Hotel*, see Bravo. Ustinov (especially p. 230) offers a sharp sense of what it was like for a foreign actor to be in Rome. Morton's comment on 'American Rome' appears in *A Traveller in Rome*, pp.75–6. Capussotti analyses post-war dreams, while Bondi and Laurenzi each comment on their underside. The case of thirteen-year-old Maria Italia is discussed by the latter on pp. 93–4. Post-war beauty contests are evaluated in Gundle, 2007, Chapters 5 and 6. On *Confidential*, see Desjardins, and Kashner and McNair, Chapter 1.

VI: Girl About Town

Anna Maria Moneta Caglio penned articles for magazines, gave interviews and wrote an autobiography dealing with her early years. Authors of books about the Montesi case have viewed her differently: some, such as Young, are openly hostile while others, including Pinkus, are more sympathetic. Probably the best contemporary portrait was offered by Melton Davis (Chapter 12), whose book rendered her vividly. Grignetti explores thoroughly the background to Silvano Muto's meeting with her, while the treatment of Adriana Bisaccia and her dealings with the journalist offered in Frignani MS is the most complete. The account of their excursion to Torvaianica is based on this source.

VII: The Marchese of San Bartolomeo

Ugo Montagna is without doubt the most intriguing and enigmatic character the case produced. His background and activities were catalogued at length in the Pompei and De Caro reports, which were reproduced in the press. On Mussolini's mistress Claretta and the Petacci family, see Bosworth pp. 363–6, Myriam Petacci's memoirs, pp. 308–14, and De Felice, 1990, pp. 1069–89. Montagna's rise to success was emblematic of the opportunities offered to the unscrupulous in the Italian transition to democracy. For this reason it is appropriate to discuss his career in terms of social history. Practices of sexual corruption and instigation to prostitution in the capital are documented in ACS Ministero dell'Interno, Dir. Gen. PS, Interpol, B.6 La tratta delle bianche (1923–49).

VIII: New and Old Rome

The portrait of Rome offered in this chapter is drawn mainly from the books listed in the 'Rome' section of the bibliography. The Padellaros' text on non-Romans in Rome is especially useful.Vidotto (Chapter 8) offers an overview, while Insolera concentrates on urban development. In Fagiolo dell'Arco and Terenzi, Miriam Mafai's essay 'Roma, dal 18 aprile alla dolce vita' connects urban development, politics and culture. The quotations from Sorlin and Levi are taken from their works in the Bibliography (respectively, pp. 118 and 121). Mafai's judgment is taken from the essay mentioned above (p. 15). The chapter makes reference to Vittorio De Sica's *Bicycle Thieves*. For two recent analyses of the film, see Gordon and Wagstaff. On drugs in Rome in the post-war period, see Musi. He argued that drug addiction in Italy is 'a phenomenon of provincial escapism, of pleasure-seeking curiosity. So, anyway, it is seen in Rome, which is the most provincial city of all because it sums up the vices and virtues of the entire Italian provinces' (p. 204).

IX: Muto on Trial

The trial of Silvano Muto is reconstructed on the basis of numerous press reports. *Il Paese* and *Paese Sera* offered the most complete accounts. The magazine *Oggi* gave much space to the circus around the case. In addition, I have used the book by his defence lawyer Bucciante, pp. 83–97, and books on the case. Coen gives his account of the photograph of Scelba and Montagna in his book, p. 137. On the controversy around Polito, see Canosa, pp. 119–20, 132. Grignetti offers a very good insight into the behind-the-scenes manoeuvres within the state.

X: A New Investigation

Grignetti and Vasile both make use of recently discovered archival materials that document the police surveillance of Raffaele Sepe during his enquiries. These papers and others relating to the Montesi case, especially the official outcomes of the instructional investigation, analysed in Chapter XVI, and the Venice trial, discussed in Chapter XVII, are now grouped together at the Archivio Centrale dello Stato in Rome and are indicated as a separate entry in the general index. I discovered Cosimo Zinza's signature at the ACS in a large volume (the only one remaining of three) of *Pensieri dei cittadini baresi su Mussolini* (Thoughts of Citizens of Bari on Mussolini) that was sent in homage to Il Duce in 1926. Fantasies of orgies run through the entire treatment of the Montesi case and it is often not easy to grasp the full range of practices covered by this term. Partridge offers the only history of the phenomenon. He argues that 'rebellion is the essence of the orgy; rebellion against accepted standards permanent or temporary' (p. 184) while accepting that it can also be a conformist letting-off of steam (pp. 7–8). An acute article referring to the cinematic influences on the orgiastic fantasy was published in *Il Borghese* as an editorial, 'L'aria di Roma', 1 April 1954. The perception of the decadence of the final phase of Fascism was informed by grotesque depictions of ageing male bodies and young female ones by artists such as Mino Maccari and Tono Zancanaro (see Cremoncini for examples). The painting by Anna Salvatore referred to in Chapter 3 belongs to this current. On Navarra and his anecdote about Mussolini's sex life, see Gundle, 2009. The account of the face-to-face confrontation between Caglio and Montagna is taken from Frignani, pp. 81–2.

XI: Via Veneto

On Caglio, see Garofalo pp. 189–90. A lengthy article by Caglio's father, Attilio, 'La mia storia di padre', was published in *Oggi*, 12 August 1954. Descriptions of the Via Veneto are based on magazine articles, memoirs and newsreels. The information on Piero Piccioni's nocturnal habits is taken from ACS, Min. Interno, Dir. Gen. P.S., Div. Pol. amm. e soc., F.1, B.454, Piccioni Gian Piero 15 December 1954. The powerful statement by Jo de Yong (Giobben Giò) appeared in 'Perchè ho mentito', *L'Europeo*, 30 May 1955. On the spirit of vice in Rome, see Laurenzi, p. 29. Frignani MS offers a vivid eye-witness account of Montagna's journey to the Regina Coeli prison (pp. 90–93).

XII: PICCIONI'S ALIBI

Young referred to Piccioni as a nonentity on p. 84 of his book. The picture of him with his nephew accompanied an article by his brother Leone, 'La verità è che mio fratello è innocente', *L'Europeo*, 27 March 1955. Piccioni almost never spoke to the press. One exception was the interview he gave to *Epoca* following the suspension of the Muto trial (issue of 4 April 1954). It was affirmed here that he 'met Montagna six or seven years ago. He was introduced to him by the nephew of a monsignor, along with a lot of other people. He found him courteous and correct to the point of deference and he never spoke about business.' The article's author, Giorgio Vecchietti, added, 'and here lies the ingenuousness or the imprudence of the young Piero Morgan, who never drew the attention of his friends, who were selected indiscriminately from all sorts of environments, to his personal position – that he was the son of a big shot – without reflecting that other more astute men never forgot that important "detail"'. The conviction among journalists that Piccioni was a drug user was conveyed to me orally by Angelo Frignani (9 September 2004). On Alida Valli's role, see Pellizzari and Valentinetti, pp. 169–90. They describe her as coming out of the case 'prostrate and destroyed' (p. 182).

XIII: THE ESTABLISHMENT FIGHTS BACK

On Secchiaroli, see Mormorio. Pinkus also offers extended discussion of him and his fellow photographers. Levy's biography of Rubirosa is good on the behaviour of the playboys. Mario Scelba's dismissal of left-wing culture was published in *Il Corriere della Sera*, 9 June 1949. It is discussed in Pizzinelli, pp. 112–13. The Sotgiu scandal was a complex intrigue in its own right. Grignetti explores the background, pp. 226–9, while Ciuffa, pp. 25–9, considers it from the journalistic angle as does Frignani MS, pp. 109–14.

XIV: A FAMILY UNDER STRESS

The account of the Montesi family is reconstructed from press reports combined with reflections on them in books about the case. Two especially useful articles by family members are: Maria Montesi, 'Wilma non conosceva marchesi, principi, figli di ministri', *Epoca*, 19 September 1954, and Giuseppe Montesi, 'La vita di Wilma non poteva avere segreti', *Oggi*, 29 April 1954. In this ghosted article he claimed, among other things, that Wilma 'was not very keen on Giuliani'. The maid Gionni's testimony is drawn from the Sepe report (see notes to Chapter XVI). On young women and sexual mores, and the Merlin campaign for the abolition of licensed brothels, see Bellassai, Introduction and Chapters 1 and 2. Revel's comment on the brutish relations between the sexes is on p. 55 of *As for Italy*. Silvana Pampanini was a fashionable star of the period. In the *Il Messaggero* archive I found a note from 1953 stating that 'the Silvana Pampanini-style girl' was the height of fashion. Rome had been invaded, the note continued, by provincial girls seeking fame and success. 'Donna Letizia' (Collette Rosselli) dispensed her advice in the press before publishing her volume *Il saper vivere* in 1960. She was married to the journalist Indro Montanelli. Silvano Muto's comments about dreams were perceptive. Capussotti comments that 'Even if, for the majority, desires remained dreams and fantasies, they stimulated the imagination with ideas of wealthy and successful lifestyles that were radically different from the destiny of women of the preceding generation' (p. 164). The writer Corrado Alvaro was a regular commentator on changing mores. Moravia's story of Irene is one of his Roman tales. Another tale on a similar theme is 'Rigoletta' in the collection *Nuovi racconti romani*. The *Los Angeles Times* described Wilma Montesi as a 'sultry-looking party girl' on 7 March 1954. Lord Kennett (Wayland Young) dubbed her a 'playgirl' and described what he saw as her role in one of my interviews with him (18 June 2004). To assess Wilma's smoking, reference may be made to a 1950 opinion poll by the DOXA organisation, which found that 31 per cent of women smoked while 59 per cent of women totally or almost totally disapproved of them doing so (quoted in Bellassai, p. 43).

XV: THE LONG ARM OF THE MAFIA

The role of the Mafia in the Montesi case, and of Ugo Montagna's possible association with organised crime, has been hinted at but never fully analysed. The role of drugs too was never clarified. A telling series of articles on Corinna Versolatto and narcotics matters appeared in *L'Unità*, 3, 16 and 18 May 1957. Felice Chilanti wrote a series of articles for *Paese Sera* about drugs in the Montesi case, which are detailed in the notes to Chapter 17. In *La mafia su Roma* he discussed Coppola on pp. 18–19. Wider comments on drug-traffickers and their influence are on p. 19 and their impact on the construction industry on p. 21. Frignani dismisses 'Red Gianna' as 'an imaginary creature who was never traced' (p. 120), but this does not tally with others' reflections. Giancarlo Fusco's comments on Don Onnis and Red Gianna are now in 'Il mondo della droga' (1957) in *Il gusto di vivere*. The comments of Piccioni's colleagues at RAI on his spliff habit are contained in ACS, Ministero dell'Interno, Dir. Gen. PS, Div. Pol. amm e soc., B.454, F.3, p.218. On Trieste and drugs in the 1950s, see ACS, Ministero dell'Interno, Dir. Gen. P.S., Centro polizia criminale. Interpol, affari generali (1946-61), B. 10, f. 25 anno 1947–48–49, which also contains reports up to 1952. For international discussions of Italy and its situation, see B.14. faldoni 1950 and 1951. Mr Pocoroba's role is referred to in letters dated 24.3.50 and 24.5.50 in B.14. 10/5122 'Anno 1950 fabbrica di "eroina": lotta contro il traffico degli stupefacenti'. The arrest of Trupia (which was reported in the *New York Times* of 26 June 1946) is cited in the 1949 report, that of Frank Callace in 1951's. Serafino Mancuso is also mentioned here, as are, in the 1947 report, the deportees Valenti and Pagliaro. Trupia's arrest was a turning point, after which Rome was seen as a major drugs centre. Salvatore Lupo discusses Frank Coppola and Lucky Luciano in *Storia della mafia*, pp. 222–65 and in *Quando la mafia trovò l'America*, pp. 149–68. The conceptual distinction between the Mafia as 'power syndicate' and as 'enterprise syndicate', elaborated by Alan Block in *East Side, West Side: Organising Crime in New York 1930–1950* (Cardiff, University College Cardiff Press, 1980) is further developed by Lupo (*Storia della mafia*, p. 223) to explain the different facets of Mafia activity, some of which may appear to have little connection to established interests and practices. Mugnani is discussed in some detail by Ciuffa. Jenny Nicholson's article was in *Picture Post*, 6 August 1955. Had a film really been made about the Montesi case in the 1950s or 1960s, no actor would have played Ugo Montagna better than Vittorio Gassman. An international production today might cast John Malkovich in the role.

XVI: Dr Sepe Reports

The two documents prepared respectively by the procurators Giocoli, Scardia and Colonnesi, and by Raffaele Sepe, are contained in ACS, Ministero dell'Interno, Dir. Gen. PS, Div Pol amm e soc, 1945–75; Busta 454. These documents, each of which is several hundred pages long, also inform the accounts of people and events in other chapters. Grignetti's account of Sepe's supposed visit to Andreotti is on p. 239 of his book. He discusses the surveillance of the magistrate and his conflicts with the Palace of Justice on pp. 182–200. Antonio Ghirelli's observation about receiving tip-offs from Fanfani is taken from Grignetti, p. 120. Montagna's article appeared in *Settimo Giorno*, 31 March 1955. For Secchiaroli's sting on Piccioni and Montagna, see Mormorio, pp. 17–18.

XVII: The Venice Trial

British embassy reports suggest that the concern of Italy's allies that the trial could result in the fall of the government had subsided by 1955. FO371, RTI 651/2 (1955) contains a Rome embassy report dated 18 March, declaring that it was a good thing that the trial had not been blocked since that would have been a gift to the Communists. It was widely expected, the report stated, that 'the three [accused] may be acquitted'; the case was 'no longer a live political issue, and no longer a threat to the life of the Scelba government'. T1651/5 contains a further report dated 23 July 1955, following the conclusion of the Sepe investigation, stating that the trial 'will probably arouse considerable public interest . . . but for the time being the public seems to have had enough'. The opening of the trial, after a long delay, did indeed re-ignite public interest. To coincide with it, *Epoca* published (27 January 1957) an interview with Maigret creator Georges Simenon, who dissected the case and dubbed Montagna 'a "cold" gangster', while Piccioni was 'interesting, tormented, pallid'. 'He has more the air of a victim than a hero,' he asserted. As for the 'footbath hypothesis' of Wilma's death, the author dubbed it too implausible to feature in any of his novels. Asked how he would react if he were to meet Anna Maria Caglio in the street, he responded bluntly, 'I would cross the road.' The account of the trial, which is largely or entirely omitted from some books on the case, is drawn from the newspapers of the time. Some specific points deserve to be mentioned. Alida Valli's account of her relations with Piero Piccioni in April 1953 was first published in *Epoca*, 26 April 1954, pp. 15–17 and reprinted during the trial. Fabrizio Menghini reflected on the case many years later in an interview with *Il Messaggero*, 24 September 1980. He claimed that he had simply reported the case, as his paper was committed neither to promoting the guilt nor the innocence of the accused. On the issue of whether Caglio inspired Muto's article instead of confirming its contents to him, see Grignetti p. 72. Although Muto admitted to Grignetti that he knew who Caglio was before meeting her, neither party has ever admitted that she was the source of his original story. Caglio's film was directed by Bruno Girolami and featured a regular supporting cast including Ferruccio Amendola (who would later dub the Italian voices of Al Pacino, Robert De Niro and Sylvester Stallone) and Carlo Delle Piane. A. Albertazzi, the critic of *Intermezzo*, described Caglio's performance as 'quite natural but neither photogenic nor expressive' in his review of 2 February 1957. Her privately published book *Una figlia del secolo* contained an extended denunciation of her mother for abandoning her husband and children for another man. She concluded by likening her fate to that of all other children of divorces, separations and out-of-wedlock unions. In *Quel che ho visto*, Swiss journalist Ingeborg Bachmann described the book as plagiarised from Françoise Sagan's *Bonjour Tristesse* (p. 72). Felice Chilanti published a series of articles on drugs and the Montesis in *Paese Sera*, beginning with 'Sul mistero dei Montesi l'ombra degli stupefacenti', 15 April 1957. Further articles were published on 16, 17, 18 and 21 April.

XVIII: The Rise Of The Paparazzi

The account of the immediate aftermath of the trial and the reactions of the interested parties are drawn from the press of the time, especially the editions of 29 May 1957. *Lascia o raddoppia?* was a hugely popular television quiz show that became a national craze. Even Parliament adjourned when it was on, and irate cinema owners saw such a drop in business that they succeeded in having it moved from its original Saturday evening slot to Thursday evenings. The written verdict of Judge Tiberi is contained in ACS, Min. Int., Dir. Gen. PS, Div. Pol. amm. e soc. B.455, F.5 Sentenza del Tribunale di Venezia (sez. penale). N.390/56. Young's reference to a bloodless revolution is on pp. 267–8 of *The Montesi Scandal*. The comments on Mario Bandini are in Christian, p. 229 and in Stajano (1959), p. 134. The account of personalities and events of the *dolce vita* is drawn from the press, mostly from the person and place files in the Centro documentazione Rizzoli. See also di Robilant, pp. 115–43, and Ciuffa. Botta comments on the mix of class and sleaze in café society (p. 6) and the men from the outlying areas who, influenced by Arena, invaded the Via Veneto (pp. 31–2). On the paparazzi, of interest is a series of articles published in *Oggi* in late 1959 and early 1960, 'Inchiesta sulla dolce vita nella capitale', especially the second article, 3 December 1959. On the break-up of the Power–Christian marriage see Guiles, p. 264, and Christian, pp. 155–6. For Novella Parigini, see interviews cited in notes to Chapter IV. On Alida Valli, see Pellizzari and Valentinetti, pp. 174–90. Flaiano's observations on a changing Via Veneto are in his *La solitudine del satiro*, pp. 5–36. Ciuffa's report of the Rugantino party appeared in *Momento-sera*. He discusses this and the event in detail, pp. 97–100. The banned *L'Espresso* issue is dated 14 November 1958. Olghina di Robilant's admission of drug use by the party set is contained in her article 'Brando ci iniziò alle pillole felici', in *Oggi, numero da collezione 'La dolce vita'*, July 2010. The scandal was picked up by all of the press, including, in an interesting comment, Bruno Ambrosi: 'Hanno avuto pubblicità a buon mercato', *La Settimana Incom*, 22 November 1958. A feature with pictures was published in *Confidential*, March 1959.

XIX: The 'Sweet Life' on Screen

Information on Fellini's preparations for, and filming of, his films is drawn mainly from Kezich's diary of the shoot and his biography of Fellini, Chapters 23 and 24. Also useful is Mingozzi's guide to the troupe and his own relations with the director. The background to the film was explored in Piero Palumbo, 'Processo alla dolce vita', *Lo Specchio*, 17 January 1960. The same magazine explored the impact of the film in articles and letters published in the issues of 17 January, and 14 and 21 February. Numerous works have evoked or celebrated the film. These include Colasanti and Siniscalchi, and De Santi listed in the 'Cinema and entertainment' section of the bibliography. The former offers a good collage of the press reactions to the film. The Trevi Fountain scene has also been recalled many times, notably by Ekberg herself. See, for example, *Il Messaggero*, 9 October 1989 and *Il Corriere della Sera*, 17 July 1991. The debate about *La dolce vita* in Parliament is recorded in Camera dei deputati, III legislatura, discussioni 1960, Vol. XIV, 12 February–13 May 1960, pp. 13222–7. The arch-moralist, Honourable Greggi, was the inspiration for a satirical film entitled *Il Moralista*, released in 1959, starring Alberto Sordi as a fervent Catholic who heads an influential lay association while running a prostitution racket on the side. See Reich on Mastroianni's transformation for *La dolce vita*. The final scene at Fregene is given a particular meaning here, connecting it to the Montesi case. In this book on Fellini's cinema, p. 296, Rondi states the the sea beast symbolised 'the putrid monstrousness of the human species explored up to that point in the film'. The magazine that featured the sea monster in Rimini in a sketch on its back cover was *La Domenica del Corriere*, issue of 29 April 1934. Kezich's comment on this scene is on p. 104 of his diary, listed here as Kezich, 1978.

XX: Aftermath

Giuseppe Montesi featured in an amply illustrated article in *Oggi*, 24 November 1960, in which his situation was reviewed. Alternative hypotheses about the fate of Wilma were rarely articulated. One magazine, *Epoca*, published an article on 6 November 1960, which claimed that Wilma had often been seen in Via Tagliamento with a man, named only as G.I., who owned an Alfa 1900. It suggested that Giuseppe knew him and was covering up for him. Nothing further came of this observation. Bertieri Bonfanti reports that in 1962 the Carabinieri uncovered a ring of five pushers of cocaine and morphine based in the Piazza Vescovio in the Salario quarter, not far from Via Tagliamento (pp. 418–19). All five were respectable and included a car dealer and a mechanic. They knew each other by nicknames and took great care not to draw attention to themselves. They were caught only after an officer overheard a suspicious conversation in a bar. Material on the changing Roman scene is drawn from Italian and international press, as well as Flaiano, 1973, Botta, and Patti, pp. 125–30. The *New York Times* comment appeared on 11 June 1961 and that of the *Los Angeles Times* on 3 August 1975. For the *Confidential* article, see Aldo Monzelli, 'Tittle-Tape Report on Rome's Dolce Vita "63"', October 1963. The Taylor–Burton affair was amply covered in the gossip press, as well as in illustrated weeklies and newspapers. I have also used biographies of the actors. The most recent treatment of their affair is in Kashner and Schoenberger.

XXI: Keys to the Case

Even in recent books and newspaper treatments of the Montesi case, the absence of hypotheses about how Wilma met her end is striking, and contrasts with the abundance of conspiracy theories surrounding other famous mysteries. There is a rich literature on Italy's numerous scandals and mysteries of later years. In the bibliography I have inserted just two books, those by Galli and Turone. Revel's comment on Italy as a police regime is on p. 51 of his volume. His later quote on the élite is on p. 58. Bernabei's reference to Wilma as a 'drug pusher' is in his memoirs, p. 48. Montanelli's comment on Italy's semi-virgins is in *Addio Wanda!*, p. 146. The description of Wilma having changed markedly since her days at college comes from Umberto Fontana, cited by Frignani, p. 28. The original title of Moravia's 1927's story is 'Delitto al circolo di tennis'. Alida Valli's career was damaged by the case but she resumed film work and continued to perform until just a few years before her death in 2006. She refused ever to collaborate with biographers and remained highly jealous of her privacy.

Epilogue

Anna Maria Caglio has been interviewed several times over the decades, including by *Gente*, 13 March 1987, and in *Il Corriere della Sera*, 15 October 1990 and 12 March 2010. Information on the deaths and burials of members of the Montesi family was obtained from the Comune di Roma, Ufficio dello stato civile. I contacted Sergio Montesi and Rossana Spissu by telephone in 2010. Both refused to meet me and declined to express any views beyond those reported here. The information on Capocotta and nudism is derived from www.ostiamediterranea.it/crea/spiaggiapa.html and www.geocities.com/bitichino nat/capocotta00.htm (both consulted 17 October 2005). The scandal of Silvio Berlusconi's alleged orgies erupted in 2009 and was fuelled by the revelations of Patrizia D'Addario. The matter is considered in Paolo Guzzanti, *Mignottocrazia* (Reggio Emilia, Aliberti, 2010) and Gundle in 'Berlusconi, Sex and the Avoidance of a Media Scandal', in E. Jones and M. Giuliani (eds), *Italian Politics: Managing Uncertainty* (Oxford, Berghahn, 2010). On the connection with the Montesi case, *La Repubblica* reported on 26 May 2009 that a government minister, Gianfranco Rotondi, had compared Noemi Letizia to Wilma Montesi, and described Berlusconi as the object of a campaign of defamation similar to that against Attilio Piccioni. The uses of '*dolce vita*' imagery are catalogued and discussed in Dufreigne.

Acknowledgements

This book has been a long time in the making and I have accumulated a number of debts of gratitude. First of all I would like to thank the four authors of previous books on the Montesi case for taking time to talk to me and, in two cases, to share materials with me. I first met the late Lord Kennett at his Bayswater home on his eightieth birthday in August 2003, having previously spoken to him several times on the telephone. As Wayland Young, he followed the Montesi case and attended the Venice trial in 1957. Following its outcome he swiftly wrote up *The Montesi Scandal*, a volume he would follow up with another dedicated to the Profumo affair. His memory was failing by the time we spoke, but he recalled with clarity aspects of the case he had followed so many years before. He kindly allowed me to see his notes and press albums. Angelo Frignani's involvement with the case dated even further back. As a young reporter on Rome's *Il Tempo*, he followed the case from the start. Having grown up in the Salario quarter, he knew the area well and drew on this knowledge in writing, in 2004, his own short book on the Montesi affair. When I met him he was 74, and long retired, but he was still active and keenly involved with *Linea*, a neo-Fascist newspaper (in this, he remained faithful to family tradition: his father had been the local Fascist boss in Ravenna before becoming director of the Bank of Naples in Rome). He talked at length with me and gave me a copy of his extended rough draft of his book, in which I found many more personal observations than are to be found in his *La strana morte di Wilma Montesi*. I am deeply grateful to him for his generous assistance. My friend Karen Pinkus published her own book on the Montesi case in 2003. Although my book is different from hers, it owes something to the connections she made between the scandal and the cinema. I have learned from her work and especially from her attention to the visual imagery of the case. Finally, Francesco Grignetti's patient archival work, which informs his book on the subject, illuminates the institutional background to the affair's development in a way that no other publication does. On a visit to London in 2008, he discussed his research with me over dinner at the White Horse pub in Fulham.

Among the people who have given me practical help, suggestions and advice, I would like to mention Cecilia Oliva and her husband Alfonso Pannone, my former neighbours in London, who accompanied me on an illuminating reconnoitre to Ostia and Torvaianica. They also introduced me to Dr Stefano Grassi, who as a young man knew Wilma Montesi by sight. Alessandra Antola and Fabrizio D'Alessio were of enormous help in tracking down information about the lives of the protagonists of the case in the years that followed. Lucia Rinaldi pointed out to me the treatment of the Montesi affair in Simone Sarasso's novel *Confine di Stato*. Ena Zannotti discussed the mores of the 1950s with me and helped me to better understand the female world of that era. I have also benefited from insights in the published works of Michela De Giorgio and Patrizia Gabrielli, scholars and friends whose knowledge of their subject is equalled only by the passion of their engagement with it.

Special thanks are due to my wife Simona Storchi, who has lived with this project almost for as long as I have. She has willingly discussed the mysteries of the Montesi case with me and put up with me stealing away to work on the manuscript when I should have been doing other things. Her ideas and suggestions have helped me shape mine.

Research for a book like this would not be possible without the resources of public libraries and national archives. It has been a pleasure to work in libraries ranging from the British Library in London to the municipal libraries of Bologna and Reggio Emilia, by way of the national libraries of Florence and Rome. The same is true for the Italian Central State Archive, the US National Archives in Washington and the Public Record Office in Kew. I am especially grateful to the Biblioteca delle donne in Bologna, which sent me a photocopy of Anna Maria Caglio's autobiography. Thanks are also due to Walter Colombo and Daniele Fullin, who kindly granted me access to the materials on people and places held by the Rizzoli and *Corriere della Sera* archives.

The book is reliant on research that I carried out in the mid-1990s with the support of a British Academy small research grant. I record here my gratitude for that important financial help. Books are rarely simply research written-up. They need to be shaped and to take a form that renders the research accessible. My agent Peter Robinson spent a long time getting me to knock this project into shape and I now appreciate, more than I did at the outset, that he was right to see that the Montesi case offered a unique way of recounting Rome in the 1950s. At Canongate, Nick Davies and his colleagues have engaged actively with the book and their enthusiasm and professionalism have helped bring it to a conclusion.

I have chosen to dedicate this book to the memory of my father. He served in the RAF during the later years of the war and was stationed in Rome in 1945, an experience he often talked about when I was a boy. I have before me as I write these words a photograph of him relaxing with fellow technicians at the Ostia Lido at that time. He died forty years ago but is still in my thoughts every day. It is also dedicated to my son Alessandro, who, even at age two, comes to tell me that it is time to close the laptop and play with him. Now, at last, I can do that.

Index

Gundle, Stephen, 1956–
Death and the dolce vita :
the dark side of Rome in the